# Society, Health, and Disease

# Society, Health, and Disease
## *Transcultural Perspectives*

**Janardan Subedi**
*Department of Sociology and Anthropology*
*Miami University of Ohio*

**Eugene B. Gallagher**
*Department of Behavioral Science*
*College of Medicine*
*University of Kentucky*

Prentice Hall
Upper Saddle River, New Jersey 07458

**Library of Congress Cataloging-in-Publication Data**
Society, health, and disease : transcultural perspectives / editors,
Janardan Subedi and Eugene B. Gallagher.
p. cm.
Includes bibliographical references.
ISBN 0-13-669094-7
1. Social medicine—Developing countries. 2. World health.
I. Subedi, Janardan. II. Gallagher, Eugene B.
[DNLM: 1. Sociology, Medical. 2. Cross-Cultural Comparison.
3. Developing Countries. WA 31 S6782 1996]
RA418.3.D48S63 1996
362.1—dc20
DNLM/DLC
for Library of Congress 95-6329
CIP

Acquisitions editor: Nancy Roberts
Editorial assistant: Pat Naturale
Editorial/production supervision: Susan Finkelstein
Copy editor: Donna Walker
Buyer: Mary Ann Gloriande

Printed in the United States of America

10 9 8 7 6 5 4 3 2 1

ISBN 0-13-669094-7

Prentice-Hall International (UK) Limited, *London*
Prentice-Hall of Australia Pty. Limited, *Sydney*
Prentice-Hall Canada Inc., *Toronto*
Prentice-Hall Hispanoamericana, S.A., *Mexico*
Prentice-Hall of India Private Limited, *New Delhi*
Prentice-Hall of Japan, Inc., *Tokyo*
Simon & Schuster Asia Pte. Ltd., *Singapore*
Editora Prentice-Hall do Brasil, Ltda., *Rio de Janeiro*

# Contents

## SECTION FOUR
## The Threat of AIDS



## SECTION FIVE
## Emerging Areas in International Health

# Preface

Editing a varied volume on health and disease from transcultural perspectives presents a challenge: Great effort is required in organizing the many chapters into a single, cohesive book that will be valued by readers interested in a global overview of health and health care.

This text will appeal to individuals from diverse disciplines and fields interested in current transcultural research regarding society, health, and disease and how they are connected. The target readership includes researchers and professors who teach courses related to the area; health planners and administrators; social workers; professionals, such as nurses and physicians; and students of health behavior, disease, and health care.

We hope that this volume will reduce some of the gaps and neglect in health research in developing countries. Furthermore, it may eliminate some "Western" biases and parochial interpretations that pervade many research studies conducted in developing countries.

The aim of this book is to lead readers to a broadened understanding of the interrelationship between health, disease, and different social settings, while increasing their awareness of the special health concerns and needs of people in developing countries.

# About the Contributors

**S. M. Nurul Alam** is a professor of anthropology at Jahangirnagar University, Savar, Bangladesh.

**Rashed J. Al-Hamdan** is a seventh-year medical student at Kuwait University and has been working as an intern at Mubarak Al-Kabir Hospital, Kuwait since July 1993.

**Hayfa H. Ali** is a seventh-year medical student at Kuwait University, Safat, Kuwait.

**Naheel S. Al-Nafisi** is a seventh-year medical student at Kuwait University. She has been working as an intern at the Al-Amiri Hospital, Kuwait since 1993.

**Richard E. Barrett** is an associate professor of sociology at the University of Illinois at Chicago.

**Jaafar Behbehani** is an assistant professor of clinical psychology in the Department of Community Medicine and Behavioral Sciences, Kuwait University, Safat, Kuwait.

**John Blangero** is a biological anthropologist. At present, he holds the position of associate scientist in the Department of Genetics, Southwest Foundation for Biomedical Research, San Antonio, Texas.

**Elizabeth Donnelly** is a research assistant in the Department of Social Medicine, School of Medicine, Harvard University.

**Mary Katharine Duffié** completed her Ph.D. in early 1994 at Washington State University, where she has been an instructor in anthropology and American Indian studies courses since 1989. She was the 1993 national winner of the W. H. R. River's Award for writing the best graduate medical anthropology paper.

**Ruth L. Fischbach** is an assistant professor of social medicine at the School of Medicine, Harvard University. In addition, she holds appointments in the Division of Medical Ethics and the Division on Aging.

**Steve Folmar** is an anthropologist who currently holds the position of research associate at the Bowman Gray School of Medicine, Wake Forest University in Winston-Salem, North Carolina.

**Gabriel B. Fosu** is an assistant professor of medical sociology, Department of Sociology/Anthropology, University of Maryland–Baltimore County, Maryland.

**Eugene B. Gallagher** is a professor of medical sociology in the Department of Behavioral Science and Sociology, University of Kentucky, Lexington, Kentucky.

**Uta Gerhardt** is a professor of medical sociology in the Department of Sociology, University of Heidelberg, Germany.

**Linda M. Hunt** is an assistant professor of medical anthropology in the Department of Medicine at the University of Texas Health Science Center at San Antonio, Texas.

**Anne C. Larme** is an assistant professor of medical anthropology at the Department of Medicine and the Texas Diabetes Institute, University of Texas Health Science Center at San Antonio, Texas.

**Nhung Le** is a doctoral student in public health at the University of California, Berkeley.

**Dana Lear** is affiliated with the School of Public Health, University of California, Berkeley. She recently has completed her Ph.D. in Public Health.

**June J. H. Lee** is a doctoral candidate in anthropology at the University of Hawaii, Manoa.

**Beth A. Macke** is currently working at the Centers for Disease Control and Prevention, Atlanta, Georgia.

**Philip M. Moody** is a professor of medical sociology and Chair of the Department of Community Medicine and Behavioral Science, Kuwait University, Safat, Kuwait.

**John O'Neill** is a professor of sociology at York University, Toronto, Ontario, Canada.

**Kathryn S. Oths** is an assistant professor of medical anthropology, adjunct professor of behavioral and community medicine, and adjunct professor of women's studies at the University of Alabama, Tuscaloosa.

**Sandra E. Paredez** is currently working in the Social and Demographic Section of the Central Statistical Office, Ministry of Finance, Belmopan, Belize.

**Usha K. Prasad** is an anthropologist who holds the position of research associate at the Graduate School and Research, University of Guam, Mangilao.

**Janardan Subedi** is an assistant professor of medical sociology at the Department of Sociology/Anthropology, Miami University, Oxford, Ohio.

**Shu-Fen Tseng** is a doctoral candidate in sociology at the University of Illinois at Chicago.

**David R. Williams** is an associate professor of medical sociology, associate research scientist in the Survey Research Center, Institute for Social Research, and faculty associate in the African-American Mental Health Research Center at the University of Michigan, Ann Arbor.

**Sarah Williams-Blangero** is a biological anthropologist and an associate scientist in the Department of Genetics, Southwest Foundation for Biomedical Research, San Antonio, Texas.

# Introduction

*Janardan Subedi and Eugene B. Gallagher*

It is accepted today that health and disease are related to, and often stem from, the structure of a society. Therefore, a systematic study of the social organization of a society, along with information about social behavior within it, are vital to understanding the influence of social and cultural phenomena on types, patterns, and distribution of disease, as well as response (both formal and informal) to disease. The study of social organization sheds light on how the social, political, and economic structures of a society affect individuals and their access to resources (e.g., wealth, availability of health care, type and quality of health care, and so on) that influence health and disease. Social behavior, on the other hand, provides information on how individuals' own experiences, lay networks, beliefs, and values shape their perceptions and responses to health and disease.

Sound knowledge about social structure and behavior must be derived from studies of different societies and drawn from various disciplines—the social sciences, epidemiology, demography—while recognizing the invaluable contribution of the medical and natural sciences.

This book addresses the social production of health and disease. Perspectives have been drawn from several countries based on research from various disciplines. Although many of the issues and perspectives used here are sociological, the readings contained herein are also drawn from other contributors, including anthropologists, behavioral scientists, biomedical educators and investigators, and professionals specializing in public health and social medicine.

## OVERVIEW OF THE BOOK

This book is divided into five sections. Section One focuses on the sociocultural context of health and disease and contains six chapters. In Chapter 1, Anne C. Larme shows how discrimination against female children and infants in two Andean communities possesses cultural and political legitimacy. Her study enables readers to understand the processes that allow gender discrimination to remain a hidden yet well-institutionalized and rationalized phenomenon in various regions of the world. Chapter 2, by June J. H. Lee, relates how various expensive "medicinal foods" have become popular among middle-class Koreans based on their own lay perceptions of health, medicine, and vulnerability to certain diseases. Mary Katharine Duffié in Chapter 3 presents a comparative analysis of the ways that five folk illnesses are used for explaining aspects of the somatization process and understanding the dynamics that underlie the expression of certain folk illnesses. Similarly, in Chapter 4, Usha K. Prasad looks at the differences in filarial disease among five Fijian, Indian, and Rotuman communities located in the Fiji islands. Her study reveals that sociocultural behavior including cultural perceptions (disease theories) and responses (health-seeking behavior) to disease contributes significantly to the difference in disease rates among groups. Gabriel B. Fosu and Janardan Subedi, in Chapter 5, discuss the high prevalence of common infectious and parasitic diseases and malnutrition among women and children in sub-Saharan Africa. These are complicated by the emerging threat of chronic diseases and the AIDS epidemic. While describing the sociocultural and behavioral contexts of the problems, the authors emphasize the importance of designing culturally appropriate and acceptable health-related programs. In the same vein, Kathryn S. Oths describes how the sociocultural, political, and natural environments contribute to certain diseases among the Chugurpampa in the Northern Peruvian Andes (Chapter 6). Through the use of case studies, the author shows how well-meaning health care programs can sometimes fail because most of them focus on what are, in a normative sense, only the most glaring health problems among disadvantaged populations. Most intervention strategies are ill adapted to the specific sociocultural, political, and environmental conditions of the target population (in this case, the highlands).

Section Two highlights some of the social, political, and economic constraints in health care delivery. In Chapter 7, Linda M. Hunt describes the national health care system of Mexico and focuses on some of the inequalities in that system. Using the example of cancer diagnosis and treatment, she highlights how resources are concentrated only in certain urban areas, hence neglecting the poorest regions of the country. Beth A. Macke and Sandra E. Paredez review utilization and cost of maternal and child health services in Belize, Central America. They find that such factors as the costs of certain types of services, location of residence, ethnicity, education, and immigrant status are predictors of access and barriers to maternal and child health service utilization (Chapter 8). Next, in Chapter 9, Shu-Fen Tseng and Richard E. Barrett discuss the results of a study of risk factors and efforts at control for hepatitis B in Taiwan and the United States. They contend that, in Taiwan, hepatitis B virus (HBV) prevention has been fairly successful where perinatal mother-to-child HBV infection is most common. However, according to them, most prevention programs have generally not been successful (e.g., in the United States) because limited medical and economic resources have not been used appropriately. The authors call for a shift from universal vaccination to the targeting of specific high-risk groups (minorities such as blacks; poor, less-educated migrants; drug users; homosexuals; active heterosexuals with multiple partners; and susceptible infants and adolescents). The authors maintain that the scope of the HBV problem is not yet recognized by doctors, political authorities, or the general public.

Section Three of this book contains chapters dealing with the psychological dimensions of health, disease, and general well-being. Numerous studies on mental health have demonstrated the relationship between an individual's psychological state and responses and the occurrence of various physical and mental diseases. Despite this fact, this area has been almost ignored in books and research on international health. Uta Gerhardt, Naheel S. Al-Nafisi et al., and Eugene B. Gallagher in Chapters 10–12 describe some of the social causes of psychological distress. Gerhardt's study is conducted in Germany, where she tries to assess how men, after early retirement due to coronary artery bypass surgery, view their quality of life (well-being). She finds that perceptions of the quality of life vary by the degree to which individuals feel that they had some control over the decision or the circumstances of their operation, subsequent early retirement, and preservation of "normal male identity." Al-Nafisi et al. in Chapter 11 analyze the impact (subjective stress) of the Persian Gulf War and occupation of Kuwait during the war on the psychological well-being of residents of Kuwait. Finally, Gallagher in Chapter 12 contrasts the expectations of patients from contemporary, individualistic Western societies with those from traditional, community-oriented ones. For this purpose, he uses the United States and Mexico as examples. Through a cultural exploration, Gallagher shows how "the medical dignity" (psychological perceptions that include feelings respected by the medical setting and satisfaction with the treatment) of individuals from these countries is based upon completely contrasting factors.

Section Four is devoted to the discussion of the important topic of AIDS, which, as the first chapter in this section (Chapter 13) by John O'Neill suggests, is a terrifying disease of global proportions and implications. The other chapters in this section (Chapters 14–16) also highlight the fact that the threat of AIDS is underestimated. Nhung Le and David R. Williams, and Steven Folmar and S. M. Nurul Alam discuss not only the context of AIDS in Vietnam and Bangladesh, respectively, to shed light on several high-risk social behaviors that are underestimated for their potential for AIDS contraction, but also the limited and/or inaccurate information regarding its transmission. Dana Lear focuses on the special conditions in Africa that make women a high-risk group for AIDS, and she stresses that many prevention strategies may not be applicable for women as long as they lack social and economic power.

Finally, Section Five describes two topics that are emerging as important areas having implications for international health. Sarah Williams-Blangero, John Blangero, and Janardan Subedi in Chapter 17 state that primary health care programs in developing countries routinely incorporate cultural information about the target population. However, they assert that the implications of the underlying intergroup variation in basic biological parameters for health care planning have received little attention. The authors also explore the potential role of genetic epidemiology in improving international health programs. In the final chapter, Ruth L. Fischbach and Elizabeth Donnelly describe the pervasiveness of domestic violence within and across cultures. The authors contend that domestic violence against women damages not only their physical well-being, but also plays a substantial role in the etiology of mental and emotional disorders.

# Society, Health, and Disease

Chapter 1

# Culture, Parental Attitudes, and Child Health in Rural Peru*

*Anne C. Larme*

Over the past 20 years, child mortality differentials have been a major concern for child survival researchers within the fields of international health, population and development, and medical anthropology. Food and health care allocation, which may differ by gender, age, or other characteristics of a child, have been postulated as proximate determinants of differential child mortality (Moseley and Chen 1984). The analysis of resource allocation within households may also provide clues regarding harder-to-observe child care practices such as selective or benign neglect (Cassidy 1980; Scheper-Hughes 1985; Scrimshaw 1978) and how these practices may affect particular groups of children.

Ethnographic data on child care attitudes and behaviors complement quantitative studies of food and health care allocation. They illuminate the cultural rationales for resource allocation within households and are an essential

*Financial support for research was provided by a National Science Foundation grant (BNS 8313190) to Bruce Winterhalder, principal investigator. Additional support was provided by the University of North Carolina Graduate School, Sigma Xi, and a NIMH postdoctoral fellowship through the Department of Behavioral Science, University of Kentucky. I wish to thank Juan Carlos Correa, Kathleen DeWalt, Eugene B. Gallagher, Margaret Graham, Sandra Kryst, Erma Lawson, Sara Quandt, Pamela Rao, Janardan Subedi, and Monica Udvardy for their assistance at various stages in the preparation of this manuscript. Special thanks go to the people of Cuyo Cuyo who participated in the study and to local research assistants who aided in data collection.

basis for planning child survival interventions and other remedial measures to enhance the lives of children and their families. Equally important, ethnographic data put a human face on issues of child survival. Under conditions of poverty and lack of access to family planning methods, parents in poorer nations may be faced with decisions about how to allocate scarce resources among family members, and ultimately which of their children may survive and prosper (Scheper-Hughes 1985, 1992). Ethnographic analysis provides a context within which to understand and evaluate such parental behaviors.

This exploratory study of health care allocation to children in highland Peru is based upon 17 months of fieldwork in the district of Cuyo Cuyo, Puno, Peru. It contributes comparative case material on the relationship of differential resource allocation to differential child morbidity and mortality in the developing world. Quantitative data on health care allocation by gender and age are presented, complemented by ethnographic data on child health, gender, child development, and family planning. In pointing out the complexity of, and contradictions in, the ways Andeans perceive and act on symptoms of ill health in their children, this analysis cautions against simplistic explanations for differential child mortality.

## DIFFERENTIAL CHILD MORBIDITY AND MORTALITY

Differentials in child morbidity and mortality, especially gender differentials, have been a focus of child survival researchers since the 1970s, spurred by an interest in gender that arose at that time in the social sciences. In South and East Asia, where much of this research has been performed, extreme differentials in favor of males have been noted (Basu 1989; Chen et al. 1981; Coale 1991; Das Gupta 1987; Jeffery et al. 1984; Johansson and Nygren 1991; Koenig and D'Souza 1986; Kumar 1989; Levine 1987; Miller 1984; Minturn 1984; Muhuri and Preston 1991). Gender differentials in child mortality have also been noted in preindustrial Europe (Johansson 1984), Africa (Cronk 1989, 1991a, 1991b; Svedburg 1990), and Latin America (Bolton 1980; McKee 1988; Scrimshaw 1978). Although discrimination is generally directed against females (McKee 1984), males are also discriminated against under certain circumstances (Cronk 1989, 1991a, 1991b; Sargent and Harris 1992; Svedburg 1990). In either case, not all members of one gender are affected. Factors such as family size, birth order, and ratio of sons to daughters appear to intervene (Das Gupta 1987; Johansson and Nygren 1991; Muhuri and Preston 1991).

Many researchers have examined food and health care allocation as proximate determinants of differential morbidity and mortality among children. Although the emphasis has generally been on nutrition (Abdullah and Wheeler 1985; Bairagi 1986; Carloni 1981; Leonard 1991a; Messer 1990, 1992; Rizvi 1991; Svedburg 1990), a few studies have focused on health care (Basu 1989;

Chen et al. 1981; Cronk 1989; Hossain and Glass 1988; Rahman et al. 1982). Researchers are increasingly moving beyond single-focus research to emphasize the complex interactions among multiple factors involved in differential morbidity and mortality, including the synergistic effects of nutrition and illness, and factors such as family size, birth order, gender ratio, marital stability, child legitimacy, family economics, support networks, mothers' education and employment, status of women, kinship and marital patterns, and acceptability of passive or active infanticide (Basu 1989; Chen et al. 1981; Das Gupta 1987; Dettwyler 1992; Johansson and Nygren 1991; Kumar 1989; Levine 1987; Muhuri and Preston 1991).

In the rural Andes, gender differentials in child mortality have also been noted, with higher survival rates for males than for females (Bolton 1980; McKee 1988; Scrimshaw 1978). Little is known about the actual mechanisms involved in higher female mortality, however. Differential food allocation does not appear to be a factor. Two separate studies of postweaning food allocation in the southern Peruvian highlands (Leonard 1991a, 1991b; Graham 1991) suggest that both male and female children receive adequate calories to meet their nutritional needs. Several researchers have suggested that active or passive infanticide, particularly of females, may be occurring in the Andes, possibly as a means of family planning or population control (Bolton 1980; Buechler and Buechler 1971; De Meer 1988; McKee 1988; Scrimshaw 1978).

Further exploration of the reasons behind gender differentials in child mortality in the Andes is needed, as well as additional case studies to enhance our understanding of differential child mortality throughout the world. Determining the role of health care allocation in addition to food allocation is important, especially to understand the complex interactions among multiple factors. Researchers of child mortality differentials have used primarily quantitative approaches to hypothesize links between sociocultural beliefs and the behaviors that influence child morbidity and mortality. To explore those links in depth, ethnographic research, or research using a combination of quantitative and qualitative methodologies, is needed.

The present study goes beyond documenting differences in the allocation of health care in rural Peru to examining, through long-term ethnographic research, how this behavior obtains legitimacy from the cultural and political economic context. Ethnomedical, gender, and child development concepts in Andean culture are shown to underlie and rationalize parental treatment of children, including the selective neglect of certain infants. These beliefs and behaviors are linked, in turn, with the social and economic marginalization of rural Andean peoples, who desire to limit family size but have little access to family planning methods.

Multilayered, contextualized research that retains a sense of the human actors involved is essential for planning culturally appropriate child survival interventions. On a broader level, clarifying how selective neglect operates within a cultural context has the potential to expand our understanding of how gender discrimination remains a hidden, unexamined, institutionalized, and rationalized phenomenon in various societies of the world.

## CUYO CUYO

The District of Cuyo Cuyo is located on the eastern Andean escarpment (3,400 m) in northern Puno, Peru. The study was conducted in two indigenous communities of the District, Ura Ayllu (population 706) and Puna Ayllu (population 1,247), which are relatively homogeneous socially, culturally, and economically, within and between the two communities. Cuyo Cuyo appears isolated geographically and in terms of access to modern conveniences such as transportation, communication, water, and electricity. Yet, past and present sociocultural and economic influences promote a fluid rural-urban identity among its inhabitants.

Cuyo Cuyeños are rural agriculturists who subsist by growing potatoes and other tubers and who practice a pre-Hispanic Andean land-use pattern known as "verticality" to adapt to their mountain environment (Brush 1977; Goland 1991; Murra 1972). However, they depend increasingly upon the entrepreneurial production of gold for their livelihood and are therefore linked to international gold markets (Recharte 1990). Although some men mine gold on community lands, others undertake lengthy seasonal migrations to mine in the Amazonian Department of Madre de Dios, located a week's journey to the north. Men's migration to gold rush communities, as well as their frequent travels to purchase goods and obtain employment in the Peruvian cities of Juliaca, Arequipa, and Lima, brings additional urban influences to Cuyo Cuyo. So do schoolteachers, policemen (*Guardia Civil*), government health personnel, agricultural technicians, missionaries, and anthropologists.

A combination of Andean, Spanish colonial, and cosmopolitan influences is evident in other aspects of life in Cuyo Cuyo. Quechua is the first language of Cuyo Cuyeños, although many are bilingual in Quechua and Spanish. The *Pachamama* (Mother Earth) and *apus* (mountain deities) feature prominently in Cuyo Cuyo religion, which has been thoroughly syncretized with Spanish folk Catholicism. More recent additions to Cuyo Cuyo religion are Seventh Day Adventism and Catholic liberation theology. Andean cultural patterns of reciprocity (*ayni*), egalitarianism, and bilaterality characterize Cuyo Cuyo social organization. Kinship, government, and economic relations also reflect the influences of Spanish colonialism and modern capitalism.

The entrepreneurial production of gold has allowed Cuyo Cuyeños to maintain a higher degree of economic and cultural autonomy than other rural Peruvians. However, there are many negative effects, especially in terms of family and gender relations. With men involved primarily in the cash economy and often absent from their families, women's workloads in subsistence, household, and community have increased. Many women and children survive without their husbands' and fathers' labor contributions—and often income—for months at a time. Gold mining and migration have also contributed to gender inequalities in Cuyo Cuyo. Women's lesser access to cash, and to the social and economic prestige that accrue to men through migration and interaction with urban culture, has in general lowered women's position in relation to men's. This has implications for the health of all Cuyo Cuyo females, including the young.

Despite a modest income from gold mining, Cuyo Cuyeños, like most rural Peruvians, survive under precarious social and economic conditions. Poor public health conditions and marginal nutrition are reflected in basic health indicators. Preliminary analysis of Cuyo Cuyo birth and death records (Larme 1992)[1] indicate an infant mortality rate of 242 deaths per 1,000 live births in the first year of life. Many infant deaths occur shortly after birth, as represented by the neonatal mortality rate (deaths in the first 4 weeks of life) of 165 deaths per 1,000 live births. Child mortality remains elevated through age five. The crude death rate (deaths per thousand population in a given year) is 27 per 1,000, and the maternal death rate is estimated at 1,022 per 100,000 live births. Life expectancy in the southern sierra region of Peru, where Cuyo Cuyo is located, averages 52 years (UDES 1987).

High-altitude stressors, including hypoxia, cold temperatures, and the highly mobile lifestyle resulting from "vertical" adaptation to the mountain environment, also impinge on the health of Cuyo Cuyeños. Hypoxia is particularly stressful in the prenatal and postnatal periods (Moore and Regensteiner 1983, pp. 291–94). Female fetuses and infants possess a greater buffering capacity than males to high-altitude hypoxia, however, as well as to illness and malnutrition (Haas et al. 1980, pp. 473–74).

Both fertility and mortality are high in Cuyo Cuyo, as in most developing societies. The women forty and older whom I studied intensively (n = 12), for example, averaged 7.4 pregnancies each but only 4.4 living children (all ages). Several reported losing half their offspring to miscarriage, stillbirth, or illness. Younger parents reported that they desired only two children, one of each gender. However, family planning methods are generally unavailable in the district, and Cuyo Cuyeños lack the knowledge and resources to use them.

Child care ideals are structured around preventing illness, promoting growth, and respecting a child's delicate nature. Infants are securely wrapped and carried nearly constantly on their mother's or an older sibling's back until well into toddlerhood. Ideally, young children should be dressed warmly; fed frequently so they do not experience hunger; carefully shielded from sunlight, noises, and brusque movements so they do not experience fright; comforted when necessary to avoid crying; and trained gently by example. Corporal punishment is frowned upon because young children are thought to be too delicate to withstand a beating and too young to understand its meaning.

Children remain primarily in their mother's care until approximately age 7, when they begin to attend school and assist their same-sex parent in agricultural, mining, or domestic activities. Grandmothers and older siblings assist mothers in child care, as do fathers when not absent due to gold mining.

## METHODS

The present inquiry was spurred by preliminary analyses of mortality statistics and ethnographic data from Cuyo Cuyo, which indicated a pervasive gender bias in Cuyo Cuyo society (Larme 1992). Mortality statistics, as previously described, showed high mortality rates through age 5, especially in the neonatal and infant periods. Did negative attitudes about females result in differential health care allocation to children, and could this be a contributing factor to gender differentials noted in mortality rates? Was age a factor in child health care decisions, contributing to the elevated mortality rates noted through age 5?

Data on child symptoms and health care were collected as part of a broader ethnographic study of health and illness in Cuyo Cuyo (Larme 1992). The overall study involved 20 families, 10 each from the communities of Ura Ayllu and Puna Ayllu. The sample of families was shared with the PSE Project, an ecological study carried out simultaneously in the District.[2] Although a convenience sample, they were chosen to represent a range of economic strategies and stages in the family developmental cycle. In other respects (income, cultural orientation, number of household heads), the families were comparable. The present analysis uses data for all children from these families between the ages of birth and 7 years. This includes 23 children: 11 males and 12 females, representing 11 of the 20 families.

Health data were collected from household heads in semistructured interviews averaging 10 per family, at intervals averaging 4.6 weeks, over the period of 1 year (February 1987 through February 1988). Parents were asked about the health status of their children since the previous interview or within the preceding month, whichever period was shorter. When a symptom or illness was reported, information was collected on perceived causes, duration, and treatments. The primary informants were mothers, who are most responsible for the care of young children in Cuyo Cuyo. Fathers, who are also knowledgeable about their children and family health matters, participated in discussions along with their wives and occasionally served as primary informants when not absent due to migration. Data were collected principally for ethnographic purposes but were also quantifiable.

Symptom and treatment data for the 23 children were converted into a quantitative data set and analyzed using SPSS. Altogether, 220 health status reports, some involving multiple symptoms, were analyzed. Symptom reports totaled 189, and treatment data were available for 178 of these. For purposes of comparison, data collected at the government health post on visits by sick children between the ages of birth and 7 years during 1984 to 1987 (n = 922) were also analyzed.[3] Frequencies were determined for both sets of data and chi ($\chi$) square tests performed to determine if significant differences existed by gender and age.

Three age groups were selected for analysis, incorporating both etic (outsider) and emic (insider) concepts: less than age 1, ages 1 through 3, and ages 4 through 6. These age groups allowed for comparison with child nutrition analyses from Cuyo Cuyo (Graham 1991). A "less than age 1" category follows etic and emic data indicating that the first year of life is the most dangerous for child survival in Cuyo Cuyo and allows for comparison with infant mortality data. The "1 through 3" category includes the entire postweaning period, a particularly risky period for child health, both etically and emically.[4] The postweaning period, when children are introduced to a variety of new foods, is especially dangerous under conditions of poor hygiene such as are found in Cuyo Cuyo, and age 3, according to Cuyo Cuyo beliefs, is considered the end of the "danger zone" for child illness and death. Finally, age 7 is an important milestone in child mental, moral, and physical development in Cuyo Cuyo, making it an appropriate endpoint for the analysis.

Quantitative data were complemented by ethnographic data on child health, gender and developmental concepts, and family planning, collected during the same semistructured interviews. Other sources of data were open-ended interviews with key informants and participant observation over 17 months in Cuyo Cuyo, including with children and parents in homes and worksites and at childhood rituals and funerals.

The analysis is limited by the small number of children for whom symptom and treatment data were collected and by their unequal distribution across the 11 families represented. These problems are minimized by the relative homogeneity of the Cuyo Cuyo population and families involved in the study and by the collection of complementary in-depth ethnographic data over a period of 17 months. Data quality may be limited by recall bias owing to the length of time between visits, and it should be noted that self-perceived (in this case, parent-perceived) morbidity data are limited as an objective measure of child health status (Kroeger 1983). The point of this study, however, is not to present an objective measure of child health status but to provide an in-depth understanding of parental perceptions and their relationship to treatment decisions for children of differing genders and ages. Parent-perceived morbidity data are therefore central to this analysis.

Finally, gender and age patterns may vary between biomedical treatment data collected in the indigenous communities and at the government health post because individuals from the district capital are overrepresented in the health post sample. Distance is not a barrier to their use of the clinic, and cultural beliefs may vary somewhat between the capital, a primarily mestizo town, and the indigenous communities.

Keeping these limitations in mind, the following quantitative and ethnographic data provide an exploratory understanding of child health care allocation in Cuyo Cuyo.

## CHILD HEALTH IN CUYO CUYO

Poor sanitary conditions and marginal nutrition jeopardize the health of all Cuyo Cuyeños, but especially that of children. Over a 1-year period, the primary symptoms (n = 189) reported for the 23 children in my sample were gastrointestinal, including parasites (42%); respiratory (33%); accidents and injuries (9%); scabies (5%); and miscellaneous other complaints (12%). Government health post data corroborate parent-reported morbidity data. Primary symptoms for children in the under-7 age group taken for treatment to the health post (n = 922) included respiratory (35%); gastrointestinal, including parasites (25%); accidents and injuries (10%); scabies (9%); and other/combined diagnoses (22%). Taken together, these two data sources provide a fairly accurate picture of the types of symptoms typically suffered by Cuyo Cuyo children.

Beyond these generalizations, distinctions are evident by gender and age. Whether a child is reported to be "healthy" or "unhealthy" is significantly related to both gender and age (Table 1–1).[5] Of 220 health status reports, girls were reported to be unhealthy 73.7% of the time, compared with 60.8% for boys ($\chi^2 = 4.19$; DF = 1; $P = 0.04$). Children under age 1 were reported to be unhealthy 83.6% of the time, compared with 92.5% of the time for the 1 through 3 age group, and 52.8% of the time for the 4 through 6 age group ($\chi^2 = 30.34$; DF = 2; $P < 0.01$).

In terms of specific symptoms, statistically significant differences were found in reported symptoms by age but not by gender (Table 1–2). For this

**TABLE 1–1. Reported Health Status by Gender and Age (n = 220)**

| | *HEALTHY* | | *UNHEALTHY* | |
|---|---|---|---|---|
| | *n* | *%* | *n* | *%* |
| *Gender** | | | | |
| Male | 40 | 39.2 | 62 | 60.8 |
| Female | 31 | 26.3 | 87 | 73.7 |
| *Age*† | | | | |
| <1 | 9 | 16.4 | 46 | 83.6 |
| 1–3 | 3 | 7.5 | 37 | 92.5 |
| 4–6 | 59 | 47.2 | 66 | 52.8 |

*$P < 0.05$
†$P < 0.01$

**TABLE 1–2. Reported Symptom Types by Gender and Age (n = 189)**

| | *GASTROINTESTINAL** | | *RESPIRATORY* | | *ACCIDENT/INJURY* | | *OTHER* | |
|---|---|---|---|---|---|---|---|---|
| | *n* | % | *n* | % | *n* | % | *n* | % |
| *Gender* | | | | | | | | |
| Male | 32 | 44.4 | 23 | 31.9 | 6 | 8.3 | 11 | 15.3 |
| Female | 48 | 41.0 | 39 | 33.3 | 11 | 9.4 | 19 | 16.2 |
| *Age*† | | | | | | | | |
| <1 | 28 | 50.0 | 16 | 28.6 | 0 | 0.0 | 12 | 21.4 |
| 1–3 | 33 | 60.0 | 11 | 20.0 | 6 | 10.9 | 5 | 9.1 |
| 4–6 | 19 | 24.4 | 35 | 44.9 | 11 | 14.1 | 13 | 16.7 |

*Includes parasites
†$P<0.01$

analysis, symptom types (n = 189) were grouped into four categories: gastrointestinal (including parasites), respiratory, accident/injury, and other. For the less-than-1 group, 50% of reported symptoms were gastrointestinal, compared with 60% for the 1 through 3 age group, and 24.4% for the 4 through 6 age group. Respiratory symptoms were 28.6%, 20%, and 44.9%, respectively; accident/injury symptoms were 0%, 10.9%, and 14.1%; and other symptoms were 21.4%, 9.1%, and 16.7% ($\chi^2 = 27.54$; DF = 6; $P<0.01$). No significant differences in symptom reports were found by gender.

In sum, parents reported that females and younger children were sicker than males and older children, and symptom types differed by age but not by gender. Differences in perceived symptoms are important because they influence parental decisions about appropriate health care for children of different genders and ages. Thus, the following questions become important for the treatment analysis: Does the greater perceived morbidity of females and younger children warrant them special consideration in the allocation of health care by parents? And, given that girls and boys are perceived to have the same types of symptoms, do they both receive equivalent health care?

## HEALTH CARE ALLOCATION TO CHILDREN

Several treatment options are available when a child becomes ill: home remedies, store/patent remedies, do-it-yourself home rituals, ritual cures by local healers, and biomedical treatments at the government health post. Some symptoms are left untreated, a final option. Most child health care is provided by women as part of their family caretaking role, often with the advice of their own mothers. Cuyo Cuyo men, except when absent due to gold mining, often participate in child health care decisions and cures, especially home rituals. No particular pattern of resort is followed. Treatments may be used alone or in combination, in sequence or simultaneously. Choice of treatment appears contingent on many factors, among them causal attribution, severity and persistence of symptom, available parental time and money, parental perceptions about the value or personal characteristics of a particular child, and preference for one or another treatment modality.

Treatment data were collected and analyzed for 178 symptoms and illnesses of children.[6] The most frequently used treatment options were inexpensive patent remedies purchased in local stores, such as cold remedies and aspirin (used in 51% of treatments), and home remedies, usually herbs grown or collected by family members (used in 50% of symptom treatments). More rarely, parents performed healing rituals themselves (used in 8% of symptom treatments). These three treatment options require a limited investment of parental time, effort, and money.

Biomedical or ritual specialists are sometimes used when a child's symptoms are serious or persistent and when the family can afford the cash outlay. When a child is taken to either a biomedical or ritual specialist, it generally means that the family is unusually concerned for a child's health and is willing to undergo considerable effort and expense for the child to be cured.

Biomedical treatments were included in 8% of treatments. A government health post in the District capital is staffed by one or two nurses or sanitarians. Access to the health post from the indigenous communities is difficult because transportation within the District is by foot only, and sick or injured children must often be carried on their parents' backs for several kilometers along steep mountain trails. Staffing and medical supplies are inconsistent, and a parent cannot be sure whether, after making the difficult journey, the child will actually receive treatment. Although the clinic fee is nominal, prescribed pharmaceuticals are costly. Biomedicine is accorded higher status than other types of health care in Cuyo Cuyo because it represents a cosmopolitan orientation and indicates that the family is sufficiently wealthy to use it. Owing to the difficulty of access and considerable expense, however, treatment at the health post is a luxury in terms of time and money that few parents from the indigenous communities can afford.

Ritual curing specialists, another extraordinary health care measure, were included in 4% of treatments. Several male, part-time ritual curers (*hampikuq*) live in each community. They generally charge a day's wages to perform a curing ritual, in addition to the cost of coca, alcohol, and other ritual supplies. Their use is generally restricted to illnesses regarded to be of supernatural origin.

To understand how specific groups of children were treated when ill, treatment data (n = 178) were analyzed by gender and age. First, treatments were divided into three categories based upon cost, hypothesizing that Cuyo Cuyo parents would invest more in the children they valued the most highly (Basu 1989). A higher economic cost generally entails a higher cost in terms of parental time and effort as well (e.g., to transport a child to the health post,

**TABLE 1–3. Reported Treatment Cost by Gender and Age (n = 178)**

| | *HOME REMEDY ONLY (NO COST)* | | *COSTS MONEY* | | *NO TREATMENT* | |
|---|---|---|---|---|---|---|
| | *n* | *%* | *n* | *%* | *n* | *%* |
| *Gender* | | | | | | |
| Male | 15 | 22.1 | 47 | 69.1 | 6 | 8.8 |
| Female | 35 | 31.8 | 64 | 58.2 | 11 | 10.0 |
| *Age* | | | | | | |
| <1 | 13 | 25.0 | 32 | 61.5 | 7 | 13.5 |
| 1–3 | 16 | 29.6 | 34 | 63.0 | 4 | 7.4 |
| 4–6 | 21 | 29.2 | 45 | 62.5 | 6 | 8.3 |

to amass ritual supplies). The three treatment categories are (1) home remedy only (home remedy exclusive of other treatment)—no cost; (2) treatments requiring a cash outlay (i.e., that include a store remedy, home ritual, ritual specialist, or biomedical specialist); and (3) no treatment.

This analysis (Table 1–3) showed that females received more "home remedy only" treatments than males (31.8% versus 22.1%), fewer treatments involving a cash outlay (58.2% versus 69.1%), and were not treated at all 10% of the time, compared with 8.8% of the time for males. However, these differences were not statistically significant. Analyzed by age, no consistent treatment pattern emerged and differences were not statistically significant.

I then analyzed each of the treatments requiring a cash outlay (n = 111; store remedy, home ritual, ritual specialist, biomedical specialist) separately, to check for gender or age differences (Tables 1–4 and 1–5). Girls received more store remedies than boys (85.9% versus 74.5%), fewer home rituals (7.8% versus 19.1%), and more cures by ritual specialists (7.8% versus 4.3%), but these differences were not statistically significant. However, girls did receive signifi-

**TABLE 1–4. Treatments Requiring Cash by Gender (n = 111)***

| | *STORE REMEDY* | | *HOME RITUAL* | | *RITUAL SPECIALIST* | | *BIOMEDICAL SPECIALIST*† | |
|---|---|---|---|---|---|---|---|---|
| | *n* | *%* | *n* | *%* | *n* | *%* | *n* | *%* |
| *Gender* | | | | | | | | |
| Male | 35 | 74.5 | 9 | 19.1 | 2 | 4.3 | 10 | 21.3 |
| Female | 55 | 85.9 | 5 | 7.8 | 5 | 7.8 | 4 | 6.3 |

*Numbers do not add up to 111 because some symptoms/illnesses received more than one treatment requiring cash.
† $P < 0.05$

**TABLE 1–5. Treatments Requiring Cash by Age (n = 111)***

| | *STORE REMEDY* | | *HOME RITUAL* | | *RITUAL SPECIALIST* | | *BIOMEDICAL SPECIALIST* | |
|---|---|---|---|---|---|---|---|---|
| | *n* | *%* | *n* | *%* | *n* | *%* | *n* | *%* |
| *Age* | | | | | | | | |
| <1 | 26 | 81.3 | 6 | 18.8 | 2 | 6.3 | 3 | 9.4 |
| 1–3 | 27 | 79.4 | 4 | 11.8 | 2 | 5.9 | 5 | 14.7 |
| 4–6 | 37 | 82.2 | 4 | 8.9 | 3 | 6.7 | 6 | 13.3 |

*Numbers do not add up to 111 because some symptoms/illnesses received more than one treatment requiring cash.

cantly fewer treatments by biomedical specialists than boys (6.3% versus 21.3%; $\chi^2 = 5.55$; DF = 1; $P = 0.02$).

Analyzing these four treatments by age revealed no statistically significant differences. However, reported use of home rituals decreased as age increased (18.8% for the under-age-1 group versus 11.8% for ages 1 through 3 and 8.9% for ages 4 through 6), and the under-age-1 group received fewer treatments by biomedical specialists than the two groups of older children (9.4% versus 14.7% for ages 1 through 3 and 13.3% for ages 4 through 6).

To understand further the use of biomedical treatments for children, I compared data from the community sample with 1984 through 1987 health post data, which included children from the entire Cuyo Cuyo District. No statistically significant gender differences were found among children under age 7 brought to the health post for treatment for whom gender was recorded (n = 905). However, there were significant differences by age (n = 922; $\chi^2 = 777.66$; DF = 2; $P < 0.01$). Markedly fewer infants less than age 1 were brought to the clinic than statistically expected (176 observed versus 441 expected). In contrast, more children in the two older age groups were brought in than expected (484 observed versus 309.2 expected for ages 1 through 3; 262 observed versus 171.9 expected for ages 4 through 6).

In general, the results of this exploratory study on health care allocation support a pattern of discrimination against female and younger children, especially infants, in Cuyo Cuyo. Females and younger children are reported to be sicker, yet they generally receive less costly treatments in terms of parental time, effort, and money. In addition, although no symptom differences between boys and girls are evident, boys and girls are given different treatments.

In the following section, I use qualitative data collected in the semistructured health interviews and through the broader ethnographic study of health in Cuyo Cuyo to reinforce these preliminary findings on health care allocation and illuminate the context of parental behavior.

## THE CULTURAL CONTEXT OF DIFFERENTIAL CHILD CARE IN CUYO CUYO

Why do Cuyo Cuyo parents distinguish among children of different genders and ages, allocating different amounts and types of health care and ultimately placing their health in jeopardy? Ethnographic data on ethnomedical beliefs, gender, child development, and family planning in Cuyo Cuyo provide a multi-faceted context for understanding differential health care allocation to children in Cuyo Cuyo.

### Child Ethnomedical Concepts

Cuyo Cuyeños perceive their bodies, health, and well-being to be in a constant state of threat from environmental forces, both natural and supernatural. This is represented by the core concept of *debilidad* (weakness, vulnerability) in Cuyo Cuyo ethnomedicine. Children are perceived to be inherently more *débil* than adults and thus more susceptible to illness and death. Protecting a child's health, as a father of seven put it, consists simply in keeping a child warmly dressed and well fed. Adequate clothing prevents illnesses from entering through vulnerable openings in the body—the head, orifices, lower back, and soles of the feet. Adequate food, which helps the body avoid hunger and *debilidad*, keeps the body invulnerable to attack by malevolent, illness-causing spirits.[7]

No matter what protective measures are taken, however, children still get sick. A major cause of child illness—in fact of all child illness, according to one parent—is thought to be *uraña*, or fright. *Uraña*[8] symptoms can be nearly anything: respiratory complaints, diarrhea, irritability, and anything inexplicable, especially symptoms that persist. Child symptoms were interpreted as *uraña* in 13% of parental reports (n = 188). This figure is undoubtedly low because *uraña* is a taken-for-granted cause of illness in young children and parents therefore may not have mentioned it specifically. They may also have been reluctant to divulge their adherence to local beliefs for fear of being seen as uneducated or backward.

The younger a child is, the more susceptible to *uraña* he or she is thought to be. Infants and young children are thought to be inherently *débil* because they have a loose connection between their physical body and its spiritual essence, or life-force. A child's life-force is easily frightened out of his or her body by loud noises, being handled too roughly, being dropped, seeing the sky, or even during the childbirth process. Without the life-force, *uraña* results. Male children are considered to be more vulnerable to *uraña*, sickness, and death than females. Accordingly, *uraña* was reported more frequently for younger children than for older ones and more frequently for males than for females, although differences were not statistically significant. The greater propensity of infants and males to suffer from *uraña* is also reflected in the numbers of ritual cures given to younger children and males than to older children and females (Tables 1–4 and 1–5).

In more extreme cases, especially when symptoms persist, a child may be diagnosed with *larpa. Larpa* symptoms appear to be those of severe malnutrition: weight loss and a gradual wasting away until death. Like *uraña,* the cause of *larpa* is reconstructed after the child becomes ill. It is most commonly attributed to the mother having seen a human corpse or dead animal while she was pregnant. The spirit of the human or animal, jealous of the life of the fetus, is thought to enter it and later cause illness.

Ethnomedical beliefs are intertwined with parental perceptions of child symptoms and therefore affect health care decisions about particular children. Culturally interpreted illnesses such as *uraña* and *larpa* explain childhood sickness and death in culturally acceptable ways and have the effect of exonerating parents from blame and alleviating their grief over child death. These effects are important, given the high risk of child sickness and death in Cuyo Cuyo due to poor hygiene, marginal nutrition, and high altitude.

### Gender and Child Health

Gender concepts in present-day Cuyo Cuyo help to explain the differential treatment of male and female children. The greater perceived vulnerability of male infants to sickness and death was powerfully expressed by one Ura Ayllu mother: "The cemetery and the tombs lie open and waiting for infant boys . . . innumerable illnesses can attack them . . . they are destined to die." She went on to explain how male infants' special vulnerability warrants them special treatment. Male newborns must be wrapped tightly (*k'irusqa*) for 3 months, compared with 2 months for females. *K'irusqa* must be done especially carefully for males so that the position of their navel is fixed and so that their limbs will grow straight. Males must not be allowed to cry or they will be very *débil* (weak, vulnerable to illness) when they grow up. Males must not be fed "stale" breast milk; that is, the mother must throw out a portion of her breast milk every time she feeds a male infant. In contrast, females can be fed any type of breast milk. Males are placed under special tents away from terrace walls while sleeping in the fields alongside their working mothers, lest they get *uraña.* Females can be placed anywhere. Young male children are favored and spoiled; females are not, although she also noted that being spoiled increased males' vulnerability to illness. If they are at any point denied what they demand, crying and getting angry as a result, they are susceptible to "grabbing" by the *Pachamama.*[9]

These data may explain why sons receive different health care than daughters in Cuyo Cuyo. Even though females are reported to be sicker and may be experiencing the same symptoms as males, male symptoms elicit a different response. Male symptoms and illnesses are perceived by parents to be more serious and life-threatening and therefore require more elaborate treatments.[10]

Differential health care allocation may also result from a higher value being placed on males than females in Cuyo Cuyo. Children of both genders are wanted and needed for economic and social reasons, but males have more economic potential than females in present-day Peru. Few cash-earning activities are open to Cuyo Cuyo females, but males can earn cash through gold mining and wage labor. Male adolescents are less of a drain on family resources because they contribute to their upkeep and education through mining gold with their male relatives, and adult males are able to help support their elderly parents. Sons are valued and treated accordingly.

Mothers say they love/want (*querer*) their male children more than their female children because girls "are born only to suffer." This refers to the hard work and childbearing adult females are destined to perform in Cuyo Cuyo and to the maltreatment and beatings they might receive from husbands. Girls are also considered more of a problem to raise than boys because of their sexual vulnerability. In the teen years, when children are most economically productive, boys can travel about freely and contribute to the family economy. Parents, however, must be vigilant over girls, lest they become pregnant out of wedlock. In general, girls are restricted in their movements and in their potential economic contributions to the family.

In sum, conceptions of greater male vulnerability, combined with a higher value placed on sons than daughters, provide a rationale for more elaborate attempts to maintain male children's health and well-being.

### Child Development and Health

Andean child development concepts provide a context for understanding the differential treatment of children by age in Cuyo Cuyo. Cuyo Cuyeños perceive a gradually strengthening life-force from birth to approximately age 7. The first few weeks of life, when the life-force is weakest, are particularly dangerous. The weakly connected life-force of a newborn or infant, as previously noted, is thought to be easily dislodged, causing sickness and death through *uraña.*

Infants with a loosely connected life force and a propensity to fright sickness are, in Cuyo Cuyo terms, not fully human, as the etymology of *uraña* suggests. This word most likely derives from the Spanish *hurañía,* meaning "diffidence, shyness, timidity, or unsociableness," a word generally associated with wild animals. Children gradually become more human as they grow and develop. The first hair-cutting ritual, which occurs at approximately age 2, can be seen as a rite of passage in which the child's acceptance into human society is symbolically acknowledged by "taming" the younger child's hair, left uncut since birth.

By age 7 a child is considered to be like a little adult, stronger and less vulnerable to illness. He or she now has a well-integrated life-force, is capable of work, and is morally responsible. Part of this view is influenced by Roman

Catholicism, which considers age 7 to be the "age of reason," when a child is capable of knowing right from wrong. Another part reflects Andean pragmatism. Children become economically productive around age 7 in Cuyo Cuyo. They have important roles in subsistence and domestic work, including herding and gathering cooking fuel, and in agricultural and mining tasks. At this point they are likely to survive to adulthood and therefore will be able to contribute to the family economy for many years.

The spiritual and pragmatic transformation of children is represented by the type of funerals given to children of different ages. Until approximately age 7, children are given a brief nighttime funeral with only immediate family members present. They are thought to be "little angels" who go directly to heaven when they die.[11] The nighttime funeral, when the spirit world is active, facilitates a child's journey to and entry into heaven. In addition, as one Puna Ayllu mother explained, before age 7, children are only *wawas* (babies) and are not worth the time and effort of a big funeral. Adults can still put in a regular day of work before the funeral. After age 7, however, children merit a daytime funeral, with the extended family and community members taking the day off to mourn.

A final piece of evidence for the different values placed on children of different ages is the inconsistent reporting and recording of neonatal deaths in Cuyo Cuyo birth and death records. As I worked with the official records, I noted many discrepancies. For some years there were death certificates for newborns, called *feto* or *nacido muerto* (fetus, born dead), but these were entered in neither the official death nor official birth registries. Only named infants were listed in the birth registry. Other years there were no *fetos* at all, even among the original death certificates. The district secretary explained that the reporting of neonatal deaths—euphemistically termed *feto* or *nacido muerto* until they were named—was optional. In Cuyo Cuyo, local values regarding neonates, reinforced at the levels of both parental reporting and official recording, are clearly evident in "official" birth and death registries.

In Andean culture, birth and human status do not coincide, as in present-day Western culture. Rather, the acquisition of human status is a gradual process taking place over several years and marked by several ritual and symbolic acts, including naming, baptizing, and the first hair-cutting.[12] These attitudes may influence the type and amount of nurturing—including health care—that a child of a particular age may receive.

### Family Planning in Cuyo Cuyo

Finally, it is important to understand differential health care allocation to children within the context of parental efforts to plan their families in Cuyo Cuyo. The term "family planning" is used here not in the conventional sense (i.e., the use of contraceptive methods), but in a broader sense that includes any efforts made by parents to control family size and composition, whether pre- or postpartum (Scheper-Hughes 1987, p. 14).

Cuyo Cuyeños, men and women alike, expressed a desire to limit family size, primarily because of limited economic resources (Maynard-Tucker 1986, 1989). The Cuyo Cuyo economy is becoming increasingly monetized rather than subsistence-oriented (Recharte 1990). Families in the research sample planted less than a half hectare of land per year (Goland 1991, p. 181). This was farmed intensively, but an adult female, an adolescent daughter or two, and occasional male labor were sufficient to care for it. Most families ran out of agricultural products (principally potatoes and other tubers) as much as 4 months before the main harvest and thus increasingly relied on cash and purchased foods for subsistence. Parents expressed an overriding anxiety about the number of mouths to feed (Graham, unpublished). In sum, land and food scarcity, lower labor needs, and increased reliance on cash are interrelated factors in the desire for smaller families in Cuyo Cuyo.

The Peruvian government, in theory, supplies birth control methods, such as oral contraceptives, at its clinics. In practice, these methods are often unavailable in Cuyo Cuyo, and when they are, Cuyo Cuyo *campesinos* lack the knowledge to use them (see also Maynard-Tucker 1986, 1989). Their desperation was evident in the many times I, as an apparently knowledgeable outsider, was asked for help to obtain them.

In the absence of artificial birth control methods, Cuyo Cuyo parents may be practicing postpartum family planning, including passive and active infanticide (as noted in other Andean locales) and sending young daughters to work as servants for urban families. Many of these practices appear to be directed at females.

Evidence for passive and active infanticide in Cuyo Cuyo is ambiguous, reflecting Cuyo Cuyeños' own ambivalent attitudes about the practice. On the one hand, infanticide is talked about matter-of-factly. One Puna Ayllu mother explained to me, for example, that it is common to leave infants, especially females, in the cold to die if they are unwanted and then blame the death on *uraña.* An Ura Ayllu father concurred: Many parents do not want female babies, so when they become ill, as infants always do, they are simply not treated and are allowed to die.

Sociocultural and economic reasons were given for infanticide. Children who present an extra burden on already strained family resources, especially excess females, excess children of either gender, and deformed infants, are generally unwanted. Twins are considered a burden because it is difficult for a mother to breastfeed and care for two infants at one time, and Cuyo Cuyeños say it is best if one dies. It is also considered best if illegitimate children die because they (and the mothers) will forever be taunted and ostracized.[13]

On the other hand, Cuyo Cuyeños demur. An Ura Ayllu mother, for example, described to me how one of her children had died of *larpa,* with symptoms that might have been Down syndrome combined with neglect. The infant had a thick tongue, cried strangely, and did not crawl at the appropriate age. It gradually wasted away and died, compounded by a severe case of scabies that was apparently left untreated.

From an etic perspective, ethnomedical beliefs appear to rationalize the deaths of less-desired children through selective neglect. The mother reconstructed the cause later: She had seen a dead animal while pregnant. Cuyo Cuyeños also acknowledge that many pregnant women see corpses without negative effects on their fetuses. However, the imputation of rationality, consciousness, and intentionality on the part of Cuyo Cuyo parents is problematic. Emically, these illnesses truly exist.

A grey area also exists between birth and parental reporting of a birth to district officials. Evidence from official birth and death registries and comments by the district secretary suggest that, especially during the crucial neonatal period, parents have limited control over whether a particular child survives to become a member of family and community. Naming a child, reporting the birth to officials, baptism, and the first hair-cutting ritual affirm a child's place in family and society. If a child does not survive, however, ethnomedical and spiritual beliefs appear to cushion negative repercussions.

Ambiguity is also reflected in the fact that, although the everyday practice of infanticide is taken for granted and politely ignored, when a specific incident of active infanticide accidently becomes public, it is negatively sanctioned. A scandal was created in the year prior to my arrival, for example, when a woman who killed her illegitimate newborn did not bury its body securely, and it was hence discovered by dogs. She was ultimately turned in to local authorities and punished. The folk illness, *lumbu wayra,* is said to be caused when a person encounters the corpse of an illegitimate baby that has been killed by its mother and hidden in an out-of-the-way place, further evidence that both illegitimacy and infanticide are negatively viewed.

The sale of female infants and young girls to families in urban areas, into what is essentially a form of indentured servitude, is a final form of postpartum family planning in Cuyo Cuyo. Parents are paid a nominal sum (in 1987, for example, the going rate for a Cuyo Cuyo infant was $20 U.S.) but are relieved entirely of the cost of childrearing. The urban family obtains a live-in servant for the rest of the child's growing years. During the PSE Project years of 1985 through 1988, 3 of the 20 research families sold, or attempted to sell, preadolescent daughters to work for families in the city, suggesting that this practice is fairly common. Several families also asked if I would "buy" their infants to take back with me to the United States. Family gender ratio appears to be important in this decision. In one of the cases, for example, the family had three daughters and one son, and then another daughter was born. When this happened they sent the 8-year-old daughter off to work for a family in the city.

In the absence of artificial birth control methods, selective neglect is likely to be the preferred form of family planning in Cuyo Cuyo. One can always claim that illness, not parental behavior, caused the death of a child. The threat of negative public sanction and the difficulty of giving up an older child are avoided.

## CONCLUSION

The ambiguity of child death in many developing countries is currently at the root of a controversy among medical anthropologists. Are poor parents forced to neglect certain children in order to survive under economically destitute conditions (Scheper-Hughes 1985, 1992)? Or do poor parents love their children yet feel powerless to control the ravages of poverty and illness on their families (Nations and Rebhun 1988)?

Data from Cuyo Cuyo show that the two positions need not be contradictory. Cuyo Cuyo parents love and care for their children, as child care ideals represent. They protect their children from illness, abstain from physical punishment, worry when their children become ill, and grieve when they die. Yet as rural Peruvians, Cuyo Cuyeños' social and economic position is precarious. The health and lives of their children suffer as a result.

Whether parents in poorer countries actually love or care for their children is not the issue we need to focus on. Instead, parental behavior must be situated within a complex, multilevel matrix of individual parental attitudes, family social and economic circumstances, and cultural and political economic factors.

The study of health care allocation is important because the manner in which health care is distributed may have a direct impact on child survival. Analyses of health care allocation are more useful, however, if their results are seen as starting points rather than ends in themselves. As demonstrated in the present study, knowledge of *which* children receive *what* type of treatment can serve as an entree to understanding *why* children of different genders and ages are treated differently by their parents, the crux of the issue.

Health care allocation and ethnographic data from Cuyo Cuyo suggest that Cuyo Cuyo parents may discriminate against females and infants in ways that jeopardize their health and well-being. Within the broader cultural and socioeconomic context, differential health care allocation and selective neglect in Cuyo Cuyo make sense. Infants suffer in the short term, but longer-term suffering for those who face an especially bleak future is avoided. The family as a whole is able to live better on limited social and economic resources. In other words, to improve the lives of their families, Cuyo Cuyo parents may be regulating family size and gender ratio through the only means available to them under current socioeconomic conditions.

Understanding the links between cultural and socioeconomic factors and parental behavior is an essential first step in planning effective child survival interventions. This knowledge is useful when applying direct interventions such as oral rehydration therapy, child vaccination, and child health care and nutrition programs. Ultimately, though, we must go even deeper.

As Cuyo Cuyo data demonstrate, if children are unwanted, direct interventions such as these are unlikely to help. Family planning programs, usually promoted under the rubric of population control and environmental protection, thus have another imperative. They prevent the untold suffering of unwanted infants, who often die lingering deaths, and of their parents, who must bear these unwanted children and grieve their loss. Women bear the brunt of these losses both physically and emotionally. Wide access to family planning methods is thus essential for child, adult female, and family well-being throughout the world.

Finally, Cuyo Cuyo data demonstrate the links between women's status and gender differentials in child care, morbidity, and mortality. Female children sicken and die disproportionately in many countries of the world. Only when women achieve economic and social parity with men will the health and well-being of female children be equally protected.

## NOTES

1. Infant, neonatal, and maternal mortality rates are calculated from 1981 through 1986 birth and death records from the District of Cuyo Cuyo, the most complete years of data available. The infant and neonatal mortality rates are averaged for the years 1981 to 1986, and maternal death rate is averaged for the years 1982 and 1984 through 1986 owing to the inconsistent quality of individual year neonatal death records and inconsistent reporting of adult causes of death. The 1981 general death rate is calculated with 1981 national census data for the district of Cuyo Cuyo and 1981 local birth and death records.

   According to the district secretary, the reporting and recording of deaths after the first few weeks of life is very accurate in Cuyo Cuyo. Infant, neonatal, and maternal mortality rates, which were calculated solely from local records, can be assumed to provide a truer picture of actual Cuyo Cuyo mortality rates than official figures might represent because care was taken to correct discrepancies in the local recording of births and infant deaths. Interpretation of the general death rate and especially of life expectancy for the southern sierra region is more problematic owing to the unreliability of vital statistics in Peru. For example, seasonal migration may affect the accuracy of census records; life expectancy rates are suspect because they are based on inaccurate local records such as those found in Cuyo Cuyo.

   See below for a more detailed discussion of the inaccuracies in local records, or refer to Larme (1992, pp. 74–76).
2. Production, Storage, and Exchange Project (National Science Foundation grant BNS 8313190), Dr. Bruce Winterhalder, principal investigator.
3. This includes children from the entire district of Cuyo Cuyo, where the two study communities are located. All visits to the health post are recorded by health post personnel. Complete data were available for 1984, 1985, and 1987; 6 months of data were available for 1986.

4. Weaning is completed by approximately age 2.
5. Health status was coded as "healthy" if the parent reported no symptoms for the child and "unhealthy" if one or more symptoms were reported.
6. Percentages do not add up to 100% because multiple treatments were used to cure some symptoms/illnesses. Altogether, 231 treatment options were used to cure 178 symptoms/illnesses.
7. This is consistent with Graham's (1991) and Leonard's (1991a, 1991b) nutritional studies in Cuyo Cuyo and Nuñoa, Puno, which show that children are not discriminated against in the allocation of food. In Cuyo Cuyo, breastfeeding on demand and allowing children to snack frequently are important preventive health concepts for children (Graham and Larme 1992).
8. The term *uraña* refers to both the name of the illness and its cause. *Uraña* interpretation overlaps with child symptoms discussed above.
9. Anger and other negative emotions may cause the *Pachamama* to "grab" and impound a child's soul in punishment, causing illness.
10. Andean conceptions of male vulnerability coincide with biologic evidence showing greater male mortality at every age (Scrimshaw 1984, p. 450; Waldron 1983), including among infants at high altitude (Haas et al. 1980, pp. 473–74).
11. This belief is common throughout Catholic Latin America (Nations and Rebhun 1988; Scheper-Hughes 1992).
12. The emphasis on process, rather than event, is a recurrent theme in Andean society and cosmology. Marriage, for example, is a process that takes place over several years (Carter 1977).
13. This is the way community members talked after a woman in one of the 20 research families became pregnant out of wedlock.

## REFERENCES

Abdullah, M., and E. M. Wheeler. 1985. "Seasonal Variation and the Intrahousehold Distribution of Food in a Bangladeshi Village." *American Journal of Clinical Nutrition* 41:1305–13.

Bairagi, Radheshyam. 1986. "Food Crisis, Nutrition, and Female Children in Rural Bangladesh." *Population and Development Review* 12:307–15.

Basu, Alaka Malwade. 1989. "Is Discrimination in Food Really Necessary for Explaining Sex Differentials in Childhood Mortality?" *Population Studies* 43:193–210.

Bolton, Ralph. 1980. "High-Altitude Sex Ratios: How High?" *Medical Anthropology* 4:107–38.

Brush, Stephen. 1977. *Mountain, Field and Family: The Economy and Human Ecology of an Andean Village.* Philadelphia, PA: University of Pennsylvania Press.

Buechler, Hans, and Judith Beuchler. 1971. P. 23 in *The Bolivian Aymara.* New York: Holt, Rinehart and Winston.

Carloni, Alice. 1981. "Sex Disparities in the Distribution of Food Within Rural Households." *Food and Nutrition* 7:3–12.

Carter, William. 1977. "Trial Marriage in the Andes?" Pp. 177–216 in *Andean Kinship and Marriage,* ed. Ralph Bolton and Enrique Mayer. Washington, DC: American Anthropological Association.

Cassidy, Claire Monod. 1980. "Benign Neglect and Toddler Malnutrition." Pp. 109–39 in *Social and Biological Predictors of Nutritional Status, Physical Growth, and Neurological Development,* ed. Lawrence S. Greene and Francis E. Johnston. New York: Academic Press.

Chen, Lincoln, Emdadul Huq, and Stan D'Souza. 1981. "Sex Bias in the Family Allocation of Food and Health Care in Rural Bangladesh." *Population and Development Review* 7:55–70.

COALE, ANSLEY. 1991. "Excess Female Mortality and the Balance of the Sexes in the Population: An Estimate of the Number of 'Missing Females.'" *Population and Development Review* 17:517–23.

CRONK, LEE. 1989. "Low Socioeconomic Status and Female-Biased Parental Investment: The Mukogodo Example." *American Anthropologist* 91:414–28.

______. 1991a. "Preferential Parental Investment in Daughters Over Sons." *Human Nature* 2:387–417.

______. 1991b. "Intention Versus Behaviour in Parental Sex Preferences Among the Mukogodo of Kenya." *Journal of Biosocial Science* 23:229–40.

DAS GUPTA, MONICA. 1987. "Selective Discrimination Against Female Children in Rural Punjab, India." *Population and Development Review* 13:77–100.

DE MEER, KEES. 1988. "Mortality in Children Among the Aymara Indians of Southern Peru." *Social Science and Medicine* 26:253–58.

DETTWYLER, KATHERINE. 1992. "The Biocultural Approach in Nutritional Anthropology: Case Studies of Malnutrition in Mali." *Medical Anthropology* 15:17–39.

GOLAND, CAROL. 1991. *Cultivating Diversity: Field Dispersion and Agricultural Risk in Cuyo Cuyo (Department of Puno, Peru)*. Ph.D. dissertation, University of Michigan, Ann Arbor.

GRAHAM, MARGARET. 1991. *Dimensions of Malnutrition and Hunger Among Children in an Andean Community*. Ph.D. dissertation, Michigan State University, E. Lansing.

______. Unpublished. "Seasonal Hunger in Andean Households."

GRAHAM, MARGARET, and ANNE C. LARME. 1992. "Food Allocation and Child Health in Rural Peru." Presented at 91st Annual Meeting of the American Anthropological Association, San Francisco, CA, December 1992.

HAAS, JERE D., EDWARD FRONGILLO, JR., CAROL STEPICK, JOHN BEARD, and LUIS HURTADO G. 1980. "Altitude, Ethnic and Sex Difference in Birth Weight and Length in Bolivia." *Human Biology*, 52:459–77.

HOSSAIN, M. MOSHADDEQUE, and ROGER I. GLASS. 1988. "Parental Son Preference in Seeking Medical Care for Children Less than Five Years of Age in a Rural Community in Bangladesh." *American Journal of Public Health* 78:1349–50.

JEFFERY, ROGER, PATRICIA JEFFERY, and ANDREW LYON. 1984. "Female Infanticide and Amniocentesis." *Social Science and Medicine* 19:1207–12.

JOHANSSON, SHELIA. 1984. "Deferred Infanticide: Excess Female Mortality During Childhood." Pp. 463–85 in *Infanticide: Comparative and Evolutionary Perspectives*, ed. Glenn Hausfater and Sarah Blafferty. New York: Aldine Publishing Co.

JOHANSSON, STEN, and OLA NYGREN. 1991. "The Missing Girls of China: A New Demographic Account." *Population and Development Review* 17:35–51.

KOENIG, MICHAEL, and STAN D'SOUZA. 1986. "Sex Differences in Childhood Mortality in Rural Bangladesh." *Social Science and Medicine* 22:15–22.

KROEGER, AXEL. 1983. "Health Interview Surveys in Developing Countries: A Review of the Methods and Results." *International Journal of Epidemiology* 12:465–81.

KUMAR, GOPALAKRISHNA. 1989. "Gender, Differential Mortality and Development: The Experience of Kerala." *Cambridge Journal of Economics* 15:517–39.

LARME, ANNE C. 1992. *Work, Reproduction and Health in Two Andean Communities (Department of Puno, Peru)*. Ph.D. dissertation, University of North Carolina at Chapel Hill.

LEONARD, WILLIAM. 1991a. "Age and Sex Differences in the Impact of Seasonal Energy Stress Among Andean Agriculturalists." *Human Ecology* 19:351–68.

______. 1991b. "Household-Level Strategies for Protecting Children from Seasonal Food Scarcity." *Social Science and Medicine* 33:1127–33.

LEVINE, NANCY. 1987. "Differential Child Care in Three Tibetan Communities: Beyond Son Preference." *Population and Development Review* 13:281–304.

Maynard-Tucker, Giselle. 1986. "Barriers to Modern Contraceptive Use in Rural Peru." *Studies in Family Planning* 17:308–16.

______. 1989. "Knowledge of Reproductive Physiology and Modern Contraceptives in Rural Peru." *Studies in Family Planning* 20:215–24.

McKee, Lauris. 1984. "Sex Differentials in Survivorship and the Customary Treatment of Infants and Children." *Medical Anthropology* 8:91–108.

______. 1988. "Controles tradicionales de la reproducción en la Sierra Ecuatoriana: Efectos en la estructura demográfica." Pp. 311–21 in *Nuevas Investigaciones Antropológicas Ecuatorianas,* edited by Lauris McKee and Silvia Arguello. Quito: Abya Yala.

Messer, Ellen. 1990. "Intra-Household Allocation of Resources: Perspectives from Anthropology." Pp. 51–62 in *Intra-household Resource Allocation: Issues and Methods for Development Policy and Planning,* ed. Beatrice Lorge Rogers and Nina P. Schlossman. Tokyo: United Nations University Press.

______. 1992. Introduction to "Intra-Household Allocation of Food and Health Care: Current Findings and Understandings." Presented at 91st Annual Meeting of the American Anthropological Association, San Francisco, CA, December 1992.

Miller, Barbara. 1984. "Daughter Neglect, Women's Work, and Marriage: Pakistan and Bangladesh Compared." *Medical Anthropology* 8:109–26.

Minturn, Leigh. 1984. "Changes in the Differential Treatment of Rajput Girls in Khalapur: 1955–1975." *Medical Anthropology* 8:127–32.

Moore, Lorna Grindlay, and Judith Regensteiner. 1983. "Adaptation to High Altitude." *Annual Reviews in Anthropology* 12:285–304.

Moseley, W. Henry, and Lincoln Chen. 1984. "An Analytical Framework for the Study of Child Survival in Developing Countries." Pp. 25–45 in *Child Survival: Strategies for Research,* edited by W. Henry Moseley and Lincoln Chen. Cambridge, UK: Cambridge University Press.

Muhuri, Pradip, and Samuel Preston. 1991. "Effects of Family Composition on Mortality Differentials by Sex Among Children in Matlab, Bangladesh." *Population and Development Review* 17:415–34.

Murra, John. 1972. "El control vertical de un máximo de pisos ecológicos en la economía de las sociedades Andinas." Pp. 429–76 in *Visita de la Provincia del Leon de Huánuco (1562), Iñigo Ortiz Zúñiga, Visitador, Tomo II.* Huánuco, Perú: Universidad Nacional Hermilio Valdizan.

Nations, Marilyn, and L. A. Rebhun. 1988. "Angels With Wet Wings Won't Fly: Maternal Sentiment in Brazil and the Image of Neglect." *Culture, Medicine and Psychiatry* 12:141–200.

Rahman, M. B., K. M. S. Aziz, M. H. Munshi, Y. Patwani, and M. Rahman. 1982. "A Diarrhea Clinic in Rural Bangladesh: Influence of Distance, Age, and Sex on Attendance and Diarrheal Mortality." *American Journal of Public Health* 72: 1124–28.

Recharte, Jorge. 1990. *Value and Economic Culture Among the Peasant Gold Miners of the Cuyo Cuyo District (Northern Puno, Peru).* Working Paper No. 3, Production, Storage and Exchange Project. Chapel Hill, NC: University of North Carolina, Department of Anthropology.

Rizvi, Najma. 1991. "Factors Affecting Inter- and Intrahousehold Food Distribution in Rural and Urban Bangladesh." Pp. 92–118 in *Diet and Domestic Life in Society,* edited by Anne Sharman, Janet Theophano, Karen Curtis, and Ellen Messer. Philadelphia, PA: Temple University Press.

Sargent, Carolyn, and Michael Harris. 1992. "Gender Ideology, Childrearing, and Child Health in Jamaica." *America Ethnologist* 19:523–37.

Scheper-Hughes, Nancy. 1985. "Culture, Scarcity, and Maternal Thinking: Maternal Detachment and Infant Survival in a Brazilian Shantytown." *Ethos* 13:291–317.

______. 1987. "Introduction: The Cultural Politics of Child Survival." Pp. 1–29 in *Child Survival: Anthropological Perspectives on the Treatment and Maltreatment of Children,* ed. Nancy Scheper-Hughes. Dordrecht, the Netherlands: D. Reidel Publishing Co.

______. 1992. *Death Without Weeping: The Violence of Everyday Life in Brazil.* Berkeley: University of California Press.

SCRIMSHAW, SUSAN. 1978. "Infant Mortality and Behavior in the Regulation of Family Size." *Population and Development Review* 4:383–403.

______. 1984. "Infanticide in Human Populations: Societal and Individual Concerns." Pp. 439–62 in *Infanticide: Comparative and Evolutionary Perspectives,* edited by Glenn Hausfater and Sarah Blaffer Hrdy. New York: Aldine Publishing Co.

SVEDBURG, PETER. 1990. "Undernutrition in Sub-Saharan Africa: Is There a Gender Bias?" *The Journal of Development Studies* 26:469–86.

UNIDAD DEPARTAMENTAL DE SALUD DE PUNO (UDES). 1987. *Informe analítico cualitativo de las acciones realizadas por la Unidad Departamental de Salud de Puno en el año de 1986.* Puno, Perú: Unidad Departamental de Salud de Puno.

WALDRON, INGRID. 1983. "Sex Differences in Illness Incidence, Prognosis and Mortality: Issues and Evidence." *Social Science and Medicine* 17:1107–23.

Chapter 2

# Transforming Society, Transforming Medicine: Lay Medical Perceptions and Self-Medication Among Contemporary Koreans*

*June J. H. Lee*

The use of Kon Gang Sik P'um (KGSP)[1] has recently been popularized among urban middle-class Koreans. This coincides with an increased public sensitivity to changing mortality patterns in Korea. Of particular interest is the fact that Korean men in their 40s and 50s have recently been a focus of public attention due to their allegedly "world-highest" mortality rate.[2] Stomach, liver, and lung cancers and chronic liver diseases are the causes of the high mortality of these Korean men (National Statistical Office 1990). In view of a perceived vulnerability to these diseases, Korean men and their families are compelled to attend to their own health maintenance and promotion. Accordingly, various health-food products as well as pharmaceuticals have become available in markets, and urban middle-class Koreans are the primary consumers of these rather expensive commodities.

A survey of health-seeking behavior among Koreans anticipated this phenomenon by showing that, at the time of the survey, 67% of respondents were taking or had taken some sort of health food for their health maintenance and that health foods are more popular among middle- and high-income households (Korea Institute for Population and Health 1988). Interestingly, only 6%

*I would like to thank Nina Etkin, Sjaak van der Geest, and Susan Whyte for their help from the inception of this research project. Special thanks go to Nina Etkin for her insightful comments on an earlier draft of this chapter. I alone am responsible for any shortcomings of this chapter.

of respondents said that they undertake exercise only for their health. In other words, the results of this survey suggest that when Koreans become conscious about their health, they are more likely to pay attention to what they eat than to whether their bodies are fit or fat.

The KGSP boom is not an entirely new phenomenon, although the scale of its commercialization and the consumer's purchasing power is unprecedented, because Koreans have a long history of using dietary items for the promotion of health as well as the treatment of various illnesses (Chun 1990; Roh 1971). In the meantime, the relatively recent influx of "Western" biomedical knowledge and pharmaceuticals has greatly affected the way Koreans understand human biology and the way in which they behave when facing illness. The rapid increase in the incidence of cardiovascular disease, various cancers, obesity, and a host of other health disorders concomitant with the rise in economic affluence is likely to perpetuate among Koreans the existing multiple use of therapeutics from diverse medical traditions, even though Korean biomedicine is predominant in the country's medical institutions (Kendall 1988; Sich and Kim 1978; Yoon 1978). This multiple therapy approach is due primarily to two facts: Biomedical therapies cannot guarantee the cure for these diseases, and the prolonged healing processes associated with these new disorders involve changes in disease manifestations that, according to Korean understanding, entail changes in therapeutic inputs and expected outcomes. In fact, Koreans tend to change their medical treatment to "traditional" Korean medicine if they have a chronic disease (Korea Institute for Population and Health 1988), and many of these newly prevalent "*hyŏn-dae-byŏng*" (modern diseases) are chronic by nature.

In view of Korea's rapid modernization and elaborated biomedical institutions, the persistent use by Koreans of nonbiomedical treatment in conjunction with biomedicine has been a nagging question for health planners (Nam et al. 1992) and an important theme for social scientists (Kendall 1988; Pang 1989; Sich and Kim 1977; Yoon 1977). Regarding Koreans' use of various medical resources, KGSP represents only the latest addition to their therapeutic repertoire. However, one could argue that a study of KGSP is more rewarding than the study of any other form of healing in contemporary Korean society. First, it provides a better opportunity to investigate lay understanding of health and medicine because most KGSPs are privately purchased and consumed. Lay medical perceptions are viewed as the most important guiding principle of Koreans' self-care through the various forms of medicine. Second, the study of KGSP leads us to the ongoing transformation of both traditional Korean medicine and biomedicine because KGSPs themselves are, for the most part, a reworking of Korean tradition with the help of modern bioscientific technologies. It is in this context of coalescing medical systems that lay medical knowledge is formulated and modified.

To investigate lay Koreans' perceptions of health and medicine, it is necessary to understand some underlying premises on which traditional Korean healing modes are based. In the first part of this chapter, those basic premises are examined in the process of reviewing the existing literature on Korean ethnomedicine. In the second part, some of the themes are introduced that have been explored in the studies of modernizing traditional medicines, such as medical pluralism, cultural construction of medicine, health commodification, and self-medication.

## ETHNOMEDICAL STUDIES ON KOREA[3]

### A Pluralistic Medical System: Biomedicine, Traditional Korean Medicine,[4] and Shamanism

Before examining what is currently known about traditional Korean medicine, I note that a postulated distinction between traditional and modern medicines is used only as a heuristic framework so as to formulate certain hypothetical propositions. This does not suggest that Korean traditional medicine has existed as an internally coherent body of inert knowledge; such an ahistorical approach to ethnomedicine has long been criticized (Nichter 1992).

The same applies for the notion of medical pluralism. As Farquhar (1987, p. 1013) notes, "It is only after a reifying division has been made that we can speak of a 'pluralistic medical system.'" In the context of multiple healing systems, a description of healing modes as bounded sets of activities does not help one understand people's pragmatic use of the healing modes, the various interpretations of their efficacy, or the ever-changing cultural significance attached to or detached from each mode. For example, Korean shamanism as a discrete domain of empirical inquiry exists only in the researcher's mind, illustrated by the fact that a shaman might recommend that her client take an antibiotic to warm a chilled body (Kendall 1988).

The introduction and spread of Western health care in Korea can be traced to the late nineteenth century, when Western culture began to be accepted slowly with much caution by the Korean people (Cha 1978; G. S. Lee 1989). During the past 30 years, however, the growth of biomedicine in Korea has been as phenomenal as the nation's rapid industrialization and modernization, owing to the perceived efficacy and practicality of pharmaceuticals and other biomedicines. Today, biomedicine in Korea enjoys a cultural as well as institutional dominance over other forms of healing such as traditional Korean medicine and shamanism (Research Institute for Health Care Policy 1992).

Nevertheless, various traditional modes of healing have been distinguished by their symbolic and religious foundations (Rhi 1973; Sich and Kim 1977), which are closely related to fundamental Korean assumptions about body, mind, individual, society, and the universe. To understand these assumptions is essential, for they have provided ordinary Koreans with various paradigms that inform health, illness, and the handling of particular kinds of suffering.

Traditional Korean medicine conceptualizes such notions as human body, mind, individual, society, and outer world, on a continuum, each quite inseparable from the other. First, a human body is considered to have *sib-i-gumun* (12 body orifices) open to the outer world's *ki* (vital energy) (Roh 1971). Not only *ki*, but also wind, cold, heat, moisture, dryness, and fire, can flow into and out of a human body, sometimes resulting in an illness due to imbalance inside the body. For instance, too much cold in a female body results in *naeng* (chill). *Naeng* is a cold imbalance in the womb, the cause of which is not appreciated by biomedicine, that brings on a heavy vaginal discharge and may cause infertility (Kendall 1987; Sich 1979).

Humoral theory, one of the most studied nonbiomedical theories of health and medicine, has been a basis for the development of traditional Korean medicine. Initially borrowed with Chinese cosmology, the hot/cold theory and the associated practices of Chinese medicine have long coexisted with an earlier indigenous Korean medicine that uses some medicinal plant treatments and shamanistic or incantatory remedies (Chun 1990; Rhi 1981). This hot/cold theory was also ground for a further elaboration to a *sasang ŭihak* (medicine of four letters/constitutions) of Korea, in which the difference in human constitution is the most important principle in the treatment of patients (Roh 1971).

In *sasang ŭihak,* the signs of health and illness are interpreted in terms of a balance of *ŭm* and *yang,* two opposing and unifying principles; the one cold, dark, and female, and the other hot, bright, and male. These properties are not immutable, however, and shift with time and space. A traditional Korean medical doctor may divide a patient's *sang* (constitution) based on his or her pulse, physiognomy, voice, odor, and so on, into four different categories: *tae-yang, so-yang, tae-um,* and *so-um.* It is according to these classifications that a doctor prescribes medications, depending on their constitutions (Pang 1989).

Second, traditional Korean medicine assumes no clear distinction between body and mind, nor any hierarchy between them (Hahm 1988), unlike biomedicine, which is predicated upon a firm body-mind dualism (Lock and Scheper-Hughes 1990). This nonduality of body and mind can be examined by the explanation and treatment of *hwabyŏng* (fire illness or anger syndrome) by traditional Korean medicine. *Hwabyŏng,* which is known as a Korean culture-bound syndrome (Lin 1983), is typically associated with suppressed anger and manifests as gastrointestinal problems, although its causes and symptoms can be extended to include a wide range of emotions and physical complaints (Pang 1990).

*Hwabyŏng* is not recognized by biomedicine; a biomedical doctor would treat only the bodily symptoms of a *hwabyŏng* patient with drugs. In contrast, traditional Korean medicine identified *hwa* as a blood-muscle lump in the epigastric region (Y. K. Kim 1982, cited in Pang 1990) and recognizes *hwabyŏng* as a somatized emotional affliction. *Hwabyŏng,* diagnosed most frequently among elderly Korean women (Pang 1989), is caused by interpersonal difficulties and socioeconomic hardship typical of what most Koreans have experienced in their post–Korean War past. In other words, *hwabyŏng* is an expression of psychosocial distress accompanied by physical manifestations, and, to be effectively cured, the practitioner's time, nurturing, and attention should follow a pharmaceutical therapy of the bodily symptoms.

As for the theoretical basis of *hwabyŏng* treatments by a traditional Korean medical doctor, emotional state is considered to be closely linked to physiologic (mal)functions. Excessive anger can cause imbalance in a person's constitution, such that too much "fire" can bring about problems related to liver, gallbladder, heart, and kidney. Conversely, balance among bodily internal organs directly involves the person's emotions, which are subject to his or her social relationships. Thus, *hwabyŏng* can be corrected by restoring balance at various levels—by the ingestion of the right substances and diet and by maintaining proper relations with other persons. In view of *hwabyŏng* treatments by traditional Korean medicine, one can conclude that a close interrelatedness between body and mind is assumed and that a "patient," rather than a "symptom," is treated in traditional Korean medicine.

Third, at the heart of biomedicine lies the notion of "bounded self and atomistic individualism" (Tambiah 1990, p. 133), whereas in Korean shamanism the boundary between an individual self and other families, as well as the shaman, is and should be blurred in order for the *kut,* the healing ceremony of a shaman, to be effective. Harvey (1976) points out that Korean shamans affect a whole family by seeing only the mothers or wives because their female clients are the embodiments of their entire families. Kendall (1988) also insightfully observes that a shaman's effectiveness as a healer comes not only from her traumatic initiation, called *sin-byŏng* (god illness), but also from her being a "knowledgeable" housewife, in terms of various medical resources as well as the diverse causes of the ailments of her fellow housewife clients.

Shamanism as a healing mode has long been of interest and has attracted a number of researchers from various disciplines, including folklorists, scholars of religion, and a group of psychiatrists who have sought to include shamanism within the theoretical framework of psychotherapy (Kim 1973, 1988). This latter approach, however, is likely to be of limited success because the adequacy and relevance of the psychotherapeutic translation of Korean shamanism have not been thoroughly examined and especially because the philosophical foundation of Korean shamanism seems quite incompatible with that of psychotherapy (J. Lee, Unpublished [a]), as outlined above.

### Lay Medical Synthesis: Multiple Use of Therapeutics

In Korea today, it is understood that traditional Korean medicine has established a more or less complementary relationship with biomedicine (Kim 1978; Pang 1989; Yoon 1977). Sich and Kim (1977) have emphasized the positive role played by traditional medicines in the process of Korea's modernization and have urged the integration of traditional medicines into the nation's health care system. Following this initiative, several multidisciplinary community medicine research efforts were made to examine whether and how this mission of medical integration can be carried out (Seoul National University 1978; Sich and Kim 1977; Yoon 1977). These projects focused on how to mobilize existing traditional medical resources to cover primary health care needs, especially in locales with inadequate or no biomedical facilities. In this context, the emphasis appears to have been a hasty application of traditional medical treatments rather than long-term efforts to understand the historical, cultural, and conceptual background of these modes of therapy.

Apart from this systematic effort to integrate traditional Korean medicine with biomedicine, successful or not, it is seldom noticed that among laypersons various forms of coalescence have already developed. (Exceptions to this are Kendall 1987 and Yoon 1983.) For instance, a folk illness such as *naeng* (Sich 1979) is an evolving concept because patients are exposed to various modes of healing and have started incorporating their experience with these different, and sometimes contradictory, explanations of illness and methods for treating its symptoms. The ultimate cause of *naeng*, according to the humoral theory of traditional Korean medicine, is a hot/cold imbalance in the womb; the immediate causes are insufficient postpartum care, constitutional vulnerability, or exposure to cold. Korean women's clinical experience with biomedical practices such as contraception and induced abortion has now added several new immediate causes to *naeng* (Kendall 1987).

Not only illness causes but also treatment choices can illustrate the "lay medical synthesis" (Kendall 1987) or "lay integration" (Yoon 1983). Koreans are reported to understand that biomedicine works quickly for acute symptoms, whereas Korean medicine is preferred for chronic diseases, as the latter are believed to strengthen the body over time (Kendall 1987; Kim 1978). It is not unusual to find patients who use several kinds of drugs simultaneously or over time (Yoon 1983). Polypharmacy is the norm rather than the exception.

Its own rationality notwithstanding, Korean health-seeking behavior has been labeled "healer-shopping," the use of a second healer without referral from the first for a single episode of illness (Kroeger 1983, p. 147). It has received mostly negative appraisals from health planners and, to a certain degree, social scientists.

Even Korean social scientists who have studied health-related issues have focused mainly on the symbolic content of healing systems or beliefs regarding disease cause and treatment, dismissing the dynamic formation of laypersons' own medical perceptions. These lay medical perceptions are formed in various clinical settings through interaction with healers of diverse medical traditions. Previous studies have resulting in reifying Korean medical knowledge into a well-bound, unchanging traditional system. In this regard, Yoon's work (1983) was a welcome exception, as he attempted to understand Korean health-seeking behavior in terms of patient integration of various medical systems.

Despite Korea's dominant biomedical institutions, people's everyday health- and/or medicine-related behavior does not necessarily conform to the bioscientific conceptualization of modern Western medicine. As illustrated in the case of *naeng,* the pluralistic medical setting of Korean society provides a context in which people easily incorporate conceptual frameworks and knowledge from different medical traditions into their own perception of health and medicine. Nevertheless, at present, little is known about the actual lay conceptualizations of medical knowledge, which are required to better understand the characteristics of the process of patient integration itself.

Additionally, lay medical knowledge is not only constantly changing but also contesting among its variants. This is exemplified by KGSP. Some members of health-food societies in Korea claim the superiority of traditional medical conceptions and dietary methods in explaining and dealing with such newly prevailing diseases as cancers and cardiovascular diseases (Yŏ-sŏng-dong-a 1992). Unlike infectious diseases, *chong-nyok kam-t'oe* (the reduction of vitality) is considered to be closely related to these new diseases. In other words, the inner bodily state at the time of outer stresses is more important with these new diseases than with infectious disease. To restore the lost vitality, treatments such as fasting and natural diet are recommended, whereas injection and medicine-taking are discouraged. These latter methods are thought to be "additive" to the already additive lifestyle—overeating and overworking—and would further aggravate the imbalance of the patient's body. However, this explanation contradicts another popular lay treatment for lost vitality—eating "hot" dishes such as "dog meat soup" and "chicken and ginseng soup" (Chun 1991). Vitality (*yang*) that is lost is supposedly compensated for by these "hearty" (*yang*) foods so that the balance between *ŭm* and *yang* is restored. One popular treatment for lost vitality recommends fasting, whereas another recommends the consumption of "hot" and "hearty" dishes.

The point is that Korean health-seeking behavior is not an irrational noncompliance (to biomedical professionals) but a rational and educated decision-making process that involves such variables as lay medical knowledge and social relationships as well as material conditions (Kim 1978; Yoon 1983). Among these variables, the importance of indigenous conceptions of illnesses that provide a basis for the dynamic process of interpreting biomedical theories and practices is stressed by Kim (1978). Kim also notes the active role of patients in negotiating and defining health care in a pluralistic medical setting. The interactive dynamics of the therapeutic efficacy of traditional Korean medicine is also hinted at when she introduces the notion of *yŏn-ttae* (Kim 1978, p. 20). *Yŏn-ttae,* a cosmologic compatibility, exists when a practitioner can empathize and communicate well with a patient so that the medicine prescribed works according to the patient's expectations. It is mostly between traditional Korean medicine practitioners and patients that a well-matched *yŏn-ttae* is observed. Thus, it is suggested that among lay Koreans therapeutic efficacy is closely related to the social relationship between a practitioner and a patient.

Therefore, a frustrating encounter with biomedical professionals could quickly make a Korean turn to other sources of health care or to self-medication.

### Kon Gang Sik P'um: Transformation of Traditional Korean Medicine and Western Biomedicine

Recent developments in medical anthropology have begun to locate medicine in its historical and cultural context and, as a result, to recognize that in most societies both traditional medicine and modern biomedicine are constantly being reinterpreted (Del Vecchio Good 1980; Etkin et al. 1990; Kleinman 1980; Logan 1973; Mitchell 1983) and innovatively syncretized into new forms of medicine (Afdhal and Welsch 1988; Bledsoe and Goubaud 1988; Jordan 1985; Waxler-Morrison 1988).

KGSP is a case in point. Koreans have believed that medicine and food are from the same sources such as plants (*sik-yag-il-ch'e* or *ŭi-sik-dong-wŏn*) and therefore have practiced taking medicinal foods. In the traditional Korean pharmacopoeia, *sangyak* (the best medicine) virtually always consisted only of dietary regimens (Huh 1991). This Korean belief in the medical efficacy of food has long been enacted in their use of *boyak* (restoring medicine). *Boyak* is used for the lack of *ŭm-aek* (*ŭm*—liquid) and *yang-ki* (*yang*—vitality). It is used, not only for the restoration of *ŭm* or *yang*, but also for the treatment of chronic as well as acute illnesses. A Korean medicine text has preserved numerous elaborate prescriptions for *boyak*, the range of application of which is quite wide. *Boyak's* popularity is further intensified by the claim that *boyak* has no side effects, unlike Western pharmaceuticals (Park 1991), because *boyak* is mostly made of plants and other food items.

Other than the professional Korean medical texts, some written documents exist on the medicinal use of dietary items in Korea (Ahn 1992; Chung 1988; Roh 1971; Sim 1974). In most cases, dietary items are identified by scientific nomenclature as well as by common names and are accompanied by cursory statements about their particular applications. Some foods are introduced as a part of Chinese materia medica, others as indigenous Korean medicines. Still others, in more recent and technical reports, are analyzed terms of their pharmacologic action on the human body. Yet these accounts are devoid of ethnographic information on the cultural contexts of such use (e.g., a preference for certain colors, tastes and shapes of plants, the importance of such concepts as *chŏng-nyŏk* (vitality or liveliness)).

If *boyak* is the food (plant) medicine of the Korean tradition, then KGSP is a modern-day hybrid medicinal food that clearly indicates the ongoing coalescence between traditional Korean medicine and biomedicine. To date, no systematic study has been done of the use of KGSP in contemporary Korean society. Several recent publications (Chun 1991; H. K. Lee 1991; S. C. Lee 1991; Sung 1989) give only a glimpse of the use of KGSP and ignore completely its sociocultural implications. Even as descriptive efforts, they lack, for instance, the classification of KGSP into subcategories such as purpose (i.e., preventive, therapeutic), form (e.g., powder, liquid, granule, capsule), and producer (e.g., pharmaceutical companies, herbalists, restaurants). Most importantly, these researchers have missed the obvious common theme of this burgeoning KGSP manufacturing industry—the scientifically approved Korean medical tradition. For instance, a great number of KGSP advertisements use biomedical terms to extol KGSP's efficacy while at the same time emphasizing the "naturalness" and safety of KGSPs.

In short, the literature of KGSP use in Korea does not reflect any social scientific rigor, and the rather static descriptions of "medicinal food" or KGSP limit their relevance for modern KGSP use. There is much discussion in popular mass media but virtually no documentation of the dynamic nature of KGSP use among Korean consumers. Nor has there been any theoretical effort to examine closely the contexts of KGSP use by linking them with how people understand bodily processes, disease pathologies, and expectations for medicine. Neither the emerging health concerns of particular age groups, such as middle-aged Korean men, nor the transformation of traditional Korean medicine and Western biomedicine has been studied in relation to KGSP use.

As exemplified in traditional Korean medicine, the therapeutic value of food items has been recognized throughout human history. The rational and adaptive basis of such food use as medicine has been investigated in many societies (Etkin 1986; Etkin and Ross 1982, 1983; Johns 1990). Whereas the use of dietary items as medicine is almost universal, definitions of health, explanations of body function, and expectations for medicine vary with place, time, and illness episode. In Korea, a medically pluralistic society with elaborate biomedical institutions, the pharmacologic effects of such medicinal foods as KGSP are much studied, and such knowledge is readily available to the public (Kang and Lee 1977; Kim et al. 1976; Lee et al. 1975; Shin 1980). Yet the availability of such knowledge and biomedical resources does not adequately explain the particular ways in which people demand and consume medicinal foods and evaluate their efficacy. To better understand the rationale underlying the thriving commercialization of medicinal food, an appreciation of popular health concerns and lay medical knowledge is required.

The interaction between lay medical understandings and practical health concerns can be examined in dietary modification for health and illness. Along with the ethnographic research on humoral theory in various cultures, a series of studies has focused on food regulations during pregnancy and puerperium (Anderson and Anderson 1975; Greenberg 1982; Ho and Chan 1985; Koo 1984; Pillsbury 1978). This research, with a focus on the cross-cultural variations of hot-cold food classifications, emphasizes that dietary modifications are to be considered, not has having a biologic origin, but as being culturally constructed (Ferro-Luzzi 1978; Laderman 1983).

For instance, in the case of Korean folk dietetics of childbirth (J. Lee, Unpublished [b]), through various culinary methods such as steaming and simmering, Korean women manipulate the intrinsic hot-cold, dry-wet properties of food items to maintain their nutritional status during critical periods without violating the symbolic classifications of food specifically assigned to pregnant and lactating women. In short, lay medical knowledge (i.e., hot-cold food classification) interacts with women's health concerns to result in the unique folk dietetics of Korea.

## TRANSFORMING SOCIETY, TRANSFORMING MEDICINE

### Coexistence of Traditional Medicine and Biomedicine: Medical Pluralism

Medical anthropologists for the past two decades have examined patterns of medicine-related behavior and the cultural interpretation of medicines. Until recently, most medical anthropologic research has focused exclusively on traditional medical phenomena. Even those anthropologists involved with public health programs in developing countries have sought more "exotic" forms of medical knowledge or practice in terms of their positive or negative effects on the acceptance of Western biomedicine (Foster 1976). Biomedicine has slowly begun to be considered as an object for cultural research (Hahn and Kleinman 1983) and explored within the purview of medical pluralism.

Several explanations have developed for the perplexing persistence of traditional medicine in spite of modernization in most developing countries. One explanation is that in a medically pluralistic society each medical system provides unique treatments for distinctive sets of illness (Kroeger 1983); for instance, biomedicine for acute illnesses and traditional medicine for chronic diseases (Colson 1971; Gould 1965; Lock 1980). Some suggest that traditional healers are particularly effective because they pay attention to the moral and social significance of illness. A facile generalization emerges, portraying traditional medical systems as being holistic and personalistic, in contrast to mechanistic and impersonalistic biomedicine (Tan 1989).

Another explanation suggests that traditional medical systems persist in the face of powerful modern biomedicine because of their structural integration with other social, economic, and political institutions of the society (Berliner 1982; Crandon 1986; Segall 1983). Some assert that in a medically pluralistic society, each medical system occupies a different position in class stratification (Frankenberg 1980), and the mixture among them is not so much a function of different therapeutic modes or their efficacy as of the dominant power structure (Elling 1981). A medical system is just another aspect of the overall socioeconomic formation of a society.

These explanations address the issue of interrelationships among various medical systems while assuming that each medical tradition is based on a distinct, internally coherent body of knowledge concerning diagnosis and treatment, and that the practice of physicians of the different types of medical systems is an expression of that knowledge. However, recent medical anthropologic studies no longer regard these assumptions as tenable. For instance, studies of Chinese medicine have revealed the multiplicity of that medical system's philosophical foundation (Unschuld 1985, 1987, 1992). They show that contemporary Chinese medicine, as represented in the country's medical integration with biomedicine (Cai 1988), is an uncritical reformulation (Farquhar 1987) and a result of the technical (e.g., acupuncture) and materialistic (e.g., some pharmaceutical regimens) reduction of the rich and sophisticated medical knowledge. Studies of modern Ayurvedic medical practices also reveal multifaceted approaches to healing within the tradition (Nichter 1989; Nordstrom 1988).

Therefore, medical pluralism can be conceived as rather ubiquitous institutional separation (Waxler 1984), which does, however, provide a context for the practice of eclectic medicine among professionals as well as laypersons. Anthropologic interest has now shifted away from the functional or structural explanations for the existence of pluralistic medical systems to dynamic negotiations and manipulations by healers and patients. In Sri Lanka, for example, indigenous medical practitioners provide all sorts of medicine, including pharmaceuticals, to cure a patient (Nordstrom 1988; Waxler-Morrison 1988). Their role is to bridge the gap between different medical traditions so that their patients can integrate the complexities of a plural medical system. Indigenous healers do not passively deliver health care services based on pure traditional medicine but rather endlessly experiment with and modify their medical theories and clinical practices (Burghart 1988; Obeyesekere 1992; Pang 1989; Trawick 1987) to meet the change in epistemologic patterns as well as the social and interpersonal needs of their patients. Lay synthesis of diverse medical tradition, however fragmentary it may be, is examined later in another section.

### Cultural Construction of Medicine in a Pluralistic Medical System

Until recently, medical anthropologists rarely included the hard core of biomedicine—pharmaceuticals—in their theoretical scope, although they have begun to research biomedicine as a cultural phenomenon (Hahn and Kleinman 1983). The question of how people in developing countries have responded to newly introduced biomedical therapeutic substances opens up a new and exciting area of study for medical anthropologists (van der Geest and Whyte 1988). People perceive imported biomedicine in relation to indigenous medicine (Etkin 1988; Etkin et al. 1990; Haak and Hardon 1988; Nichter 1980). In other words, their familiar traditional knowledge is modified and reproduced, but not replaced, by experiences with new ideas and medical products. A traditional disease pathology is, for example, expanded to explain cancer (Trawick 1991), and its pharmacopoeia appropriates penicillin into its ancient therapeutic repertoire (Burghart 1988).

The imposition of the local perspective on pharmaceuticals is dramatically exemplified in its evaluation of therapeutic efficacy. Medicines, whether belonging to traditional medicine or biomedicine, are effective if they produce required, culturally defined outcomes at particular stages of a healing process (Etkin 1988, 1992). For instance, in Hausa medicine, the signs of disease egress at the early stage of healing are very important, so the Hausa use various plant medicines and, more recently, imported pharmaceuticals to induce purgation, emesis, diuresis, and so on (Etkin and Ross 1982; Etkin et al. 1990). In the local Hausa perspective, these signs are necessary to further drug administration or to change the original diagnosis of the illness. When individuals show different responses to a pharmaceutical, the Hausa think that the drug does not accept the individual. Similar lay interpretations can be found in the Philippines (Hardon 1991) and Sri Lanka (Nichter and Nordstrom 1989).

This culturally relative approach to therapeutic efficacy explains a great deal about the use—once understood as "misuse"—of pharmaceuticals in developing countries; for example, that of chloroquine as an abortifacent in many developing countries (Bledsoe and Goubaud 1988; Browner and Ortiz de Montellano 1986). The multiple effects of medicine have been recognized by existing ethnomedical systems. The ascription of a particular effect as "primary," "secondary," and "side" depends totally on which effect is being sought at the time of application by the user and prescriber. "[A] studied appreciation of the rank ordering of medicinal (chemical and other) effects and their manipulated cascade in the management of therapeutic process" (Etkin 1992, p. 103) would help remove such pejorative terms as "misuse" and "noncompliance" from the literature on drug consumption in developing countries and reveal the underlying complexities of pharmaceutical use in many "receiver" countries.

Not only is a local understanding imposed on the evaluation of the therapeutic efficacy of existing pharmaceuticals, but it also helps shape various forms of consumer demand for new pharmaceuticals (Nichter 1989). For example, individual differentials in vulnerability to such diseases as cancer have recently highlighted the importance of *che-jil* (bodily constitution) in Korea. In view of the changing morbidity pattern from infectious diseases to chronic degenerative diseases, lay Koreans seek out the diseases' causes from their centuries-old medical theory based on human constitutions. This popular concern for bodily constitution has stimulated many pharmaceutical companies to produce various kinds of *che-jil* strengtheners, some of which are clearly revivals from the traditional Korean pharmacopoeia.

### Health Commodification and the Modernizing of Traditional Medicines

As a result of understanding the complexities of medicine usage among different peoples, medicine is now seen as a cultural construct and not merely as a biomedical substance. Medicine is a powerful healing token and as such has become an object of exchange. Although dependency on physicians among the peoples of developed countries has been growing (Illich 1976), in developing countries, the growing dependency centers more on pharmaceuticals than on physicians (Ferguson 1988; Nichter 1989).

Although this ever-increasing pharmaceutical dependency can be found virtually everywhere in developing countries, and the dominant role of transnational pharmaceutical corporations is obvious, still the individual motivations and cultural meanings underlying the use and sale of medicines are little researched. In other words, the cultural specificities of growing health commodification through medicines is yet to be appreciated.

For example, the consumer demand for medicine is to a certain extent constituted culturally (Barsky 1988; Ferguson 1981; Nichter 1989). Many people in developing countries are so impressed by the idea of injection (Reeler 1990; Wyatt 1984) as a form of drug administration that a practitioner might have to use an injection to convince a patient that he or she is offered the best treatment. In Korea, a liquid form of medicine is favored, especially "thick" liquid, which is supposedly stronger. In response to this popular penchant for a liquid form, many KGSPs are produced in a transparent gel capsule form through which the thick liquid of KGSP can be seen. This thick liquid is advertised to be directly absorbed by the organ of particular application. Underlying these consumer demands for particular drug forms is the desire for a quick fix, which has been strongly encouraged by "fast-relieving" imported pharmaceuticals.

In concert with the pharmaceuticals, therapeutics from other coexisting and competing medical traditions also contribute to the commodification of health in progress. As indigenous healers are quickly adopting new medical technologies to treat the illnesses their patients bring to them, traditional medicines, too, are undergoing a modernization process, some in their packaging, others in their "scientifically approved" efficacy. *Jamu* of Indonesia, for example, represents clearly the convergence of traditional local medicine and modern biomedicine (Afdhal and Welsch 1988). *Jamu,* a traditional and once locally prepared herbal medicine, is now produced on a large scale in the form of powders, creams, pills, and capsules. *Jamu* originates from indigenous Indonesian culture and thus symbolizes the Indonesian national identity. On the other hand, its successful marketing in and out of the country is mostly due to its modern packaging. In this modernizing process, however, *Jamu* has lost its religious connotation and is now understood simply as a medicine. Among Indonesians, *Jamu* is so much a part of daily life that it reifies health. In the case of KGSPs, as they are commercially represented in their mass media advertisements, it is the scientific revival of Korean tradition that holds appeal for their consumers. The English nomenclature for the pharmacologic constituents of a KGSP is used to extol the medical potency of the KGSP. Graphs, diagrams, and statistics are added to visualize and manipulate its efficacy. At the same time, tradition is symbolized by the Chinese character-written pharmacopoeia text that documents that particular KGSP's use in the past. In addition to that, the imagery of purity, naturalness, and safety are closely linked together to illustrate Korean tradition.

As mentioned earlier, a close interrelation exists between consumer demands and medicine production, as exemplified by KGSPs. In the case of an increased vulnerability of a particular age/gender in a society, pharmaceutical companies, in response to that vulnerability, quickly develop new products and shift their marketing focus to that particular group of people. Public anxiety over a health problem has even furthered health commodification through medicine. *Chŏng-nyŏk* (vitality), which is a polysemic word also meaning "virility," can be improved in the user by many strengthener-type KGSPs made for Korean middle-aged, white-collar men whose health, as well as their identities as fathers and husbands in their families, is in crisis. A bottle of ginseng drink with vitamin D added can give the Korean man a quick fix for lost vitality and a sense of security about his sexuality.

In summary, the ways in which health is commodified by medicine, whether traditional or modern, in various settings indicate that deep-seated cultural values and practices are indeed involved in the process. Pharmaceutical companies as agents of commercialization have played upon these popular health concerns and, to a certain degree, perpetuated them.

### Self-Medication: Further Dependency, Democratization of Healing Power, or Both?

In many developing countries a commodified health is privately appropriated through self-medication (Abosede 1984; Greenhalgh 1987; Hardon 1987; Price 1989; van der Geest 1987; Wolffers 1989). Some newly developed countries in Asia also show such a tendency; in modern Hong Kong, a wide choice of both traditional and Western non-prescription pharmaceuticals for self-medication is available. People shift their affiliation between traditional and modern forms and integrate the use of both forms in their own ways, as influenced by the type of disease (e.g., chronic/acute, everyday minor/serious), perceptions of the efficacy of different drugs, and over-the-counter drug availability (Ho et al. 1984). In Singapore, people buy prescriptions from Chinese medicine shops based on their own diagnosis without any consultation with a doctor (Ooi 1991).

Although self-medication in many developing countries may be a function of economy (i.e., lack of medical facilities and health care personnel) (Ferguson 1981), the rationale behind such a behavior is based on a long history of using plant-based home remedies (Ooi 1991; Price 1989), a custom of drug exchange as a means of expressing care and concern (Nichter 1989), and so on. A number of sociocultural contexts are woven into the self-medicating behavior of the layperson in various settings.

Even when health professionals are easily accessible, self-medication is commonly practiced (Abosede 1984), which is especially true when some positive value is attached to such behavior as "self-reliance." For example, KGSP use by lay Koreans is generally associated with modernity (although this varies according to the kind of KGSP used), health-awareness, intelligence, and wealth. Being aware of such social problems as air pollution, industrial hazards, and food contamination is highly regarded as an indication of the individual's better education and potential ability to cope with those problems. Individually fostered *che-ryŏk* (bodily strength) is described as *kug-ryŏk* (national strength). This individual self-reliance, even through medication, is tolerated, if not encouraged, by the Korean government.[5] When the Korean government announced the previously mentioned "world-highest" mortality rate for middle-aged Korean men, it did not try to modify its national health policies to accommodate the pressing need of the Korean men or to initiate a social movement for the better health of the people, as it did for the economic development of the nation. The true motivation for the government's warning about the health status of a particular group of Korean men may have been to alert the men to attend to their own health. The Korean government did not seem willing to take on the responsibility for the high mortality rate of middle-age Korean men. The point is that self-medication is not always considered negative,[6] and sociocultural, political, and economic dimensions are involved in a full understanding of the way self-medication is practiced by various social groups in different societies.

A potentially positive aspect of self-medication is that it can liberate people from unnecessary reliance on health care professionals and other members of the society (Whyte 1988). Medicines, as substances in which health and cure is reified, can be acquired by any individual. Successful self-medication can thus be a way of democratizing medical knowledge and the healing power of the medical professionals. However, it can also entail a further commodification of health through the commercial promotion of health information and education.

Self-medication is also theoretically important because examining it leads to a better picture of lay medical knowledge (i.e., definition of health, understanding of disease pathology, and perceptions of medicinal efficacy) and how such knowledge reflects interaction among different medical traditions in a society. This is not to suggest that lay medical knowledge is systematically structured and that different medical theories and healing practices always neatly complement one another. Indeed, lay medical knowledge consists of bits and pieces from various sources of information and is often internally inconsistent.

## SUMMARY

Medicines have come to be perceived as the most representative of therapeutic interventions (van der Geest and Whyte 1988). To date, the literature on medicine in developing countries records that self-medication is the most common way of taking medicines in these medically pluralistic societies. This is true of contemporary Koreans' endeavor to maintain and promote health by including much commercialized medicinal food, KGSP, in their diet. Among others, lay understanding of medicine constitutes an important principle that guides medicinal self-care through KGSP among middle-class Koreans.

## NOTES

1. KGSP, literally translated as "health food" but more correctly as "medicinal food," refers to a variety of foods distinguished by their medical benefits. Their general forms include (1) dietary items in the form of manufactured medicine (e.g., gel capsule); (2) food dishes that can be ordered at some KGSP specialty restaurants; and (3) uncooked food items, similar to "natural" or "organic" food in the United States.
2. Although mortality-based indicators are the only ones available for comparative studies of health status differentials among various populations, it is well recognized among demographers that mortality measures have a very limited applicability owing to the fact that the data on which the mortality rates are based are very often incomplete and inaccurate (Hansluwka 1987; Murray 1987; Phillips 1991). Korean mass media, ignoring the difficulties associated with the mortality rates and their comparison among different populations, reported the unusually high mortality rate of middle-aged (i.e., between the ages of 45 and 55) Korean men as the "world-highest." However, their allegation is not totally baseless: The Korean government's National Statistical Office publishes an "Annual Report on the Cause of Death Statistics," whose 1990 version records that the mortality rate of Korean men, as they approach middle age, sharply increases, to show an unusually great gender differential.
3. This review covers only those studies by trained anthropologists, with the exception of some descriptive research on Korean shamanism and traditional Korean medicine.
4. Traditional Korean medicine refers to the classic medical theory and clinical practices that have been developed by professionally educated traditional doctors. Medicines at the popular level, so-called folk medicines in Korea, have not been defined coherently nor distinguished from traditional Korean medicine by the few researchers who included the phenomenon in their studies on Korean medicine. How and even whether one can distinguish among traditional medicine, folk medicine, and shamanism in Korea have not been of scholarly interest. It is an important question to ask, however, in terms of the various healing modes' influence on the formation of lay medical perceptions among Koreans. Ethnomedicine scholars have developed several ways of differentiating local medicines (Dunn 1976; Leslie 1976; see Tan 1989 for a discussion on the labeling of these medicines).
5. See Lock (1993) for an examination of the government's influence on the ways people take care of their own or their family members' health.
6. Self-medication always has several possible negative consequences, such as overmedication, tampering of medicines, and side effects. However, in the case of KGSP use in Korea, some practical and conceptual difficulties exist in the application of these concepts. First, because the issue of whether to regulate KGSP legally is a current controversy in Korea, usable definitions of "tampering" and "side effects" of KGSP are not readily available to either lay consumers or health administrators. Second, KGSP is used by Koreans to maintain bodily balance of *ŭm* and *yang* by restoring what is lacking. Thus, it is always possible to correct any

imbalance caused by overuse of one type of KGSP by using another kind of KGSP. Hence, without focused research into KGSP use, little can be said regarding its possible misuse.

## REFERENCES


ABOSEDE, O. A. 1984. "Self-Medication: An Important Aspect of Primary Health Care." *Social Science and Medicine* 19:699–703.

AFDHAL, AHMAD F. and ROBERT L. WELSCH. 1988. "The Rise of the Modern Jamu Industry in Indonesia: A Preliminary Overview." Pp. 149–72 in *The Context of Medicine in Developing Countries,* edited by S. van der Geest and S. R. Whyte. Dordrecht, The Netherlands: Kluwer Academic Publishers.

AHN, DUK-KYUN. 1992. *Restorative Medicine of Korea.* "Hanguk ui Boyak" Seoul: Yeol-neil chaek-deol.

ANDERSON, E. N. and MARJA L. ANDERSON. 1975. "Folk Dietetics in Two Chinese Communities, and Its Implications for the Study of Chinese Medicine." Pp. 69–100 in *Medicine in Chinese Cultures: Comparative Studies of Health Care in Chinese and Other Societies,* edited by A. Kleinman, P. Kunstadter, E. R. Alexander, and J. L. Gale. Washington, DC: U.S. Department of Health, Education, and Welfare.

BARSKY, ARTHUR J. 1988. "The Paradox of Health." *New England Journal of Medicine* 318:414–18.

BERLINER, HOWARD S. 1982. "Medical Modes of Production." Pp. 162–73 in *The Problem of Medical Knowledge,* edited by A. Treacher and P. Wright. Edinburgh: Edinburgh University Press.

BLEDSOE, CAROLINE H. and MONICA F. GOUBAUD. 1988. "The Reinterpretation and Distribution of Western Pharmaceuticals: An Example from the Mende of Sierra Leone." Pp. 253–76 in *The Context of Medicines in Developing Countries,* edited by S. van der Geest and S. R. Whyte. Dordrecht, the Netherlands: Kluwer Academic Publishers.

BROWNER, CAROLE H. and BERNARD R. ORTIZ DE MONTELLANO. 1986. "Herbal Emmenagogues Used by Women in Colombia and Mexico." Pp. 32–47 in *Plants in Indigenous Medicine and Diet,* edited by N. L. Etkin. New York: Gordon and Breach.

BURGHART, RICHARD. 1988. "Penicillin: An Ancient Ayurvedic Medicine." Pp. 289–98 in *The Context of Medicines in Developing Countries,* edited by S. van der Geest and S. R. Whyte. Dordrecht, the Netherlands: Kluwer Academic Publishers.

CAI, JINGFENG. 1988. "Integration of Traditional Chinese Medicine with Western Medicine: Right or Wrong?" *Social Science and Medicine* 27:521–29.

CHA, SUNGMAN. 1978. "Korean Heritage in Medicine: A Glimpse of History." *Yonsei Medical Journal* 19:75–84.

CHUN, SEOK-JO. 1991. "What Is Wrong With Restorative Foods?" "Kongangsikp'um, Mueosi Muncheinga?" *Issue Paper* 12:39–45. Seoul: Research Institute for Health Care Policy.

CHUNG, MIN-SEONG. 1988. *Rediscovery of Folk Medicine [of Korea].* "Minjok Uihak ui Chaebalkyon." Seoul: Hakminsa.

______. 1990. *History of Korean Medicine.* "Hanguk Uihak ui Yoksa." Seoul: Hakminsa.

COLSON, ANTHONY C. 1971. "The Differential Use of Medical Resources in Developing Countries." *Journal of Health and Social Behavior* 12:226–37.

CRANDON, LIBBET. 1986. "Medical Dialogue and the Political Economy of Medical Pluralism: A Case from Rural Highland Bolivia." *American Ethnologist* 13:463–76.

DEL VECCHIO GOOD, MARY-JO. 1980. "Of Blood and Babies: The Relationship of Popular Islamic Physiology to Fertility." *Social Science and Medicine* 14(B):147–56.

DUNN, FRED. 1976. "Traditional Asian Medicine and Cosmopolitan Medicine as Adaptive Systems." Pp. 133–58 in *Asian Medical Systems,* edited by C. Leslie. Berkeley: University of California Press.

ELLING, RAY H. 1981. "Political Economy, Cultural Hegemony and Mixes of Traditional and Modern Medicine." *Social Science and Medicine* 15:89–99.

ETKIN, NINA L. (ed.). 1986. *Plants in Indigenous Medicine and Diet: Biobehavioral Approaches.* New York: Gordon and Breach.

______. 1988. "Cultural Construction of Efficacy." Pp. 299–326 in *The Context of Medicines in Developing Countries,* edited by S. van der Geest and S. R. Whyte. Dordrecht: Kluwer.

______. 1992. "'Side Effects': Cultural Constructions and Reinterpretations of Western Pharmaceuticals." *Medical Anthropology Quarterly* 6:99–113.

ETKIN, NINA L., and PAUL J. ROSS. 1982. "Food as Medicine and Medicine as Food: An Adaptive Framework for the Interpretation of Plant Utilization Among the Hausa of Northern Nigeria." *Social Science and Medicine* 16:1559–73.

______. 1983. "Malaria, Medicine, and Meals: Plant Use Among the Hausa and Its Impact on Disease." Pp. 231–59 in *The Anthropology of Medicine,* edited by L. Romanucci-Ross, D. E. Moerman, and L. R. Tancredi. New York: Praeger Publishers.

ETKIN, NINA L., PAUL J. ROSS, and IBRAHIM MUAZZAMU. 1990. "The Indigenization of Pharmaceuticals: Therapeutic Transitions in Rural Hausaland." *Social Science and Medicine* 30:919–28.

FARQUHAR, JUDITH. 1987. "Problems of Knowledge in Contemporary Chinese Medical Discourse." *Social Science and Medicine* 24:1013–21.

FERGUSON, ANNE E. 1981. "Commercial Pharmaceutical Medicine and Medicalization: A Case Study from El Salvador." *Culture, Medicine and Psychiatry* 5:105–34.

______. 1988. "Commercial Pharmaceutical Medicine and Medicalization: A Case Study from El Salvador." Pp. 19–46 in *The Context of Medicine in Developing Countries,* edited by S. van der Geest and S. R. Whyte. Dordrecht, the Netherlands: Kluwer Academic Publishers.

FERRO-LUZZI, G. EICHINGER. 1978. "More on Salt Taboo." *Current Anthropology* 19:412–15.

FOSTER, GEORGE M. 1976. "Medical Anthropology and International Health Planning." *Medical Anthropology Newsletter* 7:12–18.

FRANKENBERG, RONALD. 1980. "Medical Anthropology and Development: A Theoretical Perspective." *Social Science and Medicine* 14:197–207.

GOULD, HAROLD A. 1965. "Modern Medicine and Folk Cognition in Rural India." *Human Organization* 24:201–8.

GREENBERG, LINDA. 1982. "Midwife Training Programs in Highland Guatemala." *Social Science and Medicine* 16:1599–1609.

GREENHALGH, TRISHA. 1987. "Drug Prescription and Self-Medication in India." *Social Science and Medicine* 25:307–18.

HAAK, HILBRAND and ANITA P. HARDON. 1988. "Indigenized Pharmaceuticals in Developing Countries: Widely Used, Widely Neglected." *Lancet* 2:260–61.

HAHM, PYUNG-CHOON. 1988. "Shamanism and the Korean World-View, Family Life Cycle, Society and Social Life." Pp. 60–97 in *Shamanism: The Spirit World of Korea,* edited by C. Yu and R. Guisso, Trans. K. Suh and H. Im. Berkeley, CA: Asian Humanities Press.

HAHN, ROBERT and ARTHUR KLEINMAN. 1983. "Biomedical Practice and Anthropological Theory: Frameworks and Directions." *Annual Review of Anthropology* 12:305–33.

HANSLUWKA, HARALD E. 1987. "Measuring the Health Status of a Population: Current State of the Art." *Population Bulletin of the United Nations* 23/24:56–75.

HARDON, ANITA. 1987. "The Use of Modern Pharmaceuticals in Fillippino Village: Doctor's Prescription and Self-Medication." *Social Science and Medicine* 25:277–93.

______. 1991. "That Drug is Hiyang for Me: Lay Perceptions of the Efficacy of Drugs in

Manila, Philippines." Presented to International Conference on Social and Cultural Aspects of Pharmaceuticals. Zeist, the Netherlands, 17–21 October.

HARVEY, YOUNG-SOOK K. 1976. "The Korean Mudang as a Household Therapist." Pp. 191–98 in *Culture-Bound Syndromes, Ethnopsychiatry, and Alternate Therapies,* edited by W. P. Lebra. Honolulu: University of Hawaii Press.

HO, SUZANNE C. and S. Y. CHAN. 1985. "Dietary Beliefs in Health and Illness Among a Hong Kong Community." *Social Science and Medicine* 28:223–30.

HO, SUZANNE C., K. C. LUN, and W. K. NG. 1984. "The Role of Chinese Traditional Medical Practice as a Form of Health Care in Singapore: Health Conditions, Illness Behavior and Medical Preferences of Patients of Institutional Clinics." *Social Science and Medicine* 18:745–52.

HUH, CHEONG. 1991. "Sociocultural Background of Restorative Medicine Taking." "Boyak ui Sahoemunhwachok Baegyong." *Issue Paper* 12:1–6. Seoul: Research Institute for Health Care Policy.

ILLICH, IVAN. 1976. *Medical Nemesis: The Expropriation of Health.* New York: Pantheon.

JOHNS, TIMOTHY. 1990. *With Bitter Herbs They Shall Eat It.* Tucson, AZ: University of Arizona Press.

JORDAN, ROY E. 1985. *Folk Medicine in Madura* (Indonesia). Ph.D. thesis. Rijksuniversiteit, Leiden, the Netherlands.

KANG, YOUNG-HEE, and JUNE-SEUNG LEE. 1977. "Plant Nutritional and Physiological Studies of Korean Ginseng." *Journal of National Academy of Sciences* 16:27–62. Seoul: National Academy of Sciences.

KENDALL, LAUREL. 1987. "Cold Wombs in Balmy Honolulu: Ethnogynecology Among Korean Immigrants." *Social Science and Medicine* 25:367–76.

______. 1988. "Healing Thyself: A Korean Shaman's Afflictions." *Social Science and Medicine* 27:445–50.

KIM, BYONG-KAK, HEE-KYUNG CHOI, and EUNG-CHIL CHOI. 1976. "Studies on the Constituents of Higher Fungi in Korea." *Journal of National Academy of Sciences* 15:211–20. Seoul: National Academy of Sciences.

KIM, KWANG-IEL. 1973. "Shamanist Healing Ceremonies in Korea." *Korea Journal* 13:41–47.

______. 1988. "Kut and the Treatment of Mental Disorders." Pp. 131–61 in *Shamanism: The Spirit World of Korea,* edited by C. Yu and R. Guisso. Trans. K. Suh and H. Im. Berkeley, CA: Asian Humanities Press.

KIM, SEONG-NAE. 1978. "Traditional Medical Culture Under Acculturation in a Korean Rural Village." *Anthropological Study* 4:3–57. Seoul: The Anthropological Society of Seoul National University.

KLEINMAN, ARTHUR. 1980. *Patients and Healers in the Context of Culture.* Berkeley, CA: University of California Press.

KOO, LINDA. 1984. "The Use of Food to Treat and Prevent Disease in Chinese Culture." *Social Science and Medicine* 18:757–66.

KOREA INSTITUTE FOR POPULATION AND HEALTH. 1988. *A Feasibility Study on the Integration of Traditional Medicine into Primary Health Care in Korea.* Seoul: Korea Institute for Population and Health.

KROEGER, AXEL. 1983. "Anthropological and Socio-Medical Health Care Research in Developing Countries." *Social Science and Medicine* 17:147–61.

LADERMAN, CAROL. 1983. *Wives and Midwives: Childbirth and Nutrition in Rural Malaysia.* Berkeley, CA: University of California Press.

LEE, GRANT S. 1989. "The Growth of Medicine and Protestantism Under Persecution: The Korean Experience." *Korea Journal* 29:36–51.

LEE, HYUNG-KOO. 1991. "Restorative Medicine and Health (Boyak kwa Kongang)." *Issue Paper* 12:29–34. Seoul: Research Institute for Health Care Policy.

LEE, JUNE J. H. 1993. Unpublished(a). "An Open Question: How Can We Translate 'Korean Shamanism' into Western Psychiatry?" Department of Anthropology, University of Hawaii, Manoa.

______. 1993. Unpublished(b). *Folk Dietetics of Childbirth in Korea.* Master's thesis. Department of Anthropology, University of Hawaii, Manoa.

LEE, SANG-CHONG. 1991. "Korean Medicine and Strengtheners" (Hanguk Uihak Kwa Kangjangche)." *Issue Paper* 12:7–14. Seoul: Research Institute for Health Care Policy.

LEE, SANG-SUP, BYUNG-SUL YU, BYONG-KAK KIM, and NAK-DOO KIM. 1975. "Studies on Hypotensive Ingredients in Korean Crude Drugs." *Journal of National Academy of Sciences* 14:275–292. Seoul: National Academy of Sciences.

LESLIE, CHARLES. 1976. *Asian Medical Systems.* Berkeley, CA: University of California Press.

LIN, KEH-MING. 1983. "Hwa-Byung: A Korean Culture-Bound Syndrome?" *American Journal of Psychiatry* 140:105–107.

LOCK, MARGARET. 1980. *East Asian Medicine in Urban Japan.* Berkeley, CA: University of California Press.

______. 1993. "Ideology, Female Midlife, and the Greying of Japan." *Journal of Japanese Studies* 19:43–78.

LOCK, MARGARET and NANCY SCHEPER-HUGHES. 1990. "A Critical-Interpretive Approach in Medical Anthropology: Rituals and Routines of Discipline and Dissent." Pp. 47–72 in *Medical Anthropology: Contemporary Theory and Method,* edited by T. Johnson and C. Sargent. New York: Praeger.

LOGAN, MICHAEL. 1973. "Humoral Medicine in Guatemala and Peasant Acceptance of Modern Medicine." *Human Organization* 32:385–95.

MITCHELL, M. FAITH. 1983. "Popular Medical Concepts in Jamaica and Their Impact on Drug Use." *Western Journal of Medicine* 139:841–47.

MURRAY, CHRISTOPHER, J. 1987. "A Critical Review of International Mortality Data." *Social Science and Medicine* 25:773–81.

NAM, EUN-WOO, SEUNG-HYUN KIM, and SANG-HYO NAM. 1992. "A Study on the Integration of Korean Traditional Medicine and Biomedicine." *Korean Hospital Association Newsletter* 21:51–56.

NATIONAL STATISTICAL OFFICE. 1991. *Annual Report on the Cause of Death Statistics.* Seoul: National Statistical Office.

NICHTER, MARK. 1980. "The Layperson's Perception of Medicine as Perceptive into the Utilization of Multiple Therapy Systems in the Indian Context." *Social Science and Medicine* 14(B):225–33.

______. 1989. "Pharmaceuticals, Health Commodification, and Social Relations: Ramifications for Primary Health Care." Pp. 233–77 in *Anthropology and International Health,* edited by M. Nichter. Philadelphia, PA: Gordon and Breach.

______. 1992. *Anthropological Approaches to the Study of Ethnomedicine.* Philadelphia, PA: Gordon and Breach.

NICHTER, MARK and CAROLYN R. NORDSTROM. 1989. "The Question of Medicine Answering: The Social Relations of Healing in Sri Lanka." *Culture, Medicine and Psychiatry* 13:367–90.

NORDSTROM, CAROLYN R. 1988. "Exploring Pluralism: The Many Faces of Ayurveda." *Social Science and Medicine* 27:479–89.

OBEYESEKERE, GANANATH. 1992. "Science, Experimentation and Clinical Practice in Ayurveda." Pp. 160–76 in *Paths to Asian Medical Knowledge,* edited by C. Leslie and A. Young. Berkeley, CA: University of California Press.

OOI, G. L. 1991. "The Persistence of Chinese Medicine." *Social Science and Medicine* 32:261–66.

PANG, KEUM-YOUNG C. 1989. "The Practice of Traditional Korean Medicine in Washington, D. C." *Social Science and Medicine* 28:875–84.

______. 1990. "Hwa-Byung: The Construction of Korean Elderly Immigrant Women in the United States." *Culture, Medicine and Psychiatry* 14:495–512.

PARK, CHAN-WOONG. 1991. "Boyak." *Issue Paper* 12:21–28. Seoul: Research Institute for Health Care Policy.

PHILLIPS, DAVID R. 1991. "Problems and Potential of Researching Epidemiological Transition: Examples from Southeast Asia." *Social Science and Medicine* 33:395–401.

PILLSBURY, BARBARA L. K. 1978. "'Doing the Month': Confinement and Convalescence of Chinese Women After Childbirth." *Social Science and Medicine* 12:11–22.

PRICE, LAURIE J. 1989. "In the Shadow of Biomedicine: Self-Medication in Two Ecuadorian Pharmacies." *Social Science and Medicine* 28:905–15.

RESEARCH INSTITUTE FOR HEALTH CARE POLICY. 1992. "Biomedical Facilities in Korea: Comparison With Developed Countries." *Issue Paper* 13 (a special issue). Seoul: Research Institute for Health Care Policy.

REELER, ANNE V. 1990. "Injections: A Fatal Attraction?" *Social Science and Medicine* 31:1119–25.

RHI, BOO-YOUNG. 1973. "Problems of Medical Cultural Adjustment in Korea." *Neuropsychology* 12:98–109.

______. 1981. "Illness and Healing in the Three Kingdom Period: A Symbolical Interpretation." *Korea Journal* 21:4–12.

ROH, CHUNG-WOO. 1971. "Chinese Medicine in Korea." *Korea Journal* 11:24–35.

SEGALL, MALCOLM. 1983. "On the Concept of a Socialist Health System: A Question of Marxist Epistemology." *International Journal of Health Services* 13:221–25.

SEOUL NATIONAL UNIVERSITY, SCHOOL OF PUBLIC HEALTH. 1978. *Choon-sung Community Medicine Project.* Seoul: Seoul National University Press.

SHIN, HAY-DONG. 1980. "Purisiri (Mountain Ginseng) in Folkloristic Aspect." *Annual Newsletter of the Scandinavian Institute of Asian Studies* 14:3–17.

SICH, DOROTHEA. 1979. "Naeng: Encounter with a Folk Illness During Modern Gynecological Consultations in Korea." *Transcultural Psychiatry Research Review* 18:45–46.

SICH, DOROTHEA and YOUNG-KEY KIM. 1977. "A Study on Traditional Healing Techniques and Illness Behavior in a Rural Korean Township." *Anthropological Study* 2:75–111. Seoul: The Anthropological Society of Seoul National University.

______. 1978. "A Study on the Childbearing Behavior of Rural Korean Women and Their Families." *Transaction of Royal Asiatic Society, Korea Branch* 53:27–55.

SIM, SANG-NYONG. 1974. *Natural Medicinal Food* (Yak I Toenun Chayonsik). Seoul: Changjosa.

SUNG, NAK-EUNG. 1989. *About Health Food* (Kongangsikp'um e Taehayo). *Issue Paper* 5:49–54. Seoul: Research Institute for Health Care Policy.

TAMBIAH, STANLEY. 1990. *Magic, Science, and the Scope of Rationality.* New York: Cambridge University Press.

TAN, MICHAEL L. 1989. "Traditional or Transitional Medical System?: Pharmacotherapy as a Case for Analysis." *Social Science and Medicine* 29:301–307.

TRAWICK, MARGARET. 1987. "The Ayurvedic Physician as Scientist." *Social Science and Medicine* 24:1031–50.

______. 1991. "An Ayurvedic Theory of Cancer." *Medical Anthropology* 13:121–36.

UNSCHULD, PAUL. 1985. *Medicine in China: A History of Ideas.* Berkeley, CA: University of California Press.

______. 1987. "Traditional Chinese Medicine: Some Historical and Epistemological Reflections." *Social Science and Medicine* 24:1023–29.

______. 1992. "Epistemological Issues and Changing Legitimation: Traditional Chinese Medicine in the Twentieth Century." Pp. 44–61 in *Paths to Asian Medical Knowledge,* edited by C. Leslie and A. Young. Berkeley, CA: University of California Press.

VAN DER GEEST, SJAAK. 1987. "Self-Care and the Informal Sale of Drugs in South Cameroon." *Social Science and Medicine* 25:293–305.

VAN DER GEEST, SJAAK and SUSAN R. WHYTE (eds.). 1988. *The Context of Medicines in Developing Countries.* Dordrecht, the Netherlands: Kluwer Academic Publishers.

WAXLER, NANCY E. 1984. "Behavioral Convergence and Institutional Separation: An Analysis of Plural Medicine in Sri Lanka." *Culture, Medicine and Psychiatry* 8:187–205.

WAXLER-MORRISON, NANCY E. 1988. "Plural Medicine in Sri Lanka: Do Ayurvedic and Western Medical Practices Differ?" *Social Science and Medicine* 27:531–44.

WHYTE, SUSAN R. 1988. "The Power of Medicines in East Africa." Pp. 217–33 in *The Context of Medicines in Developing Countries,* edited by S. van der Geest and S. R. Whyte. Dordrecht, the Netherlands: Kluwer Academic Publishers.

WOFFLERS, IVAN. 1989. "Traditional Practitioners' Behavioral Adaptations to Changing Patient's Demands in Sri Lanka." *Social Science and Medicine* 29:1111–19.

WYATT, H. V. 1984. "The Popularity of Injections in the Third World: Origins and Consequences for Poliomyelitis." *Social Science and Medicine* 19:911–15.

YŎ-SŎNG-DONG-A. 1992. "Health Food Societies in Seoul." "Seoul ui Kongangsikp'um moimdeol." July. Seoul: Dong-A-Il-Bo-Sa.

YOON, SOON-YOUNG. 1977. *An Ethnomedical Anthropological Study of Rural Community's Utilization of Folk and Modern Health Facilities (Sudong Report).* Seoul: Ewha Woman's University Press.

______. 1978. *Korean Rural Health Culture.* Seoul: Ewha Woman's University Press.

______. 1983. "A Legacy without Heirs: Korean Indigenous Medicine and Primary Health Care." *Social Science and Medicine* 17:1467–76.

Chapter 3

# Intrapsychic Autonomy and the Emotional Construction of Biocultural Illness: A Question of Balance

*Mary Katharine Duffié*

Biocultural illness is the tendency to experience socially conditioned emotional states in terms of physical symptoms. The literature on folk illness suggests that "nerves-nevra-nervios-'Uzr" (a term respectively derived from English, Greek, Spanish, and Egyptian words) is a culturally constructed emotional distress message, transmitted symbolically through the human body into one's social system. The symptoms appear at the interface of chronic emotional distress and culturally ordered imbalances in power distribution, be they social or economic (Davis 1990; Dunk 1989; Guarnaccia and Farias 1988, 1989; Morsy 1978a, 1978b; Van Schaik 1989). When emotional distress is repressed for whatever cultural reason, physiologic processes are stimulated, producing culture-specific somatic symptoms.

As a physical illness with a psychosocial origin, nerves-nevra-nervios-'Uzr is of interest to medical anthropologists because it defies the mind-body dualism in the epistemology of Western biomedicine. Constrained by science, the biomedical model separates mind from body, tending to "categorize and treat human afflictions as if they were either wholly organic or wholly psychological in origin" (Lock 1990, p. 53), with little or no attention paid to the social context that gives rise to symptom expression. The tendency to separate mind from body has proved effective in dealing with diseases that have a known biologic or genetic origin, such as communicable and hereditary illnesses. However, the biomedical model breaks down in consideration of socially constructed physical illnesses—illness that results from a psychophysiologic reaction to a stimulus in one's social system, as is the case with nerves-nevra-nervios-'Uzr. The dualism in the biomedical model often results in symptoms being medicalized, such that there is a tendency to transform a social cause into a biologic one.

The failure of the biomedical model to successfully relate individual psychologies to the physical body and further to the respective social system has prompted much criticism in medical anthropology. Margaret Lock and Nancy Schepher-Hughes (1990) suggest that medical anthropologists and clinicians should "struggle to view humans and the experience of illness and suffering from an integrated perspective" (p. 53). They recognize, however, that as professionals we lack a precise vocabulary with which to do so—one that deals effectively with mind-body-society interconnections. They argue that fragmented concepts like "biocultural" and "psychosomatic" are "feeble ways of expressing the many forms in which the mind speaks through the body, and ways in which society is inscribed on the expectant canvas of human flesh" (p. 53).

The idea that folk illness does not operate in a vacuum is well established in medical anthropology, but beyond this it has traditionally been up to individual ethnographers to describe and interpret the various illness contexts. Consequently, we have a collection of very good folk illness ethnographies, well written with penetrating insight but unorganized in being related to a common structure.

Building on the findings of prominent folk illness researchers and bringing together threads of the critical and phenomenologic theory traditions, I propose an interpretive model that provides such an organizational framework. The model interprets a specific set of integrated relations linking the processes in psyche, soma, and culture, which together reflect biocultural illness. In doing so, I am pursuing a more inclusive rational basis (broader than the traditional biomedical/psychoanalytic models). Thus, the model provides an intellectual foundation that conceives of oppositions such as mind/body and individual/society (an integral part of a discussion on nerves-nevra-nervios-'Uzr) as existing in a complementary relationship (i.e., psychobiology *and* society), instead of the traditional contrastive one (i.e., mind *or* body, individual *or* society). In this light, traditional Euro-American oppositions, such as mind and body, are viewed as two sides of the same coin that phenomenologists call "being in the world" (D'Aquili et al. 1990).

The model is adequate for use with comparative data taken from five folk ethnographies. It suggests a common blueprint or fundamental structure underlying the dynamics of folk illness in some of its various forms, making it possible then to superimpose ethnographic details related to the various illness contexts. The structure itself remains constant despite cross-cultural variation in symptom repertoire and value orientations.

First, I review several well-known case studies, the details of which come from five frequently referenced ethnographies. Next, a distillation of relevant theoretical considerations from critical theory and phenomenology is presented to establish an intellectual basis for components of the model. Finally, I introduce a concept uniting the three variables of biocultural illness—psyche, soma, and culture—fundamentally.

The synthesis of theoretical forms with ethnographic interpretation comprises what is original in the analysis. My major point is that nerves-nevra-nervios-'Uzr is manifested at the intersection of three impaired expressions of "existential balance": (1) At the level of psyche, a lack of "intrapsychic autonomy," which would otherwise provide mental representations of enduring sources of self-esteem, comfort, and self-knowledge (Ewing 1991), makes individuals depend on inappropriate social contexts for these; (2) at the level of physiology, homeostatic regulating and counterregulating mechanisms that fail to respond adequately to the flight/fight response produce somatic symptoms associated with the major biologic systems; and (3) at the level of culture, asymmetric power relationships in the political economy interdict certain social, economic, and psychological needs of individuals.

## ETHNOGRAPHIC CONSIDERATIONS

The following review of nerves-nevra-nervios-'Uzr ethnographies is organized in terms of the context that gives rise to various symptomatology, including the cultural considerations contributing to emotional distress. Following are basic characteristics epitomizing the folk illness ethnographies reviewed here, and most others (including cases where the researcher has included not only the traditions, values, and attitudes of the culture in question, but also the class relations and influence of the political economy in the social production of illness). (1) Nerves-nevra-nervios-'Uzr is socially constructed as the afflicted select from a mutually agreed upon, dynamic array of ailments and complaints called "symptom repertoires." Shorter (1982) defines *symptom repertoire* as "a range of physical symptoms available to the unconscious mind for the physical expression of psychological conflict" (p. 547). (2) The symptom symbolism of nerves-nevra-nervios-'Uzr places human suffering in a meaningful context. Whether the cultural focus is a set of somatic symptoms or a symptom discourse, individuals use nerves-nevra-nervios-'Uzr as a culturally appropriate vehicle for using their support system. The body is an "idiom of distress" (Nichter 1981; Parsons 1984) because attacks are intended to provide relief—either through the mobilization of the individual's emotional support network or by withdrawing from ordinary routine activities. (3) Nerves-nevra-nervios-'Uzr manifests primarily, although not exclusively, among women in social contexts characterized by some kind of cultural oppression borne of power inequities. Its genesis lies not in an individual's physiology, but rather in the lived experience of culturally ordered, structural imbalances in the social system and/or the political economy. "The large body of research on nerves-nevra-nervios-

'Uzr in medical anthropology can be interpreted not merely as culturally constituted idioms for the expression of distress, but also as a dominant, widely distributed and flexible metaphor for negotiating relations of power" (Lock 1990, p. 70).

***Immigrant Greek women in Montreal—"nevra"*** Dunk studied 100 first-generation Green immigrant families in Montreal to understand the meaning of "nevra" according to the Greek cultural experience. Her findings suggest that nevra is the reason most women do not remain healthy. The symptom repertoire for nevra includes headaches, dizziness, a heat sensation starting at the back of the neck and moving down the spine, and a pain radiating from the heart.

As a contextual background, concepts of honor and shame are organizing principles in the Greek experience. Men are expected to be providers and to protect the family honor. Women are expected to protect their modesty and sexuality through carefully controlled behavior. Because social worth is constantly being scrutinized by other families, discussion of psychological problems with others is discouraged.

Nevra's expression stems from economic and social pressures within the social system. According to Dunk, a traditional division of labor exists "with women, even those holding full-time jobs (mostly at a local garment factory), responsible for the domestic routine of cooking, looking after children and household chores" (p. 31). In addition to low wages, pressure from the garment factory to work at home or lose their jobs, and responsibilities of child care, immigrant women lose support from extended family/community upon emigration from Greece, where they worked collectively in village squares and malls. In Montreal, day-to-day contact with other women is reduced while emotional dependence on the husband is increased. For women working outside the home, job and household responsibilities prevent extra time for leisure and social activities. Dunk reasons that, in addition to these problems, immigrant women experience psychological pressures linked to language difficulties, alienation in a new country, poor working conditions, long work hours, and perhaps husbands who drink and/or have extramarital affairs. Her informants agreed that nevra symptoms are worse in Canada than in Greece, owing to economic and psychological pressures. Because it is not considered appropriate for Greek women to complain about their emotional problems, these women are "supposed to handle it by [themselves], go for a walk, lie down, or visit extended family to restore 'tranquility,'" (p. 38), all of which are usually ineffective.

***Egyptian village women—"'Uzr"*** Morsy (1978a and 1978b) studied the folk illness "'Uzr" among Egyptian women in Fateha, a peasant community composed of 3,200 farming families on the Nile Delta halfway between Cairo and Alexandria. Unlike nerves-nevra-nervios, this folk illness follows "the general pattern described in the literature of spirit possession. . . 'Uzr entails the invasion of a person's body by a spiritual agency" (1978a, p. 600). However, 'Uzr is similar to nerves-nevra-nervios insofar as disturbing emotional experiences precipitate somatic symptoms. The symptom repertoire is "diffuse and variable" and may include any or all of the following: nausea, coughing, headache, chills, excessive sleep or insomnia, loss of balance, back pain, chest pain, or a lump in the throat (1978a, p. 614). "The ultimate cause of 'Uzr is (found) in the affected person's social relations. The affliction is known to be induced by a variety of negative emotional experiences, including sadness, quarrels, fight and anger" (p. 614).

Morsey deduces that power differentials associated with forced marriage, the threat of divorce, social isolation, and domineering affines as the social origins of 'Uzr. Morsy reasons that "differential access of males and females to the major material and nonmaterial sources of prestige and power—such as material wealth, personal autonomy, culturally sanctioned decision making power, and political and religious leadership" (p. 604) contribute to the onset of 'Uzr. In Fateha, women contribute substantially to agricultural subsistence, but men regulate access to the products of women's labor and therefore retain control of culturally sanctioned power bases (p. 605). Women generally have no say in their choice of marriage partners, and there is a prevailing belief in their inherent physical, mental, and moral weakness. In newly married couples, wives are subservient to husbands who are "definitely at the center of authority" (p. 607). Women are not permitted to leave their homes after sunset without the expressed permission of their husbands or affinal older women. Consequently, women are socially more isolated than men. Beating is considered legitimate punishment for women's transgressions, and young women often live under the threat of divorce. Power inequities ease considerably as the woman matures, but her innate inferiority remains inextricably connected with the stresses of everyday life.

***Appalachian men and women—"nerves"*** Van Schaik (1989) studied a broad range of somatic symptoms among Kentuckian men and women coal miners living in the Appalachian mountains in the United States. "Nerves" is a folk illness category in Appalachia that, as in the other examples, is linked systematically to the afflicted's social relations. Van Schaik interprets nerves using a critical paradigm, viewing illness as a reflection of asymmetric power relations related to the class struggle in American culture. The daily lives of Appalachian individuals who complain of nerves are characterized by "continuous struggles to cope with the responsibilities of family life in an Appalachian context of poverty, restricted opportunities for employment, and limited sources of emotional support" (p. 15). Individuals select from a variety of culture-specific, psychosomatic complaints. The psychological symptoms of nerves include feelings of nervousness, anger, impatience, fearfulness, and depression. The somatic symptom repertoire includes gastrointestinal disturbances, weight loss, increased heart rate, headaches, and blackouts. Although some individuals complained only of headaches or fainting, all of Van Schaik's informants "reported physical agitation, restlessness, itching, and internal quivering and jerking" (p. 19). Nerves are described as chronic reaction, marked by periods of activity and remission, some episodes being more salient than others.

Van Schaik's study revealed entrenched economic exploitation, insofar as eastern Kentuckians are "deprived of ownership of the means of production, first by the timber industry and then by local coal companies" (p. 23). Appalachians are chronically underemployed and do not retain local control of institutions and services. Van Schaik observed that asymmetric power relations prevent individuals from comprehending the social outcomes they experience. ". . . It is important to account for the powerful inequalities that exist between social security disability petitioners and psychiatrist, (and) coal miners and physicians which reproduce the notion that access to the production of medical knowledge, as with access to the means of producing a livelihood, is naturally and inevitably restricted" (p. 23). Medicalization maintains class conflict, configuring a context in which human suffering produces psychological and physical symptoms but whose systemic origins remain obscured from individual consciousness.

***Newfoundland fishing families—"nerves"*** Newfoundland, a province of Canada where fishing families have lived in a culture of poverty for 200 years, was the subject of a 1990 study on nerves. Some of the poorest people in Canada who also experience the lowest level of public services can be found there. Fishing families are continually in debt to merchants who advance supplies in the form of goods in exchange for their catches. The village that was studied is geographically isolated and occupationally homogeneous, with no identifiable middle class. According to the author (Davis), no agreement exists among her informants on the exact nature of nerves. Patterns regarding its quality do emerge, however, from analyzing the discourse. First, nerves is a relatively minor but chronic complaint. Symptoms are associated with worry over some problem, and an intense emotion. The symptom repertoire includes crying, sleep disturbance, upset stomach, "pins and needles" in limbs, and headaches (p. 70). Eighty percent of the women surveyed exhibited such symptoms regularly.

A great amount of worry is associated with the fishing lifestyle; thus, the concept of "woman as worrier" is fairly institutionalized (p. 73). An attack can keep husbands home from fishing trips, bringing relief for the women from household chores. Davis theorizes that their way of life to them seems to be static and unalterable, and so it is necessary to find cultural mechanisms that obscure the macrorealities of power inequities. Thus, a great emphasis is put on the individual's ability to cope with his or her situation. A large and meaningful discourse has thus evolved around nerves symptoms—a discourse that allows women the chance to show great inner strength by verbalizing the ability to "control their 'nerves'" (p. 74). Conversations relating to nerves symptoms serve also to reveal private experiences with adversity to friends and family, which is otherwise *not* encouraged. "Those who bear their 'nerves' in a stoic fashion are positively judged." Through the language of nerves, women can create a sense of self-worth as they gain status and respect for the careful expression of their nerves.

***Latinas living in the United States—"nervios"*** Guarnaccia and Farias (1988, 1989) studied "nervios" among Latinas who had illegally immigrated from war-torn El Salvador. They suggest that nervios among Latinas has a variety of meanings. As in the preceding four examples, nervios somatically expresses psychic tension and pain. The symptom repertoire includes dizziness, heat in the body, aches, headaches, choking, and eye problems. They suggest that at one level, "heat in the body is both a description of a sensation, and an idiom for anger" (p. 1229). At another level, the authors suggest that nervios is a mirror for family relations of conflict and abuse. The expression of "'nervios' is the antithesis of ideal family life, which supports everyone in living tranquilly."

Latinas' psychological distress can be traced to hard factory work in sweat-shop-like conditions. These women are required to endure long hours under tough, scrutinizing supervisors. Financial pressure due to economic hardship and illegal status forces Latinas to work in these conditions. Additionally, they are emotionally strained from alienation in a new, large society. Their suffering also stems from being separated from friends and family (whose safety back home in El Salvador is a daily source of concern) and/or being subjected to abuse or abandonment by spouse. These anxieties culminate in a deep sense of daily insecurity, "expressed in both concrete and metaphorical terms" in the experience of nervios (p. 1229).

## THEORETICAL CONSIDERATIONS

As we have seen from the ethnographic descriptions, cross-cultural somatization involves social actors enmeshed in certain political/economic realities amid relationships that, through social circumstances, negatively impact their psychological constitutions. When cultural sanctions prevent individuals from *meaningfully* communicating their resultant distress, the mind speaks through the body, and somatization is the result. Nerves-nevra-nervios-'Uzr is therefore a "form of communication—the language of the organs—through which nature, society and culture speak simultaneously" (Lock 1990, p. 71). To deal effectively with the three broad variables in any somatization analysis—psyche, soma, and culture, it is necessary to consider theory forms not constrained by science and able to handle many variables. That is why I have chosen threads from critical-interpretive anthropology and phenomenology as the principal means of organizing the above data.

The authors mentioned herein have outlined the theoretical foundations of the critical-interpretive approach. The three-body concept of the critical tradition provides a working template onto which we can apply aspects of the illness context to organize the burgeoning collection of data. As an alternative to the reductionism in the biomedical model, the critical tradition considers illness simultaneously through the lenses of three bodies: (1) the individual body, or the lived experience of the body-self; (2) the social body, or the physical body as a symbolic intersection between family, community, society, and self; and (3) the body politic, or the regulative body, which interdicts the other two. The three-body concept "provides the key to the development of a new epistemology and metaphysics of the body, and of the emotional, social, and political sources of illness and healing" (Lock 1990, p. 71). Despite its help, however, the three-body concept cannot sufficiently show the dynamics that interconnect psyche, soma, and culture; it merely describes them in terms of a holistic investigation into the illness context. That is why I have also chosen to discuss phenomenology.

Phenomenology comes ultimately from the work of Edmund Husserl (1859–1938), Martin Heiddeger (1889–1976), and Jean Paul Sartre (1905–1980). It is concerned with uncovering fundamental structures (at the most basic, common level of analysis) that order human experience. It is not dualistically motivated and therefore represents a radical shift from the empirical sciences, which often take lived experience for granted. Boss (1979), a modern phenomenologist, suggests that the terminology and jargon of Western medicine and psychology have made too many assumptions, obscured the truth, and limited the direction in which the disciplines might evolve (i.e., the underlying assumption in medicine and psychology that humans experience their bodies as self-contained units separate from their minds). As an alternative to the dualistic, positivist approach, he attempts to reunite mind and body, using his own description of conscious experience, and in so doing links the two. In *Existential Foundations of Medicine and Psychology,* he cites several innate, fundamental characteristics that condition the conscious experience of a social world, although in a Western sense. I would like to superimpose these characteristics over the three-body paradigm and add the data along with my own analysis.

***The individual body*** The individual body is the mind and body considered together as a single operating unit, or, put another way, conscious experience and physical bodyhood analyzed simultaneously—an unlikely synthesis in the Eurocentric tradition. "We may reasonably assume that all people share at least some intuitive sense of the embodied self as existing apart from other individual bodies" (Lock 1990, p. 53). In a phenomenologic sense the body-self really means embodied consciousness. D'Aquili et al. (1990) are neurophenomenologists whose definition of consciousness is appropriate for biocultural illness because it links the mind to the body. "Consciousness is a term referring to the ongoing stream of experience mediated by a neural complex called conscious network. It is constantly transforming itself through the entrainment and disentrainment of neural networks to model our conscious world" (p. 90). Using the five sense, neural brain networks extract information from the environment, then compare that with mental models based on past experience to facilitate the development of new ones (Weiss 1990, p. 297). Conscious network therefore maps an intensely personal but, at the same time, culturally relevant model of reality for each individual.

From what ethnographers have described about the respective biocultural illness contexts, we may assume that the quality of individual neural models are characterized by slight emotional discomfort on one end of the continuum and extreme strain, stress, and conflict on the other. Boss (1979) commented on the emotional quality of these models. Boss specifies space as the seat of human experience—that is, embodied conscious experience dwells in space, extending beyond the body conceived of merely as a self-contained biologic unit.[1] Emotional attunement or mood, he suggests, conditions the character of this space, such that the relative depth and width of one's conscious experience has an ontologic correlation with affect. The underlying assumption is that either expanded or constricted apertures of being in the world respectively correspond to positive and negative emotional states. Every experiential moment "is by itself attuned to happiness whenever all its innate potential ways of being stand open" when one is "in love" or "ecstatic" (p. 110).

The degree to which one remains "open" or "closed" conditions creativity and receptivity in a necessarily social world. For example, an expanded aperture of being broadens the possibilities for responsiveness to self, social relationships, and the larger cultural landscape. If these relationships are dependable and meaningful, one retains the psychological freedom to remain open. Conversely, being constricted narrows these possibilities, as well as inhibits necessary psychological freedom over the appropriate degree of openness required for each experiential moment. For Boss, human bodyhood is always the "bodying forth" into the social world of the ways in which we are dwelling in space—expanded or constricted according to our particular mood or attunement (p. 100).

Another way of conceiving of Boss's ideas, one that anthropologists might better understand, is to consider the work of Douglas (1966). She analyzed constrictedness at the macro level, suggesting that when human groups are socially threatened they respond by increasing the number of social controls that regulate the groups' boundaries (Lock 1990, p. 65). McCarthyism, Japanese workcamps in World War II, modern trade wars, and the Salem witch trials of the seventeenth century are examples of this type of boundary regulation in the United States. During those times, the nation turned inward, constricting its own aperture of being in response to some perceived global threat. Just as nation-states who believe they are in some way compromised constrict their field of relations, so too do body-selves when their immediate relationships are not meaningful or, do not provide dependable sources of comfort and security. Using the embodied consciousness idea, we may assume that folk illness considered at the level of the individual body is due in part to emotionally distressful internal models of reality mapped by neural networks resulting from the undependability of important social relationships.

***The social body*** What is referred to as the social body is the human body and society considered simultaneously, such that each is seen as a reflection of the other. At one level, the human body is a collective metaphor—the site "where social truths and social contradictions are played out, as well as a locus of personal and social resistance, creativity and struggle" (Lock 1990, p. 71). That is, in most societies the human soma is often a cognitive template, or map, which charts aspects of social structure for a given cultural universe. When collective representations of the human soma are analyzed by anthropologists, "other natural, supernatural, social and even spatial relations" become visible within a given social system (p. 60). For example, the body-as-machine metaphor reflects the technologically oriented West in colloquial expressions used to describe somatic states such as "I'm drained" or "I couldn't call it up," terms primarily referring to machines or computers (p. 60).

In terms of biocultural illness, the bond that unites the human body and society is visible in terms of somatic symptoms, insofar as they are a collective metaphor that reflects certain truths about social relations within the larger cultural landscape. Symptoms are indicative of emotional distress, serving as a kind of language for the expression of certain socially conditioned psychological states—states often ironically maintained by the social system itself. For example, Guarnaccia and Farias (1988, 1989) suggest that Latinas with nervios who symptomatically feel the floor rocking or who fear falling down without warning, are communicating somatically that their place in society is neither safe nor stable (p. 1229).

At another level the social body is literally society itself—a nexus of social relationships organized in terms of power distribution (Foucault 1980). Kardiner (1945) classified two useful orders of cultural structure that phenomenologically provide a foundation onto which we can superimpose ethnographic details of the illness context. The social body, according to Kardiner, is organized in terms of two basic orders—primary and secondary social structures. Primary social structure is composed of population subunits—parts of a larger human whole containing certain familiar and nonfamiliar members who share at least one or more similar value orientations. These are, for example, family, community, and society—any classes of interpersonal relationships that systematize, structure, and organize ordinary human routines. In terms of biocultural illness, the social body often contains relationships that are unstable, capricious, and undependable. For women, this is most often illustrated by being not only responsible for an overwhelming domestic routine at home but also the pressures of work at an outside job.

***The body politic*** Kardiner also identified secondary social structure—what the critical tradition calls the body politic or the political economy—composed of organizations, institutions, and ideology whose activities regulate and condition the affairs of individual and social bodies. The body politic "provides codes and social scripts for the domestication of the individual body in conformity to the needs of the social and political order" (Lock 1990, p. 67).

Consideration of the body politic is necessary because it completes a holistic analysis of the illness context. Somatization is very often related to power differentials—asymmetric relationships between classes of rich and poor, male and female, educated and illiterate, or any such polarizations, which govern the social production of illness. Body politic analyses have been called the missing link in medical anthropology because they go beyond informant-centered narratives, which rely almost exclusively on local explanations, to bring into clearer focus economic and political processes that administrate, regulate, and control the experience of health, illness, and healing (Morsy 1990, p. 43).

## DISCUSSION

### Existential Balance: The Mediatrix for Psyche, Soma, and Culture

Building on the critical and phenomenologic theory traditions as above, I propose a concept for explaining the interconnections among psyche, soma, and society in terms of folk illness. I suggest that the presentation of sociogenic, somatic symptoms exist as the interface between three expressions of impaired "existential balance": (1) the lack of "intrapsychic autonomy," such that neural models of reality fail to provide enduring sources of comfort and self-esteem at the level of consciousness (Ewing 1991, p. 133); (2) neuroendocrine imbalances that fail to regulate homeostatic mechanisms influence biologic systems, inducing various symptomatology at the level of bodyhood (Gold et al. 1988); and (3) disparities in power distribution at the level of the body politic and the social body (Foucault 1980).

***Existential balance in conscious experience*** Psychoanalytic models that account for psychological disturbances have been problematic where the studies of cultures and psyches meet (Ewing 1991). This is because particular manifestations of emotional distress (anxiety, depression, folk illness) are culturally patterned and therefore do not always conform to Western theories, whose dualism may conflict with the values of the culture in question. It is necessary, then, to continue in the existential phenomenologic tradition, which can handle a mind/body analysis simultaneously.

Existential phenomenologists have suggested that emotional distress is the direct result of abandoning one's "authentic self." Delmonte (1989) defines the authentic self as "one's true identity which is threatened by erosion from the demands of the mob, horde or society" (p. 83). It refers to a sense of well-being formed by stable internal conceptions of self-worth that are sustained despite the daily impositions of cultural mores and the social role. Ewing's (1991) notion of "intrapsychic autonomy" is a useful theoretical basis for conceptualizing authentic self. "Intrapsychic autonomy is the ability to maintain enduring mental representations of sources of self-esteem and comfort, permitting a more flexible adaptation to the vicissitudes of the immediate environment" (p. 132). Speaking neurophenomenologically, then, authentic self derives from mental models mapped by conscious network that provide stable sources of self-worth, self-esteem, and emotional comfort and nurturing. When an individual is intrapsychically autonomous, he or she is free from an inauthentic reliance on some perceived external authority or context. However, when an individual lacks intrapsychic autonomy, depending primarily instead on the capricious social context, "self-esteem is too easily threatened, the ability to perceive others accurately and to function effectively is also likely to be impaired" (p. 149).

Existential balance in conscious experience is defined, then, as an agency that mediates an inauthentic dependence on an inappropriate external context as a primary source of emotional comfort and self-worth. When existential balance is intact, authentic self is consistently experienced as one's being less dependent on the environment and therefore less vulnerable to the moods and dictates of others. When existential balance is impaired, as in the case of biocultural illness, an individual relies heavily on relationships, events, and situations, which often fail to provide meaningful, stable sources of emotional comfort.

***Existential balance and bodyhood*** The biologic process known as homeostasis mediates the organic systems (i.e., circulatory, reproductive, immune, and digestive) to conform to the demands of the external environment by maintaining a sensitive control of hormone levels to balance such things as hunger against satiation, sexual desire against gratification, thirst against fluid retention, and sleep against wakefulness, all via the neuroendocrine system. The neuroendocrine system is composed of chemicals excreted by the pituitary and hypothalamus, which contain biologic information necessary for interceding between interior functionings and external circumstance. "The hypothalamic and pituitary systems maintain normal, internal stability in an organism by coordinating the responses of the organ systems that compensate for environmental changes" (Turner 1983, p. 245). A classic example of this process is the flight/fight response. When an individual is emotionally distressed, homeostasis is altered in response to the external situation producing the anxiety (e.g., an angry family member). In a functional sense, adaptive neural pathways activated by the endocrine system promote attention, arousal, and aggression. At the same time, these chemicals inhibit nonadaptive hormones that would stimulate inappropriate activities such as sleeping and reproduction. When the external stimulus diminishes, counterregulating hormones (balancers) ordinarily enter the picture to soothe the inflammatory response and promote the restoration of homeostasis. However, when emotional distress is chronic (such as when one consistently depends on anxiety-producing contexts for sources of self-esteem in lieu of stable internal mental representations), the counterregulating hormones are never secreted. In this case, various systems in the body are affected.

The immune system has received recent research attention in this regard. A study by Gold et al. (1988) suggests prolonged secretion of particular neurohormones that fail to respond to homeostatic regulation exist in a triangular relationship with chronic emotional distress and the presentation of somatic symptoms. Their research found that if neuroendocrine imbalances persist for certain periods of time, the immune system becomes depressed and is unable to fight off pathogens in a normal, consistent manner. This is because effective homeostatic regulation depends on a balanced neuroendocrine system—one that secretes both regulating and counterregulating hormones. Because the neuroendocrine system intercedes amid the composite of biologic systems (i.e., immune, respiratory, circulatory), Gold et al. conclude that "many other illnesses in clinical medicine can be attributed to adaptive physiological processes that fail to respond normally to homeostatic regulation" (p. 419).[2]

Existential balance at the level of physiology is defined, then, as an agency/process that mediates a functional neuroendocrine complex influencing the various human biologic systems. When existential balance in physiology is impaired by chronic emotional distress, homeostatic mechanisms fail to respond adequately with counterregulation to soothe the flight/fight response. Therefore, the neuroendocrine system ineffectively mediates a dysfunctional homeostatic complex, producing symptoms associated with the major biologic systems.

***Cultural expression of existential balance*** Morsy (1990) suggested that the political economy, or the structural relationship among the economic infrastructure, political power, and their ideologies, should be considered when interpreting the illness context. The political economy of health views class-linked power differentials as circumscribing the social production of sickness and healing, and this analysis is key to understanding the systemic factors that give rise to biocultural illness.

Foucault (1980) commented on the political economy in his classic analysis on power relations. He observed that institutions of the body politic, such as government, religion, medicine, economy, and education, are insidious networks of power in control of vital information, knowledge, and access to important resources. With no singular focal point, he observed that institutions exert hegemony—the predominance of ideology over individual needs and lives—in an endless complex of interpersonal relations. Foucault saw social structure containing microcontexts within which are visible various aspects ascribed to the macroscope. In a microcontext such as a visit to a health clinic, the power/knowledge matrix infiltrates minds and bodies often without the conscious recognition of individuals.

Existential balance in culture is defined as an agency/process that mediates power relations within the microcontext. When intact, the institutions of the body politic organize but do not regulate against fundamental economic, social, and psychological needs of individual and social bodies (such as access to a decent livelihood). When impaired, ideology and the cultural infrastructure interdict these requirements such that institutions exert hegemony within the many microcontexts characteristic of the attendant culture. Microcontexts are cultural loci where power relations among the social body, body politic, and individual bodies are directly experienced. The word "context" actually comes from the Latin word meaning *to weave;* it refers to a situational event that fuses the individual body with the regulations, dictates, and various other interdictions of the body politic (e.g., a visit to the physician, an 8-hour day at the factory, a counseling session with a local priest or psychiatrist). When ideology does not take precedence over economic and psychological needs of individuals in these various contexts, power relations may be thought of as symmetric or balanced. However, in the case of nerves-nevra-nervios-'Uzr ethnographies, where economic and psychological needs are submerged in favor of institutional hegemony, power relations may be considered unbalanced. When symptoms are labeled and then medicalized by a physician, for example, without consideration of the structural factors that give rise to their expression, power relations are out of balance. In this light, individuals participate in the mystification their own illness experience (Van Schaik 1989, p. 20).

Figure 3–1 illustrates all of the theory forms I have distilled from the literature, as well as three expressions of existential balance shown intact. The institutions and ideology of the body generate microcontexts that do not necessarily regulate against the economic, social, and psychological needs of individual bodies. The individual shown here exhibits intrapsychic autonomy such that he or she does not depend on inappropriate contexts for self-esteem and emotional comfort. His or her aperture of being is thus open, responsive to a social world in which relationships are meaningful and emotionally stable. When emotional stress *is* experienced, it is judged to be an acute rather than a chronic condition of experience. Thus, homeostatic mechanisms respond appropriately to the flight/fight response, mediating a functional neuroendocrine complex that in turn influences healthy biologic systems. Common variables and themes are evident in all of the aforementioned cases of nerves-nevra-nervios-'Uzr. These themes are more visible when the data is organized in terms of critical and phenomenologic theory traditions that view variables such as psyche-soma-society interconnections inclusively. For each respective variable, psyche-soma-culture, imbalances exist that govern the mechanics of

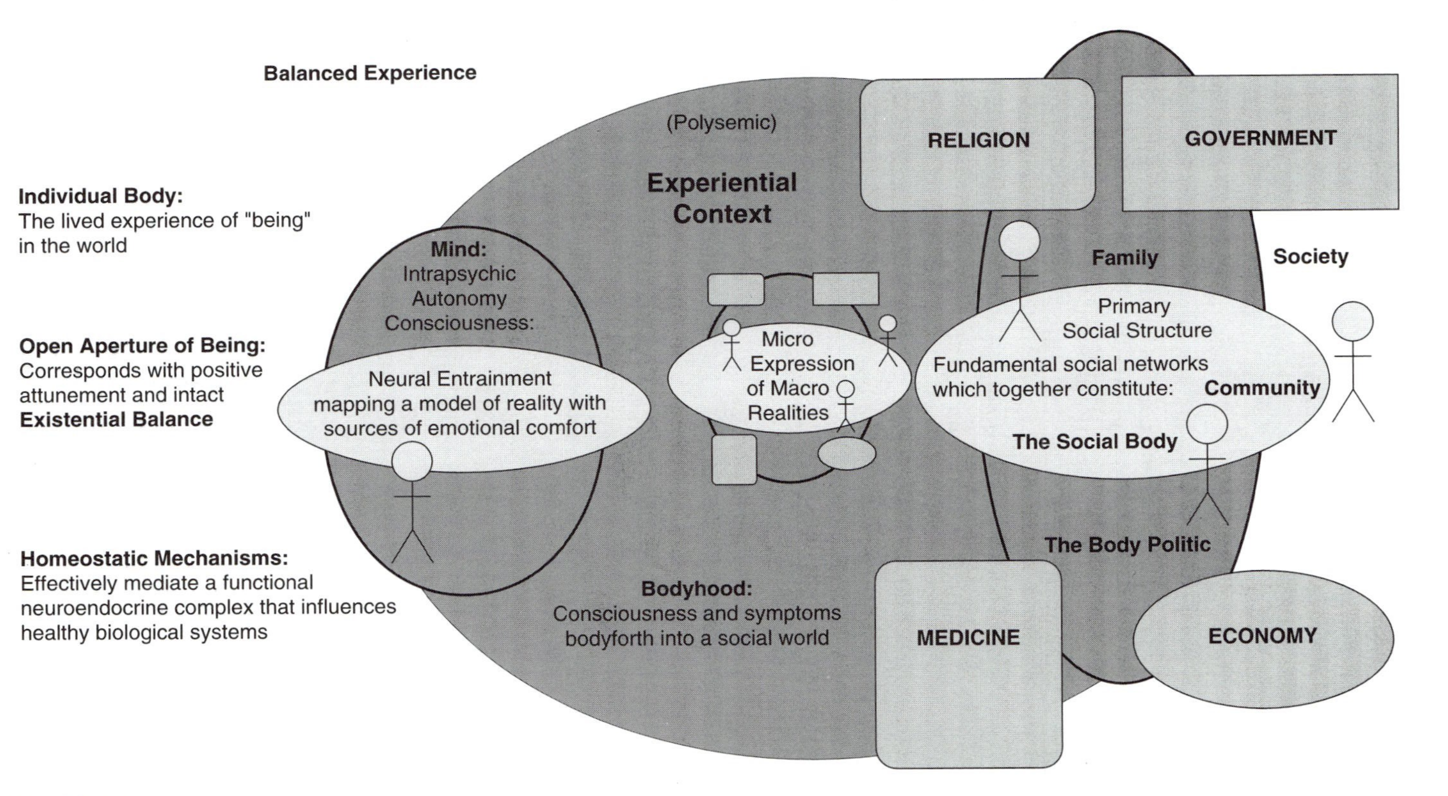


FIGURE 3–1. Generic.

their respective functions. Folk illness results when three expressions of these imbalances exist simultaneously. At the level of psyche, the afflicted are intrapsychically dependent on various inappropriate social circumstances, rather than on internal mental representations for enduring sources of self-esteem, comfort, and emotional nurturing. When situational contexts do not adequately provide these, the afflicted's mood diminishes, making emotional distress a chronic rather than an acute condition of existence. Their aperture of being constricts, inhibiting psychological freedom for the appropriate degree of openness required for each context while narrowing the possibilities for authentic responsiveness to important relationships such as spouse, family, and work. At the level of soma, healthy biologic systems depend upon, among other things, a balanced neuroendocrine system—one that secretes both regulating and counterregulating hormones during the flight/fight response. When emotional distress is chronic, the flight/fight response is ineffective such that counterregulating hormones are not secreted to soothe the inflammatory reaction. Gold et al. (1988) have shown that this process depresses the immune system, producing biologic symptoms, and further suggest that because other major biologic systems are also involved, many additional clinical illnesses can be traced to this failure.

At the level of culture, asymmetric power relations are visible in the situational contexts generated by the institutions of the social body and political economy. These contexts represent microloci, sites where individual bodies intersect and fuse with the ideology and power relations of the body politic, such as a visit to the physician. When this context interdicts certain psychological, social, or economic needs of individuals, such as the development of adequate mental representations for emotional comfort and self-esteem, self-worth and self-esteem are submerged in favor of the ideologic maintenance of the body politic itself (as in the case of medicalization).

Based on the preceding analysis, Figure 3–2 charts the course that results in biocultural illness for five represented ethnographies. In all of these examples, the illness context is a window into aspects of the lived experience which result in biocultural illness. The illness context reveals microexpression of macro power differentials (disparities that represent the systemic origins of somatization), a lack of intrapsychic autonomy, and a dysfunctional neuroendocrine complex that produces symptomatology.

In Figure 3–2a, the medicalization of immigrant Greek women's symptoms demonstrates a lack of intrapsychic autonomy. Instead of obtaining community relief via extended friendship circles, which would otherwise restore internal representations of emotional comfort and self-worth, immigrant Greek women must rely on an impersonal authority—the physician. Although it is probable the physician has their best interests in mind, he is most likely removed from their everyday existence and is thus prevented from correlating their symptoms with the respective systemic origins. Greek immigrant women are nevertheless dependent on this context as a principal source of emotional

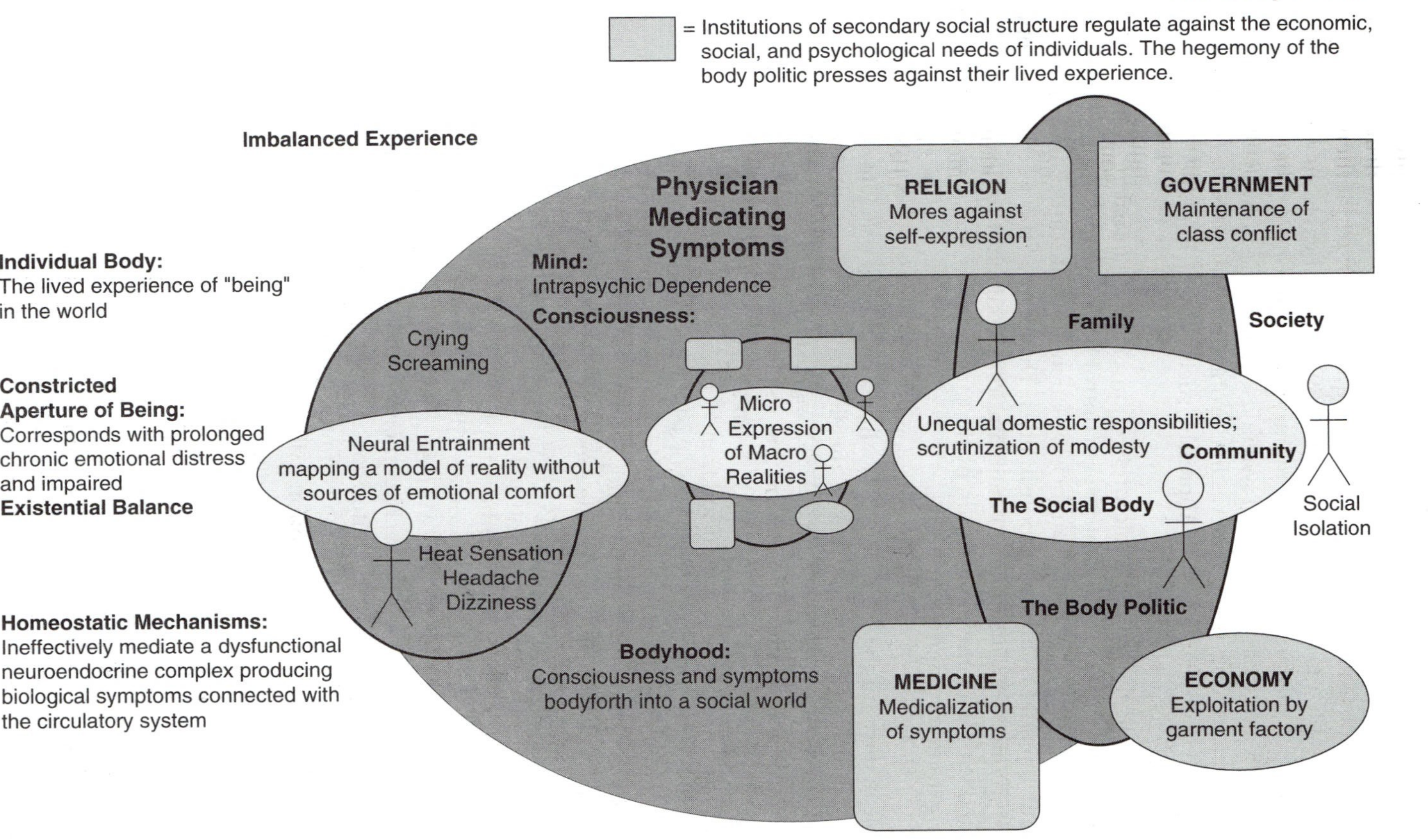


**FIGURE 3–2a.** Greek women in Montreal—nevra.

comfort, which of course takes the form of a short discussion about symptoms and the subsequent prescription of tranquilizers and antidepressants for an uncomfortable emotional state (Dunk 1989). In most cases, drugs are a temporary, poor substitute for enduring intrapsychic autonomy when the symptoms have their genesis in the social system itself. Such medication will lift the "fog"; however, as long as she believes her problems result from her own inferiority and not from reaction to an oppressive social system, her biocultural symptoms are likely to persist.

Medicalization is a microreflection of power imbalances in the macroscope insofar as prescription drugs control her symptoms enough to maintain the class conflict in Canadian society—an inequitable distribution of resources and unequal domestic responsibilities. Drugs treat the women's emotional symptoms, allowing them to maintain long hours and underpayment associated with both the exploitation by the garment factories and the overwhelming domestic routines at home.

In Figure 3–2b intrapsychic dependence among Egyptian women is visible in terms of the "sick role." Born into a culture in which men control access to culture-specific power bases, the sick role becomes the surrogate for intrapsychic autonomy. Morsy (1978a) suggests that the sick role serves to temporarily alleviate psychic tension and somatic symptoms because it is a "strategy of indirect control" (p. 611). As an alternative power base, it provides the afflicted with a short suspension from ordinary oppressive realities—ones that regularly prevent the experience of self-understanding and self-worth. In lieu of mental representations of emotional comfort, which are either absent or unavailable in their conscious mind, Fatehan women are inauthentically dependent on the sick role to provide these.

The sick role is a microreflection of macroimbalances because symptoms are given a special female status. 'Uzr harbors an inferior character reflecting an ideologic belief in the inherent physical, mental, and moral weakness of women generally. Egyptian women's illness thus legitimizes and reinforces the social system's view of them: Women are inherently weak and inferior.

In Figure 3–2c Appalachian men's and women's symptoms are medicalized. Because they have limited social support networks and endure marital and family tensions linked to economic hardship, Appalachians seek psychiatrists for help with their emotional distress. Like the Greek women, their symptoms are then medicalized, making them inauthentically dependent on an external authority for sources of self-esteem and emotional comfort. Appalachian men and women are characteristically denied access to medical knowledge and educational pursuits. The availability of these would otherwise support the (*re*)construction of internal models of reality that facilitate self-understanding, self-worth, and emotional comfort.

Related to this, medicalization is also a microreflection of macroimbalances. Medicalization is to the creation of enduring representations of self-worth and emotional comfort, what class conflict and economic inequalities

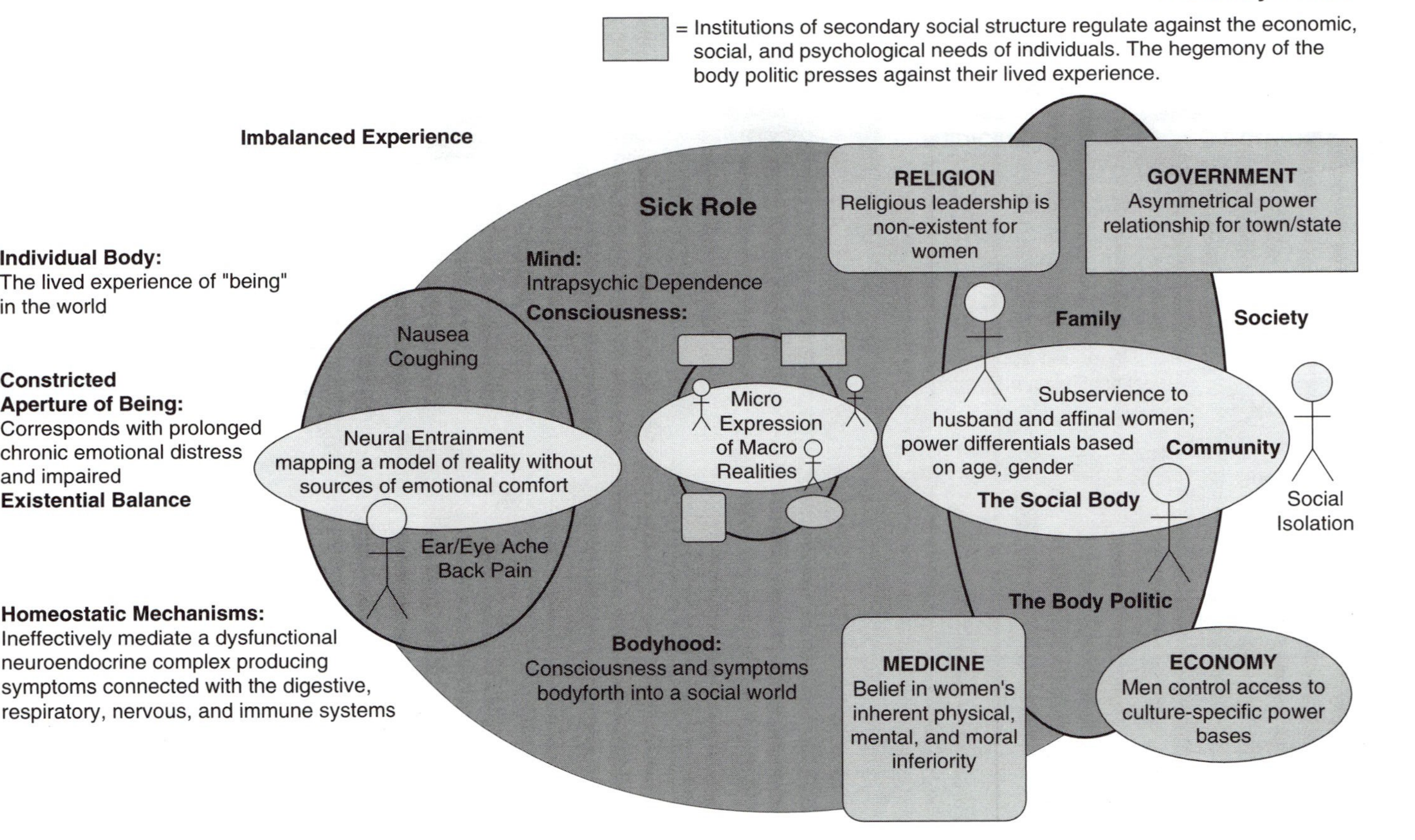


**FIGURE 3–2b.** Egyptian village women—'Uzr.

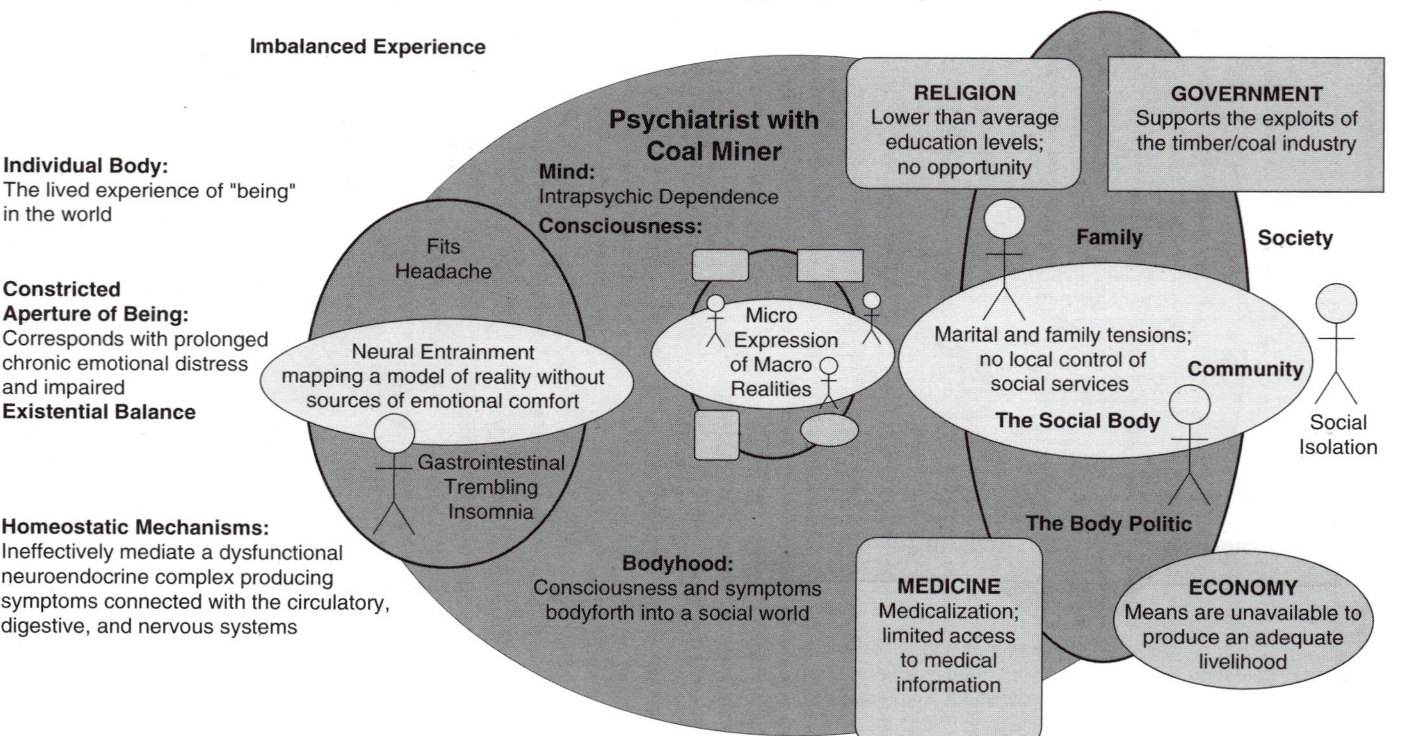


FIGURE 3–2c. Appalachian men and women—nerves.

are to creating and maintaining a decent living. The class-based relationship between the psychiatrist, who is in a superior position owing to income and access to information, and the coal miner replicates the limitations inherent in producing an adequate livelihood in Appalachia (Van Schaik 1990).

In Figure 3–2d a symptom discourse shows an inauthentic reliance on an external context for sources of self-esteem and comfort and therefore a lack of intrapsychic autonomy. Thus, a symptom discourse is a maladaptive impression management scheme that exists as a surrogate for mental representations that would otherwise produce sources of enduring emotional comfort and self-esteem (Davis 1990).

A symptom discourse is also a microreflection of imbalances in the body politic. Economic exploitation via merchant middlemen keep families and individuals continually in debt and out of control of their finances. A symptom discourse gives Newfoundlanders pseudocontrol over symptoms—one of the only areas in life which an individual exercises control of any kind.

In Figure 3–2e Latinas are medicalized. Like the Greek and Appalachian examples, Latinas in the northeastern United States are inauthentically dependent on the physician as a source of self-esteem and self-worth. Medicalization alone is a poor substitute for the creation of internal representations, which would otherwise generate sources of emotional comfort useful in stressful situations.

Medicalization is a microreflection of macroimbalances because it prevents a correlation of symptoms with the structural factors that contribute to a "loss of tranquility." It thus reproduces helplessness within the larger society, powerlessness stemming from racism, hard factory work under strict supervisors, language difficulties, and loss of family ties.

## SUMMARY

This chapter presents a model that synthesizes the relationships among self-perceptions of individuals, neuroendocrine responses, and the structures of inequality characteristic of a society and its attendant culture, resulting in illness in the individual. The model does not purport to be the complete picture, as every theory or model has its recognized limitations. It is meant as a starting point for comprehending the psychological, somatic, and systemic factors that, when taken together, result in the biomedical anomaly known as nerves-nevra-nervios-'Uzr. I suggest that existential balance governs the processes of the three variables common to all ethnographies—psyche, soma, culture. In the preceding analysis, nerves-nevra-nervios-'Uzr represents the interface among three stated expressions of impaired existential balance: (1) a lack of intrapsychic autonomy (Ewing 1991), making individuals reliant on some inappropriate external circumstance for enduring sources of self-esteem and emotional comfort; (2) homeostatic mechanisms that fail to respond adequately with

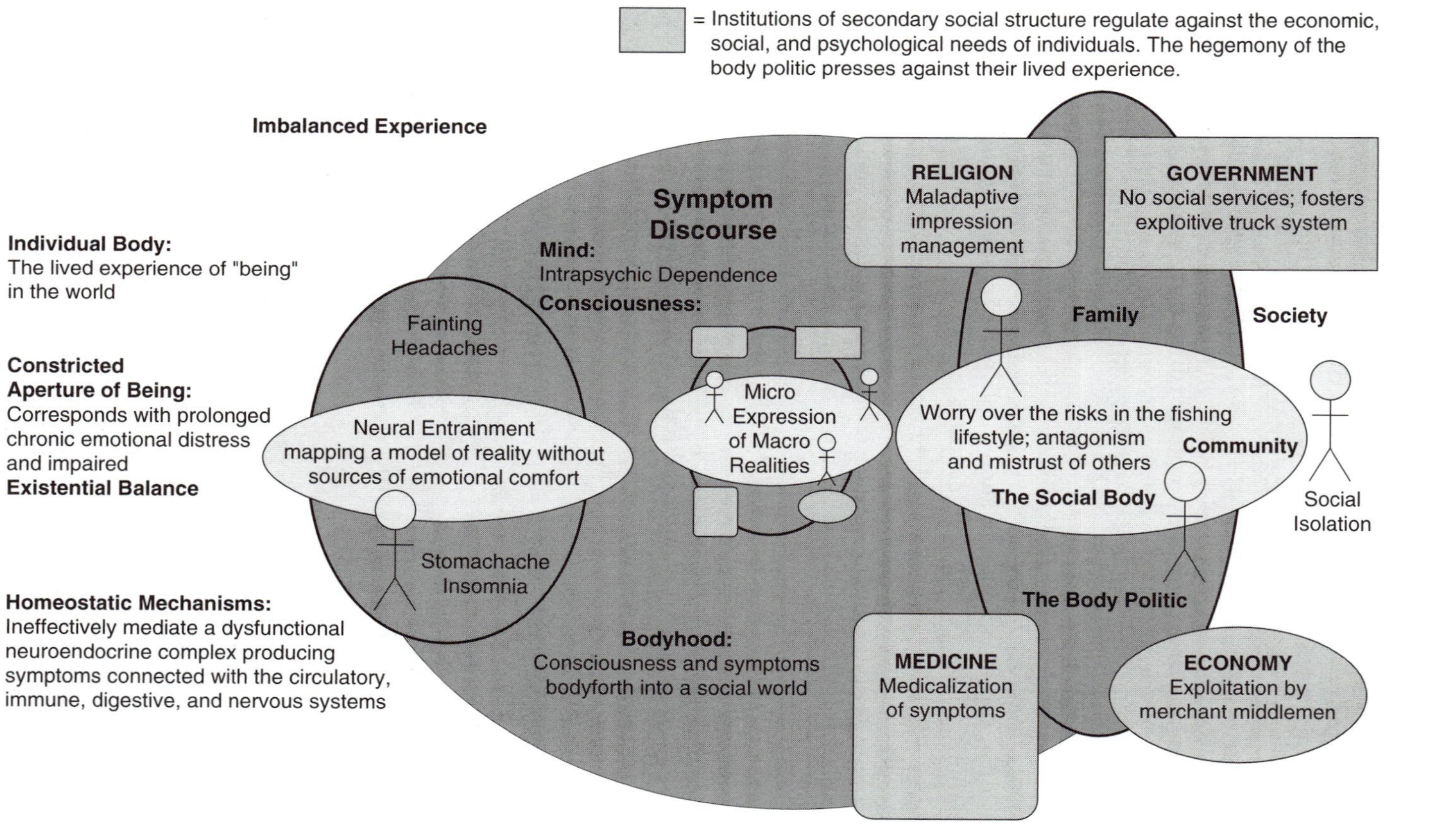


**FIGURE 3–2d**. Newfoundland fishing families—nerves.

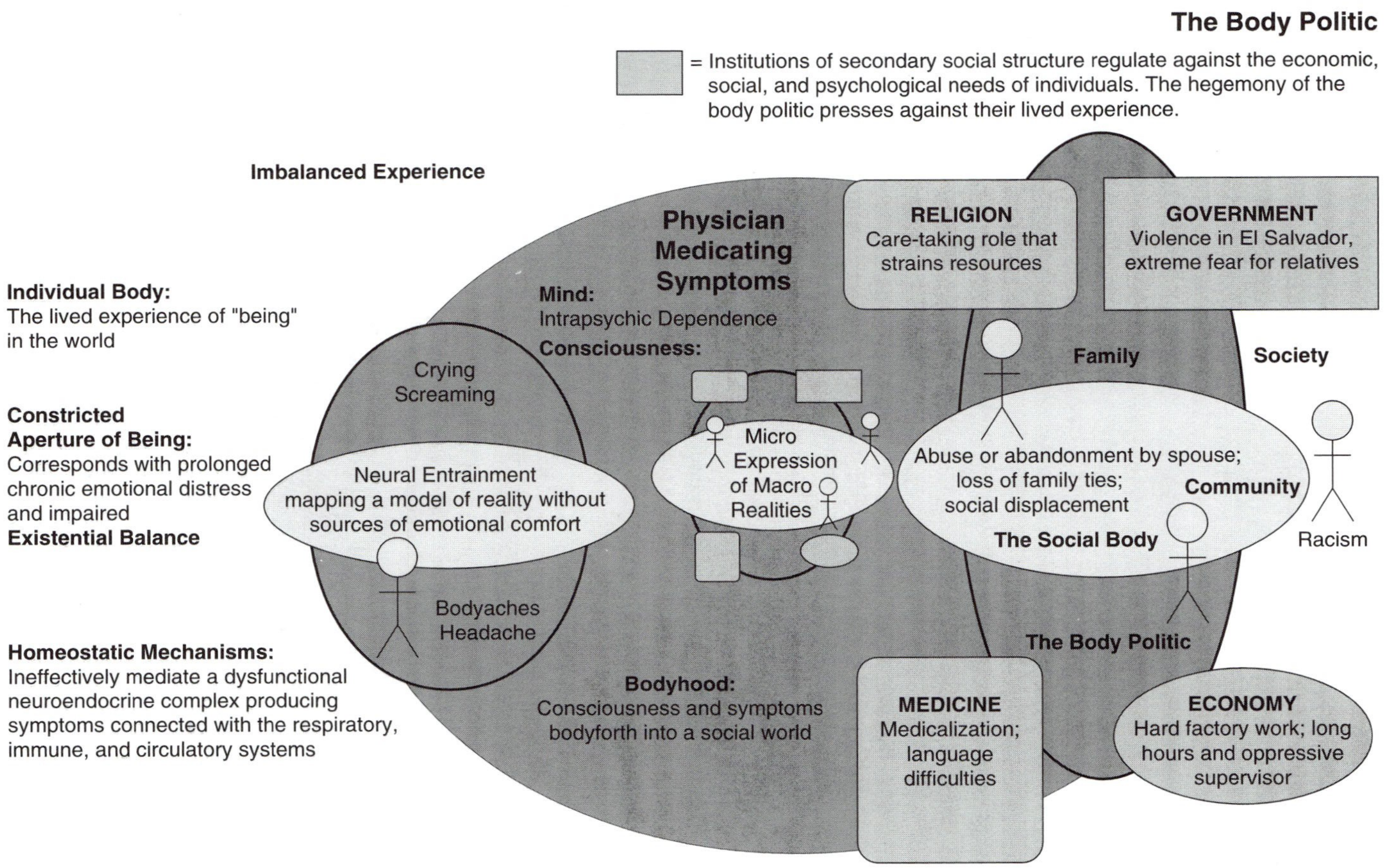

**FIGURE 3–2e.** Latinas living in the United States—nervios.

counterregulating hormones to soothe the flight/fight response and ineffectively mediate a dysfunctional neuroendocrine complex, producing symptoms associated with the major biologic systems; and (3) inequities in power distribution that sabotage the lived experience of self-worth and self-understanding such that the ideology, desires, and dictates of the body politic take precedence over the economic, social, and psychological needs of individuals.

## NOTES

1. For proof of this he uses memory as an example: "We extend ourselves into one of three temporal dimensions—extensions or ecstasies of the past, present or future. . ." (100).
2. Homeostatic regulation and neuroendocrine imbalances provide an important window for understanding the association between emotional distress and various symptoms. However, it does not go far enough to suggest reasons for the appearance of mutually agreed upon, varying culture-specific symptom repertoires characteristic of somatizations, i.e., backache in one culture, and numbness in limbs in another. Bergman (1969) has proposed that the neuroendocrine system is also a transducer, or a psychophysiological encoder, which converts a cognitive set of information into a physiologic chain of events. Psychoneuroimmunology is a relatively new field that is seeking an understanding of neurochemistry and its relationship to emotional states and physiologic systems (see Dubos, Sobel, and Pert [all 1990]). However, the jury is still out as to whether the transducer hypothesis or a version of it will prevail.

## REFERENCES

BERGMAN, K. 1969. "Phycomyles." *Bacteriology Review* 33:99–157.

BOSS, M. 1979. *Existential Foundations of Medicine and Psychology.* New York: Jason Aronson.

D'AQUILI, EUGENE, et al. 1990. Pp. 17–74 in *Brain, Symbol and Experience: Toward a Neurophenomenology of Human Consciousness.* Boston: New Science Library.

DAVIS, D. 1990. "The Variable Character of Nerves in a Newfoundland Fishing Village." *Medical Anthropology* 11:63–78.

DELMONTE, M. 1989. "Existentialism and Psychotherapy: A Constructivist Perspective." *Psychologia* 32(2):81–89. Japan: Kyoto University.

DOUGLAS, M. 1966. *Purity and Danger.* New York: Praeger.

DUBOS, R. 1990. "Self-Healing: A Personal History." In *The Healing Brain,* edited by Robert Ornstein and Charles Swenciones. New York: Guilford Press.

DUNK, P. 1989. "Greek Woman and Broken Nerves in Montreal." *Medical Anthropology* 11(4):29–45.

EWING, K. 1991. "Can Psychoanalytic Theories Explain the Pakistani Woman? Intrapsychic Autonomy and Interpersonal Engagement in the Extended Family." *Ethos* 19(2):131–37.

FOUCAULT, M. 1980. *Power Knowledge: Selected Interviews and Other Writings.* New York: Pantheon.

GOLD, F., et al. 1988. "Clinical Manifestations of Depression: Relation to the Neurobiology of Stress." *New England Journal of Medicine* 319:413–20.

GUARANACCIA, P., and P. FARIAS. 1988. "The Social Meanings of Nervios: A Case Study of a Central American Woman." *Social Science and Medicine* 26:1223–31.

______. 1989. "Multiple Meanings of Ataques de Nervios in a Latino Community." *Medical Anthropology* 11(4):47–62.

KARDINER, A., et al. 1945. *The Psychological Frontiers of Society.* New York: Columbia University Press.

LOCK, M. 1990. "A Critical-Interpretive Approach in Medical Anthropology: Rituals and Routines of Discipline and Dissent." With N. Scheper-Hughes. Pp. 47–72 in *Medical Anthropology: Contemporary Theory and Method,* edited by Thomas Johnson and Carolyn Sargent. New York: Praeger.

MORSY, S. 1978a. "Sex Differentials and Folk Illness in an Egyptian Village." In *Women in the Muslim World,* edited by L. Beck and N. Kiddie. Cambridge, Mass.: Harvard University Press.

______. 1978b. "Sex Roles, and Illness in an Egyptian Village." *Medical Anthropology* 5:137–50.

______. 1990. "Political Economy in Medical Anthropology." In *Medical Anthropology: Contemporary Theory and Method,* edited by Thomas Johnson and Carolyn Sargent. New York: Praeger.

NICHTER, M. 1981. "Idioms of Distress: Alternatives in the Expression of Psychological Distress: A Case Study from India." *Culture, Medicine and Psychiatry* 5:379–408.

PARSONS, C. 1984. "Idioms of Distress." *Culture, Medicine and Psychology* 8:71–93.

PERT, C. 1990. "The Wisdom of the Receptors; Neuropeptides, Emotions, and Body-Mind." In *The Healing Brain,* edited by R. Ornstein and C. Swenciones. New York: Guilford Press.

SHORTER, E. 1982. "Paralysis: The Rise and Fall of an Hysterical Symptom." *Journal of Social History* 19:547–82.

SOBEL, D. 1990. "The Placebo Effect: Using the Body's Own Healing Mechanisms." Pp. 63–74 in *The Healing Brain,* edited by R. Ornstein and C. Swenciones. New York: Guilford Press.

TURNER, V. 1983. "Body, Brain and Culture." *Zygone* 18:245.

VAN SCHAIK, E. 1989. "Paradigms Underlying the Study of Nerves as a Popular Illness Term in Eastern Kentucky." *Medical Anthropology Quarterly* 11(4):15–28.

WEISS, R. 1990. "Shadows of Thoughts Revealed." *Science News* 138(19):297.

WUNTHROW, R., et al. 1984. P. 8 in *Cultural Analysis: The Work of Peter L. Berger, Mary Douglas, Michel Foucault and Jurgen Habermas.* London: Routledge and Kegan.

Chapter 4

# A Cross-Cultural Comparison of Filarial Disease in the Fiji Islands*

*Usha K. Prasad*

Filariasis is a highly endemic, mosquito-transmitted disease found throughout the tropics. It is estimated that nearly 300 million people, most of them living south of the equator, suffer from this disease (Dasgupta 1978). Filariasis is commonly diagnosed as a short-term fever accompanied by some lymphatic swelling. Elephantiasis occurs as the most advanced stage of the disease, often resulting in permanent swelling of the limbs.[1]

Like many South Pacific Islands, Fiji has a high prevalence of bancroftian filariasis caused by the nematode *Wuchereria bancrofti* of the subperiodic type. Subperiodic forms of *W. bancrofti* vary their activity and appearance in human blood and tissue. To date, no animal reservoirs have been reported for bancroftian filariasis (Ottesen 1984). However, at least five species of mosquito vectors are known in Fiji. Of these five, *Aedes polynesiensis, Ae. pseudoscutellaris, Ae. fijiensis,* and *Culex fatigans* are found in the main Fiji group, whereas *Ae. rotumae* is found only on Rotuma Island (Iyengar 1960).

Methods to control the disease include environmental measures aimed

*Fieldwork for this project was funded by National Science Foundation, Grant No. BNS8503130. While in Fiji, assistance was provided by the Institute of Natural Resources, University of the South Pacific, and Dr. Jonu Mataika of the Wellcome Virus Laboratory.

at eliminating the vector population and chemotherapy with diethylcarbamazine[2] (DEC) aimed at reducing the human reservoir of infection. Environmental measures have had little long-term effect in changing vector densities. Moreover, in some islands the "bush" mosquitoes, considered the primary vectors of filariasis, are becoming peridomestic (Pillai and Urdang 1979). *W. bancrofti* is also becoming increasingly prevalent in urban situations where the vectors *C. quinquefasciatus* and *C. pipens* are breeding prolifically in polluted water (White 1989). Furthermore, use and effectiveness of DEC in developing areas are still in question (Ottesen 1987; Sasa 1976), especially since mass drug administrations have met with little success. Follow-up surveys of mass drug administrations with DEC in Fiji (Mataika et al. 1971, 1985), as well as in Samoa and Tonga (R. Desowitz, personal communication, 1989), reveal high recurrence rates of filariasis in all three island groups. In Fiji, rates are highest in the Fijian and Rotuman communities, where filariasis affects primarily the male population.

Fiji comprises 320 islands that vary from densely populated, high, volcanic islands, such as Viti Levu, to uninhabited low-lying coral atolls that become partially submerged at high tide. Over 90% of the population (approximately 715,000) live on the islands of Viti Levu and Vanua Levu, which together comprise 87% of the total land area (Deo and Schoeffel 1987). Fiji's multiethnic population consists of indigenous Fijians who share both a Melanesian and Polynesian ancestry, East Indians brought for plantation labor in the late 1800s, Rotumans who are Polynesians, part-Europeans, Chinese, and other Pacific Islanders. Approximately 46% of the population is Fijian, and 48% is Indian (Deo and Schoeffel 1987). The remaining 4% consists of Rotumans, part-Europeans and Europeans, Chinese and other Pacific Islanders. The majority of Rotumans (approximately 8,000) live in the Suva district of Viti Levu (Bryant 1974), while approximately 2,400 remain on Rotuma Island 240 miles to the north-northwest of Fiji. Except in town centers such as Suva and Nadi, Fijians and Indians live in separate, distinct rural communities. As the major mosquito-transmitted disease in Fiji, filarial infections are reported primarily in the rural areas. Villages throughout Fiji and Rotuma show high prevalence rates, whereas rural Indian communities show significantly lower rates of filariasis. Fijians, Indians, and Rotumans living on Rotuma Island were chosen for this study because they form the largest rural ethnic communities in Fiji and because prevalence data were available for all three groups.

This chapter examines the factors contributing to ethnic differences in disease rates and recurrence rates of filariasis in Fiji. It begins with a summary of materials and methods used for gathering data, then proceeds to discuss the characteristics of disease and disease vectors, patterns of vector-host contact, and cultural perceptions and reactions to filariasis as a disease. A summary follows, pointing to cultural adaptation as the primary cause of observed differences in filarial disease in Fiji.

## MATERIALS AND METHODS

The study discussed here (Prasad 1989) was conducted between June 1985 and June 1986. Intensive fieldwork was done in two Fijian, two Indian, and one Rotuman community. The Fijian communities consisted of Vunibau village on Viti Levu and Lalati village on Beqa Island. The Indian communities consisted of Waidova and Wainibokasi settlements on Viti Levu. On Rotuma Island, data were gathered primarily from Motusa village; interviews with patients were conducted throughout the island (Fig. 4–1).

Additionally, interviews were conducted on Vanua Levu and Taveuni Islands with Fijian and Indian plantation workers who had developed elephantiasis.[3] Some data were also collected while accompanying a World Health Organization (WHO)–sponsored survey of Kadavu Island. All five communities chosen for intensive fieldwork had individuals affected by filariasis and/or vector mosquitoes and included representative samples of the Fijian, Rotuman, and Indian populations. Additional factors considered in the selection process included similarity of the physical environments and geographic proximity of the study site to sources of biomedical care.

Both quantitative and qualitative data were gathered. The qualitative portion consisted of ethnographic information gathered through participant-observation, formal and informal interviews, and questionnaires. The interview and questionnaire forms were designed to obtain general demographic data, followed by specific questions regarding filariasis and elephantiasis. The quantitative portion consisted of vector samples, monitoring human behavior in vector zones, epidemiologic data on filariasis provided by the Wellcome Virus Laboratory, survey data from the Kadavu project, and medical data from each study site. To identify the filarial vectors and their activity patterns, each study site was divided into four activity (vector) zones described in the Vector-Host Contact section of this paper. Mosquito collections (using human bait) to identify vectors by species and habitat were done in each zone over a 24-hour period. After mosquito/vector samples were collected, human activity was monitored in the four designated vector zones for a period of two weeks. The remaining medical data were obtained through medical records and survey reports.

## CHARACTERISTICS OF DISEASE AND DISEASE VECTORS

Although filariasis appears to have a fairly predictable age distribution, diagnosis of infection can be extremely difficult because individual resistance and response to infection vary. Clinical manifestations reflect the interaction of multiple factors such as genetic and immunologic responses of the host and the species, strain, and infective dose of the parasite (Mak and Dennis 1985). In endemic areas clinical symptoms range from uninfected, asymptomatic

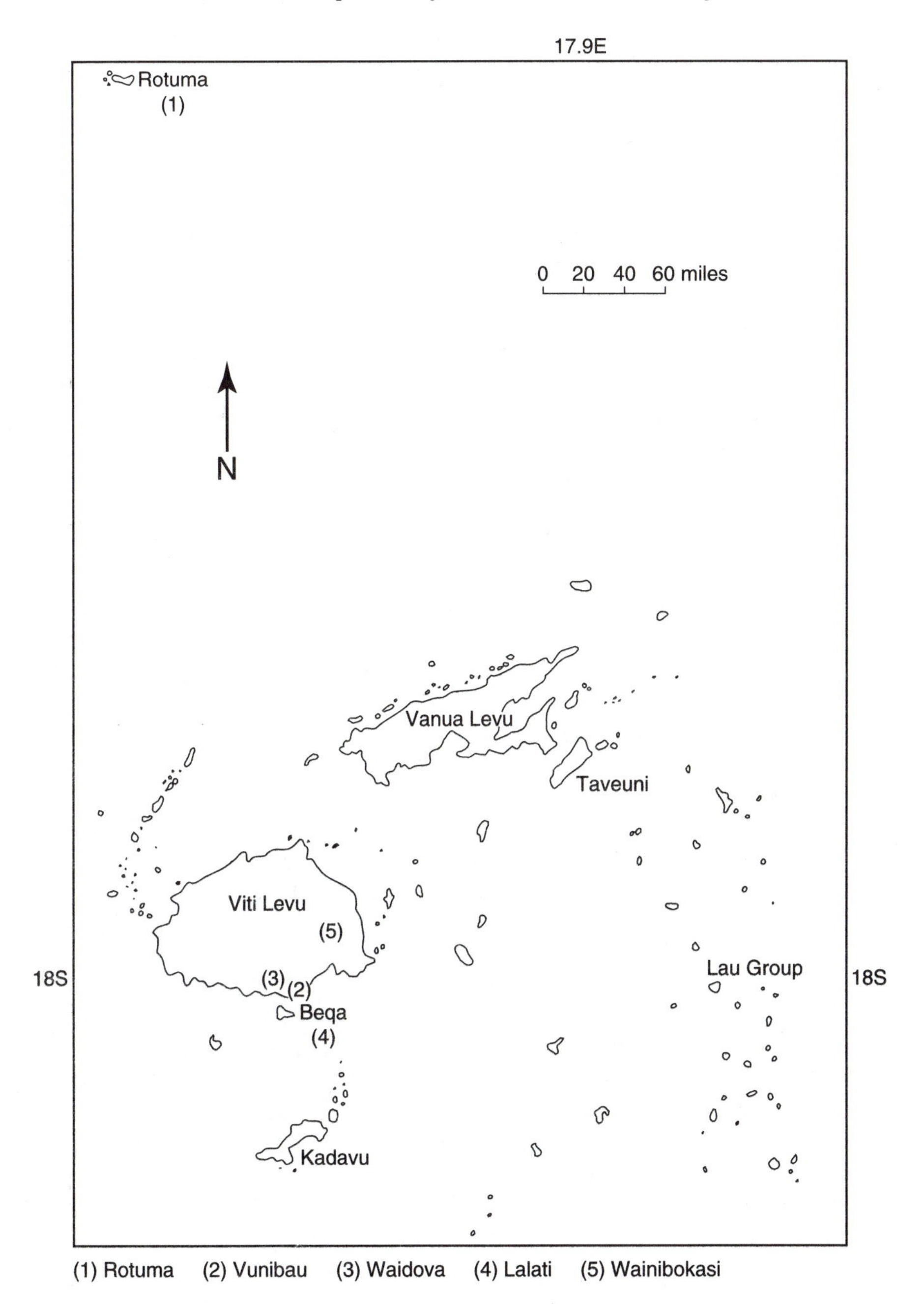


**FIGURE 4–1.** Map of the Fiji Islands showing the study areas.

microfilaremia and "cryptic" infections to chronic pathology such as elephantiasis and tropical eosinophilia (Ottesen 1984, 1987). Diagnosis of infection is determined almost exclusively by parasitologic techniques demonstrating microfilariae in the blood or tissue.[4]

Infection is believed to occur as a result of intense, prolonged exposure to infective larvae (Ottesen 1984; White 1989). As a general rule, the microfilaraemia rate shows a gradual but continuous rise in the 1 to 4 year age group, peaking in the 15 to 20 year age group, with signs of the disease most common in the 20 to 29 year age group (Wilcocks and Manson-Bahr 1978). "There is a slow and steady rise in the prevalence of elephantiasis beyond the age of 20 years, with the peak incidence between the ages of 25 to 45 years" (Mak and Dennis 1985, p. 439). In Fiji, the youngest elephantiasis patient was a 14-year-old Indian boy from the island of Taveuni.[5]

The incidence of filarial infection is higher among males in most countries (Wilcocks and Manson-Bahr 1978). In Fiji, the Indian, Fijian, and Rotuman males have higher rates of infection than their female counterparts. Fijian and Rotuman males have greater potential for contact with vectors than females because they perform more subsistence activities in the village-family–owned coconut plantations, where the principal filarial vector breeds. An exception to this gender bias is found among Fijian and Indian women exhibiting rates of filariasis similar to males in Vanua Levu and Taveuni Islands. Women in these areas engage in economic activities alongside men, probably accounting for these similarities. One could assume that, in the absence of a division of labor, the expected rates of filariasis would be very similar for males and females.

Although results from the latest (1985 to 1990) WHO survey[6] of the islands are not yet available, data are available from previous surveys of blood tests showing microfilarial density and distribution. In 1983, a WHO-sponsored survey (Mataika et al. 1985) was done in the islands of Rotuma, the Lau group, Oni-i-lau, and Kadavu. This survey showed that men on Rotuma and Lau Islands had the highest rates of microfilaremia known to date. Indians were not included in the 1983 survey, but field observations indicated that they continue to show significantly lower rates than either Fijians or Rotumans. The lowest rates of microfilaremia are found among Indian females. Table 4–1 shows the ethnic distribution of filariasis based on microfilariae rates.

The 1983 survey also revealed a high recurrence of filariasis, especially in Rotuma. Infection rates among Rotuman males had dropped to 7.9% in 1975 after mass administrations of DEC. Results of the 1983 survey, however, showed that infection rates had increased to 30% (Mataika et al. 1985). The high recurrence or increase in infection rates was most probably due to an increase in the human reservoir population (J. Mataika, personal communication, 1985). High recurrence rates may also be partially attributed to the remoteness of these islands, which limits their access to continuous biomedical services such as DEC treatment and surgery for lymphatic swellings.

**TABLE 4–1. The Ethnic Distribution of Filariasis**

| | *FIJIANS* | *ROTUMANS* | *INDIANS* |
|---|---|---|---|
| Males | 30% (1983) | 33% (1983) | 9.2% (1971) |
| Females | 11.6% (1983) | 21.2% (1983) | 7.3% (1971) |

Both surveys (1971 and 1983) represent the latest prevalence data available for each ethnic group. The data were obtained from the Wellcome Virus Laboratory in Suva. The rates for Fijians are averages based on combined results from the islands included in the 1983 survey (rates vary between and among individual islands).

Prior to discussing how human behavior and cultural practices directly influence the outcome of filariasis, it is important to consider the behavior or activity patterns of the pathogen because its presence in human blood and tissue determines infection rates.

## THE PERIODIC NATURE OF THE PATHOGEN

The disease transmission cycle of filariasis depends on timing, or a "synchronized" connection between the host, vector, and pathogen. Filarial nematodes that show rhythmic variations in microfilarial density during the 24-hour cycle are termed periodic or subperiodic (Sasa 1976). This variation can be seen by the presence and absence of microfilariae in human blood and tissue samples. Only the diurnally subperiodic form of *W. bancrofti,* which is most active during early morning and early evening hours, is present in Fiji (Symes c. 1957). Because of its activity pattern, to determine infections with *W. bancrofti,* blood samples must be collected during the times when the microfilariae are present (active) in the peripheral blood.

In Fiji, activity patterns of *W. bancrofti* generally correspond with the combined activity periods of the *Aedes* vectors. *Ae. pseudoscutellaris, Ae. polynesiensis, Ae. rotumae,* and *Ae. fijiensis* are all day-biting mosquitoes (Iyengar 1960). Whereas the first three are most active during the early morning hours, the last is most active during late afternoon–early evening hours. *C. fatigans,* which is primarily a night biter, is not considered to be a major vector of filariasis in Fiji (Kessel 1961). Figure 4–2 shows the activity patterns (biting rhythms) of the four filariasis vectors in Fiji. The activity patterns of *Ae. rotumae* and *Ae. pseudoscutellaris* are very similar (Iyengar 1960). Figure 4–3 shows the correlation between microfilarial periodicity and the biting rhythm of *Ae. polynesiensis.* This figure demonstrates the highly adaptive nature of the parasite to its vector. In sum, periodicity directly influences the transmissibility of the parasite to the vector and also influences accurate diagnosis of infection in the human host.

Timing and activity are also important for contact between vector and

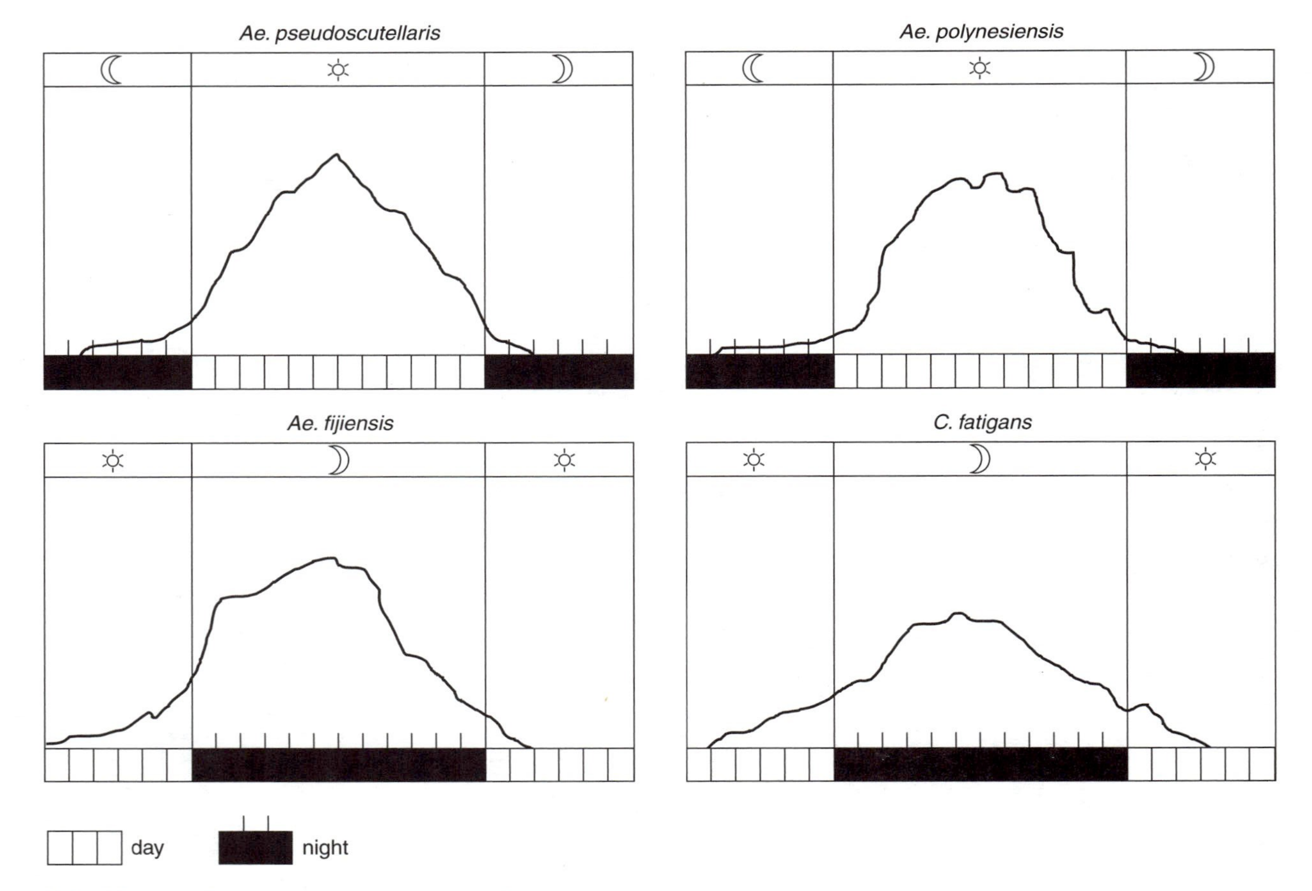


**FIGURE 4–2.** The 24-hour biting cycles of Filariasis vectors in Fiji.

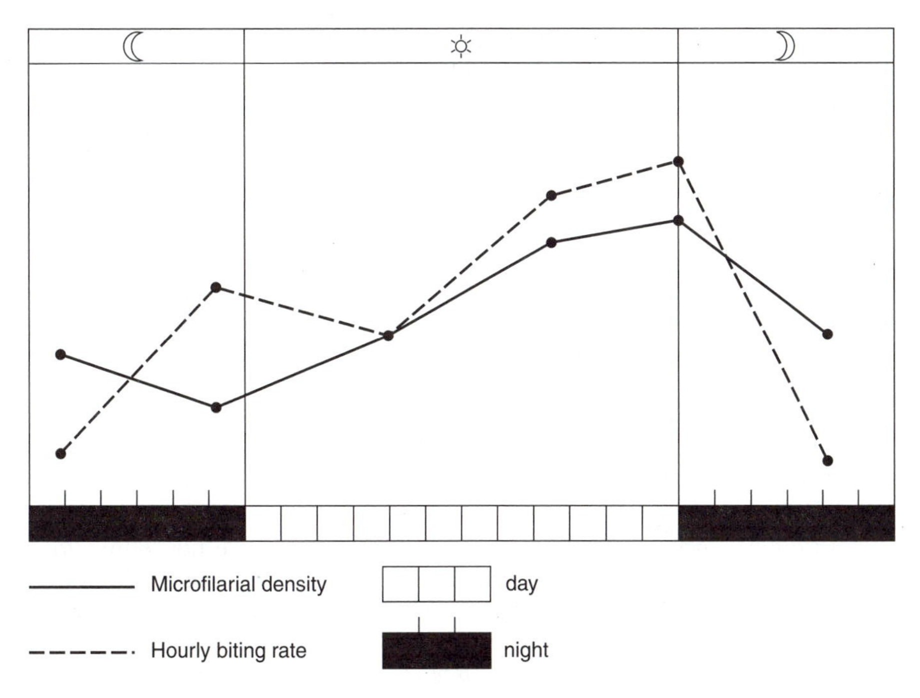


**FIGURE 4–3.** Correlation between microfilarial periodicity and the biting rhythm of vector—subperiodic *W. bancrofti* and *Ae. polynesiensis*. (Adapted from Mattingly, 1969.)

host. The following discussion presents a summary of contact between the mosquito vectors and humans, as observed in the five study sites.

## PATTERNS OF VECTOR-HOST CONTACT: AGE, GENDER, AND ETHNIC GROUP EFFECTS

Based on data gathered during this study, disease rates appear to reflect the amount and frequency of human contact with vector mosquitoes. To monitor the occurrence and frequency of contact between humans and vectors, each study site was divided into four observable, spatially controlled units (vector zones) in which human activities leading to contact with vector mosquitoes could be observed. While a means of controlling the parameters of comparative data, these zones also included specific environmental features in which vector concentrations could be measured.

The four zones were identified as indoor (I), household compound (II), village/community (III), and garden/plantation (IV). The village/community zone included open, semiopen, and some fully enclosed structures such as churches. Vector collections revealed that the garden/plantation zone (IV), followed by the household compound (II), had the highest densities of vector mosquitoes.

In general, the types of social and economic activities of Fijians, Indians, and Rotumans did not vary as much as the distance of the activity site from the household. Distance of activity sites varied largely according to the spatial organization of communal Fijian and Rotuman villages, which differ significantly from the self-contained, single-household units of Indians.

Once the vectors had been identified and the activity (presence) periods were known for each zone,[7] human activities within these zones were monitored. Table 4–2 summarizes the results of monitoring vector-host contact by gender and ethnic group.

## SUSCEPTIBILITY OF WOMEN TO VECTOR CONTACT

Fijian women have greater contact with vectors outside the household zone than either Rotuman or Indian women (Table 4–2). In contrast, the daily activities of most Rotuman and Indian women keep them closer to the household. Fijian women also travel most frequently to perform daily activities, including fishing, maintaining vegetable gardens and pandanus patches, and tending pigs. Fishing is a major activity of Fijian women living in coastal villages such as Lalati and Vunibau. Women fishing in open water, usually from a canoe, are less likely to be bothered by mosquitoes. However, women sitting and

**TABLE 4–2. Exposure According to Time Spent in Vector Zones**

| | *ZONE I* | | *ZONE II* | | *ZONE III* | | *ZONE IV* | |
|---|---|---|---|---|---|---|---|---|
| | *M* | *F* | *M* | *F* | *M* | *F* | *M* | *F* |
| Rotuma | 9 | 14 | 2 | 4 | 4 | 3.5 | 9 | 2.5 |
| Vunibau | 10.5 | 12.5 | 1 | 3 | 4 | 3.5 | 8.5 | 5 |
| Lalati | 9 | 13 | 1 | 4 | 4.5 | 3 | 9.5 | 4 |
| Waidova | 10 | 15.5 | 1 | 3 | 1 | .5 | 12 | 5 |
| Wainibokasi | 11 | 15.5 | 1 | 4 | 2 | 2.5 | 10 | 2 |

Zone I = **Indoor** (living, sleeping, and eating quarters)
Zone II = **Household compound** (immediate area surrounding the house, including kitchen gardens)
Zone III = **Village/community** (schools, churches, markets, and other community activity areas adjacent to the village compound)
Zone IV = **Garden/plantation** (coconut plantations, rice fields, pigsties, and roads and paths leading to these areas of primary economic activity)

fishing along shorelines and mangrove swamps are continuously bitten by mosquitoes. Cleaning and washing activities also expose many Fijian women to vectors. In Lalati, where only one communal tap provided fresh water for the entire village, tap water was used exclusively for cooking while the freshwater streams were most often used for bathing and cleaning.

Rotuman women have less contact with vector mosquitoes than do Fijian women (Table 4–2). The women from Motusa village most frequently came into contact with vectors while gathering pandanus, usually done once or twice a week. Contact with vectors also occurs when feeding pigs. Although it is usually a man's job, some Rotuman girls also share the responsibility of pig feeding. Older Rotuman women often fish in the lagoon and make mats, while younger women tend to the household chores unless they are working outside the home. There was very little travel involved in the daily activity patterns of most Rotuman women observed during this study.

Indian women are the least likely to travel outside their household compound for any major activity. Except for younger women working in the towns, Indian women from Waidova and Wainibokasi settlements primarily worked in the rice fields and vegetable gardens adjacent to their houselots. They also tended farm animals if children were unavailable or unable to do so. Kitchen gardens, a very common feature in household compounds, also form a part of the major outdoor activity of Indian women. These gardens provide the basic vegetables and spices for daily use.

Based on these observations, it is highly likely that under similar environmental conditions and similar activity patterns, all three groups of women would be equally susceptible to vector contact.

## SUSCEPTIBILITY OF MEN TO VECTOR CONTACT

In all three groups, men had more frequent and more consistent contact with vector mosquitoes in the highest vector density zone (IV) than women. In Rotuma, income from copra[8] is very important, and men can spend 3 to 4 days a week gathering, husking, and shelling coconuts. Except for sabbath day, Rotuman men spend the remaining days in their vegetable gardens and working around the home, performing communal labor and other social activities. However, the time spent in the coconut plantations is the single most important activity in terms of vector-host contact. Preliminary observations indicated that some men from Motusa village whose activities showed greater or more frequent exposure and contact with vector mosquitoes also had fairly high counts of microfilariae. Microfilariae infection rates were obtained from patient medical records maintained at Rotuma Hospital.[9]

Similar economic activities make Fijian men equally susceptible to vector contact. Although there was very little difference in the amount of time Fijian men from Lalati or Vunibau spent in each vector zone, the men from Vunibau had a wider range of economic possibilities that often took them into the towns. However, even if part of their daily activities was performed in the towns, these men tended to communal and household gardening activities after returning home. The work performed in the village and surrounding areas, such as pandanus and coconut groves, brought the men into frequent contact with vectors.

Using small-engine boats, a few men from Lalati also commuted to work on Viti Levu during the day. Although Beqa in Lalati is only 4.3 miles from Viti Levu, it remains socially isolated from the greater community of Viti Levu. As a result of this relative isolation, the island of Beqa has undergone little development. For instance, travel between villages is primarily by boat or footpaths, and economic activities are limited to fishing, subsistence farming, and, to a lesser degree, firewalking.

In Lalati, the two primary vectors of filariasis, *Ae. pseudoscutellaris* and *Ae. polynesiensis,* were found in high densities. Large numbers of these vectors were also found in the neighboring villages of Dakuni and Daquibeqa. The last filariasis survey done in Beqa (1955) revealed extremely high rates of filariasis (Desowitz and Southgate 1973). Similar observations were made again during a brief visit to the island in 1986 (Brian Southgate, WHO advisor, personal communication, 1986).

As shown in Table 4–2, Indian men from the Waidova and Wainibokasi settlements spend more time in the garden/plantation zone than Rotuman and Fijian men. However, these men still have less contact with vector mosquitoes because their plantations consist of corn, rice, and sugar cane, considered unsuitable breeding places for the *Aedes* vectors (Toohey et al. 1981). Although Indians in Waidova settlement and Fijians in Vunibau village live in close proximity to the vector *Ae. fijiensis,* their economic and social activities lead to a difference in contact with the vector.

The success of filarial vectors in isolated areas where constant human reservoirs are available and breeding habitats are abundant is reflected in the high rate of filarial infection seen in Beqa and Rotuma. For instance, on Matuku and Lakeba Islands, where copra is the main source of income and where vectors such as *Ae. polynesiensis* breed prolifically, surveys reveal very high rates of microfilaremia (Mataika et al. 1985). Fijian men on these islands showed rates of 19.4% and 12.1%, respectively, the highest rates found among Fijians on a single island. Vector-host contact is not determined solely by the environment or type and duration of activities. Another factor is how well protected an individual is from mosquito bites. Observations not only revealed that men have more frequent contact with vector mosquitoes, but also that they use fewer protective measures. Protecting oneself from mosquito bites is a matter of social importance first, economics second, and convenience last.

## PROTECTIVE MEASURES: SEX AND ETHNIC GROUP EFFECTS

A variety of direct and indirect protective measures were observed during the study period. Direct measures are intended to protect the individual from mosquito bites. Indirect measures are environmental features and cultural practices that, in themselves, are not intended to protect but incidentally provide such benefits. Table 4–3 summarizes the more apparent/observable protective features found in the five Fijian, Rotuman, and Indian communities included in the study. This summary also illustrates the cultural differences in using and creating such measures. For comparison, this summary generalizes from specific household data collected at each of the study sites.

Direct protective measures are taken by those who perceive or feel the need to protect themselves from mosquitoes. As Table 4–3 indicates, Indians take more direct protective measures and also have greater protection from indirect measures. This is partially due to the need Indians feel to protect themselves from mosquitoes. Equally important is the desire to have indoor plumbing and window screens, both of which are social and economic indicators of status. Although such features may also serve as indicators of status in some Fijian and Rotuman households, indoor plumbing and screens on windows are not necessarily desirable. Fijian and Rotuman villages are primarily communal

**TABLE 4–3. Direct and Indirect Protective Measures**

| | *FIJIAN* | *ROTUMAN* | *INDIAN* |
|---|---|---|---|
| *Direct Measures* | | | |
| Mosquito nets | * | ** | *** |
| Mosquito coils, sprays, incense, and repellent | * | ** | *** |
| Window screens | * | ** | *** |
| Clothing | | | ** |
| Bush clearing | * | * | * |
| *Indirect Measures* | | | |
| Kitchen smoke | ** | ** | * |
| Clothing | * | * | *** |
| Bush clearing | * | *** | *** |
| Location of outhouse | ** | ** | ** |
| Indoor plumbing | | * | ** |
| Incense | | | * |
| Location of pets and farm animals | * | ** | * |

* = rarely used
** = used when available
*** = used regularly

organizations in which houses are often clustered together. The proximity of houses, housing structure, and materials generally reflects this sense of community. In comparison, Indian households, although perhaps in close proximity with other relatives' houses, are self-reliant units constructed with individual preferences in mind.

In general, Fijians do not perceive mosquitoes as harmful pests and rarely use protective measures such as mosquito nets while sleeping. The most common Fijian clothing items are sulus and shirts/blouses which, although well suited for the tropics, provide little protection from hungry mosquitoes.

Some Rotumans, especially those who have participated in filariasis and trachoma[10] education programs, are likely to use some protective measures such as window screens and mosquito nets. It appears that gaining some knowledge and acceptance of mosquitoes as agents of disease has at least some temporary effect on behavior patterns. Permanent behavioral change, however, is not likely to happen unless there is constant reinforcement coupled with education, environmental control, and some visible aspects of the positive impact of change.

The factors contributing to the occurrence and recurrence of disease are primarily those bringing the pathogen, vector, and host into contact. However, perpetuation of the disease cycle is strongly influenced by people's beliefs and responses after infection has developed.

## PERCEPTION AND REACTIONS TO FILARIASIS AS A DISEASE: ETHNIC GROUP EFFECTS

The events that take place after the individual has become ill with filariasis are very important in determining the outcome of disease. These events are basically dictated by cultural behavior, which in turn affects known and observed prevalence rates. In Fiji, health-seeking behavior appears to reflect the general world-view of the individual's cultural belief system. Culture can and does influence disease patterns in several ways: (1) how good and ill health are defined, (2) how the individual and community can deal with health and disease, and (3) offering possible solutions. In addition to the traditional ethnomedical system, beliefs and forms of therapy are also influenced by changes brought on by acculturation and contact with other medical systems. The dominant form of medical care in Fiji is the Western biomedical system, established as the national health care system under colonial rule. Ethnomedical practices also remain among the different cultures of Fiji.

Filariasis as a health problem was a part of the Fijian, Rotuman, and Indian societies long before contact with Europeans and Western biomedical care.[11] The historical existence and acknowledgment of this disease have created a special place in the ethnomedical lore of each group. In contrast, the introduction of biomedically based knowledge and treatment of filariasis is relatively recent. Furthermore, filariasis is confined primarily to the traditional rural settings, whereas the "scientific" explanation and treatment of filariasis are found largely in the nontraditional, urban setting. For instance, the only filariasis laboratory in the islands is located in Suva, Fiji's urban center. Because this is the only facility in Fiji, its centralized location is necessary, yet travel to Suva, especially from the small outer islands, is very difficult. This leaves a large proportion of the human reservoir, those segments of the population where disease rates are the highest, with little or no access to the treatment facility.

## FILARIASIS IN THE FIJIAN COMMUNITY

Based on data from earlier surveys, filariasis appears to be prevalent in many Fijian communities, particularly those socially and geographically isolated from the main islands, where vector presence is high. The Fijian term for filariasis is *waqaqa;* the term for elephantiasis is *tauna. Waqaqa,* a common term in the Fijian vocabulary meaning fever with swelling, is also used by Rotumans and Indians. *Tauna* is less commonly used, and younger Fijians were generally unfamiliar with the term.

Fijian disease theories place filariasis in the category of illnesses caused by the "mate vaka vanua," or spirits of the land (Spencer 1941). These spirits can be of the living or the dead. However, accusations against the living are less common than those against the dead. Most often, sickness is blamed on carelessness and/or misconduct by the sick individual. Explanations of how these spirits caused *waqaqa* were associated with water, cold air, food, yagona (kava), spells, and spiritual possessions. Filariasis is not thought to be a disease transmitted by mosquitoes unless the mosquito acted as an agent or was a spirit in disguise.

Health-seeking behavior indicates that traditional healers are preferred over biomedical doctors for the treatment of filariasis. The diseases caused by the mate vaka vanua are most often treated by a *dauvagunu,* or traditional healer. During this study, 49 of the 83 people who acknowledged having had filariasis at some time in their life sought the advice of a traditional healer first. Table 4–4 provides a summary of health-seeking behavior in five Fijian communities: the two study areas of Lalati and Vunibau and three other Fijian communities briefly visited (Taveuni, Kadavu, and Vanua Levu Islands).

The popularity of traditional healers reflects causal explanations for the disease as well as a higher level of trust and confidence in local healers. In contrast, there is less confidence in biomedical practitioners, including both doctors and nurses. This lack of confidence is partially attributed to the negative side effects of DEC, as well as possible misdiagnosis and/or incorrect treatment of infections.

Most Fijians make little or no association between filariasis and elephantiasis. When recurring filarial symptoms included swelling, there was some un-

**TABLE 4–4. Health-Seeking Behavior of Fijians in Response to Filariasis**

| *STUDY AREAS* | *TRADITIONAL HEALER* | *MEDICAL PRACTITIONER* | *HOME REMEDIES* |
|---|---|---|---|
| Lalati | 12 | 2 | 4 |
| Vunibau | 6 | 5 | 1 |
| Kadavu | 11 | 4 | 6 |
| Vanua Levu | 8 | 3 | 4 |
| Taveuni | 12 | 3 | 2 |
| TOTALS | 49 | 17 | 17 |

derstanding that this swelling would ultimately lead to elephantiasis. However, elephantiasis generally is considered a separate disease because the near-permanency of elephantiasis afflictions is not associated with the recurring short-term infections caused by filarial fever. The lack of association between the separate stages of the disease was evident in people's responses. Biomedical terms and explanations for labeling filarial fever or elephantiasis were cited primarily by patients and younger community members. Both groups include individuals who have learned the terminology and/or disease process through their exposure to biomedical care.

Perhaps the most significant observation made of Fijians afflicted with elephantiasis is their participation in daily, routine village life. They are not outcasts in the community and are not prohibited or excluded from any activities except those which they are physically incapable of doing.

## FILARIASIS IN THE ROTUMAN COMMUNITY

Rotuman disease theories generally do not reflect the vector-host relationship of filariasis. Nor are their theories bound by social explanations, as seen among their Fijian neighbors. This is largely due to the changes which have been brought upon Rotuman society. As Howard explains, "despite the history of resistance, Rotumans did in fact ultimately accept most of the medical innovations forced on them through the authority of colonial administrators, and by 1960 their responses to most medical problems were distinctly secular" (Howard 1970, p. 271).

Filarial fever in Rotuma is known as *tau te'*; however, the Fijian term *waqaqa* is more commonly used. Many of the herbal remedies and plants used for treating filarial disease were borrowed or learned from Fijians living on the island. Of the several traditional healers interviewed on Rotuma, a 43-year-old Fijian woman married to a Rotuman man was one of the most popular.

Between 1981 and 1985, 57 individuals (38 men and 19 women) came to the public health nurses's station for DEC treatment. Of these 57, only 21 returned for a second dose, and only 9 of these individuals continued to come on a regular monthly basis for their tablets. The majority of those not returning were young men who said that DEC brought on additional discomfort. They felt that if left alone, the fever would eventually pass. Additionally, when taking DEC, patients are discouraged from taking diuretics. The prohibition of yagona and other diuretics such as orange wine is another reason some Rotuman men do not take DEC. Another reason is that young Rotuman men rarely, if ever, visit the hospital. Hospital visits are considered more appropriate for women.

Rotuman women were more cooperative with DEC treatment than men. These women's primary concern was the effects of DEC on unborn children. As a rule, DEC treatment was discontinued after the first trimester owing to the drug's possible negative effects on the fetus (Viliame, personal communication, 1986). The fear of DEC's potential harm to children, and perhaps ultimately adults, worried these women.

Several individuals on Rotuma have elephantiasis. Elephantiasis is referred to as either *fefe* (the Rotuman term) or *tauna* (the Fijian term). Again, no association is made between elephantiasis and the earlier stages of filariasis. Those who have elephantiasis go about their daily activities no differently than anyone else. They are not teased or ridiculed. They may even have special services rendered to them because of their condition, but only as the need for such services arises. As in Fijian society, Rotumans with elephantiasis are active members of the society who receive little or no attention because of their physical disabilities.

## FILARIASIS IN THE INDIAN COMMUNITY

The variety and number of traditional Indian healers outnumber, by far, their Fijian and Rotuman counterparts. The pundit is the primary healer and the provider of traditional health care. There are numerous bone-setters, dais (traditional midwives), seers, and herbalists. Fiji Indians do not fully participate in biomedical care because they still rely on traditional healing methods. A common Indian belief about biomedical care is that modern medicines do not fully heal illness.

The range of causal explanations for filarial disease in Fiji's Indian communities varies with geographic, economic, and social issues. Causal explanations are often influenced by religious beliefs, superstitions, educational background, and familial observations of illness behavior. Men generally are more inclined to give "naturalistic" explanations—for example, filarial fever is caused by cold air—whereas women are more likely to give social or religious explanations—for example, filarial fever results from breaking or not observing taboos. Explanations also differ among healers, which in turn determines the mode of treatment used in a given situation. Although there is consistency in the types of treatment for specific diseases, these are often also accompanied by "tailor-made" explanations.

The health-seeking behavior of Indians reveals that both traditional and biomedical care are sought for the treatment of filariasis. In general, Indians tend to use the combined services of traditional healers and biomedical practitioners more regularly than their Fijian and Rotuman counterparts. However, most Indians first seek a traditional healer within their own community before seeking biomedical treatment. Of the 24 Indian patients with filariasis, 21 had or were currently taking DEC. The remaining 3 either never completed the first course of DEC or did not return for further treatment. All 3 of these individuals, however, continued to observe social restrictions prescribed by their traditional healer.

Most Indians made little or no association between filariasis and elephantiasis. They often used the term *waqaqa* when referring to filarial fever, which in some cases denoted their categorization of it as a "fijian" disease. Filariasis falls into the category of short-term afflictions, whereas the permanent disfigurement resulting from elephantiasis is thought to be brought on by more serious causes. Further, any chronic disease that manifests itself with physical impairment is automatically placed in a serious category. Among some Indians, death is seen as a lesser means of punishment than permanent disfigurement. Therefore, a person who suffers from elephantiasis can be viewed as a constant reminder of the punishment incurred as a result of action that cannot be amended.

Based on observations, Indians who suffer from elephantiasis often become social outcasts within their own household and community. Although not every person with elephantiasis is treated in the same manner, avoidance and isolation were common reactions to the five observed cases of elephantiasis on Vanua Levu and Taveuni Islands. Family and public reaction toward the two women were more negative than toward the three men. This may to some degree reflect the fact that two of the men were still the primary providers for their individual families and their physical disabilities were overlooked because of their economic roles. Interviews with all but one man, who met with the investigator in public, were conducted in the privacy of the person's home.

## SUMMARY

It is now recognized that any human disease or disorder is the result of many factors within what may be described as a "causal web," a web of determinants . . . within any such causal web, many of the determinants of disease and disorder are behavioral (Dunn and Janes 1986, p. 3).

This chapter has looked at two factors that contribute to the prevalence of filariasis in Fiji: human behavior leading to contact with vector mosquitoes and the varied perceptions and reactions to the disease. Through direct and indirect behavior, Fijian and Rotuman men have more frequent contact with vectors, which in turn significantly contributes to the higher rates of filariasis in those groups. Indian men, on the other hand, because of lesser contact with vectors, exhibit much lower infection rates. Women from all three groups have lower rates of filariasis. However, differences in behavioral patterns also contribute to Fijian and Rotuman women having higher rates than their Indian counterparts.

The second factor contributing to the prevalence of filariasis encompasses the varied disease theories and health-seeking behaviors in response to filariasis. Even though Western biomedical care is the "national" health care system in Fiji, culture-bound explanations are still more common then scientific explanations. Traditional healers still serve an important role in each culture's repertoire of healing practices and are often sought or preferred over biomedical practitioners. Chemotherapeutic efforts are not fully accepted or adhered to. In general, Indians are more compliant with DEC treatment than Fijians and Rotumans. Although biomedical care exists at the national level, treatment for filariasis is still influenced by social and geographic factors. Traditional health care or ethnomedicine, on the other hand, is readily available and accessible.

To better understand the disease cycle, other factors examining the more biologic aspects of the disease, although beyond the scope of this work, need to be considered. These include (1) the accuracy of blood tests in determining the distribution of the disease, (2) questioning whether the presence or absence of microfilariae alone determines the existence of disease, (3) individual resistance and susceptibility to infection, and (4) the distribution and abundance of mosquito vectors, particularly those of the genus *Aedes,* which have proven to be highly adaptive to transient environmental conditions (Spielman and Rossignol 1984).

It is quite apparent from this study that culture has, in varying ways, influenced how Fijians, Rotumans, and Indians have learned to live with filariasis. Indians treat filariasis as a health hazard and take protective measures against mosquito bites. Fijians treat filariasis as a recurring event but not a serious health problem and do not perceive mosquitoes to be harmful pests. Lastly, Rotumans tolerate filariasis as a nuisance and, although it is not a serious problem, more concern over proper precautions and treatment is exhibited.

## NOTES

1. Hydrocele in the form of scrotal inflammation has also been reported throughout the island.
2. Diethylcarbamazine (DEC, also known as Hetrazan), a filaricide that kills microfilariae, was discovered in 1947 by Hewitt et al. Repeated courses of DEC may de-

stroy adult filarial worms (Wilcocks and Manson-Bahr 1978), but its efficacy is still questionable.

3. Dr. Kenneth Gilchrist, a British surgeon brought in to treat patients with elephantiasis in the 1940s recalled that this disease was common among both Fijian and Indian plantation workers on Vanua Levu and Taveuni Island.
4. Laboratory studies to determine the cause of filarial parasites are still difficult because *Wucheria bancrofti* and *Onchocerca volvulus,* the two most important parasites, cannot be maintained in laboratory animals (Ottesen 1978).
5. Elephantiasis from Brugian filariasis has been reported among 6- and 7-year-olds in Africa and Southeast Asia.
6. The Vector and Biological Control Unit of WHO has sponsored several antifilariasis campaigns in Fiji. Most of these campaigns, led by Dr. Jonu Mataika and the staff of the Wellcome Virus Laboratory, involve blood tests followed by mass administrations of DEC.
7. Climatic changes influenced the presence and density of vectors, with the highest vector densities found during calm periods immediately following rainshowers. Periods of heavy winds revealed the lowest vector densities.
8. Copra is the dried meat of coconuts from which coconut oil is extracted. Copra production was initiated by various colonial administrations throughout the Pacific Islands.
9. Attempts to compare medical record data for all Lalati residents was unsuccessful because their clinic records did not include information on filarial infections. No attempts to check medical records for the other study populations were made because these individuals had access to a variety of medical facilities.
10. Trachoma is a major health problem in Rotuma, and attempts are being made to control the island's fly population. Preventive measures such as the use of trash incinerators have been initiated by the New Zealand Army Medical Team.
11. Filarial infections caused by both *W. bancrofti* and *Brugia malayi* are found throughout India (Wilcocks and Manson-Bahr 1978). It is likely that the laborers and migrants who came to Fuji in the late 1880s already had some exposure to this disease.

## REFERENCES

Bryant, Jennifer J. 1974. "Rotuman Islanders Living in Fiji." Ph.D. dissertation, University of Otago, New Zealand.

Dasgupta, A. 1978. *Progress in Filariasis I.* India: Ankur Publishing House.

Deo, Indra and Penelope Schoeffel. 1987. "Country Profile—Fiji." Paper presented to the Nutrition Challenges in a Challenging World Conference, University of Hawaii, Honolulu, Hawaii.

Desowitz, Robert S. and Brian A. Southgate. 1973. "Studies on Filariasis in the Pacific. 2. The Persistence of Microfilaraemia in Diethylcarbamazine-Treated Populations of Fiji and Western Samoa: Diagnostic Application of the Membrane-Filtration Technique." *Southeast Asian Journal of Tropical Medicine and Public Health* 4:179–83.

Dunn, Frederick L. and Craig R. Janes. 1986. "Introduction: Medical Anthropology and Epidemiology." Pp. 1–39 in *Anthropology and Epidemiology,* edited by C. R. Janes, R. Stall, and S. Gifford. Holland: D. Reidel Publishing Company.

Howard, Alan. 1970. *Learning to Be Rotuman.* New York: Columbia Teachers College Press.

Iyengar, M. O. T. 1960. "A Review of the Mosquito Fauna of the Pacific: (*Diptera Culicidae*)." Technical Paper No. 130, Noumea: South Pacific Commission.

KESSEL, JOHN F. 1961. "The Ecology of Filariasis." Pp. 45–71 in *Studies in Disease Ecology,* edited by J. M. May. New York: Hafner Publishing Co.

MAK, J. W. and D. T. DENNIS. 1985. "Lymphatic Filariasis." Pp. 431–50 in *Epidemiology and the Community Control of Disease in Warm Climate Countries,* edited by Derek Robinson. New York: Churchill Livingstone.

MATAIKA, J. U., B. C. DANDO, G. F. S. SPEARS, and F. N. MACNAMARA. 1971. "Mosquito-Borne Infections in Fiji I. Filariasis in Northern Fiji: Epidemiological Evidence Regarding Factors Influencing the Prevalence of Microfilaraemia of *Wuchereria bancrofti* Infections." *J. Hyg. Camb.* 69:273–86.

MATAIKA, J. U., M. V. MATAITOGA, and E. KIMURA. 1985. "Recent Situation of Filariasis in Lau and Rotuma Provinces in Fiji." *Fiji Medical Journal* 13:211–15.

MATTINGLY, P. F. 1969. *The Biology of Mosquito-Borne Disease.* London: George Allen and Unwin Ltd.

OTTESEN, ERIC A. 1984. "Filariasis and Tropical Eosinophilia." Pp. 390–423 in *Tropical and Geographical Medicine,* edited by Kenneth S. Warren and Adel A. F. Mahmoud. New York: McGraw-Hill.

______. 1987. "Introduction." Pp. 1–5 in *Filariasis: Ciba Foundation Symposium.* New York: John Wiley and Sons.

PILLAI, J. S. and J. URDANG. 1979. "The Discovery of the Mosquito *Aedes Aegypti* on Tokelau Group." *New Zealand Medicine* 90:212–13.

PRASAD, USHA K. 1989. "A Cross Cultural Comparison of Filarial Disease in the Fiji Islands." Ph.D. dissertation, University of Hawaii, Honolulu.

SASA, MANABU. 1976. *Human Filariasis.* Baltimore: University Park Press.

SPENCER, DOROTHY M. 1941. *Disease, Religion and Society in the Fiji Islands.* Washington: Seattle University Press.

SPIELMAN, ANDREW and PHILIPPE A. ROSSIGNOL. 1984. "Insect Vectors." Pp. 167–82 in *Tropical and Geographical Medicine,* edited by Kenneth S. Warren and Adel A. F. Mahmoud. New York: McGraw-Hill.

SYMES, C. B. c. 1957. "Observations on the Natural History of Human Filariasis in Fiji: A Report to the Secretary of State and Colonies on Investigations Conducted over the Period 1954–1956." Suva, Fiji: Government Printers.

TOOHEY, M. K., M. S. GOETTEL and J. S. PILLAI. 1981. "A Review of the Prospects of Using Biological Control Against Mosquito Vectors of Subperiodic Filariasis and Arboviruses in Polynesia." *South Pacific Journal of Natural Science* 2:4–43.

WHITE, G. B. 1989. "Lymphatic Filariasis." Pp. 23–34 in *Tropical Distribution of Anthropod-borne Diseases and their Principal Vectors.* Vector Biology and Control Division, World Health Organization, Switzerland.

WILCOCKS, CHARLES and P. E. C. MANSON-BAHR. 1978. *Manson's Tropical Diseases,* 18th ed. London: Bailliere-Tindall.

Chapter 5

# The Demographic, Cultural, and Behavioral Contexts of Maternal and Child Health in Developing Countries

*Gabriel B. Fosu and Janardan Subedi*

The demographic, epidemiologic, and cultural transformations occurring in developing countries are creating a complex health profile of the populations. For instance, the high prevalence of the common infectious and parasitic diseases and malnutrition is complicated by the emerging threats of chronic diseases and the AIDS epidemic. As developing countries try to attain the goal of universal health by the year 2000, it is becoming increasingly clear that the current health care systems have not been and will not be adequate for dealing with the growing complexity of health needs. Apart from the fact that the health sector is competing with other sectors for very scarce financial resources, limited access to health care services still leaves large segments of the population with little or no health coverage. There is an urgent need, therefore, to understand the current health-illness patterns and to identify the diseases that will dominate the future health care scene so that we can anticipate the future requirements of the health care system, set up our priorities, and plan our strategies for effective administration of the system. The purpose of this chapter is to examine the demographic and epidemiologic trends and to suggest how they may influence both the demand for and the provision of maternal and child health care services in developing countries. The trends in selected sub-Saharan African countries are used to illustrate the situation.

## CONCEPTUAL MODEL

The links between health, culture, and population processes are complex. Each influences the other in several ways, and all are influenced by socio-economic and political processes. Three models based on "transitions" are important in understanding such links. These are the demographic transition (DT), the epidemiologic transition (ET), and the health transition (HT). Demographers initially proposed the demographic transition theory to describe the differences in demographic patterns of countries with different levels of social and economic development (Notestein 1945, 1983). This theory recognizes the central role that the timing and interdependence of the secular decline in birth and death rates played in the outcome of Western demographic structures. It assumes that the social organization of an underdeveloped society is conducive to high fertility and mortality rates, which result in little or no population growth. According to Notestein (1945), high fertility was necessary for survival in pre-modern societies; otherwise, the very high mortality rates would have resulted in population extinction. Hence, a whole series of societal and cultural "props" were maintained to keep fertility high. If these props do not change when mortality rates decline, fertility may remain high. However, as a society undergoes industrialization, improvements in nutrition and health standards tend to reduce mortality while fertility remains high, thereby producing population growth. Furthermore, as urbanization and other social changes associated with industrialization occur, pressures are created that favor smaller families. Consequently, the birth rate gradually falls, approaching a balance with the death rate. These processes take place in three transitional stages: high fertility and high mortality; high fertility and low mortality; and low fertility and low mortality.

The epidemiologic transition theory (Omran 1971) also posits a series of interrelated and complex changes in the disease pattern that occur in specific human populations over time and are closely related to social, economic, and demographic transformations. The evolution of disease patterns in European countries spanned more than a century and fell into three distinct stages or eras. The first stage, the age of pestilence and famine, was marked by the persistence of infectious diseases related to poverty, malnutrition, and poor personal and environmental hygiene. Life expectancy was low, between 20 and 39 years. This gave way after the early part of this century to the second stage, the era of receding pandemics. During that era, the disease pattern was still dominated by infectious diseases and malnutrition, although major mortality fluctuations were less common. The increasing control of biologic pollution of the environment, as a result of improved sanitation and declining rates of infection, contributed to a rise in life expectancy to between 30 and 50 years. The third stage, the era of degenerative and "man-made" diseases, reflects a growing concern with human-induced diseases, such as cardiovascular diseases, cancer, and diabetes due to exposure to environmental pollution, as well as lifestyle factors such as drug addiction and violence. Life expectancy rose to over 50 years. A fourth stage of delayed degenerative diseases and lengthening life but poorer health has recently been proposed (Olshansky and Ault 1986).

The most salient criticism of both transitional models is that no justification exists for postulating that the relationship between modernization and demographic or epidemiologic processes is universal, linear, and unidirectional (Caldwell 1976; Frenk et al. 1989). The historical conditions of developing countries are different from the experiences of the now-developed or industrialized countries. For instance, whereas developed nations passed through the three stages over more than a century, developing nations are confronting all three simultaneously. It may be useful, therefore, to view the "model" in a more dynamic perspective rather than in the classic unilinear evolutionary perspective, by which all societies are expected to follow the Western pattern. Similarities and differences should be identified. Similarities may be found in the processes whereas differences may be identified in particular paths to the processes.

Recently, Frenk and associates (1989) have suggested two phenomena to be considered in the context of epidemiologic transitions: (1) health conditions, or the processes of health and disease that define the epidemiologic profile of a population; and (2) the changing organized social response to those conditions, that is, health care transition—dealing with the way the health care system is organized to deliver its services. To give due recognition to both components, Frenk and associates use the term "health transition." Their aim is to focus on important social, cultural, and behavioral aspects that have been neglected in favor of biomedical explanations. In their view, the health care transition evolves partly in response to epidemiologic transitions and partly from social, cultural, economic, and political changes, as well as from technologic and scientific developments in disease recognition, prevention, and treatment. In the course of its evolution, therefore, every society develops a system for coping with disease and ill health, which must be given due emphasis in any discussion of a nation's health care system.

This change of emphasis has three implications: (1) it recognizes that good health depends on the resources, values, and behavior of individuals, households, and communities; (2) it implies a shift from disease-specific and medical interventions to an examination of determinants of health in general, including nutrition, hygiene, and sanitation; and (3) it implies a focus on very broad issues of social evolution, such as education, equity, and empowerment (Cleland 1990).

However, despite the wider emphasis of health transition on social, cultural, and behavioral determinants of health and its attempts to clarify the complexities and realities of demographic and epidemiologic changes in the last 20 years, health transition should not be divorced from the broader concerns of the demographic and epidemiologic transitions. For example, the usefulness of both the demographic transition and the epidemiologic transition lies in pointing out the relationships among industrialization, health, and population processes and their relevance to health care planning (Phillips 1994). From the viewpoint of the health planner, the size and structure of the population, as well as the rate of change, are among the most important determinants of demand for health care. The disease spectrum and consequent needs for health care vary by age and gender. Hence, planning for the health needs of children, mothers, or the elderly must be based on the size of these groups, as well as their anticipated changes, which to a large extent depend on the three components of population (fertility, mortality, and migration). Also, as Phillips (1994) has succinctly discussed, the epidemiologic transition can provide a formal framework within which to set health and health care strategies over the medium to long term. In many developing countries, for instance, rich, middle-income, and poor citizens live in different epidemiologic worlds. Levels of care and standards of provision can be brought into focus in discussion of future epidemiologic patterns if such varied experiences are recognized and used as guides for resource allocation, especially where resources are scarce.

Even though each model facilitates the analysis of specific interventions, in reality health care planners must use a more integrated approach and consider several options. In examining the maternal and child health in developing countries, therefore, we use an integrated framework incorporating the strengths of each of the three transition models. Within this framework, three components are highlighted: demographic structure, epidemiologic trends, and cultural and behavioral response.

## DEMOGRAPHIC TRENDS

The United Nations estimates that the world's population in 1998 will be 6 billion and that annual additions for the next decade will be 97 million (United Nations 1991). Nearly all this population growth will be in Africa, Asia, and Latin America. Thirty-four percent of the world's population growth will be in Africa alone, with another 18% in south Asia. Since 1965, the population of sub-Saharan Africa has been growing at the rate of more than 2.5% annually (Table 5–1). The average annual growth of 3.1% between 1988 and 1991 is five times the population growth rate in high-income countries such as the United States, Great Britain, and Canada. Contrary to common assumptions, such phenomenal growth is due to persistent high fertility rather than to declining mortality rates. A look at the total fertility rates, the number of children a typical woman would have during her reproductive lifetime if she were to follow current fertility rates, reveals interesting trends. For Africa south of the Sahara as a whole, the total fertility rate has averaged 6.4 since the mid 1960s. Even though the rate is expected to decline to 5.9 by the year 2000, the total number of births is not expected to change substantially because of the *momentum* of population growth; that is, the mothers of the children who will be born in the year 2000 have already been born. The number of children and women, under such circumstances, cannot easily be ignored in the delivery of health care.

**TABLE 5–1. Population Growth, Fertility, and Maternal Mortality in Sub-Saharan Africa**

| *COUNTRY* | *AVERAGE ANNUAL GROWTH OF POPULATION (%)* | | *TOTAL FERTILITY RATE* | | *MATERNAL MORTALITY (PER 100,000 LIVE BIRTHS)* |
|---|---|---|---|---|---|
| | *1988–1991* | *1991–2000* | *1991* | *2000* | *1988* |
| Low income | 2.0 | 1.8 | 3.8 | 3.2 | 308 |
| Middle income | 1.8 | 1.5 | 3.2 | 3.1 | 107 |
| High income | 0.6 | 0.5 | 1.8 | 1.7 | — |
| Sub-Saharan Africa | 3.1 | 3.0 | 6.4 | 5.9 | 686 |
| Uganda | 2.5 | 3.3 | 7.3 | 6.6 | 550 |
| Mali | 2.6 | 3.1 | 7.0 | 7.0 | 2,325 |
| Burkina Faso | 2.6 | 3.0 | 6.5 | 6.3 | 810 |
| Kenya | 3.8 | 3.5 | 6.5 | 5.5 | — |
| Nigeria | 3.0 | 2.8 | 5.9 | 5.0 | 800 |
| Ghana | 3.2 | 3.2 | 6.2 | 5.1 | 1,000 |
| Togo | 3.4 | 3.1 | 6.6 | 5.5 | — |
| Zimbabwe | 3.4 | 2.3 | 4.7 | 3.4 | 77 |
| Senegal | 3.0 | 2.8 | 6.1 | 6.3 | — |
| Botswana | 3.5 | 2.8 | 4.8 | 3.1 | — |

Source: World Bank. *World Development Report 1993: Investing in Health.* New York: Oxford University Press, 1993.

In Ghana, for instance, the proportion of children under 5 years to the total population has been relatively high and steady around 18% since 1950. This is projected to decline to about 11% in 2025 (Fig. 5–1). However, in absolute numbers, the under-5 population in 2025 (4 million) will be fourfold that of 1950, which was less than 1 million. In Kenya, on the other hand, the proportion of 17.4% in 1950 has risen to the current levels of over 21%. This is expected to decline to about 12% by 2025. This decline, however, masks the fact that by 2025 the population of children under 5 in Kenya will be 4.5 million, an increase of about 3 million over the child population in 1950. The provision of child health care services in both countries, as in all sub-Saharan African countries, therefore remains an important concern.

Closely linked to the need for child health care services is the need for maternal health care services. In both Ghana and Kenya, a large number of women enter the reproductive age each year. As Figure 5–1 shows, the proportion of childbearing women in Ghana over the years had been about 22% of the total population. The current level of 22.8% is expected to rise to 27% by 2025, representing a threefold increase from 2.4 million (1980) to almost 10 million in just under 50 years. The change in Kenya is even more dramatic.

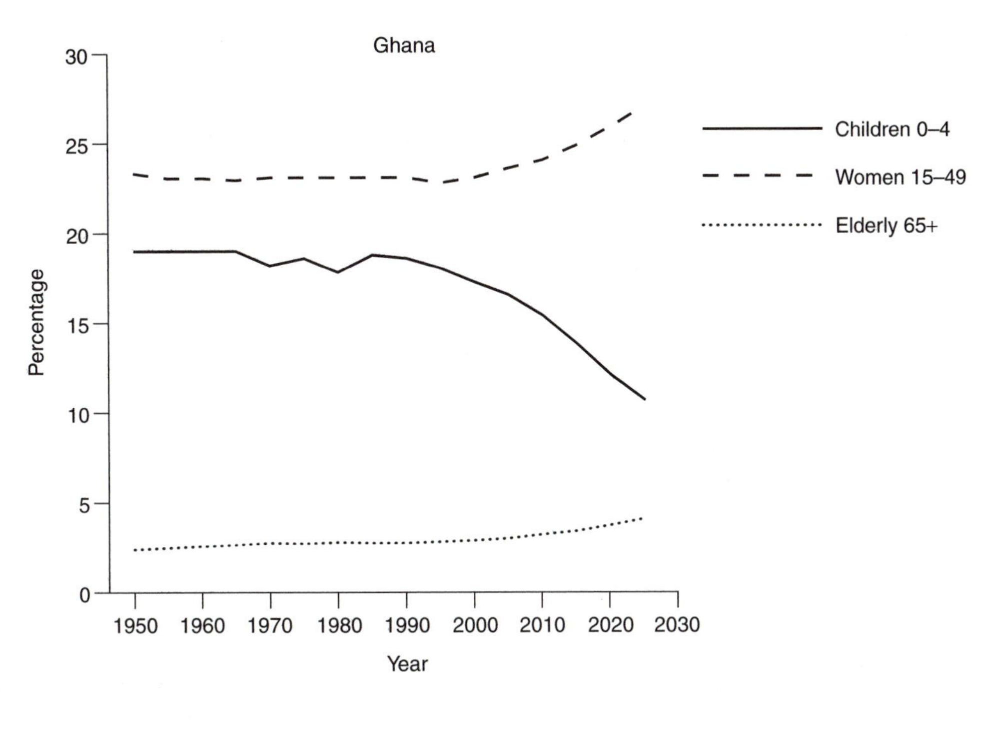


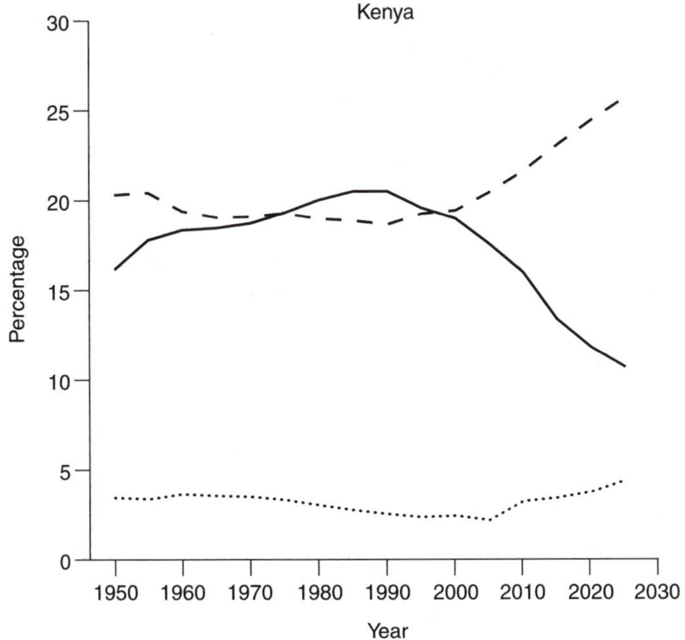


**FIGURE 5–1.** Percentage distribution of children (0–4), women of child-bearing age (15–49), and the elderly (65+) in Ghana and Kenya: 1950–2025. (Source: United Nations. Global Estimates and Projections of Population by Age and Sex: The 1988 Revision. New York: United Nations, 1989.)
Note: Projections from 1990 based on medium variant.

The 1980 level of 20% (3.3 million) is expected to increase to 27% (21 million) by 2025. Compared with 1980, therefore, the projected growth indicates a sevenfold increase in absolute numbers in just half a century. When data on the increasing size of childbearing women are examined together with continuing high levels of fertility and low usage levels of family planning services, it becomes clear why mothers should be seen not only as vehicles for child health but also as primary health care beneficiaries in their own right.

## MATERNAL MORTALITY

The World Health Organization (WHO) estimates that about 500,000 women die each year of complications related to childbearing. Thirty percent of such deaths occur in sub-Saharan Africa. In Mali, for instance, which has one of the highest maternal mortality rates, 2,325 women die out of every 100,000 live births (Table 5–1). Also, for every woman who dies, about 10 others have impaired health due to obstetric complications (Paul 1991). Maternal deaths have several causes, including hemorrhage, sepsis, toxemia, and obstructed labor. Most of these are preventable. The availability of prenatal care, for instance, could minimize problems such as obstructed labor and sepsis. Furthermore, poor socioeconomic conditions increase the risk of pregnancy-related morbidity and deaths.

The need to prevent such unnecessary maternal deaths led to a conference on Safe Motherhood hosted by the Government by Kenya in 1987 and sponsored by the World Bank, WHO, and the United Nations Fund for Population Activities. The conference called for action on four fronts:

> Improve economic opportunities for women. This could be done through income-generating activities, education and training, improved nutrition, and increased production of subsistence crops. Such actions will also ensure that the next generation of mothers are stronger, healthier, and more knowledgeable when they enter the childbearing years.
> Strengthen health services at community level—to provide prenatal care, more effective help during delivery, and family planning. Prenatal care can help reduce anemia and otherwise strengthen women; it can also help prevent problems before they become costly and difficult to manage by identifying women at high risk so that they can be referred to clinical facilities before childbirth.
> Strengthen maternal health care at the first referral level of health facilities, usually the district hospital. Women with high-risk pregnancies or those developing serious complications during pregnancy need more advanced medical care if they are to survive.
> Develop an "alarm" and transport system that would link the community level and first referral services so that women with high-risk pregnancies or obstetric complications could be attended to rapidly (Herz and Measham 1987, p. 45).

**TABLE 5–2. Life Expectancy and Children's Health Status in Sub-Saharan Africa**

| | *LIFE EXPECTANCY AT BIRTH (YRS)* | | *INFANT MORTALITY RATE (PER 1,000 LIVE BIRTHS)* | | *BABIES WITH LOW BIRTH WEIGHT (%)* | *PREVALENCE OF MALNUTRITION (UNDER 5)* |
|---|---|---|---|---|---|---|
| | *FEMALE* | *MALE* | | | | |
| *COUNTRY* | *1991* | *1991* | *1970* | *1991* | *1985* | *1990* |
| Low income | 58 | 61 | 109 | 71 | — | — |
| Middle income | 71 | 65 | 80 | 38 | — | — |
| High income | 80 | 73 | 20 | 8 | — | — |
| Sub-Saharan Africa | 52 | 49 | 144 | 104 | — | — |
| Uganda | 47 | 46 | 109 | 118 | 10 | 45 |
| Mali | 50 | 47 | 204 | 161 | 17 | 31 |
| Burkina Faso | 50 | 46 | 178 | 133 | 18 | 46 |
| Kenya | 61 | 57 | 102 | 67 | 13 | — |
| Nigeria | 53 | 50 | 139 | 85 | 25 | — |
| Ghana | 57 | 53 | 111 | 83 | 17 | 36 |
| Togo | 56 | 52 | 134 | 87 | 20 | 14 |
| Zimbabwe | 62 | 59 | 96 | 48 | 15 | 12 |
| Senegal | 49 | 46 | 135 | 81 | 10 | 22 |
| Botswana | 70 | 66 | 101 | 36 | 8 | 15 |

Source: World Bank. *World Development Report 1993: Investing in Health.* New York: Oxford University Press, 1993.

## INFANT AND CHILD MORTALITY

In sub-Saharan Africa as a whole, life expectancy at birth in 1991 was 53 years for women and 49 years for men, a difference of 24 to 28 years compared with that of high-income countries (Table 5–2). This reflects the excessive rates of infant and child mortality in sub-Saharan Africa despite recent declines. In Mali, for instance, which has one of the highest rates, 161 infants out of 1,000 live births die before their first birthday, compared with an average of 8 infant deaths in developed countries like Canada. The irony is that these infant deaths in sub-Saharan Africa are preventable through relatively inexpensive child survival interventions (UNICEF 1991). Malnutrition is an underlying as well as a contributing cause of infant and child morbidity in sub-Saharan Africa. Maternal malnutrition before and during pregnancy is a major cause of low birth weight and fetal growth retardation. As noted in Table 5–2, between 8% and 25% of babies born in 1985 had low birth weights, a factor associated with higher mortality in childhood. Similarly, malnutrition in children is estimated to contribute to one third of all child deaths in sub-Saharan Africa. In 1990, for instance, 45% of all children under 5 in Uganda and 46% of those in Burkina Faso had a deficiency or an excess of nutrients that interfered with their health and genetic potential for growth.

Studies that have documented the excessive levels of maternal, infant, and child mortality have also identified the causes of such deaths (Boerma and Bicego 1991; Feachem et al. 1991; Fosu 1986; Jamison et al. 1993). Socioeconomic, cultural, biologic, and demographic factors interact in a complex manner to adversely influence maternal and child survival. Barriers that limit access to health and family planning services play a critical role. Similarly, behavioral and cultural determinants of utilization are important components of maternal and child survival. In the next section, therefore, we examine the provision and use of health-related services to improve maternal and child survival.

## HEALTH SERVICES FOR MATERNAL AND CHILD HEALTH

A major objective of "health for all by the year 2000" is to increase the political commitment of governments in developing countries to improve the health of their people through primary health care (PHC). However, the provision of health care services does not necessarily mean that the people for whom they are intended will use the services. Several factors influence the use of health care services. These include objective need due to the presence of a disease that requires service; the perception that this need exists; the accessibility of the services with regard to acceptability, distance, cost, and time; barriers to the acceptance of services due to negative attitudes and competing services; the quality of services provided; and whether the group is satisfied with the services

(Andersen 1968; Kroeger 1983; Rosenstock 1966; Subedi 1989). Utilization data, therefore, are important for planning the extension and improvement of health care services. They can clarify the fit between the health needs of a population and the health care system and suggest how to design a more effective health care system so as to reduce inappropriate medical care.

Until recently, however, the lack of comparable data on the provision and use of health care services was one of the biggest challenges to the evaluation of the progress of PHC. To address this need, the Demographic and Health Surveys (DHS) program was started in 1984 with funding from the United States Agency for International Development (USAID) and other donor agencies. It has gone through three phases, and about 60 surveys are planned, 39 of which have been completed. The DHS also used a core questionnaire and, in addition to a birth history similar to the World Fertility Survey (WFS), also collected data on immunizations, health care behavior, and several aspects of child health. The WFS and DHS population-based surveys have information on users and non-users of public services and have generated a wealth of information on health status, risk factors, and use of health care services. However, neither the WFS nor the DHS collected detailed economic data on households. The World Bank's Living Standards Measurement Survey (LSMS) was undertaken to provide such information. The survey collects information on the relationships among income, poverty, health, education, and nutrition. These three standardized surveys are excellent examples of how international agencies can assist governments of developing countries in collecting health data necessary for monitoring health status and health outcomes. The critical question is how such rich data can enable governments in developing countries to move away from the urban-based, hospital-oriented health care system (Fosu 1989) to a health care system that is just and benefits the majority of the people, especially women and children.

## USE OF MATERNAL HEALTH SERVICES

The use of antenatal care services enables health care providers to identify high-risk women and to manage any pre-existing or new problems. Also, it facilitates nutrition education and postpartum family planning to prevent high-risk pregnancies. The attendance of women during labor and delivery by trained providers tends to reduce complications of sepsis and hemorrhage, a major cause of maternal mortality in Africa. Nevertheless, poor access to and low use of such services continue to be critical factors in maternal and child morbidity and mortality. The DHS data, therefore, are invaluable in examining behavioral and user-related factors in health services use.

Table 5–3 shows the percentage of live births for which women in sub-Saharan Africa received antenatal care and delivery care between 1985 and 1990. In almost all countries, coverage was higher for antenatal care than for

**TABLE 5–3. High-Risk Births and Maternal and Child Health Care in Sub-Saharan Africa, 1985–1990**

| *COUNTRY* | *CONSISTENT USE FOR LAST AND ANY PREVIOUS BIRTHS/DELIVERIES (%)* | | *HIGH-RISK BIRTHS (%)* | *UNMET NEED FOR CONTRACEPTION TO PREVENT HIGH-RISK BIRTHS (%)* | *% CHILDREN < 1 YEAR FULLY IMMUNIZED (1990–1991)** | |
|---|---|---|---|---|---|---|
| | *ANTENATAL* | *DELIVERY* | | | *DPT3* | *MEASLES* |
| Uganda | 81.7 | 27.6 | 71.1 | 62.6 | 77 | 74 |
| Mali | 23.7 | 25.1 | 71.9 | 61.1 | 35 | 40 |
| Kenya | 72.6 | 34.9 | 70.6 | 47.6 | 36 | 36 |
| Ondo State | 76.8 | 49.8 | 67.9 | 58.1 | 65 | 70 |
| Ghana | 75.3 | 27.8 | 59.1 | 53.8 | 39 | 39 |
| Togo | 71.2 | 40.9 | 63.1 | 41.7 | 73 | 61 |
| Sudan | 65.6 | 64.1 | 72.4 | 59.4 | 63 | 58 |
| Senegal | 55.4 | 33.6 | 66.8 | 45.0 | 60 | 59 |
| Zimbabwe | 85.0 | 54.7 | 61.2 | 35.3 | 89 | 87 |
| Botswana | 87.4 | 65.4 | 53.5 | 33.7 | 90 | 89 |

Sources: Demographic and Health Surveys. *Comparative Studies 8*. Columbia, MD: DHS/Macror Systems, 1993.

*World Bank. *World Development Report 1993*. New York: Oxford University Press, 1993.

delivery care. The proportion of births for which mothers received prenatal care ranged from 87% in Botswana to 23% in Mali. The coverage for delivery care ranged from 65% in Botswana to 25% in Mali. Coverage for both services was lower among women with no education and those living in rural areas (Govindasamy et al. 1993). The proportion of women with access to maternity care services in most of the sub-Saharan African countries is not enough to ensure a healthy pregnancy outcome for both mothers and children.

## HIGH-RISK BIRTHS

The prevention of high-risk pregnancies can potentially reduce both maternal and infant deaths. The DHS examined fertility-related risk factors and their relationship to infant and maternal mortality. High-risk birth was defined by the following: (1) the mother is less than 18 years or more than 34 years of age at the time of the birth; (2) the woman has already had three or more live births; or (3) the birth occurs within 24 months of a previous live birth. As Table 5–3 indicates, overall 72% of women in sub-Saharan Africa were classified as being in a high-risk group, compared with 57% of women in Asia and 53% in Latin America and the Caribbean.

One intervention to reduce both maternal and infant deaths associated with high-risk births is to target family planning services to women who, because of their age, parity, or close birth spacing, are in a high-risk group. Family planning in this context may be an important tool for improving maternal and infant and child survival, especially in sub-Saharan Africa where reproductive rates are high, health care facilities are inadequate, and fertility-related morbidity and mortality are excessively high.

In an analysis involving only sexually active women who are not currently using contraception, the unmet need for contraception to prevent the occurrence of high-risk births ranges from a low of 33.7% in Botswana to a high of 63% in Uganda. A breakdown of the socioeconomic characteristics of sexually active women in the high-risk groups who are not currently using contraception indicates that the unmet need for family planning to avoid high-risk births is most acutely felt among poorly educated, currently unemployed, rural women in sub-Saharan Africa. Increasing contraceptive use among women with known risks requires changes in attitudes and behaviors as well as changes in the delivery of services. Areas that need emphasis are discussed in the last section.

## HEALTH CARE FOR INFANTS AND CHILDREN

One of the most innovative strategies to reduce childhood morbidity and improve child survival is the "Child Survival Revolution" initiated by the United Nations Children's Fund (UNICEF) and supported by WHO, USAID, the

World Bank, and many private and voluntary groups. Elements of the "Child Survival Revolution" include the GOBI-FFF (growth monitoring, oral rehydration, breast feeding and immunization–female family planning, female education, food supplementation). These are relatively simple, low-cost preventive measures (Fosu 1994).

Substantial progress has been made in these areas. For instance, immunization coverage against diphtheria, whooping cough, and tetanus (DPT) has reached 90% in Botswana, and 89% for measles (Table 5–3). On the other hand, in some countries like Mali, Kenya, and Ghana, immunization is not gaining ground, partly because of the lack of basic health services at the grassroots level and partly because of the shortage of trained and motivated health personnel. However, an even more important obstacle that goes beyond these two involves social, cultural, and behavioral factors.

## REFOCUSING UPSTREAM: THE ROLE OF SOCIOCULTURAL FACTORS IN MATERNAL AND CHILD HEALTH

Studies by Polgar (1963) and others have convincingly shown the importance of cultural factors in the delivery of public health programs. Polgar (1963) identified four fallacies afflicting public health programs of the period: the fallacy of empty vessels—the assumption that client populations did not have preexisting health customs; the fallacy of the separate capsule—health beliefs and practices were assumed to be separate and independent of the remainder of culture; the fallacy of the single pyramid—a trickle-down theory of communication; and the fallacy of the interchangeable faces—all clients are alike (Raharjo and Corner 1990).

However, three decades later, public health officials still seem to gloss over the importance of culture. Gaisie (1990) aptly describes this sentiment:

> The failure of the family planning program in the region is an unpleasant reminder of the need to review the existing theories and develop hypotheses that accept the fact that the social structures of sub-Saharan Africa do not comprise "traditional" and "modern" sectors as polar opposites but as interpenetrating and integrated through complex social, economic and political factors, reflecting the interplay of forces, both traditional and modern, which make up contemporary African societies. Pluralism, cultural conservatism and resilience make these societies more complex and diverse than those in the other parts of the world. Studies of Africa conducted on premises derived from the study of other societies have not yielded useful results to provide frameworks for efficient management of development programs including those of family planning and health (Gaisie 1990, p. 625).

Although we do not suggest a return to ethnocentrism, we do agree with Polgar and others that cultural sensitivity can assist health planners to design culturally appropriate and acceptable health-related programs. A good example is the spread of AIDS among women in sub-Saharan Africa. In an insightful discussion of this issue, Ulin (1992) argues that AIDS prevention campaigns have not yet taken into account the cultural, social, and economic constraints on most African women's ability to comply with advice to limit partners and use condoms.

> Trends in the incidence of HIV/AIDS infection among women in sub-Saharan Africa suggest this population is increasingly at risk. Many of the same factors that have predisposed rural African women to ill health in the past now increase their vulnerability to AIDS, including poverty and malnutrition, uncontrolled fertility, and complications of childbirth. As men travel out from rural communities to urban centers in search of employment, their sexual contacts multiply; many will acquire the HIV virus and carry it back to infect wives at home. Women, too, are leaving rural areas for the promise of a better life in the cities and commercial centers along the way. Their struggle for economic survival and personal autonomy has led many to form relationships with new sexual partners, with a consequent increase in HIV seroprevalence among women once considered at low risk of infection (Ulin 1992, p. 63).

The interaction of several risk factors tends to produce effects that are greater than their sum. However, very often the delivery of health services in sub-Saharan Africa is organized on a national basis rather than in stages, such as rural/urban or by age groups. Efforts should be made to provide services that target special groups. A rural focus is more useful than an urban focus, and a risk approach may be more beneficial than a global approach. Focusing on children and women who are at risk heightens the community's awareness of the health problems and strengthens its resolve to overcome them. In the long term, it may become an invaluable instrument of equity as it establishes the rationale for redirecting resources to the populations, such as women and children, with the greatest needs.

## REFERENCES


Anderson, R. 1968. *A Behavioral Model of Families Use of Health Services.* Center for Health Administration Studies, Research Series No. 25. Chicago: University of Chicago.

Boerma, J. T. and G. T. Bicego. 1992. "Preceding birth intervals and child survival: Searching for pathways of influence." *Studies in Family Planning* 23:243–56.

Caldwell, John C. 1976. "Toward a Restatement of Demographic Transition Theory." *Population and Development Review* 2:321–66.

Cleland, J. 1990. "The Idea of Health Transition." p. xviii in *What We Know About Health Transition,* Vol. 1, edited by S. Caldwell et al. Canberra: Australian National University.

Feacham, R. G., D. T. Jamison, and E. R. Bos. 1991. "Changing Patterns of Disease and Mortality in Sub-Saharan Africa." Pp. 3–27 in *Disease and Mortality in Sub-Saharan Africa,* edited by R. G. Feacham and D. T. Jamison. New York: Oxford University Press for the World Bank.

Fosu, Gabriel B. 1986. "Implications of Mortality and Morbidity for Health Care Delivery in Ghana." *Sociology of Health and Illness* 8:252–77.

Fosu, G. B. 1989. "Access to Health Care in Urban Areas of Developing Societies." *Journal of Health and Social Behavior* 30:398–411.

Fosu, G. B. 1994. "Childhood Morbidity and Health Services Utilization: Cross-National Comparisons of User-Related Factors from DHS Data." *Social Science and Medicine* 38:1209–20.

Frenk, J., J. L. Bobadilla, J. Sepulveda, and M. Cervantes. 1989. "Health Transition in Middle-Income Countries: New Challenges for Health Care." *Health Policy and Planning* 4:29–39.

Gaisie, S. K. 1990. "Culture and Health in Sub-Saharan Africa." Pp. 609–27 in *What We Know About Health Transition,* Vol. II, edited by J. Caldwell et al. Canberra: Australian National University.

Govindasamy, Pavalavalli, M. Kathryn Steward, Shea O. Rutstein, J. Ties Boerma, and A. Elizabeth Sommerfelt. 1993. *High Risk Births and Maternity Care.* DHS Comparative Studies No. 8. Columbia, MD: Macro International Inc.

Herz, B. K. and A. R. Measam. 1987. "Maternal Health and Development." *Finance and Development* 24(2):44–45.

Jamison, Dean T., W. Henry Mosley, Anthony R. Measham, and Jose-Luis Bobadilla (eds.). 1993. *Disease Control Priorities in Developing Countries.* New York: Oxford University Press.

Kroeger, A. 1983. "Anthropological and Socio-medical Health Care Research in Developing countries." *Social Science and Medicine* 17(3):147–61.

Notestein, Frank W. 1945. "Population: The Long View." In *Food for the World,* edited by T. W. Schultz. Chicago: University of Chicago Press.

______. 1983. "Population Growth and Economic Development." *Population Growth and Economic Development* 99:345–60.

Omran, A. R. 1971. "The Epidemiologic Transition: A Theory of the Epidemiology of Population Change." *Milbank Memorial Fund Quarterly* 49:509–38.

Olshansky, Jay S. and Brian A. Ault. 1986. "The Fourth Stage of the Epidemiologic Transition: The Age of Delayed Degenerative Diseases." *Milbank Quarterly* 64:355–91.

Paul, B. M. 1993. "Maternal Mortality in Africa: 1980–87." *Social Science and Medicine* 37:745–52.

Phillips, D. R. 1994. "Does Epidemiological Transition Have Utility for Health Planners?" *Social Science and Medicine* 38(10):vii–x.

Polgar, S. 1963. "Health Action in Cross-Cultural Perspective." Pp. 397–419 in *Handbook of Medical Anthropology,* edited by H. E. Freeman, S. Levine and L. G. Reeder. Englewood Cliffs, NJ: Prentice Hall.

Raharjo, Y. and L. Corner. 1990. "Cultural Attitudes to Health and Sickness in Public Health Programs: A Demand-Creation Approach Using Data from West Aceh, Indonesia." Pp. 522–33 in *What We Know About Health Transition,* Vol. II, edited by J. Caldwell et al. Canberra: Australian National University.

Rosenstock, L. M. 1966. "Why People Use Health Services." *Milbank Memorial Fund Quarterly* 44:94–124.

Subedi, J. 1989. "Modern Health Services and Health Care Behavior: A Survey in Kathmandu, Nepal." *Journal of Health and Social Behavior* 30:412–20.

Ulin, P. R. 1992. "African Women and AIDS: Negotiating Behavioral Change." *Social Science and Medicine* 34:66–73.

UNICEF. 1991. *The State of the World's Children.* New York: Oxford University Press.

United Nations. 1991. *Global Estimates and Projections of Populations by Age and Sex: The 1988 Revision.* New York: United Nations.

World Bank. 1993. *World Development Report 1993: Investing in Health.* New York: Oxford University Press.

Chapter 6

# Ecologic and Macrolevel Influences on Illness in Northern Peru: Beyond the International Health Paradigm*

*Kathryn S. Oths*

The efforts of international health organizations most often center on the most glaring health problems among disadvantaged populations worldwide. For example, in the 1980s, child survival was the focal point of international aid agencies and applied social scientists, with topics such as infant diarrhea, oral rehydration therapy (ORT), immunization, infant mortality, nutrition, and breastfeeding receiving prominent attention (Mosley et al. 1990; Nichter and Kendall 1991; Nightingale et al. 1990; Scheper-Hughes 1987; UNICEF 1989; WHO 1986b). Of late, the World Health Organization (WHO) and other agencies have widened their child survival agendas to incorporate acute respiratory infections in some parts of the world (Mull 1990, p. 40). For some populations, however, social, political, and natural environments contribute to an illness pattern that varies greatly from that for which international aid agencies gear their intervention strategies.

Recently some researchers with a long history of committment to the study of international health problems have called for a re-evaluation of the goals and perspectives of those working to improve health in developing coun-

*This research was carried out with the support of grants from the Inter-American Foundation and the National Science Foundation. I am indebted to Nanette Barkey, William Dressler, Jennifer McGehee, and an anonymous reviewer for their helpful comments on several versions of this manuscript.

tries. Bicknell and Parks (1989), Mull (1990), Mosley et al. (1990), and Feachem et al. (1992) question a sole focus on children to the exclusion of adults. They cite a need for a comprehensive primary health care initiative that does not pit the needs of children against the needs of the community as a whole. In the context of tobacco production for and consumption by Third World peoples, Nichter and Cartwright (1991) note the irony of saving children only to subject them to the prospect of being cared for by unhealthy, especially chronically ill, parents. Ill health in adults may be especially harmful to children in the household and has been associated with higher infant and childhood mortality in developing countries (Feachem et al. 1992).

Some international health care advocates have also suggested that a focus on infectious disease in children serves to distract attention from the economic, social, and political contributions to the production of illness. Nichter and Kendall (1991) argue that the time has arrived to explore not only individual agency, but also the role of economic and social structural interactions in creating the conditions for an improvement in health. Applying this sort of logic, Brown (1987) discusses the costs of the exploitative peasant agricultural labor system in Sardinia and shows how, in terms of factors such as energy expenditure and number of work days lost, the costs of "macroparasitism" (i.e., exploitative labor relationships) far exceed those of the "microparasitism" of the endemic infectious disease malaria. Thus, a singular focus on infant and childhood infectious disease agents that disregards adults and larger macrosystemic influences on health not only serves to obfuscate the real conditions underlying poor health, but derails sincere efforts to achieve an effective and lasting solution to health problems in parts of the developing world.

The hamlet of Chugurpampa in the northern Andes of Peru can help illustrate some of these issues. In Chugurpampa there is little justification for an exclusive focus on infant health. Communicable childhood diseases are virtually absent from the community as the result of an established, effective program of immunization in the province. Older children and adults are as afflicted as infants with respiratory and other types of health problems. For children, respiratory illnesses (especially influenza, head colds, and bronchitis) predominate over gastrointestinal ailments (colic, diarrhea) in frequency and severity. Yet neither illness category is a major contributor to mortality for this population.

Elsewhere the author has addressed some of the cultural particulars of the medical system, health behaviors, and illness management in Chugurpampa (Oths 1991, 1992, forthcoming). In this chapter several issues are addressed that expand upon the critique of the emphases of international health. First, the distribution of illnesses and illness episodes in a developing society, one that does not fit the typical pattern of underdevelopment and health as described in the international health literature, is presented. Second, the ecologic and political-economic factors that contribute to this particular morbidity profile are discussed. Third, through case studies, this chapter examines how well-meaning health care programs that are ill adapted to the real conditions of the community are destined to fail. The aim of examining these data and issues is to improve the planning and implementation of future international health policies.

## THE SETTING

As mentioned above, the setting for this account is a highland hamlet of peasants (comunidad campesina[1]) in Northern Peru, in the Department of La Libertad, where an intensive investigation of health care and treatment choice was performed from 1987 to 1989. Chugurpampa, in the western escarpment of the Andes, covers an altitude range of 2,875 to 3,750 meters (approx. 9,450 to 12,300 ft.). Homes in the community are scattered across the steep mountainsides, covering more than 1,000 hectares (approx. 2,470 acres) of land. The semi-arid environment supports a principal but sparse vegetation of cacti and eucalyptus, a lush green during the rainy season, brown and dusty during the dry months. Large diurnal temperature fluctuations make the days warm and often wet, and the nights invariably damp and cool to freezing.

The principal occupation of peasants in this region is agriculture. Potatoes are produced as the main subsistence crop for household consumption, as well as the principal cash crop for trade with the coastal market. Market participation is extensive. Other occupations include mining and commercial ventures.

Nine hundred and two permanent residents populate the 166 Chugurpampino households (442 female; 460 male). A random sample of 32 households (166 individuals) was selected for the collection of illness case histories and discussion of highland beliefs and practices. The households were visited at 2-week intervals for 24 weeks.

## THE DISTRIBUTION OF ILLNESS IN CHUGURPAMPA

Contrary to what is reported for many impoverished and Third World populations, Chugurpampinos suffer from relatively few serious infectious and childhood diseases. The absence of such problems can be attributed primarily to (1) an uncontaminated spring-fed water supply due to their position atop a mountain peak, (2) a plentiful diet, as this agricultural zone is the breadbasket of the country, (3) the high altitude, which inhibits bacterial growth, and (4) the disposal of human fecal waste and garbage at a distance from the house, reducing the possibility of direct contamination of the habitat. The latter can be credited to the dispersed nature of housing settlement, which contrasts with more densely settled town and urban areas.

The low infectious disease rate is reflected in an infant mortality rate of

31 per 1,000 in Chugurpampa, compared with the national average of 94 per 1,000 and over 200 per 1,000 in other Andean areas. The death rate is 6 per 1,000, compared with 11 per 1,000 for Peru in general and over 20 per 1,000 for other highland communities (Population Reference Bureau 1987; Oths 1993). According to the estimates of the local health post doctor who delivered care and kept vital records throughout the research period, the most frequent illnesses attended to in the district for children under 5 years of age are, in descending order of frequency, (1) respiratory illness, (2) skin illness, (3) diarrhea, and (4) intestinal parasites.

In the study sample, there were eight infants less than a year old at any point during the 24-week case-collection period. Tables 6–1 and 6–2 contain data on the respiratory and gastrointestinal disease episodes for infants under 1 year of age in Chugurpampa. Illnesses were rated on a three-point scale of severity: mild, moderate, and grave. An illness designated as mild was one that was neither serious nor disabling, moderate was one for which the affected person was bedridden or unable to perform regular activities, and grave was one in which the person was threatened with the loss of life or limb.

In Chugurpampa, cases of respiratory illness outweigh gastrointestinal cases at a ratio of higher than 3:1. Although gastrointestinal illnesses last longer on average than respiratory ones (25 versus 12 days), the respiratory cases tend to be more severe, especially the cases of bronchitis. However, no illnesses resulted in death. The illness rates for Chugurpampa are not unusual for this area of northern Peru. A comparison of the vital statistics of the hamlet with the surrounding district shows similar rates.[2]

Table 6–3 categorizes all reported illnesses by the organ system most affected. Because some illnesses affected two systems more or less equally, 37 cases were given two categorical designations. When viewing the illness patterns for the sample as a whole regardless of age, respiratory illnesses are the most salient, although only 3% of these were considered grave. Musculoskeletal illnesses were the second most common, although again consisting primarily of mild cases. Gastrointestinal complaints, although not the most numerous, were much more likely to be grave (13%), usually in adults.

**TABLE 6–1. Number of Cases and Severity of Respiratory Infection in Chugurpampa Infants (n = 8) during 24-Week Case-Collection Period**

| | *SEVERITY* | | | |
|---|---|---|---|---|
| *TYPE OF COMPLAINT* | *LIGHT* | *MODERATE* | *GRAVE* | *TOTAL* |
| Gripe | 11 | 3 | 2 | 16 |
| Bronchitis | — | 4 | 2 | 6 |
| Cough | 1 | 2 | — | 3 |
| TOTALS | 12 | 9 | 4 | 25 |

**TABLE 6–2. Number of Cases and Severity of Gastrointestinal Ailments in Chugurpampa Infants (n = 8) During 24-Week Case-Collection Period**

| | *SEVERITY* | | | |
|---|---|---|---|---|
| *TYPE OF COMPLAINT* | *LIGHT* | *MODERATE* | *GRAVE* | *TOTAL* |
| Diarrhea | 2 | — | 1 | 3 |
| Empachado | 1 | 1 | 1 | 3 |
| Stomachache | 1 | — | — | 1 |
| Dry heaves | 1 | — | — | 1 |
| TOTALS | 5 | 1 | 2 | 8 |

Although the rates of infectious disease are unremarkable, the degree and pattern of morbidity among the highlanders are not inconsequential. As seen in Table 6–3, respiratory, musculoskeletal, and gastrointestinal illnesses indeed occur with regularity in the highlands. Several of the unique ecologic and social factors impinging on the health of Chugurpampinos and thus ostensibly contributing to the disease rates in Table 6–3 are dealt with below.

## ECOLOGIC CONDITIONS

International health care programs are generally paradigmatic, being implemented worldwide according to universal standards and criteria. These programs often give little consideration to the conditions unique to the target population. The flexibility to tailor programs to the actual and perceived needs of a people would be a huge first step in increasing program effectiveness. The following discussion details some of the factors that any health care team would do well to consider when designing primary health care for highland populations in the Andes, and possibly elsewhere. The extensive work of Heath, Ward, Monge, and other highland biologic researchers is drawn upon here.

The environmental conditions unique to sierrans, such as extremes of hot and cold temperature, low barometric pressure, high levels of ultraviolet (UV) radiation, as well as hypoxia and other physiologic responses to high altitude, greatly influence the types of diseases from which people suffer. The ambient temperature falls at a rate of approximately 1°C with each altitude increase of 150 meters (Ward 1989). Heath and Williams (1989) detail cold stress at high altitude, pointing out that the body loses heat to its surroundings in four ways. Convection carries heat away by means of high wind velocity and windchill. The body radiates heat and also conducts heat through contact with cold objects. Evaporation of water from the body, a process which occurs at a rapid pace in the sierra, is another means of heat loss.

**TABLE 6–3. Prevalence of Illness by Subcategory in Chugurpamp During 24-Week Study Period***

| *ILLNESS CATEGORY* | *SUBTOTAL* | *TOTAL* | *PERCENT* |
|---|---|---|---|
| Respiratory | | 239 | 40 |
| gripe | | 222 | |
| bronchial | 13 | | |
| chronic cough | 4 | | |
| Musculoskeletal | | 106 | 18 |
| stress | 68 | | |
| injury | 38 | | |
| Gastrointestinal | | 85 | 14 |
| stomach | 43 | | |
| intestinal | 31 | | |
| liver | 8 | | |
| gall bladder | 3 | | |
| Head | | 78 | 13 |
| headache | 33 | | |
| eyes | 18 | | |
| cerebro | 14 | | |
| ears | 13 | | |
| Skin | | 41 | 7 |
| laceration | 24 | | |
| infection | 17 | | |
| Genitourinary | | 25 | 4 |
| gynecological | 13 | | |
| kidney | 12 | | |
| Oral | | 21 | 4 |
| dental | 19 | | |
| sores | 2 | | |
| Emotional-psychiatric | | 16 | 3 |
| susto | 11 | | |
| other | 5 | | |
| Systemic infection | | 8 | 1 |
| Other | | 9 | 2 |
| | | 628 | 106 |
| Coded into two categories | 37 | | |
| TOTAL ILLNESSES | | 591 | |

*Percentages based on actual number of illness episodes (n = 591) across the 32 households.

The wet and windy rainy season and frequent cold temperatures, combined with typically crowded living quarters, make for the maintenance and easy transmission of viral respiratory infections. Respiratory problems, mainly influenza and colds, account for 40% of illnesses recorded and constitute by far the largest class of illnesses in Chugurpampa.

Large diurnal temperature changes force the body to be in a state of constant temperature flux. People are exposed to the cold while bathing, washing clothes, pasturing animals at dawn, or getting caught in the rain. Cultural adaptations such as wearing warm clothing, especially loose-fitting layers of wool garments, or consuming heated food and drink can reduce cold stress (Ward 1989, p. 52) but does not eliminate it. The effects of the cold are especially notable on the muscles, joints, and nerves and the respiratory and gastrointestinal tracts (Ward 1989), thus accounting for the high incidence of musculoskeletal disorders, colds and flus, ulcers, colic, and other abdominal complaints.

Water loss or dehydration occurs rapidly at high altitude owing to a very low absolute humidity. Ventilation and sweating with exertion compound the effect. Pugh (1964) estimates that, at 5,500 meters, 1 liter of water is lost for every 5 hours of exercise. Warm drinks such as the ubiquitous herbal teas of the sierrans help to prevent hypothermia and replace vital fluids lost through dehydration (Ward 1989).

UV radiation is both a bane and a blessing: it reduces germs, but it also causes a host of highland-specific illnesses and symptoms. The exposure to UV radiation increases linearly both with higher altitude and with lower longitude (WHO 1979, 1986a). Therefore Chugurpampa, lying at a range of altitude from 2,875 to 3,750 meters and at 8° south of the equator, has one of the highest ambient levels of UV radiation on earth. Sometimes the sun can burn the skin like a flame, reminiscent of the feeling of holding a magnifying glass over one's hand on a sunny day. The amount of UV radiation absorbed depends on a person's dress. Hats are mandatory to protect the top of the head from exposure, but wearing a shirt is no guarantee of protection, as up to 50% of UV radiation can pass through it. Sierrans do not take a siesta, thus increasing their risk of overexposure, as the highest intensity of radiation occurs around midday (WHO 1979).

Highland-specific symptoms caused by UV radiation include headache, backache, sunstroke, mountain sickness (Ward 1989), and eye and skin irritation and damage (Gates 1966; Heath and Williams 1989; Taylor et al. 1989) among other problems. The loci of these complaints follow logically from the fact that the head and neck receive maximum exposure to sunlight (Blum 1948; Urbach et al. 1966). Conditions such as toothache, insect bite, and earache are believed to be aggravated by exposure to the sun. Any "weak" person such as an infant or postpartum woman is also thought to be highly susceptible to harm, even death, from the sun's rays.

Infectious bacterial and parasitic diseases are relatively uncommon in the high altitudes owing to a combination of ecologic factors. Buck et al. (1968) and Baker (1978) also report a low rate of infectious disease in the Andes. This is because high UV radiation along with cold temperatures inhibits bacterial growth (Heath and Williams 1989, p. 25; Ward 1989, p. 57). This results in a low incidence of systemic infectious diseases despite what some might judge to be poor hygienic practices by the highlanders. Baker (1978, p. 334) concurs on this point. However, growth of human microbial flora of the skin, throat, and feces has not been shown to be affected by atmospheric UV radiation (Weiser 1969, as cited by Heath and Williams 1989, p. 255). UV radiation, cold climate, and a low atmospheric pressure inhibit bacterial growth. Combined with a sufficient childhood immunization coverage, these factors together likely account for the virtual absence of childhood infectious diseases. Also, parasitic and dust- and water-borne diseases endemic in other parts of Peru such as malaria, leishmaniasis, tetanus, hepatitis, and cholera are also virtually unknown in Chugurpampa because the organisms and their vectors do not survive at high altitude.[3] Tuberculosis, with exception, is not uncommon in the highlands because of the hardiness of the tubercle bacterial spore harbored in the dirt floors of shaded, poorly ventilated living spaces.

Monge's disease, or chronic mountain sickness, is a condition identified by the researcher Carlos Monge in 1925 (Monge 1943). Apparently some highlanders living above 3,300 meters lose their natural acclimatization with advancing age, developing a chronic case of what is otherwise normally experienced as temporary mountain sickness, or *soroche.* As Ward states, "vague neuropsychological complaints" such as headache, dizziness, mental confusion, weight gain, and swelling of the tissue especially around the eyes and fingers are the most typical signs of Monge's disease (Ward 1989, p. 405; Heath and Williams 1989). There were a few probable mild cases of Monge's disease in this study sample, judging from reported symptoms and by comparing appearances with those of textbook cases. Mountain sickness in general would help explain the frequent complaints of many of the informants, especially the older ones, of headache, dizziness, lightheadedness, weakness, swelling of tissue, and so on.

Other highland illnesses mimic Monge's disease to some degree, suggesting that they too are a result of the unique highland ecologic conditions. The complex culture-bound illness *debilidad* (debility) shares many of the physiologic features of Monge's disease, although it is much more than simply a reaction to aging at high altitude. *Debilidad* can be described as weakness or exhaustion resulting from the accumulated toils and various losses in one's life. The low frequency of Monge's disease in women reported by Ward (1989, p. 410) does not correspond to the high frequency (almost 30%) of *debilidad* among postreproductive women in this study. The sudden onset of *chucaque* (embarrassment illness) in children and *terración* (adult version of chucaque) in adults could be a result of or aggravated by the special atmospheric conditions of high altitude (possibly stomach and blood gas from low barometric pressure plus hypoxia from nervous embarrassment). These high-altitude ailments are characterized by head and stomach symptoms, especially headache and vomiting.

Other ailments or physiologic malfunctioning attributable to the varied stresses of high-altitude living include a higher incidence of gastric ulcers at high altitude (so far inexplicable, possibly related to expanded bodily gases from lower barometric pressure and an acid-base disequilibrium from hypoxia and dehydration), nasal and retinal bleeding from capillary fragility and pulmonary edema (often upon return from low altitude) (Heath and Williams 1989; Ward 1989). Ringing ears may also be an effect of barometric pressure. All of the above are well represented in the illness cases collected in Chugurpampa.

Health problems not often seen at high altitude include coronary artery disease, myocardial infarction, high blood pressure, obesity, bronchial asthma, allergies from pollen or mold spores, and anemia. A high-calcium diet (Baker and Mazess 1963) combined with high vitamin D synthesis from sun exposure (Ward 1989) may account for the rareness of bone breaks and fractures (there were none in the study sample despite numerous injuries). Cancers occur infrequently, and despite the high solar intensity skin cancer is not prevalent owing to the protective effect of skin melanin and pigmentation (Gates 1966).

## NUTRITIONAL FACTORS

Contrary to what is generally reported for Latin America and other parts of the Andes, diet and nutritional status are good in Chugurpampa. The Otuzco area is part of the breadbasket of the country. Peasants produce a variety of foodstuffs for market despite their continually eroding economic situation. Unlike other agricultural economies, which produce one major luxury cash crop such as tobacco, coffee, or cotton and are thus tied to the vagaries of international commodity prices, Chugurpampinos can subsist on their cash crop, the potato, and thus avert nutritional disaster in times of market downturn.

Overall the diet of most families is complete and well balanced. The sierran diet, while principally dependent on the potato, consists of a wide variety of tubers, cereals, and legumes with some vegetable, fruit, meat, and dairy products. Meat consumption is sporadic. A substantial portion of protein intake is in the form of quinoa, a chenopod with the highest protein content of any known vegetable (it contains all eight essential amino acids), and certain food combinations that make complete proteins (e.g., peas and wheat). This high-carbohydrate, low-fat diet is considered the most suitable for high-altitude living (Picón-Reátegui 1978). Much evidence indicates that metabolic rate and energy expenditure are greater at high altitude, demanding the high-calorie diet typically found there (Picón-Reátegui 1978; Ward 1989).

Chugurpampinos are tremendously preoccupied with eating well and in large quantities. Sickness is believed to occur promptly if meals are skipped, skimped on, or even eaten past the normal hour (*a mala hora*). One constantly hears admonitions to eat more. A commonly encountered illness complaint is lack of appetite, which is cause for alarm and remedial action such as appetite-stimulating tonics and preparation of choice foods, especially meat and fruit. Thinness to the highlander is not a sign of beauty, but rather a less-than-optimal state. It connotes sickliness, weakness, and possibly endangered health. However, obesity as such is not considered desirable either; rather, a rosy plumpness is the ideal. Morbidly obese people are rare in the highlands and are looked upon with incredulity.

Maintaining adequate weight is, of course, critical for newborns and children under 5. Small children often begin to eat their meal ahead of the adults, as it takes them longer to consume the massive quantities of heavy, high-calorie foods needed at high altitude. Because it is difficult to fulfill their intake needs in one sitting, children are encouraged to snack freely between meals from leftovers, wild fruits, edible presents from compadres, and basically anything else they can scavenge.

Although the overall diet of Chugurpampinos is adequate and healthful, some health problems nonetheless stem from specific foods and medicines that people ingest. Excessive consumption of processed foods and over-the-counter medications as well as easily obtainable "prescriptions" can be considered an example of what Nichter and Cartwright (1991) call "the pathogenic trends in life-style which accompany 'defective modernization'" (after Simonelli 1987).

Habitual consumption of sugar and refined foods, combined with poor oral hygiene, leads to tooth decay. Dental caries are on the increase through South America and most developing countries. This increase parallels the increase in consumption of sugar (Akpabio 1990). Even though they represent only a fraction of the total illness, dental caries are a problem of major importance, as the inability to masticate well contributes heavily to digestive disorders and nutritional inadequacies in adults. To give an idea of the severity of the problem, the average tooth loss by adult age group in this sample is listed in Table 6–4.

Gastrointestinal disorders of the stomach, liver, and gallbladder have multiple origins, yet the contribution of diet is likely substantial. Aji No Moto° (a popular flavor enhancer, monosodium glutamate), alcohol, antibiotics and sulfa drugs (Janowitz 1989), overuse of patent bicarbonates such as Alka Seltzer (alone or compounded with other factors such as dehydration), heavy and greasy foods, increased stomach gases from altitude, digestion-impeding tooth loss, or emotional upset all may cause the various gastrointestinal problems common in Chugurpampa. Heavy use of antibiotics may also lead to bowel disorders and colitis (Janowitz 1989).

Some metabolic disorders may also be diet related at high altitude. Low blood glucose or hypoglycemia prevalent in the highlands (Bolton 1981, 1984)

**TABLE 6–4. Edentulousness by Selected Age Groups in Chugurpampa**

| *AGE (YRS)* | *N* | *MEAN NUMBER OF TEETH LOST* | *INDIVIDUALS WITH NO LOSS* |
|---|---|---|---|
| 17–19 | 10 | .5 | 70% |
| 20–29 | 18 | 2 | 39% |
| 30–39 | 16 | 3 | 38% |
| 40–49 | 12 | 4 | 8% |
| 50–59 | 9 | 8 | — |
| 60–69 | 10 | 14 | — |
| 70–79 | 6 | 17 | — |
| 80+ | 1 | 28 | — |

is characterized by headache of the *cerebro* (brain stem area), dizziness, and weakness. This is likely a result of the body's high metabolism at high altitude (Picón-Reátegui 1978, pp. 230, 279; Ward 1989, pp. 55, 356), which quickly depletes energy reserves if one is active. These headaches, apparently caused by low blood glucose, are frequently a result if meals are late or missed. Hypoglycemia would also explain the rapid effect of popular remedies used for the above symptoms, such as *suero* (bottles of intravenous glucose rehydration fluid people drink rather than inject), vitamin tonics (many of which contain alcohol), liquors, beer, and rich foods.

## POLITICAL-ECONOMIC AND SOCIAL INFLUENCES ON HEALTH

Two major occupations that are open to the highlander—agriculture and mining—both bring with them a set of conditions that are conducive to the illnesses from which Chugurpampinos suffer.

Potato agriculture requires constant stooping and the lifting, carrying, and swinging of heavy loads (100 to 150 lbs.) and sharp tools. During harvest, for example, men, women and children alike may typically fill, lift, and carry their weight in sacked potatoes at 15-minute intervals throughout an 8- to 10-hour workday. This easily figures to one ton of potatoes per day. The result of such arduous labor with little respite under harsh climatic conditions is a high incidence in sierran populations of physical degenerative illnesses, such as musculoskeletal aches, pains and strains, injuries, lacerations, arthritis, and kidney problems.

The physical problems created by such work are further complicated by inclement weather and foot travel over steep, rough terrain, stressing feet, back, and legs, and especially knees. Jurmain (1975), Landy (1983), Anderson

(1984), Finerman (1985), and Sorofman and Tripp-Reimer (1989) all report similar types of work-related physical complaints for agricultural and/or highland populations. Heavy physical labor also aggravates the above-mentioned high-altitude stress (Fuchs 1978).

The heavy use of pesticides should not be overlooked as another potential agricultural contributor to the categories of respiratory (through inhalation) and gastrointestinal (through ingestion) illness (Bull 1982).

It is characteristic of peasant populations that food production be directed by the politically dominant, nonproducing elite. Agricultural production of potatoes for the market finds the sierran peasants caught in a vicious circle of spiraling costs of petrochemicals and deflating market prices, requiring ever-increasing production to stay ahead. The price of potatoes remains so deflated that peasants barely recoup the cost of their investment. They "break their backs" in the process of feeding the nation for free (Simonelli 1987, p. 26).

Since fertilizers and pesticides were introduced by government extension agents a few decades ago, fields have become eroded of nutrients and prey to insects to the point that high yields are impossible without them. The government, through exploitative agricultural policies (controlled fertilizer and pesticide prices, exorbitant interest on agrarian loans—70% in 1988) and artificially low prices to pacify coastal consumers, keeps potato production unprofitable and sierrans working overtime in what Camino (1989) has called "the planned impoverishment" of the people.

When asked, for example, why 150-pound potato bags are used instead of something more manageable and less back-rending, the highlander answers that ENCI (Empresa Nacional para la Comercialización de Insumos), the Peruvian Department of Agriculture, requires that standard size. The official bags must be purchased from ENCI. Highlanders then sell their potatoes in bulk to middlemen, who buy them by the pound. The middlemen deduct—previously 3, then 5, now 10—kilos from the weight of each full sack "for the weight of sack" (which weighs at most 3 or 4 ounces). Sales, the highlanders reason, would be even less profitable if smaller sacks were used. Furthermore, the sierran's meager savings, largely earned during one brief harvest period, are routinely gouged by hyperinflation as the year progresses (Oths 1991). The words of an elder Chugurpampino sum up the sierran condition: "We poor Christians![4] The same poverty that makes us ill obliges us to work hard." Lamentably, the superhuman effort needed for economic survival takes its toll on the body over time.

National policies have never favored the advancement of Peru's native peoples. Until the social, political, and economic conditions change to become more favorable for the sierran agriculturalist—even if only to provide a fair price for goods produced—the physical burden of their existence will not be eased and their illness conditions can be expected to remain chronic. Increased production, stimulated by government propaganda and promises, will continue to be seen as the only solution to lower prices when in fact bumper crops serve to deflate market prices all the more. A few have opted out of the market to produce only for subsistence. They then find themselves without the cash needed for purchases such as notebooks, pencils, and uniforms for their school children, laundry soap or a bottle of beer, not to mention for participation in important social events like community feasts.

In contrast to agriculture, which in and of itself is gratifying work to the sierran, mining is an occupation seen as highly undesirable. Nash (1979) and Taussig (1980), among others, have documented the abysmal conditions of industrial mining in the Andes. Chugurpampinos are well aware of the physical and mental health consequences of such labor. Therefore, only the poorest and the landless resort to mining when there are no other economic options.

In times past, before land reform more equitably distributed plots among families and before the introduction of fertilizers allowed increased yields on sparse soils (albeit at a prorogated cost), many poor young sons of Chugurpampinos worked in Quiruvilca, a silver mining center one day's journey east of the hamlet. Only a few young Chugurpampinos migrate to work there today. When it becomes difficult to survive from livestock herding during the slack season of bad years, the men migrate. Once employed, they find it difficult to leave the mines. Benefits include complete health care for worker and extended family. Yet the value of all past health services rendered for anyone other than the worker himself must be reimbursed by the employee if he terminates with the company. Four ex-miners, now older, were in this sample. Not coincidentally, these four were the sickest of my sample and the only ones for whom past or current alcoholism was acknowledged, despite the near-ubiquitous use and occasional abuse of alcohol by Chugurpampino men. The marked toll on their health is described by the following vignette of one of them.

*The Case of Jhoni*

> One of the ex-miners, Jhoni, can no longer find the only pharmaceutical cream that has ever helped his pain, prescribed by a physician at the Quiruvilca mining company hospital years ago. He has never lost hope for a cure, however. Jhoni looks like a famine victim, his skin stretched taut over pronounced indigenous cheekbones. I was stunned to find he was 57, not the 80 I had guessed. He, like other miners, suffers from severe damage to his nerves and joints, chronic respiratory problems, and limbs numbed by a cold that never thaws. He has been in this condition for 25 years since working at the mines in the bitter cold Puna region of Quiruvilca. There, for 5 years, his job required him to stand in icy water the day long. He wore a wet suit, yet the water left scars on his hands still visible today. Despite his physical frailties, he perseveres valiantly without complaint, as he must provide for his wife and the seven children still at home, one an infant. His 15-year-old son helps him in the fields when not at school, but the other boys are still young. Jhoni went to the mines because he was poor, and he remains poor to this day. On his last trip to the doctor in Trujillo, he walked the last 8-hour leg of the return trip to save the 30-cent fare.

## INAPPROPRIATE INTERVENTION

Some specific ecologic, dietary, and political-economic conditions that contribute to disease in Chugurpampa have been detailed above. The negligence of health care workers in perceiving the relevant local cultural, material, and environmental conditions and adjusting their program initiatives accordingly is a problem that has plagued international aid efforts since their inception nearly 50 years ago (Paul 1955).

Wellin (1955), in one of the classic contributions to the field of applied anthropology, explicated the resistance of coastal Peruvians to water-boiling, a health measure that was being heavily promoted for its "obvious" benefits by hygiene workers in a rural town. Simply being taught that unboiled water caused infectious diseases like typhoid was insufficient impetus for women to change their practices. Ecologic conditions (scarcity of fuel, humorally "hot" and "cold" climatic conditions) were identified as a primary determinant of continued crude water consumption. Little has changed since Wellin's insightful study.

Eighteen months in the field allowed me to observe the implementation of health care interventions by national and foreign entities in the Otuzco region. Whether hailing from the Peruvian coastal cities or from overseas, the representatives of these health care programs had little knowledge of (and a remarkable disinterest in learning about) the climate, customs, or illnesses of high-altitude people.[5] Health care workers (mostly outsiders) outlined their programs on the assumption that particular illnesses (diarrhea, malnutrition) would be the primary illnesses contributing to infant and childhood mortality, assumptions not backed up by sound local epidemiologic data.[6]

The result was much wasted effort expended on introducing well-meaning programs that were meaningless to the people they were intended to serve. Concrete examples of such child survival programs in Chugurpampa included organizing a (1) mothers' club (club de madres), (2) community garden (huerto comunal), and (3) height and weight monitoring of children (control de peso de niños infantiles).

The mothers' club was organized by the Ministry of Health with the expressed intent of providing a conduit through which to deliver health messages to the community. In the words of one of the health post personnel, "How are we going to reach the mothers to teach them about nutrition, family planning and so on if they're not organized?" Mothers' club meetings were (intended to be) monthly reunions of hamlet mothers centered around lectures by health care representatives on the topics of infant diarrhea and homemade oral rehydration therapy (ORT), family planning, and nutrition. Nutritional instruction, for instance, included lessons on cooking as well as identification of the four food groups.[7] Mothers felt that the information provided about child care and about food, especially how to cook, was irrelevant (even insulting to some) because they were quite efficient at these tasks already.[8]

On the instigation of the international aid agency working in Chugurpampa, a community garden was planted near the school to provide hot school lunches. Mothers were to come on a rotating basis to prepare the food. The implication was that children were malnourished in their own home and thus inattentive during the school day. For many students it was too far to walk home at noon, so they brought cold lunches, adding to their purported malnutrition. The schoolteachers, hired primarily from the coastal cities, rented rooms near the school for living quarters. These teachers filched from the community garden with the tacit approval of the school principal. Meanwhile, the mothers heavily supplemented the lunch menus from their own food stores. Although the project donated some utensils and commodity foodstuffs, the mothers had to haul cooking ware, stoves, fuel, and food across long distances and back to successfully implement the meal program.

The common belief of the international aid community that children's inattentiveness in primary school is a result of poor nutrition at home serves as the rationale for development projects such as the school garden and lunch program. On the contrary, by the reckoning of community mothers, it is precisely a young child's presence in school that can cause sickliness, debility, and weight loss. Day-long school attendance curtails the young ones' habit of constant snacking between meals to fulfill energy needs, leading to the observed drowsiness of some pupils.

In addition to the communal garden, the international aid agency also carried out a program of height and weight monitoring of infants under 1 year of age. The aim was to identify high-risk babies and educate their mothers in proper infant care. Besides the problem of uncalibrated scales and poorly trained health worker aids producing erratic growth curves, the wisdom of modifying standard height and weight expectations for different populations was absent. Upon monthly measurement, nearly all babies (healthy or not) were pronounced malnourished, with mothers categorically being admonished to feed themselves and their babies more.[9]

The initiation of the above-mentioned programs coincided with my stay in Chugurpampa. From my vantage point as full-time community resident and participant-observer, I witnessed the efforts to round up unwilling and time-pressed mothers for scheduled meetings. I witnessed the acquiescent, compliant posture of the Chugurpampinos before their prestigious visitors and reactions of a quite different sort once the project vehicles had pulled away. The programs met with reactions ranging from mild amusement or consternation to suspicion, defensiveness, and anger: "How funny that the health care workers did not come today because the road between Chugurpampa and Julcan (the district capital) was washed out. If they are so healthy, why don't they walk over on the trail like the rest of us?" "Why were these city folks trying to teach us to cook their dishes. I already know how to cook!" (Some ingredients used in the demonstrations were not available locally.) "My baby is malnourished? She's healthy! She nurses constantly, has gained weight steadily, and she's not sickly."

When a raffle was organized by health care workers through the mothers' club to raise money for their programs, one mother complained: "If they're going to help, why go around taking money from us already-poor people?" Rumors flew around the hamlet that the mothers' club was introducing communism. The sentiment was: "We don't need help. We've been poor and we'll stay poor before accepting aid, especially aid from foreigners." Women participated in the health programs out of a sense of obligation, never out of any true enthusiasm that could be detected. They simply viewed the program aims as irrelevant. It is not surprising that within 1 year of their initiation the programs were functioning in name only. Instead of a participatory spirit, a distrust of aid workers had been instilled in the community members, certain to disadvantage any future intervention efforts.

Community participation in health care efforts is an ideal espoused by the major international aid agencies, although its actual success has been limited so far (Mull 1990; WHO 1991). One reason for this has been that community participation has not begun in the development and planning stages of a program. Interventions that enlist community input only at the implementation stage, when the identification and definition of health problems have already been established by outsiders, are not successful, as international aid experiences during the 1980s have shown (Green and Barker 1988). Involvement of Chugurpampinos in the identification and definition of health problems that need to be addressed would result in a list of problems very different from that produced by the Ministry of Health and foreign aid agencies. Judging from the concerns expressed on a daily basis in the community, people really wanted advice and therapy for prevalent problems such as dental, respiratory, musculoskeletal, and stomach ailments. Infant and childhood illnesses and malnutrition certainly would not be isolated as the only, or even the major, health risks that these highlanders face. The participation of community members in programs designed to ameliorate the problems locally defined as prevalent would be more readily forthcoming.

## SUMMARY

A variety of factors—ecologic, dietary, political, and economic—contribute to the distinct illness pattern observed within this Andean hamlet. However, these factors are not among the typical morbidity risks considered within a paradigm of international health that emphasizes child survival, infectious and parasitic diseases, and an atomistic view of health behaviors.

Interactions between humans and their environments at high altitude that trigger illness include exposure to the elements (heat, cold, water, wind, UV radiation, low barometric pressure). Illnesses stemming from these conditions include influenza, colds, headache, dizziness, backache, sunstroke, mountain sickness, and other hypoxia-related illnesses, as reflected in the illness rates (Table 6–3). One beneficial consequence of highland living conditions is a reduced exposure to bacteria and thus a lower incidence of some infectious diseases, especially among children.

Illnesses that can be attributed to dietary factors, while conspicuously not including malnutrition or obesity, include dental caries, hypoglycemia, and gastrointestinal, especially stomach, disorders.

The effects of brutal working conditions imposed by the political and economic domination and exploitation of the highland peasants by the societal elite are clearly visible. Degenerative and musculoskeletal complaints and lacerations stemming from arduous labor account for 22% of reported health problems of highlanders. These include ache, strain, injury, laceration, arthritis, and kidney pain. The heavy use of pesticides may contribute to respiratory and gastrointestinal illness as well. Mining destroys a highlander's health in myriad ways, not the least of which are through nerve and joint damage, respiratory problems, and possibly alcoholism.

International health paradigms are atomistic in that they emphasize individual pathways of disease exposure and individual health behaviors to deal with the disease experience. This model cannot be used to understand, much less intervene in, the processes influencing health in the Andean community studied here or in other communities like it. An emphasis on individual health behaviors and hence the assumed individual responsibility for one's health and that of the household is important in accounting for the illness pattern in the Andes. Individual and cultural adaptations such as proper clothing, better hygiene, a sugar-free diet, or the circumspect adoption and use of pharmaceuticals might help alleviate several health problems of the Chugurpampinos. Yet without structural and infrastructural changes in the larger society, little can be done to alter the conditions conducive to poor health. Some political-economic forces that hold highlanders in the stalemate of poverty, back-breaking productivity, and poor health include the market-oriented promotion of deleterious consumer goods (e.g., refined foods, pesticides) and the promulgation of national policies—labor, agriculture, health care, and education—that are exploitative and unfair to indigenous peoples.

Illustrative of the individualistic focus on illness causation is the popular notion among international health care specialists that infectious disease and malnutrition can be adequately controlled through the change in behavior of a single individual, namely the female head of household. Maternal education as a causal factor has been emphasized in much of the literature on treatment choice and the epidemiology of infant illness and mortality in developing societies (cf. the recent discussion of maternal education and health by Ware et al. 1992 and Mosley et al. 1990). Several dimensions of maternal education believed to contribute directly to child health and survival pertain to health beliefs and domestic practices. These include, among others, the hypotheses that more educated mothers are thought to (1) provide more nutritional meals, (2) maintain a more hygienic household living environment, (3) more correctly identify symptoms, (4) be able to administer some treatments themselves in life-threatening situations (e.g., ORT), and (5) recognize when a child should be taken to a physician. It is not surprising, then, that international health programs target efforts in health education campaigns at female heads of household, as seen in the above case examples from Chugurpampa (e.g., mothers' clubs, school lunches, lectures on infant feeding, ORT).

The larger political, economic, and social forces affecting health are ignored at the peril of health intervention program success (Walsh 1988). The social relationships of production and redistribution controlled by the state heavily influence the individual illness patterns seen in the Andes. As noted earlier, Brown (1987), examining the infectious disease malaria, made a similar argument, using household productivity as an outcome variable. He showed that, to satisfy the demands of a distant market and absentee landlords, more productive days were lost by a household to exploitative productive relationships than were lost to the malaria parasite itself. This observation led him to use the term "macroparasitism."

The analysis of illness in Chugurpampa parallels Brown's, the difference being that the synergistic effects of the natural highland environment and political economy are measured by actual morbidity patterns rather than lost productivity, although clearly these two outcomes are related. Following Brown's logic and the distinctions between infectious and chronic disease, one might thus posit the notions of "macro–risk factors," or perhaps even "macro–degenerative disease" in highland epidemiology (Oths 1993).

Thus, the discussion of the ecologic and political influences on health in Chugurpampa is useful as a critique of the international health paradigm. It points out the error of concentrating selectively on specific problems such as infant diarrhea, malnutrition, and communicable childhood diseases and of prescribing individualistic behavioral measures to alleviate them. This is not an idle concern. Large amounts of resources have been unwisely invested on the assumption that a model paradigm of child survival, complete with solutions for problems such as infant diarrhea and malnutrition, is inherently applicable everywhere there are poor people. However, populations such as those in parts of the northern Andes suffer a morbidity profile that should not be ignored in international health policy. Cognizance of the social, political, and economic stresses on a community will not make health care workers capable of correcting such intractable problems, but it may sensitize them to what they can accomplish—accurate assessments of extant problems. Solutions for the illnesses that do exist may then be devised.

International health care initiatives such as child survival are borne of the health problems faced by inhabitants of tropical and semitropical lands with dense populations (e.g., Bangladesh, Brazil, and Nigeria). Thus, the health problems of impoverished peoples living in temperate (woodland, grassland, desert), not to mention some high-altitude, climates,[10] environmental zones that support roughly 38% of the world's population, are overlooked. Programs designed for the former are likely to meet with incomprehension and resistance by inhabitants of the latter. Furthermore, the problem of implementing paradigmatic programs is not limited to ostensibly atypical populations. A flexibility in design and implementation of programs as they are applied from any one context to another is sorely needed (Taylor and Jolly 1988; Nabarro and Chinnock 1988). As Justice (1989) has painstakingly documented for Nepal, institutional imperatives at the highest levels of the international aid organizations to get the job done quickly and efficiently are often responsible for the inflexibility of program design.

In view of the information gathered here, three recommendations can be made for those active in international health care endeavors. First, community participation must be elicited in problem definition and program planning (as opposed to implementation only) to define problems in a way relevant to the people served. This is a necessary first step if programs are to be made viable for a particular people in a particular place and time. Second, a careful epidemiologic survey and prioritization of the effective problems and conditions of the host population are imperative during the planning stages of any program (Green and Barker 1988). As experience has repeatedly shown, the wholesale importation and application of health care solutions devised in an office in Geneva or Washington for a "typical" population is not successful everywhere (Justice 1989). Last, it is imperative to recognize that the health of the whole community will determine, in large part, the health of its weakest and most dependent members. There is no reasonable justification for adult health to be sacrificed to that of infants and children. Human morbidity, not infant mortality alone, is the appropriate problem to be addressed (Mosley et al. 1990; Feachem et al. 1992).

Returning to the issue of policy, an international health paradigm focusing narrowly on infectious and communicable diseases, which represent only a small fraction of illness complaints, or on individual health behaviors that might alleviate such perceived distress has little to offer this highland community (or other communities like it) for improving the health of its members. These communities offer a special challenge to researchers in international health and to policy advocates whose goal is to intervene in fundamental disease processes to reduce the burden of morbidity and mortality in the developing world. Those disease processes may simply be beyond the grasp of a view of health that does not extend beyond the individual.

## NOTES

1. A *comunidad campesina* is a free peasant community with communal land rights.
2. During a 6-month time period, roughly coterminous with my case-collection period, the health post doctor recorded 38 mild, 59 moderate, and 3 grave respiratory infections, for a total of 100 cases. Of diarrheal illnesses, there were 36 regular and 19 with dehydration, for a total of 55. Note that the above figures do not represent all illness episodes, but only those cases deemed serious enough to warrant biomedical intervention. According to the doctor, who signed all death certificates, the only infant death recorded in the entire district (approximate pop-

ulation = 37,000, including 390 infants) during this time period was one of the infants treated for diarrhea by the health post.

3. Highland populations, however, may suffer from these illnesses to the extent that their people migrate. Often seasonal migrant workers import cases of infectious disease contracted in the lowland cities or jungle areas.
4. In Peru Christian (Christiano) is a term meaning "civilized person" or, loosely, "citizen," used in contrast to gentile (gentil), meaning "heathen." The latter term is usually used to refer to prehistoric peoples.
5. In all fairness to the international aid agency active in Chugurpampa, the director of the program was one of the most enlightened, caring health care workers I have ever met. He was sensitive to cultural differences and local constraints and wished desperately to overcome many of the problems mentioned herein, although his paradigmatic thinking, program imperatives, and employee apathy impeded his efforts.
6. Health care agencies conducted a few of their own independent local illness surveys, in my opinion of questionable reliability. The high disease rates they "found" reflect the bias of persons committed a priori to the existence of certain diseases. Thus, they found what they were looking for. I witnessed physical health examinations in highland schools and clinics. Identical to the yearly health examination scene in the educational film, *Viracocha: The Aymara of the Bolivian Highlands* (AUFS 1974), children in Chugurpampa were lined up and inspected by a visiting doctor, who told each in turn what was wrong with him or her by a cursory visual inspection. Each child had to have something to fill out the chart and was assigned an illness promptly and in seemingly arbitrary fashion: intestinal parasites, malnutrition, anemia . . . intestinal parasites, malnutrition, anemia . . .
7. For instance, the meat category was limited to pictures of seldom-eaten beef and pork, while guinea pig, mutton, rice and legumes, and quinoa—the most common sources of protein in Chugurpampa—were missing.
8. Ironically, the same health care workers who came to teach the mothers how to grow food, prepare meals, and keep their kids nourished seldom arrived at the hamlet unannounced, so that mothers would have time to organize a festive highland lunch for them. They were vocally annoyed when, on occasion, the anticipated food did not materialize.
9. There is considerable debate in the scientific community as to the applicability for children of all ethnic groups of height and weight requirements standardized on European populations (Frisancho 1990). Many highland researchers support a "small but healthy" theory. Birth weights lower than normal for sea level populations have actually been found to be optimum for survival of Andean newborns (Beall 1976). Although the Chugurpampan children fell into the low-normal range for NCHS standards, none had been born underweight. The crucial factor was that the plot of weight gain formed a consistently upward curve from birth onward for all infants.
10. Health conditions in the high altitudes of South America vary tremendously from community to community (Oths 1993).

## REFERENCES

Akpabio, S. Prince. 1990. "Achieving Oral Health by the Year 2000." Pp. 227–51 in *Issues in Contemporary International Health,* edited by T. A. Lambo and S. B. Day. New York: Plenum Medical Book Company.

Anderson, Robert. 1984. "An Orthopedic Ethnography in Rural Nepal." *Medical Anthropology* 8:46–59.

BAKER, PAUL T. 1978. "The Adaptive Fitness of High-Altitude Populations." Pp. 317–50 in *The Biology of High-Altitude Peoples,* edited by P. T. Baker. Cambridge, UK: Cambridge University Press.

BAKER, PAUL T. and RICHARD B. MAZESS. 1963. "Calcium: Unusual Sources in the Highland Peruvian Diet." *Science* 14:1466–67.

BEALL, CYNTHIA. 1976. *The Effects of High Altitude on Growth, Morbidity, and Mortality of Peruvian Infants.* Ph.D. dissertation. State College, PA: Penn State University, Department of Anthropology.

BICKNELL, WILLIAM J. and CINDY LOU PARKS. 1989. "As Children Survive: Dilemmas of Aging in the Developing World." *Social Science and Medicine* 28:59–67.

BLUM, H. F. 1948. "Sunlight as a Causal Factor in Cancer of the Skin of Man." *Journal of the National Cancer Institute* 9:247–58.

BOLTON, RALPH. 1981. "Susto, Hostility, and Hypoglycemia." *Ethnology* 20:261–96.

______. 1984. "The Hypoglycemia-Aggression Hypothesis: Debate Versus Research." *Current Anthropology* 25:1–53.

BROWN, PETER J. 1987. "Microparasites and Macroparasites." *Cultural Anthropology* 2:155–71.

BUCK, ALFRED A., TOM T. SASAKI, and ROBERT I. ANDERSON. 1968. *Health and Disease in Four Peruvian Villages and Contrasts in Epidemiology.* Baltimore: Johns Hopkins Press.

BULL, DAVID. 1982. *A Growing Problem: Pesticides and the Third World Poor.* Oxford, UK: OXFAM.

CAMINO, ALEJANDRO. 1989. "The Potential of Indigenous Technologies for Supporting Conservation and Development in the Andean Uplands of Peru." Paper presented at American Anthropological Association Meetings, Washington, DC, November 15–19.

FEACHEM, RICHARD G. A., TORD KJELLSTROM, CHRISTOPHER J. L. MURRAY, MEAD OVER, and MARGARET A. PHILLIPS. 1992. *The Health of Adults in the Developing World.* New York: Oxford University Press.

FINERMAN, RUTHBETH D. 1985. "Health Care Decisions in an Andean Indian Community: Getting the Best of Both Worlds." Ph.D. dissertation. Los Angeles: University of California, Department of Anthropology.

FRISANCHO, A. ROBERTO. 1990. *Anthropometric Standards for the Assessment of Growth and Nutritional Status.* Ann Arbor: University of Michigan Press.

FUCHS, ANDREW. 1978. "Coca Chewing and High Altitude Stress: Possible Effects of Coca Alkaloids on Erythropoiesis." *Current Anthropology* 19:227–91.

GATES, D. M. 1966. "Spectral Distribution of Solar Radiation at the Earth's Surface." *Science* 151:523–29.

GREEN, ANDREW and CAROL BARKER. 1988. "Priority Setting and Economic Appraisal: Whose Priorities—the Community or the Economist?" *Social Science and Medicine* 26:919–29.

HEATH, DONALD and DAVID WILLIAMS. 1989. *High-Altitude Medicine and Pathology.* London: Butterworth and Company.

JANOWITZ, HENRY D. 1989. *Your Gut Feelings: A Complete Guide to Living Better with Intestinal Problems.* London: Oxford University Press.

JURMAIN, ROBERT D. 1975. "Stress and the Etiology of Osteoarthritis." *American Journal of Physical Anthropology* 46:353–66.

JUSTICE, JUDITH. 1989. *Policies, Plans and People: Foreign Aid and Health Development.* Berkeley: University of California Press.

LANDY, DAVID. 1983. "Medical Anthropology: A Critical Appraisal." Pp. 185–314 in *Advances in Medical Social Science,* Vol. 1, edited by J. Ruffing. New York: Gordon and Breach Science Publishers.

MONGE, M. CARLOS. 1943. "Chronic Mountain Sickness." *Physiological Reviews* 23: 166–84.

Mosley, Henry, Dean T. Jamison, and Donald A. Henderson. 1990. "The Health Sector in Developing Countries: Problems for the 1990s and Beyond." *Annual Review of Public Health* 11:335–58.

Mull, J. Dennis. 1990. "The Primary Health Care Dialectic: History, Rhetoric, Reality." Pp. 28–47 in *Anthropology and Primary Health Care,* edited by J. Coreil and J. D. Mull. Boulder, CO: Westview Press.

Nabarro, David and Paul Chinnock. 1988. "Growth Monitoring—Inappropriate Promotion of an Appropriate Technology." *Social Science and Medicine* 26:941–48.

Nash, June. 1979. *We Eat the Mines and the Mines Eat Us.* New York: Columbia University Press.

Nichter, Mark and Elizabeth Cartwright. 1991. "Saving the Children for the Tobacco Industry." *Medical Anthropology Quarterly* 5:236–56.

Nichter, Mark and Carl Kendall. 1991. "Beyond Child Survival: Anthropology and International Health in the 1990s." *Medical Anthropology Quarterly* 5:195–203.

Nightingale, Elena O., David A. Hamburg, and Allyn M. Mortimer. 1990. "International Scientific Cooperation for Maternal and Child Health." Pp. 113–33 in *Issues in Contemporary International Health,* edited by T. A. Lambo and S. B. Day. New York: Plenum Medical Book Company.

Oths, Kathryn S. 1991. "Medical Treatment Choice and Health Outcomes in the Northern Peruvian Andes." Ph.D. dissertation. Cleveland, OH: Case Western Reserve University, Department of Anthropology.

______. 1992. "Some Symbolic Dimensions of Andean Materia Medica." *Central Issues in Anthropology* 10:76–85.

______. 1993. "The Diversity of Ecological and Macrolevel Influences on Illness in the Andes: Challenging International Health Assumptions." Paper presented at the American Anthropological Association Meetings, Washington, DC, November 17–21.

______. 1994. "Health Care Decisions of Households in Economic Crisis: An Example from the Peruvian Highlands." *Human Organization* 53(3):245–54.

Paul, Benjamin D. 1955. *Health, Culture, and Community: Case Studies of Public Reactions to Health Programs.* New York: Russell Sage Foundation.

Picón-Reátegui, E. 1978. "The Food and Nutrition of High-Altitude Populations." Pp. 219–50 in *The Biology of High-Altitude Peoples,* edited by P. T. Baker. Cambridge, UK: Cambridge University Press.

Population Reference Bureau. 1987. "World Population Data Sheet." Washington, DC.

Pugh, L. G. C. E. 1964. "Animals in High Altitude: Man Above 5000 Meters—Mountain Exploration." Pp. 861–68 in *Handbook of Physiology, Section 4, "Adaptation to the Environment,"* edited by D. B. Dill, E. F. Adolph, and C. G. Wilber. Baltimore, MD: Waverly Press.

Scheper-Hughes, Nancy (ed.). 1987. *Child Survival: Anthropological Perspectives on the Treatment and Maltreatment of Children.* Dordrecht, the Netherlands: Kluwer Academic Publishers.

Simonelli, Jeanne. 1987. "Defective Modernization and Health in Mexico." *Social Science and Medicine* 24:23–36.

Sorofman, Bernard and Toni Tripp-Reimer. 1989. "Health Care Choices in an Iowa Old Order Amish Community." Paper presented at the American Anthropological Association Meetings, Washington, DC, November 15–19.

Taussig, Michael. 1980. *The Devil and Commodity Fetishism in South America.* Chapel Hill: University of North Carolina Press.

Taylor, Carl and Richard Jolly. 1988. "The Straw Men of Primary Health Care." *Social Science and Medicine* 26:971–77.

TAYLOR, H. R., S. K. WEST, F. S. ROSENTHAL, B. MUÑOZ, H. S. NEWLAND, and E. A. EMMETT. 1989. "Corneal Changes Associated with Chronic UV Irradiation." *Archives of Ophthalmology* 107:1481–84.

UNITED NATIONS INTERNATIONAL CHILDREN'S EMERGENCY FUND (UNICEF). 1989. *The State of the World's Children.* New York: Oxford University Press.

URBACH, F., R. E. DAVIES, and P.D. FORBES. 1966. "Ultraviolet Radiation and Skin Cancer in Man." *Advances in the Biology of Skin* 7:195–215.

WALSH, JULIA. 1988. "Selectivity Within Primary Health Care." *Social Science and Medicine* 26:899–902.

WARD, MICHAEL P. 1989. *High-Altitude Medicine and Physiology.* Philadelphia: University of Pennsylvania Press.

WARE, NORMA C., NICHOLAS A. CHRISTAKIS and ARTHUR KLEINMAN. 1992. "An Anthropological Approach to Social Science Research in the Health Transition." Pp. 23–38 in *Advancing Health in Developing Countries: The Role of Social Research,* edited by L. C. Chen, A. Kleinman, and N. C. Ware. New York: Auburn House.

WELLIN, EDWARD. 1955. "Water Boiling in a Peruvian Town." Pp. 71–103 in *Health, Culture and Community,* edited by P. Benjamin. New York: Russell Sage Foundation.

WORLD HEALTH ORGANIZATION (WHO). 1979. *Environmental Health Criteria 14: Ultraviolet Radiation.* Helsinki, Finland: WHO.

______. 1986a. *Evaluation of the Carcinogenic Risk of Chemicals to Humans: Some Naturally Occurring and Synthetic Food Components, Furocoumarins and Ultraviolet Radiation.* IARC Monograph Vol. 40. Lyon, France: WHO.

______. 1986b. *Health Research Strategy for Health for All by the Year 2000.* Advisory Committee on Health Research. Geneva, Switzerland: WHO.

______. 1991. *Community Involvement in Health Development: Challenging Health Services.* Technical Report Series No. 809. Geneva, Switzerland: WHO.

Chapter 7

# Inequalities in the Mexican Health Care System: Problems in Managing Cancer in Southern Mexico*

*Linda M. Hunt*

As more countries continue to industrialize, chronic and degenerative diseases are becoming increasingly prominent health concerns (Evans et al. 1981; Litvak et al. 1987). The improvements in nutrition, sanitation, and disease control that accompany industrialization often result in a demographic transition toward an aging population. Death rates due to infectious disease begin to decline, and therefore people live longer. As countries experience this general age shift in the population, their primary health problems become increasingly those of chronic degenerative diseases such as cancer and heart disease rather than those of acute infectious diseases. This sociodemographic shift often introduces new and serious problems in health care delivery owing to the lim-

*This paper is based upon research supported in part by the National Science Foundation under grant no. BNS8916157, Wenner-Gren grant no. Gr.5183, and a grant from the Fundación México en Harvard. Any opinions, findings, conclusions, or recommendations expressed in this paper are mine and do not necessarily reflect the views of these foundations. An earlier version of this paper was presented at the National Meetings of the American Public Health Association, Washington, DC, November 1992. I wish to express my gratitude for the cooperation and support of the Centro de Investigaciones de Salud de Comitán, Chiapas, México. I am indebted to Atonio Escobedo Aguirre of INEGI, Aguascalientes, Mexico, and Margo Guitierrez of the University of Texas, Austin Libraries for their help locating statistical information. Enrique Griego and Rolando Medina made many useful suggestions on the manuscript. I am especially grateful to the physicians and patients of southern Mexico who shared their experiences and insights with me in the course of this research.

ited availability and expense of high-technology and high-maintenance treatments. The problems associated with these diseases in the industrializing world are far from trivial and merit serious consideration in policy planning in these countries (Chen and Cash 1988).

Most existing models for health care delivery in the industrializing world have been designed to address acute, communicable diseases such as diarrheal disease and malaria (Navarro 1982) and are not well suited for the special problems associated with long-term degenerative disease. These include diseases whose biomedical management often requires extended access to advanced diagnostic and treatment technologies. Rather than develop delivery systems specifically designed for these problems, most commonly the already existing health care system is used. No explicit adjustments in the system are made, and it is basically left to ad hoc innovations of administrators and health care personnel to find ways to diagnose and treat these diseases within the constraints of the existing system. What too often results is a passive process of adaptation wherein acute care delivery systems are stretched and manipulated to meet the special requirements of chronic disease.

This process of ad hoc adaptation of the health care system tends to produce far-reaching inequality in health care. The distribution of expensive health resources in often highly politicized. It is therefore common for extensive health care to be concentrated in large cities and towns as rewards for key occupational groups, whereas the services available to more marginalized groups remain minimal. Marginal groups are provided primary care services, but the system may contain no overt mechanism for the higher-level treatment needs of these populations (Sherraden and Wallace 1992). This process thereby tends to reproduce local social hierarchies within the context of health care, which reflect existing social inequality based on cultural, ethnic, educational, and gender differences.

Mexico, which in recent years has undergone a process of rapid industrialization, is a good example of the demographic transition and the associated change in disease incidence described above. Life expectancy in Mexico has been increasing steadily, and mortality rates have been dropping. In 1940, for example, the average Mexican life expectancy was 39 years, rising to a 1990 average of 70 years (*Statistical Abstracts of Latin America* 1960, 1992). This trend toward an aging population has been accompanied by an increasing incidence of degenerative disease. Cancer, for example, was Mexico's sixth leading cause of death in 1973, its third in 1986, and its second in 1990, behind coronary disease and surpassing the previous leading causes—infectious disease and accidents (INEGI 1993; PAHO 1990). However, the nation's health care system has not kept pace with these demographic trends. As a result, tremendous social and geographic inequity exists in accessibility of treatment for these diseases.

This chapter describes the development and current status of the Mexican health care system, then considers some features of social and political life in Mexico that affect the distribution of resources and the implications of unequal distribution for the management of diseases requiring access to high technology. In doing so, however, this chapter does not attempt to assess the adequacy of the system for addressing acute versus chronic disease, but rather examines some examples of the specific difficulties that arise in clinical practice when trying to handle chronic degenerative illness when the system is not designed to do so. The diagnosis and treatment of cancer in one hospital in Southern Mexico are used to illustrate some of the practical and ethical problems that arise when adjusting the system to serve the changing health needs of a population.

## THE MEXICAN NATIONAL HEALTH CARE SYSTEM

Mexico has had a longstanding commitment to socialized medicine. In 1861, as part of a sweeping reform movement, the federal government took control of the nation's hospitals from the Catholic Church. During the turbulent period of the 10-year Mexican revolution, the Academia Nacional de Medicina was established (1912) and in the 1917 Mexican Constitution the provision of health care to the remote areas of the country was declared a priority in the national program for social justice. This goal was left largely unaddressed until 1938, when President Cárdenas instituted the Social Insurance Act, guaranteeing health care to all workers. With the intense industrialization in Mexico during World War II and the resultant increase in the gross national product, the country was finally able to begin to establish a series of institutions for fulfilling these commitments (Finkler 1991).

During World War II the Mexican government began building numerous hospitals and clinics in the larger cities throughout the country. In 1940, in response to demands from workers' organizations, the Instituto Mexicano del Seguro Social (IMSS) was established, which provided retirement and health care benefits for state and private industry workers. The Secretaría de Salubridad y Asistencia (SSA) was established in 1943 to coordinate government institutions providing health care for uninsured citizens. In 1960 government employees demanded and received a separate insurance system, splintering off from the IMSS to establish the Instituto de Seguridad y Servicios Sociales de los Trabajadores del Estado (ISSSTE). Since then a number of smaller insurance systems, both public and private, have been established, as well as numerous public programs for the rural and urban poor. SSA, IMSS, and ISSSTE remain the major public health care institutions in Mexico (Alvarez 1974; Barry 1992; Finkler 1991; Gonzalez-Block 1988b; López Acuña 1987; Ovalle and Cantu 1985; PAHO 1990; Sepúlveda 1981; Zschosk 1986).

In 1983 President de la Madrid signed a constitutional amendment declaring health care a universal right. Massive expansion of health services throughout the country followed, including the building of 3,000 rural primary care clinics in 2 years. However, owing to a generally weak national economy, federal expenditure for health has been steadily decreasing.[1] Nevertheless, the Mexican health care system today provides at least minimal access to biomedicine to nearly all Mexicans (Frazier 1981; Horn 1983; Rubel 1990; Stebbins 1986; Zschosk 1986). Although approaching the ideal of universal health care, centralization and inequality remain hallmarks of this system.

Recent estimates for Mexico[2] indicate that private medicine serves about 5% of the population and consumes about 34% of national health care resources. The social insurance system, including IMSS, ISSSTE, and several smaller plans,[3] provides direct service for affiliated workers. In 1990 about 60% of the nation's population was covered by social insurance (INEGI 1993). These plans consume about 50% of the national health care budget. The public assistance sector, administered primarily by the SSA,[4] cares for about 35% of primarily rural and marginally employed people and accounts for 16% of the national health care budget (Ovalle and Cantu 1985, p. 152).

Table 7–1 shows the approximate coverage by each of the three tiers of the health care system for the nation, for Mexico City, and for the states of Oaxaca and Chiapas. Consistent with their status as the two poorest and most underserved states in Mexico, Oaxaca and Chiapas fall well below the national average in coverage by the two higher tiers of the system (private and social security insurance). Less than a quarter of the population in either state is covered by insurance plans, compared with the nearly 80% in Mexico City, where most of the nation's wealth is concentrated. These poorer regions must depend almost exclusively on public assistance health care systems (e.g., SSA), more than doubling the national average for reliance on this kind of health service.

**TABLE 7–1. Approximate Population Covered by Major Sectors of the Mexican Medical System: Private, Social Security Insurance, and Public Assistance for the Nation and for Three Regions 1991***

| | *NATIONAL* | *MEXICO CITY* | *STATE OF CHIAPAS* | *STATE OF OAXACA* |
|---|---|---|---|---|
| Private[†] | 5% | 8% | >1% | >1% |
| Social Security insurance | 60% | 71% | 19% | 23% |
| IMSS | 49% | 52% | 12% | 14% |
| ISSSTE | 10% | 18% | 6% | 8% |
| Other | 1% | 1% | >1% | >1% |
| Public assistance (e.g., SSA)[‡] | 35% | 21% | 80% | 72% |

*Source: INEGI: "Información Estadística del Sector Salud y Seguridad Social." Cuaderno Núm. 9. Aguas Calientes, AGS, México: INEGI.

[†]Unavailable for 1991, these figures are extrapolated from figures published by Barry (1992), Gonzalez-Block (1988a), and Ovalle and Cantu (1985).

[‡]Calculated as the remaining, uninsured population.

The inequality in the distribution of health resources between these systems illustrates a national trend to concentrate resources in the major urban areas and among the middle and upper classes (Barry 1992; Breu 1986; Felix 1983; Portes 1985; Selby et al. 1990). Public policies based on the logic of providing the greatest good for the greatest number and heavily influenced by political interests have resulted in pronounced disparities between services available in the major urban centers like Mexico City, Guadalajara, and Monterrey and those available in the smaller urban centers in the outlying areas of the country. The tendency for doctors and health resources to concentrate in urban areas is common worldwide but is especially pronounced in Mexico.[5] Oaxaca and Chiapas, with their largely rural and indigenous populations, are especially affected by these inequities. These two states rank last nationally in almost every measure of health resource investment, whereas the region of Mexico City ranks first in all measures. These patterns are well illustrated in Table 7–2, which shows the extreme cases and the national average in the distribution of some key health resources. The numbers of doctors and hospital beds per 100,000 for Mexico City are more than four times those of the state of Oaxaca and five times those of the state of Chiapas.

Public health care in Mexico is organized as a multilevel regional system. The central administration of the various health services (IMSS, ISSSTE, or SSA) defines geographic regions of service and allocates personnel and resources within each region while setting policies and establishing a system for evaluation of needs and services (Sepúlveda 1981). At the first level are small community and neighborhood outpatient clinics that deliver primary health care services in almost every locality in the country. If a patient should need more sophisticated care, he or she is referred to the next-level institutions, which are general hospitals providing basic inpatient services in surgery, gynecology, and internal medicine. At the next level are the so-called specialty hospitals, which offer at least some access to specialized care. However, the

**TABLE 7–2. Distribution of Some Health Resources for the Nation and for Three Regions, 1991***

| | *PERCENT POPULATION COVERED BY SOCIAL INSURANCE* | *DOCTORS PER 100,000 POPULATION* | *HOSPITAL BEDS PER 100,000 POPULATION* |
|---|---|---|---|
| National total | 60% | 120.60 | 83.32 |
| Mexico City | 71% | 289.33 | 203.91 |
| State of Chiapas | 19% | 59.92 | 39.18 |
| State of Oaxaca | 23% | 72.22 | 50.83 |

*Source: INEGI: "Información Estadística del Sector Salud y Seguridad Social." Cuaderno Núm. 9. Aguas Calientes, AGS, México: INEGI.

level of care available in most of these hospitals is quite limited. These low-level specialty hospitals must refer many patients to regional hospitals, where complete specialty units are located.

Technology and training for more intensive treatments and specializations are concentrated in the high-level specialty hospitals of the major urban centers of the country. These institutions have the most specialized personnel and the resources to perform the most advanced diagnostic and treatment procedures available in Mexico. In theory, the service regions for these hospitals are defined primarily by concentrations of population. However, because the largest cities are also the most politically influential, the distribution of resources also reflects the concentration of political and economic power existing in the country.

Table 7–3 shows the unequal distribution of hospitals nationally, for Mexico City, and for the states of Chiapas and Oaxaca. Although both Oaxaca and Chiapas have a large number of outpatient clinics, they suffer from a serious lack of more sophisticated services. Mexico City alone has as many general hospitals and a staggering 30 times the number of specialty hospitals as are in Chiapas and Oaxaca combined. Indeed, 45% of all specialty hospitals in the entire nation are located in Mexico City. Clearly, the more sophisticated services are highly concentrated in the urban center and simply do not exist in the outlying regions.

The current national distribution of diagnostic and treatment resources for chronic degenerative disease also exhibits this trend. Nearly all expensive, high-technology equipment and specialized personnel are located in a few large cities like Mexico City, Monterrey, and Guadalajara. The poor southern states of Oaxaca and Chiapas, where the majority of rural and indigenous peoples of the country live, have been virtually excluded. There are several large hospitals in the major cities of Oaxaca and Chiapas and although some offer limited specialty services like oncology, their ability to treat chronic degenerative disease is quite limited. Many patients must be referred to out-of-state hospitals for at least some phase of their care. No true high-specialty hospitals ex-

**TABLE 7–3. Distribution of Hospitals for the Nation and for Three Regions, 1991***

| | *OUTPATIENT CLINICS* | *GENERAL HOSPITALS* | *SPECIALTY HOSPITALS (LOW AND HIGH, COMBINED)* |
|---|---|---|---|
| National | 13,040 | 638 | 134 |
| Mexico City | 647 | 46 | 60 |
| State of Chiapas | 755 | 25 | 0 |
| State of Oaxaca | 751 | 21 | 2 |

*Source: INEGI: "Información Estadística del Sector Salud y Seguridad Social." Cuaderno Núm. 9. Aguas Calientes, AGS, México: INEGI.

ist in the states of Oaxaca and Chiapas. Patients requiring more advanced services in these states must travel great distances to far-away large cities to the high-specialty hospital assigned to their region.

Thusfar, we have seen that, historically, the strategy for complying with the national law that health care be available to everyone has followed a model of providing minimal primary care services in the outlying areas and higher-level care predominantly in the major urban centers. In the past, when the problems of infectious disease were by far the most pressing health problems in the rural areas, the availability of higher-level care in the outreaches of the country was less urgent than was ensuring access to very basic treatments like antibiotics and rehydration therapies. However, with the recent demographic changes in Mexico and the accompanying increase in chronic degenerative disease, the inaccessibility of higher-level care for whole sectors of the nation has become a more serious health problem. Cancer treatment in Oaxaca and Chiapas provides a striking example of the problems that arise as a result of the way the health care system currently addresses chronic diseases.

## THE LOCAL CONTEXT: OAXACA AND CHIAPAS

Of the approximately 400 oncologists practicing in Mexico at the time of this research, only three practiced in the entire state of Oaxaca and one in the state of Chiapas. There were about 95 radiation therapy machines in Mexico, but only two were in the southern part of the country and none was in either Oaxaca or Chiapas.[6]

Although people from Oaxaca and Chiapas do have access to the advanced diagnosis and treatments available in the major medical centers, they can access this care only if they are willing and able to travel to receive the services. For cancer patients in these states, receiving treatment often entails up to 2 days' travel to distant metropolitan areas. Patients must then find a way to live in those cities, sometimes for 3 or 4 months at a time, to complete a treatment protocol. Such a trip, of course, is a virtual impossibility for great numbers of poor patients. The national medical system therefore effectively excludes them from care.

It is left to individual physicians treating cancer patients in these areas to negotiate this gulf between the formal structure of available care and its practical limitations. Physicians face profound contradictions between their professional mandate to diagnose and treat disease and the actions possible in the setting where they work. In trying to diagnose and treat cancer, they are routinely engaged in adapting biomedical concepts and protocols reliant on high technology to a resource-scarce environment. This requires a continual process of interpretation, alteration, and modification to the specific local context in which they are working, with its distinct system of power, economics, morality, and social hierarchy. Mostly, this adaptation process is completely implicit, shrouded behind a rhetoric of equal access to health care when actual access is in fact vastly unequal, reproducing broadly based social and cultural inequities.

## THE STRUCTURE OF INEQUALITY IN MEXICO

It is unmistakable in Mexico that there is truth to the popular observation that there are "many Mexicos." It is a country of great geographic, ethnic, cultural, and socioeconomic variation. There is a wide range of living conditions in the country. In major urban areas the trappings of the "international middle class," like private automobiles, air transportation, university education, imported goods, and personal services, are relatively accessible and inexpensive. However, there coexists another Mexico where inequality is extreme, where subsistence farming, unemployment, and underemployment are frequent, and where devastating urban and rural poverty with their attendant problems of health and welfare persist for masses of the population.[7]

As is common throughout Latin America, access to the upper strata of Mexican society frequently falls along ethnic lines. Vestiges of the racism that was the formal basis of social stratification during the colonial period persist in spite of postrevolutionary official doctrine aimed at breaking down ethnic barriers[8] (Bonfil Batalla 1981; Friedlander 1975; Graham 1990; Knight 1990). It is not surprising that the two most impoverished of Mexico's states, Chiapas and Oaxaca, are also the two most "eminently indigenous"[9] (Barry 1992; Hernández Díaz 1988; INEGI 1986, 1993; Kunz et al. 1986; Programa Nacional "Mujer, Salud y Desarrollo" 1990). These states are ranked last in the country on every standard-of-living indicator, including infant and maternal mortality, urban infrastructure, illiteracy, level of education, non-Spanish monolingualism, and health resources (INEGI 1986).

A great deal of ambivalence exists among the Mexican middle and upper classes toward the lower-class citizens of their country. Reflecting a long heritage of *patron* relationships between the classes, a sense of entitlement and obligation is a central feature of interclass interactions, often expressed in paradoxical mixtures of revulsion and pity, resentment and commitment.

This ambivalence is particularly evident in the attitudes of upper status Mexicans toward the *indígenas* of Mexico.[10] *Indígenas* continue to be discriminated against for their cultural and ethnic identity while simultaneously admired for being the "real soul" of Mexico and proof of a noble past (Bartra 1974, 1987; Knight 1990). Images of the venerated cultures of the Aztecs and Mayans are regularly invoked as central icons of Mexican national identity. Reproductions of the great public art of those ancient cultures are ubiquitous in Mexico, appearing on nearly every public building, in company logos, and even on the national currency. The regional dances and dress of various indigenous groups are represented in every public pageant. This tendency to idealize indigenous material culture is particularly pronounced in Oaxaca and Chiapas, where tourism, a major industry of the area, relies on maintaining interest in the local indigenous crafts, culture, and archeological sites.

At the same time, disdain for the living *indígenas* is highly visible among middle and upper class Mexicans. Blatant expressions of ethnic prejudices are not uncommon, and the use of derogatory references to indigenous ethnicity are an accepted part of social life. For example, in discussing the illness of indigenous patients, medical staff frequently blame them for their own demise, citing their ignorance, filth, and erroneous beliefs.

Many studies have shown that educational, ethnic, and socioeconomic differences between patients and physicians profoundly influence clinical interaction and the course of treatment in cancer care (GIVIO 1986; Good 1988, 1990; Good et al. 1993; McIntosh 1974). As in most of Latin America, the Mexican physicians are primarily from the urban middle class (Collado Ardón 1976; Rubel 1990). Indeed, in this study the physicians were all from solidly middle-class families, whereas the patients they cared for included a great number of illiterate, rural poor, many of whom were *indígenas*. In the observations made for this study, these social differences interacted with the broader political-economic constraints of the health care bureaucracy and had an important effect on how physicians adapted and modified the health care system in their effort to treat cancer. These factors often resulted in serious practical and ethical problems. The way that cancer patients were treated in one provincial hospital in southern Mexico is used as an illustration.

## VISTA HERMOSA

The town of Vista Hermosa[11] is a market center of about 100,000 people in the southernmost part of Mexico. Its main health care institution is a secondary hospital, the Vista Hermosa General Hospital, which serves one of the poorest and least industrialized areas of Mexico. Its catchment area includes nearly 500,000 people, about 25% of whom are ethnically Mayan and maintain many Mayan traditions.

Because it is the most complete hospital in the area, the physicians at the Vista Hermosa Hospital handle referrals for a wide variety of conditions, including numerous cases of cancer. In the past 2 years, more than 350 cases of cancer were diagnosed and treated there by nonspecialized surgeons and internists.

The hospital is drastically underfunded and must rely on very limited resources and antiquated equipment. These limitations seriously undermine the staff's ability to address any illness, but make their efforts to manage cancer a particularly frustrating and futile undertaking. A larger hospital in the state capital 2 hours away is meant to offer specialized care for the state's population. In fact, however, the resources in that hospital are not much better than those of Vista Hermosa. For example, at the time of the research, there was only rudimentary x-ray equipment in the capital's hospital, no mammography or radiation therapy equipment, and no staff with the capacity to prescribe or administer chemotherapy. Thus the specialized techniques and personnel required for cancer management were available nowhere in the state.

A few patients each year are transferred from Vista Hermosa to well-equipped hospitals in Mexico City and other large cities, but support for such transfers has been quite limited. A trip of this kind presents an immense burden for patients and their families. For people who have little cash income, the cost of travel and related expenses can be prohibitive. Additionally, many poor rural people in this area fear Mexico City as a dangerous and confusing place. Families also are anxious that the patient not die far from home, where the costs of processing and transporting the deceased might be extremely high. For these reasons, the vast majority of cancer patients included in this study received only what limited care could be marshalled in the Vista Hermosa hospital itself.

The "front-line" physicians of Vista Hermosa had to make critical treatment decisions based on preliminary and rudimentary diagnostic information. Because the national health care plan included no explicit support or realistic recommendations for primary care physicians treating diseases like cancer, the treatment process relied completely on the innovations and adaptations of individual physicians and administrators. This gap allowed the cultural background and social prejudices of individual physicians implicitly to come into play in a central way, reflecting their assumptions about the intelligence, resources, and life options of patients. They often relied on culturally based moral and social concepts about the traditionalism and ignorance of patients to rationalize and explain the limited options on which they could count (Hunt 1992, 1994).

For example, the family of a young boy who had metastasized bone cancer and had recently lost a leg to the disease refused to take him to Mexico City for palliative radiation therapy, instead opting to bring him home against medical advice. From the staff's viewpoint, this reflected the family's inability to understand the medical diagnosis and recommended treatment. The staff thought the family's decision was rooted in their belief that witchcraft was a cause of the illness. The staff therefore made no effort to convince the family nor to find a way to help them make the trip, owing to their conclusion that the family had "given up" on medical treatment. However, the real reason for not seeking treatment in Mexico City was because the family had already spent everything they owned, including land and animals, in unsuccessful attempts to cure the child. Thus the family was simply unable to muster any more resources for the trip (Hunt 1993).

Another set of serious problems encountered in treating cancer patients in Vista Hermosa revolved around the use of surgical biopsy as a diagnostic tool. In the absence of mammography and other advanced diagnostic techniques, biopsy was one of the few procedures available for diagnosing tumoral cancer. However, biopsy results were often virtually useless in managing cases of cancer. The Vista Hermosa hospital had no pathology department, so specimens had to be sent to the public hospital in the state capital for analysis. It commonly took about 30 days to get a biopsy result. By then many patients had already died, and nearly all had returned to their villages without being informed of the findings.

Even if patients were to return to the hospital, there was no assurance that the biopsy result would be incorporated into their management. Owing to staffing shortages in the medical records department in Vista Hermosa, biopsy results were not normally filed with a patient's medical record. They were entered only when they were specifically requested by a physician. Often the attending physician was unaware that a biopsy had ever been performed and did not request the report. As a result, hundreds of biopsy reports were stacked in a drawer in medical records and never affected the treatment of the patient.

The seriousness of this practice can be seen in the following example. A young man, a 24-year-old farmer, had been brought to the hospital with abdominal pain and anal bleeding. He was thought likely to have gastric cancer, a common condition in southern Mexico (Halperin et al. 1988). A few months later, when reviewing the stack of biopsy reports, I learned that his biopsy had been negative and he did not have cancer. Coincidentally, a few days later the patient was readmitted to the hospital. He was being treated for suspected gastric cancer again, and a nurse pointed him out to me as a possible participant in my study. I recognized him as a patient I had already excluded because of his negative diagnosis and informed the unaware attending physician. Only then was the case management for this particular patient changed.

According to the physicians in the Vista Hermosa hospital, the lack of access to biopsy results is not a problem in treating patients. Accustomed to working without a pathology department, physicians are skilled at making diagnoses based only on clinical and surgical data. Despite being superfluous to patient care in this clinical setting, biopsies were regularly taken from cancer patients in Vista Hermosa. These patients were often in very advanced stages of disease. Many never recovered from the biopsy surgery and died shortly afterward. Even patients with more positive prognoses received little benefit from the biopsies, partly because patients and their families were rarely informed about the purpose of the surgery. As a result, many assumed that the biopsy had been a treatment for the disease. When the patient failed to improve, the family interpreted it as an indication that the treatment had failed and simply waited for the patient to die rather than bring him or her back to the hospital.

Another example provides an interesting contrast between a family's and medical staff's perceptions of a biopsy. The patient was a 64-year-old farmer from a small, remote village near the Guatemalan border. He had a very long history of severe abdominal pain and swelling. Eventually he was brought to the Vista Hermosa hospital, where a biopsy was performed and cancer of the liver was found. He became very ill, weak, and jaundiced following the procedure. The attending nurse said the family had been told that the patient would die if they took him home, but they didn't understand and brought him home anyway. In an interview with me 1 month after the biopsy, the family described the events quite differently. They called the procedure an "operation" (*operación*), rather than a "biopsy" (*biopsia*). Furthermore, the family had been told that the patient had a "grave illness," that it was cancer, which they believed was an incurable disease. The physicians were always in a big hurry and never stopped to explain anything. Seeing that the patient was extremely ill after the surgery and that the "operation" had not helped him, and believing that the physicians had already done all they could, the family took the patient out of the hospital so that he could die at home. He died 2 days after being brought home.

One may wonder why biopsies were performed with regularity at this hospital, given their marginal utility and associated danger. One reason is the lack of other options in addressing cancer. By virtue of biomedical training and professional responsibility, physicians face a moral mandate for action (Engelhardt 1974; Hahn 1985; Young 1976). They are impelled to act. However, in cancer treatment appropriate action is highly technology-dependent. Thus, in trying to diagnose and treat cancer in settings where technologies are simply unavailable, possible actions are quite limited in number. As there was no real access to advanced diagnostic techniques such as mammography or CAT scan and virtually no access to chemotherapy, radiation treatment, or advanced surgery, biopsies were conducted because they were one of the few concrete things that physicians had at their disposal.

## DISCUSSION

This chapter examines some of the ways that physicians in a poorly equipped hospital, far from the resource centers of the country, must adapt the system to address the special problems associated with cancer. No major overt adjustments have been made to the health care system to accommodate these diseases in the outlying areas of the country. This lack of concrete planning has resulted in reliance on the ad hoc decision making of "front-line" physicians.[12] By leaving this process implicit, the basis of screening and treating these diseases is left to the influence of local systems of knowledge, morality, social hierarchy, and political-economic power.

The limited scope of the present study does not make it possible to say whether the problems and processes observed in the management of cancer in southern Mexico can be generalized to other chronic degenerative diseases or to other geographic areas or socioeconomic situations. Yet, it is clear that in Mexico, as in the United States, high-level planning in the health care system continues to follow an agenda in which political and economic issues are often more central than a real concern for addressing the changing health care needs of a changing population. Any real adaptation to these changes requires a reorganization of the system into one capable of addressing two major issues: (1) directly confronting the special requirements of chronic degenerative disease like cancer and (2) providing adequate access to treatment to all sectors of the population.

## RECOMMENDATIONS

This chapter raises some difficult questions: How can diseases requiring tremendous resource investment be equitably dealt with by a country with a limited resource base? How can a medical system designed primarily for dealing with the pressing issues of acute infectious disease be efficiently and adequately adjusted to explicitly address the equally urgent needs surrounding the diagnosis and treatment of chronic degenerative disease? There are no simple answers, but a set of short-term solutions based on observations of successful adaptations made by oncologists, surgeons, and general physicians of southern Mexico is provided. Many of these strategies and adaptations, although clearly not optimal, may prove useful in generating short-term solutions to similar problems in other contexts.

A major problem encountered by physicians in similar regions is patients' frequent arrival in very advanced stages of illness. According to physicians, late diagnosis is caused in part by the rural and indigenous patients themselves, who spend much time with traditional folk medicine before consulting physicians. However, I found that most patients consulted with biomedical physicians soon after symptoms appeared, but often these local physicians were unable to diagnose cancer in its early stages. Misdiagnosis was quite common owing to lack of access to diagnostic techniques and poor training of local physicians in the early diagnosis of cancer. Tumors were often noted only when they became quite obvious. To help reduce this problem, visiting workshops could be held throughout the country for nonspecialist physicians working in small clinics. These workshops would be specifically set up to train physicians to recognize possible cancers using medical interview and physical examination rather than emphasizing the use of diagnostic equipment. In this way, more timely referrals could be made to specialty hospitals.

Another low-cost strategy to improve early diagnosis could be the use of mobile diagnostic units.[13] A limited number of specialized technicians and equipment could be made available to a wide geographic area on a rotating basis. Based on symptomatology, family history, and age, preliminary screening could be done by local physicians. At-risk people could then be gathered to maximize the benefit of the mobile unit's presence in a particular community. Again, this would enhance timely referrals to specialty hospitals.

Another serious problem in treating cancer in southern Mexico is the frequent failure of patients to return for test results or refusal to pursue treatment protocols. Many physicians assume that this is a result of patient ignorance or traditional fears and beliefs. However, in this study, patient misunderstandings or beliefs were rarely important barriers to complying with physicians' recommendations. Issues of access to technology and medications were much more important factors affecting compliance. Sensitivity to the magnitude of the social and economic resource demands placed on patients by treatment recommendations might help health care workers recognize some important barriers to treatment and encourage them to try to identify practical alternatives.

Access to radiation therapy and chemotherapy is quite limited in southern Mexico. To receive radiation therapy, patients must travel great distances and live for extended periods away from their homes. Unfortunately, there are no low-cost local remedies for this situation. Staff might try to develop specific strategies to facilitate and encourage patients to make the necessary trips for treatment. These include educating patient families about the value of the therapy, helping them overcome their fears of the city, and, perhaps most importantly, helping them identify and obtain resources for offsetting costs. For example, publicly supported housing accommodations (*albergues*) can sometimes be found near major hospitals. Furthermore, charitable organizations associated with some of the major hospitals have limited funds available to help cancer patients receive treatment. Information about these options can be gathered in advance by contacting the hospital social worker of the referral hospital.

A major problem for uninsured patients in Mexico, as in most countries, is the very high cost of chemotherapy drugs. Older protocols are sometimes less expensive and more easily obtainable than new or experimental treatments and may therefore sometimes be more feasible alternatives for treating patients with limited resources. Also, some patients are solely responsible for the support and maintenance of their family. Such persons often stop chemotherapy when they discover that they cannot care for their family because of debilitating side effects of the treatment or the need to travel to the hospital for treatment. For patients facing these problems, treatments with reduced side effects should be considered even if they are not the most effective available. Finally, more support staff could be trained throughout the country to administer and monitor chemotherapy protocols prescribed by specialists so that patients need not make frequent long journeys to receive treatment.

These recommendations suggest some ways that cancer treatment might be made less burdensome and more accessible, given the local conditions of areas like southern Mexico. The central theme of these strategies is placing a high priority on the development of culturally appropriate and economically efficient ways of diagnosing and treating illnesses in areas of scarce resources. Similar adjustments might be made for the short-term resolution of the problems encountered in treating other chronic degenerative diseases as well. Adaptations on this level, however, produce only stop-gap solutions. The increasing problem of treating chronic degenerative diseases like cancer in industrializing countries is a complex undertaking influenced by an intricate web of local, national, and international factors. Long-term solutions that genuinely address these issues require a major redistribution of resources and major adjustments in the overall strategy for health care delivery. A prerequisite to developing a health care strategy that would truly fulfill national commitments to universal health care is the development of explicit and realistic policies that include a real commitment to serving the needs of marginal populations suffering from chronic degenerative diseases.

## NOTES

1. In 1982 Mexico entered a serious economic crisis. Over the next 6 years the peso was drastically devalued, the national debt was 17% to 19% of the GNP, wages were reduced by more than 40% and inflation hovered around 150% annually (Selby et al. 1990). Initially, the government increased public services to compensate for the overall burden on the population. However, in recent years, they have drastically reduced health care spending.
2. Health statistics of all kinds are notably unreliable in Mexico. Except where otherwise noted, the figures cited in this section are approximations, based on readings of a number of sources citing inconsistent figures for 1978 through 1987 (Báez 1988; Finkler 1991; Gonzalez-Block 1988a, 1988b; Horn 1983; López Acuna 1987; Ovalle and Cantu 1985).
3. IMSS is by far the largest social insurance program, covering 80% of the nation's insured workers. ISSSTE ranks second, covering 17%. All other programs combined account for only 3% of the insured workers (INEGI 1993).
4. The SSA is the largest arm of the Mexican Public Health Ministry, which also includes a number of smaller programs. For simplicity in this chapter, when referring to the public assistance health sector, the author will use SSA unless it is not applicable.
5. For a review of this phenomenon both internationally and historically within Mexico, see Collado Ardón 1976.
6. IMSS, for example, has radiation equipment available in only seven cities of the nation. Their policy goal for 1991 was to have one machine for every 1 million people of the 17 million they serve. By 1990 they had exceeded this goal, having 20 machines, but these were concentrated in the wealthy cities of the north and around Mexico City. There was only one machine south of Mexico City, in Merida, Yucatan. Both a private and a public radiation clinic were under construction in the city of Oaxaca at the time the research was completed. However, on returning in 1991 for a visit, I found that neither had yet installed equipment or begun operations.
7. Many studies show that income inequality in Mexico is increasing with increased industrialization, indicating that the benefits of a growth economy are concentrated in the upper strata of society (Breu 1986; Felix 1983; Portes 1985; Selby et al. 1990).
8. During the colonial period, careful caste-like divisions based on race were maintained throughout the Spanish Empire in the New World. After Mexico won independence from Spain in 1821, official doctrine granted all citizens equality; however, a strong racist disposition persisted in Mexican law and policy. With the

Mexican revolution beginning in 1910, the *indígenas* were at once drawn into the ideology of resistance and reform and objectified and marginalized by the very policies meant to aid them. After 70 years of postrevolutionary *indígenista* policies, racism has declined in Mexico, but many real barriers exist. For a fascinating discussion of these historical trends and their intended and actual effects, see Knight 1990.

9. Knowing an indigenous language is generally taken as an indicator of indigenous ethnic identity in Mexican demographic studies. In the 1990 census, 40% of the state of Oaxaca and 27% of Chiapas were reported to speak an indigenous language. These are very high proportions, compared with 8% nationally and 2% in Mexico City (INEGI 1992).
10. For a review of relevant literature and an insightful critique, see Bartra 1987.
11. All proper names are pseudonyms.
12. I wish to stress that the physicians practicing in marginal hospitals like Vista Hermosa are profoundly ethical and professionally committed people. Their decision to work in an outlying area such as this attests to their moral commitment to provide service to a population in need, rather than work in the more comfortable, better paying hospitals of the major urban areas of the country. However, they are faced with serious contradictions between their professional mandate and possible action.
13. My thanks to Dr. Enrique Griego for this suggestion.

## REFERENCES

ALVAREZ, JOSÉ (ed.). 1974. *Enciclopedia de México,* Vol. 8. México D.F.: Enciclopedia de México, S.A.

BÁEZ, GUADALUPE. 1988. "Durante el Presente Sexenio han Disminuido Cerca de 40 Por Ciento los Gastos en Servicios de Salud." *Uno Más Uno,* June 13.

BARRY, TOM. 1992. *Mexico: A Country Guide.* Albuquerque: The Inter-Hemispheric Education Resource Center.

BARTRA, ROGER. 1974. "El Problema Indígena y la Ideología Indigenista." *Revista Mexicana de Sociología* 36:459–82.

______. 1987. *La Jaula de la Melancolía: Identidad y Metamorfosis del Mexicano.* México: Grijalbo.

BONFIL BATALLA, GUILLERMO. 1981. *Utopía y Revolución: El Pensamiento Político Contemporáneo de los Indios en América Latina.* México, D.F.: Editorial Nueva Imagen.

BREU, WERNER. 1986. "Growth in Inequality: The Case of Brazil and Mexico." *Latin American Research Review* 21:197–207.

CHEN, LINCOLN and RICHARD CASH. 1988. "A Decade after Alma Ata: Can Primary Health Care Lead to Health for All?" *New England Journal of Medicine* 319:946–47.

COLLADO ARDÓN, ROLANDO. 1976. *Médicos y Estructura Social. Fondo de Cultura Económica.* México, D.F.: UNAM.

ENGELHARDT, H. 1974. "Explanatory Models in Medicine: Facts, Theories and Values." Texas Reports on Biology & Medicine 32:225.

EVANS, JOHN et al. 1981. "Shattuck Lecture—Health Care in the Developing World: Problems of Scarcity and Choice." *New England Journal of Medicine* 305:1117–27.

FELIX, DAVID. 1983. "Income Distributions and the Quality of Life in Latin America." *Latin American Research Review* 18(2):3–33.

FINKLER, KAJA. 1991. *Physicians at Work, Patients in Pain: Biomedical Practice and Patient Response in Mexico.* Boulder, CO: Westview Press.

Frazier, Robert. 1981. "Progress in the Delivery of Health Care in Mexico." *Pediatrics* 67:155–57.

Friedlander, Judith. 1975. *Being Indian in Hueyapan: A Study of Forced Identity in Contemporary Mexico.* New York: St. Martin's Press.

GIVIO (International Group for Cancer Care Evaluation) Italy. 1986. "What Doctors Tell Patients with Breast Cancer about Diagnosis and Treatment: Findings from a Study in General Hospitals." *British Journal of Cancer* 54:319–26.

González-Block, Miguel Angel. 1988a. "Traslape de Demandes en el Sistema Nacional de Salud de México: Limitaciones en la Integración Sectorial." *Salud Publica Mexicana* 30:804–14.

______. 1988b. "Health Services Decentralization in Mexico: Policy. Relevant Aspects of its Formulation, Implementation and Results." Paper Presented at the Annual Meetings of the American Public Health Association.

Good, Mary-Jo DelVecchio. 1988. "The Practice of Biomedicine and the Discourse on Hope: A Preliminary Investigation into the Culture of American Oncology." Paper prepared for Anthropologies of Medicine: A Colloquium on West European and North American Perspectives. Hamburg, Germany.

______. 1990. "Oncology and Narrative Time." Paper presented at the Annual Meetings of the American Anthropological Association. New Orleans, LA.

Good, Mary-Jo DelVecchio, L. M. Hunt, T. Munakata, and Y. Kobayashi. 1993. "A Comparative Analysis of the Culture of Biomedicine: Disclosure and Consequences for Treatment in the Practice of Oncology." In *Health and Health Care in Developing Societies: Sociological Perspectives,* edited by P. Conrad and E. Gallagher. Philadelphia: Temple University Press.

Graham, Richard (ed.). 1990. *The Idea of Race in Latin America, 1870–1940.* Austin: University of Texas Press.

Hahn, Robert. 1985. "A World of Internal Medicine: Portrait of an Internist." In *Physicians of Western Medicine,* edited by R. Hahn and A. Gaines. Dordrecht, the Netherlands: D. Reidel Publishing Company.

Halperin, D. C., M. Belgrade, and A. Mohar. 1988. "Stomach Cancer Cluster in Mexico." *Lancet* 1(8593):1055.

Hernández Díaz, Jorge. 1988. *Ensayos Sobre la Cuestión Étnica en Oaxaca.* Oaxaca: Instituto de Investigaciones Sociológicos, Universidad Autónoma "Benito Juárez" de Oaxaca.

Horn, James. 1983. "The Mexican Revolution and Health Care, or the Health of the Mexican Revolution." *Latin American Research Perspectives* 10(4):24–39.

Hunt, Linda. 1992. "Living with Cancer in Oaxaca Mexico: Patient and Physician Perspectives in Cultural Context." Ph.D. dissertation. Cambridge, MA: Harvard University, Department of Anthropology.

______. 1993. "The Metastasis of Witchcraft: The Interrelationship between Traditional and Biomedical Concepts of Cancer in Southern Mexico." *Collegium Antropologicum* 17:249–56.

______. 1994. "Practicing Oncology in Provincial Mexico: A Narrative Analysis." *Social Science and Medicine* 38:843–53.

INEGI (Instituto Nacional de Estadística Geografía e Informática). 1993. "Información Estadística del Sector Salud y Seguridad Social." Cuaderno Núm. 9. Aguas Calientes, AGS, México: INEGI.

______. 1992. "XI Censo General de Población y Vivienda, 1990." Resumen General. Estados Unidos Mexicanos. Aguas Calientes, AGS, México:INEGI.

______. 1986. "X Censo General de Población y Vivienda, 1980." Resumen General. México, D.F.: INEGI.

INI (Instituto Nacional Indigenista). 1991. *Programa Nacional de Desarrollo de los Pueblos Indios 1991–1994.* México, D.F.: INI.

KNIGHT, ALAN. 1990. "Racism, Revolution and *Indigenismo*: Mexico 1910–1940." Pp. 71–113 in *The Idea of Race in Latin America, 1870–1940,* edited by R. Graham. Austin: University of Texas Press.

KUNZ, IGNACIO, MARIO CONTINA and M. A. GONZÁLEZ-BLOCK. 1986. *Regionalización Socioeconomico-Demográfica y de Salud de la República Mexicana.* México, D.F.: Secretaria de Salud.

LITVAK, JORGE et al. 1987. "The Growing Non-Communicable Disease Burden, a Challenge for the Countries of the Americas." Pan American Health Organization *Bulletin* 21:156–71.

LÓPEZ ACUÑA, DANIEL. 1987. *La Salud Desigual en México.* México, D.F.: Siglo Veintiuno Editores.

MCINTOSH, JIM. 1974. "Processes of Communication: Information Seeking and Control Associated with Cancer: A Selective Review of the Literature." *Social Science and Medicine* 8:167–90.

NAVARRO, VINCENT. 1982. "The Nature of Imperialism and Its Implications in Health and Medicine." In *Imperialism, Health and Medicine.* London: Pluto Press.

OVALLE FERNÁNDEZ, IGNACIO Y ARTURO CANTU (coordinadores). 1985. *Necesidades Esenciales en México: Situación Actual y Perspectivas al Año 2000.* México. D.F.: Siglo Veintiuno Editores.

PAHO (PAN AMERICAN HEALTH ORGANIZATION). 1990. *Health Conditions in the Americas,* Vol. I. Scientific Publication 524. Washington, DC: World Health Organization.

PORTES, ALEJANDRO. 1985. "Latin American Class Structure: Their Composition and Change During the Last Decades." *Latin American Research Review* 20:7–39.

PROGRAMA NACIONAL "MUJER, SALUD Y DESARROLLO." 1990. *La Salud de la Mujer en México.* México, D.F.: Secretaria de Salud.

RUBEL, ARTHUR. 1990. "Compulsory Medical Service and Primary Health Care: A Mexican Case. Pp. 137–53 in *Anthropology and Primary Health Care,* edited by J. Coreil and J. D. Mull. Boulder, CO: Westview Press.

SELBY, HENRY, ARTHUR MURPHY and STEPHEN LORENZEN. 1990. *The Mexican Urban Household.* Austin: University of Texas Press.

SEPÚLVEDA, BERNARDO (coordinador). 1981. *Seminario Sobre Problemas de la Medicina en México.* México, D.F.: El Colegio Nacional.

SHERRADEN, MARGARET SHERRARD and STEVEN WALLACE. 1992. "Innovation in Primary Care: Community Health Services in Mexico and the United States." *Social Science and Medicine* 35:1433–43.

*STATISTICAL ABSTACT OF LATIN AMERICA.* 1992. Vol. 29. Los Angeles: UCLA Latin America Center Publishers.

______. 1960. Vol. 4. Los Angeles: UCLA Latin America Center Publishers.

STEBBINS, K. R. 1986. "Politics, Economics and Health Services in Rural Oaxaca." *Human Organization* 45:112–19.

YOUNG, ALLAN. 1976. "Some Implications of Medical Beliefs and Practices for Social Anthropology." *American Anthropologist* 78:5.

ZSCHOSK, DIETER. 1986. "Medical Care Under Social Insurance in Latin America." *Latin American Research Review* 21:99–122.

Chapter 8

# Utilization and Cost of Maternal Child Health Services in Belize, Central America*

*Beth A. Macke and Sandra E. Paredez*

Belize, a small country located south of Mexico and east of Guatemala, is somewhat unique in Central America. Formerly British Honduras, Belize acquired its independence from Great Britain in 1981. Belize has a population of just under 200,000, one of the lowest population densities (persons per square mile) in the region (Central Statistical Office 1992). Most of inland Belize is forest and lacks an extensive network of all-weather roads. The government of Belize is patterned after the British system, consisting of a ceremonial head of state, a prime minister, an elected House of Representatives, and an appointed Senate, and it has been remarkably stable. Suffrage is granted to all adult citizens. The stability of the Belizean government is noteworthy because it is a major provider of maternal child health services.

## CULTURE

The population is composed of four major ethnic groups: Creoles, Mestizos, Garifuna, and Maya. The Creoles are principally African and English, the descendants of eighteenth- and early nineteenth-century slaves, African immi-

*We would like to acknowledge the contributions of Paul Stupp, Richard Monteith, Sylvan Roberts, and Leo Morris. The opinions expressed here are those of the authors and do not represent the Centers for Disease Control and Prevention, the Central Statistical Office of Belize, or the United States Agency for International Development.

grants, and British settlers (Bolland 1986). The Mestizos, primarily a mixture of Spanish and Indian (Grant 1976), have emigrated to Belize in waves over the past two centuries as a result of wars in neighboring countries (Bolland 1986; Everitt 1984; McCommon 1989). The Garifuna, or Black Carib, are a mixture of African and Carib Indians who were transported forcibly by the British from the Windward Islands to the area in 1796 (Gonzalez 1988). The Maya have been on Belizean soil from as early as 1500 B.C. but were devastated by early contact with Spanish explorers and British logcutters (Bolland 1977). Most of the Mopan and Kekchi Maya who inhabit Belize today have immigrated from Mexico or Guatemala over the past two centuries. The official language of Belize is English, which is taught in all schools. However, Spanish is spoken by an increasing percentage of the general population.

## ECONOMY

The major industries in Belize are agriculture, forestry, and fishing (Bolland 1986), but tourism is becoming an increasingly important part of the economy, especially on the coast. Because of Belize's small population, there is not a large enough market to sustain production of its own goods; therefore, Belize relies on imports. This contributes to a lack of employment opportunities, especially for women, and has resulted in a steady stream of Belizeans migrating to the United States to find work. As with most developing countries, Belize has a large foreign debt and is struggling for self-sufficiency. Consequently, resources for maternal child health services are scarce at both the individual family level and the government level. However, Belize has moved beyond the early stages of development, where demand for maternal child health services far exceeds those available, as its fertility rates have fallen to 4.5 per woman (Monteith et al. 1992) and its infant mortality rate is estimated to be 34 per 1,000 live births (Figueroa unpublished).

## WOMEN IN BELIZE

Women's economic and educational status is below that of men's (Barry 1992, p. 120) but generally higher than that of most of the surrounding Latin American countries. This is important because the health status of mother and children is correlated (both in the developed and developing world) with the economic and educational status of the parents, particularly that of the mother.

Underemployment, associated with the lack of opportunities for upward mobility, is a problem for Belizean women (*Belize Today* 1991). According to the 1991 Belize census, approximately 30% of the female adult population are currently in the labor force. Although the current female workforce participation rate for Belize seems low, it is consistent with rates found in neighboring countries (United Nations 1985). Almost half (45%) of the currently working women are in occupations that require some technical training such as typists and data entry clerks, whereas 44% are in jobs that require no formal training, such as housekeeping. Only 10% of working women are in professional jobs requiring education beyond grade 10. The median income for working Belizean adults (men and women) falls between BZ $5,760 and $7,199, or US $2,880 and $3,595 (Central Statistical Office 1992).

## BELIZE FAMILY HEALTH SURVEY

The field research for the Belize Family Health Survey was conducted by the Central Statistical Office of Belize in conjunction with the Ministry of Health of Belize, the Belize Family Life Association, with technical assistance from the Division of Reproductive Health of Centers for Disease Control and Prevention (CDC), and was funded by the United States Agency for International Development (USAID). This survey was the first maternal child health survey done in Belize with a pervasive national scope. The sample was a national household probability frame from which urban and rural domains were sampled independently. The interviews took 5 weeks to complete during January and February 1991, in which time 4,566 household were visited. Interviews were conducted with one woman between the ages of 15 and 44 in each household. Data were gathered on a variety of topics, including the demographic background of the respondent and her household, birth history, contraceptive use, and, where applicable, children's health. Complete interviews were obtained in 94% of the households that had an eligible respondent (N = 2,656), 1,790 being with women married or in consensual unions (Monteith et al. 1992).[1]

## BARRIERS TO SERVICE UTILIZATION

Principal barriers to health service utilization in developing countries are language, area of residence, education, and immigrant status. Each of these barriers is discussed in the Belizean context.

One barrier to receiving services in the Belizean context is language. Most health services in Belize are provided by English or Creole speakers; thus, Spanish, Garifuna, and Maya speakers may have difficulty in obtaining health care. In addition, more general cultural barriers may exist, especially for the Maya, whose norms discourage women from making decisions, including the seeking of care from outsiders, without approval from the male elders (Macke unpublished).

Area of residence can also be a factor in obtaining health services. Pre- and postnatal care, along with immunizations and treatment for acute respiratory illness and diarrhea, are provided to rural communities through mobile clinics every 6 weeks. This accounts for 40% of the service delivery in maternal child health care provided by the Ministry of Health (Figueroa unpublished). Nevertheless, the tropical terrain and lack of roads, especially all-weather roads, in rural areas may act as obstacles to rural women in obtaining health care. In good weather, it can sometimes take up to 8 hours to go 150 miles, and in rainy season some roads become impassable. According to the 1991 Belize census, the majority of the Maya (91%) and over half of the Mestizos (62%) live in rural Belize. In contrast, 69% of the Creoles and nearly 77% of the Garifuna live in urban areas (Central Statistical Office 1992). Therefore, if residence is a barrier to obtaining health care in Belize, this would necessarily affect the Maya the most and the Mestizo population to a lesser extent.

The Creole are the most educated of all the ethnic groups, with 26% having more than 8 years of formal education (Central Statistical Office 1992). They are followed by the Garifuna, 20% of whom have achieved more than 8 years of education. In contrast, only 14% of the Mestizos and 4% of the Maya reported having more than 8 years of education. Because education is positively correlated with the utilization of maternal child health services, the Mestizos and the Maya again may be at the greatest disadvantage.

Being born outside Belize may also be an obstacle to obtaining health care, especially if the immigrant does not understand how the government health system works or if the immigrant is an illegal alien who fears reprisal if he or she is discovered. According to the Family Health Survey, 31% of the Mestizos and nearly 10% of the Maya reported that they were born outside of Belize. The survey did not determine their legal status in Belize or how recently they had immigrated. Guatemala and El Salvador were the principal countries of birth among the Mestizos born outside of Belize, while Guatemala and Mexico were the principal countries of birth among the Maya.

## TRENDS IN UTILIZATION

### Prenatal Care

An overwhelming majority (96%) of survey respondents who have had a live birth within 5 years of interview had prenatal care. This proportion is constant for urban and rural women, women at all education levels, and women of all ethnic groups.

The majority of women who obtained prenatal care reported going to a government facility (87%). Rural women were only somewhat more likely to obtain care from a government facility (89% versus 85%). Less than 1% of either urban or rural women used a midwife/traditional birth assistant for prenatal care. Women with 9 or more years education, however, were three times as likely to get care from a private facility as were women with less than 7 years of education. Garifuna and Maya were more likely to use a government facility for prenatal care than a private facility. This may reflect a lack of private facilities in the areas where the Garifuna and Maya live.

The timing of the first prenatal visit is important because delaying care past the first trimester can increase the risk of complications for a pregnancy. Regarding timing, about 43% of women sought prenatal care in their first trimester and 43% in their second trimester. The rest of the respondents either waited until their third trimester or were unsure of the timing of their first visit. Three-fourths of the respondents made five or more prenatal care visits. The number of visits did not vary substantially by location of residence, years of education, or ethnicity, although urban women and women with secondary education reported a slightly higher number of visits.

### Delivery

Regarding location of birth, 70% of the respondents said that they delivered in a government hospital, 22% delivered in their home, and 6% delivered at a private hospital. Urban residents were much more likely to give birth in a hospital (90%) than were rural women (57%); a substantial number of rural women gave birth at home (40%). Only 4% of women with some secondary education delivered at home whereas 30% of women with less than 7 years of education delivered at home. About 90% of both Creole and Garifuna women delivered at a hospital, whereas 70% and 50% of the Mestizos and Maya, respectively, delivered at a hospital.

Nurse-midwives (60%) and traditional birth assistants (17%) assisted at the majority of births, whereas physicians assisted at 17% of births. This is not surprising, given the scarcity of physicians in developing countries. Nurse-midwives go to formal schooling whereas traditional birth assistants (TBAs) have more informal training. Both types of delivery assistants work in cooperation with the Ministry of Health as well as the local hospital, if there is one in the area. Approximately 80% of all TBAs have been trained and are monitored by the Ministry of Health. Creoles, Mestizos, and Garifuna have similar utilization patterns for nurses/TBAs versus doctors. The Maya, however, are only half as likely to have doctors assist at delivery as any other ethnic group.

### Postpartum Care and Newborn Check-Up

The majority of women reported that they did take their child for a newborn check-up (58%), whereas only a minority of women said that they had received postpartum care (40%). Rural women were less likely than urban women to have either a newborn check-up (40% versus 74%) or postpartum care (31% versus 48%). Women with secondary education were nearly twice as likely to get their newborn checked and to have postpartum care for themselves as women with less than 7 years of education. Mayas were the least likely to get a postpartum check-up (25%) or a newborn check-up (39%). The Creoles and the Garifuna were the most likely to report getting a postpartum check-up (55% and 56%) and a newborn check-up (79% and 78%); the proportion of Mestizos getting their newborn checked and postpartum care was 50% and 35%, respectively.

### Cost of Services

An attempt was made to ascertain costs of prenatal care and delivery expenses for the two most recent children of the respondent. To minimize recall bias, this discussion is limited to the most-recent child. Owing to extreme values for both prenatal and delivery expenses, the median instead of the arithmetic mean is used. Respondents were asked separately about the cost of their visits and medicines or vitamins, because visits to government facilities are free, whereas prenatal vitamins and medications must be bought, often at high prices, in the private sector. The overall median expense for visits and medicines together is BZ $115, or US $58. The most striking difference in prenatal care expense is between government and private prenatal care. Women using government facilities reported spending an average (median) of BZ $65 for prenatal care, whereas women using private facilities reported they spent BZ $250 on prenatal care. The sample size of women using traditional birth assistants or neither facility was too small to estimate a median cost.

The overall median for delivery expense is BZ $32. It is notable that the delivery expense did not vary by location of birth. For hospital births, the average expense was BZ $33; for home births, the average was BZ $30. Delivery expenses ranged from BZ $30 to BZ $36, irrespective of residence, education, ethnicity, or immigrant status. However, the expenses do vary significantly by the type of assistance at the birth. In births attended by medical doctors, the average delivery expense was BZ $95. In contrast, the cost of births attended by either a nurse-midwife or a lay midwife/traditional birth assistant was BZ $30. The obvious explanation is that doctors cost more. Alternatively, it may be that births attended by medical doctors are those with complications and therefore take more time and financial resources.

Rural women pay substantially less for their prenatal care, BZ $60, than do urban women (BZ $150). Given that only 5% more urban than rural women use private facilities, though, it may mean that care in urban areas, even when government facilities are used, is more expensive. An alternative explanation, supported by the data, is that urban women make more prenatal care visits and purchase more vitamins and medications than do rural women, thus incurring a higher cost. Rural residents, according to the Belize Census, have lower incomes than do urban residents, so they would have less to spend on care (Central Statistical Office 1992).

Women with less than a primary education, on average, pay BZ $75 for prenatal care, whereas women with 8 years of education pay BZ $98 and women with at least some secondary education pay BZ $183. This relationship can be explained in part by the positive relationship between number of visits and years of education and points out that more educated women are able to spend more on prenatal care and are able to make more visits, which can improve pregnancy outcomes, especially for high-risk pregnancies.

When examining costs by ethnic group, prenatal care utilization patterns are further elucidated. Creoles and Mestizos pay the most, on average, for prenatal care, BZ $108 and BZ $150, respectively, whereas Garifuna pay BZ $50 and Maya pay BZ $57. These costs reflect the differential utilization of government versus private facilities discussed earlier. It may be that the higher cost for the Mestizos relative to the Creole is due to higher transportation costs or higher rates of complications.

Immigrants paid, on average, BZ $144 for prenatal care versus Belizean natives who paid BZ $111. It is not clear from the data why immigrants would pay more, because they have the same utilization patterns in terms of source of prenatal care as natives. It is possible that immigrants have more complications or high-risk pregnancies, which are costlier.

### Determinants of Utilization

Because prenatal care is nearly universal in this sample, no analyses of determinants of prenatal care utilization could be carried out. However, predictors of utilization of hospital births, postpartum check-up, and newborn check-up were analyzed in a previous work (Stupp et al. 1993). All else being equal, Mayans who speak Maya (as opposed to Spanish), immigrants, and rural residents were significantly less likely to give birth in a hospital. Conversely, women with secondary education were significantly more likely to give birth in a hospital. Although Spanish-speaking Mestizos and Spanish-speaking Mayas were just as likely to deliver in a hospital as the Creoles, they were significantly less likely to get either a postpartum check-up for themselves or a check-up for their baby. Rural women were no different from urban women in terms of the postpartum check-up but were significantly less likely to get a newborn check-up. Women with some secondary education were more likely to get a postpartum check-up and a newborn check-up.

These analyses highlight several important points. One is that, although Spanish speakers have no apparent problems in obtaining prenatal care or hospital delivery, there seems to be some type of barrier in terms of postpartum and newborn care, although the nature of this barrier cannot be determined from the data at hand. One possibility is that these services are not accessible to Spanish speakers; another is that using these services is not the norm for Spanish speakers. That Maya are significantly less likely to deliver in a hospital also points to possible access and/or cultural barriers. The same may be said for immigrants.

Secondary education, on the other hand, is a clear positive predictor of service utilization. This may be due to increased resources to spend on such care or an increased awareness of the importance of care.

## SUMMARY

This chapter gives the reader an overview of the utilization patterns and cost of maternal child health services in Belize. One strength of the survey and census data used here is that it is representative of the population at hand. These data enable us to get a look at the overall picture of health services, such as the critical role that government facilities and midwives play in the provision of affordable health care for Belizean women. In addition, the data show that residence location, ethnicity, education, and immigrant status are also associated with the likelihood of using maternal child health services. However, there are limitations. For instance, the exact explanation for the large increase in delivery expenses by type of assistance at birth cannot be known from these data. Nor can we know the reason why Maya-speaking Maya are less likely than other cultural groups to deliver in a hospital or why Spanish speakers are less likely than Creole speakers to get a postpartum check-up or newborn check-up. Qualitative research must be conducted at the organizational, that is, health center and community, level to answer these questions in depth (Moss et al. 1992). However, the difficult climate and terrain make any study difficult, and the country's economic situation means that internal resources for such research are extremely limited. Nevertheless, to improve access to and utilization of maternal child health services in Belize, more queries are needed.

## NOTE

1. Because each woman's probability of selection was inversely proportional to the number of eligible women in the household, the responses have been weighted to compensate for their unequal probability of selection.

## REFERENCES

BARRY, TOM. 1992. *Inside Belize.* Albuquerque, NM: The Inter-Hemispheric Education Resource Center.

BELIZE TODAY. 1991. "Women Gain Recognition." *Belize Today* 5(11/12):28–29.

BOLLAND, NIGEL O. 1977. *The Formation of a Colonial Society.* Baltimore, MD: Johns Hopkins University Press.

______. 1986. *Belize.* Boulder, CO: Westview Press.

CENTRAL STATISTICAL OFFICE. 1992. *1991 Population Census: Major Findings.* Belmopan, Belize: Government Printery.

EVERITT, JOHN C. 1984. "The Recent Migrations of Belize, Central America." *International Migration Review* 18:319–25.

FIGUEROA, RAMON. Unpublished. Data from the 1992 Maternal and Child Health Department, Ministry of Health, Belize City, Belize.

GONZALEZ, NANCIE L. 1988. *Ethnogenesis and Ethnohistory of the Garifuna.* Urbana: University of Illinois.

GRANT, C. H. 1976. *The Making of Modern Belize.* New York: Cambridge University Press.

MACKE, BETH A. Unpublished. Field notes.

MCCOMMON, CAROLYN S. 1989. "Refugees in Belize: A Cauldron of Ethnic Tensions." In *Conflict, Migration and the Expression of Ethnicity,* edited by N. L. Gonzalez and C. S. McCommon. Boulder, CO: Westview Press.

MONTEITH, RICHARD S., PAUL W. STUPP, BETH A. MACKE, and SANDRA PAREDEZ. 1992. *Belize: 1991 Family Health Survey, Final Report.* Atlanta, GA: U.S. Centers for Disease Control.

MOSS, NANCY, MICHAEL C. STONE, and JASON B. SMITH. 1992. "Child Health Outcomes Among Central American Refugees and Immigrants in Belize." *Social Science and Medicine* 34(2):161–67.

STUPP, PAUL W., BETH A. MACKE, RICHARD MONTEITH, and SANDRA PAREDEZ. 1993. "Ethnicity and the Use of Health Services in Belize." *Journal of Biosocial Science* 26:165–177.

UNITED NATIONS. 1985. *Women's Employment and Fertility.* New York: United Nations.

Chapter 9

# Hepatitis B in Taiwan and the United States: A Sociologic Analysis of Comparative Risk Factors and Efforts at Control

*Shu-Fen Tseng and Richard E. Barrett*

The hepatitis B virus (HBV) is blood-borne and has modes of transmission similar to the human immunodeficiency virus (HIV). A general recognition of the risk of HBV infection has come about recently in the United States. In general, the potential for HBV transmission is much greater than for HIV transmission. For example, in the workplace, the risk of infection with HIV following one needle-stick exposure to blood from a patient known to be infected with HIV is approximately 0.5%, compared with a 6% to 30% risk of infection for persons who receive one needle-stick exposure from an HBV-positive person (CDC 1989a).

HBV infection is particularly important because those who become HBV carriers are at high risk for liver diseases. An especially important manifestation of chronic HBV infection is hepatocellular carcinoma (HCC), a disease that is very common in Africa, China, and Southeast Asia. A strong correlation has been shown between HCC and HBV infection or carriage in both high- and low-prevalence areas of the world (Pastorek 1989). In a prospective study of 22,707 men in Taiwan, Beasley (1988) found that the risk of HCC is much higher in HBV carriers than in noncarriers, and the relative risk for HBV carriers to develop HCC is 98.4 times higher than for noncarriers. Worldwide, HBV is probably the causative agent for 75% to 90% of primary liver cancers (Beasley 1988). In addition, chronic carriers with chronic active hepatitis

(CAH) may go on to suffer cirrhosis, hepatic failure, and early mortality from liver disease (Pastorek 1989).

There are estimated to be more than 300 million carriers of HBV worldwide (Maynard 1990; Sherlock 1990). The infection rate and transmission patterns of HBV vary markedly in various parts of the world. The endemicity of HBV infection can be considered high in those areas of the world where the prevalence of HBsAg (hepatitis B surface antigen) is 8% to 15% and where 70% to 95% of the population have serologic evidence of previous infection. These highly endemic areas include China, Southeast Asia, sub-Saharan Africa, Pacific islands, parts of the Middle East, and South America. In most developed parts of the world (North America, western Europe, and Australia), HBV infection is a disease of low endemicity, and the overall prevalence of HBV infection is relatively low, with HBsAg chronic carrier rates of less than 1% and overall infection rates of 4% to 6%. The remaining parts of the world, such as eastern Europe, the Mediterranean countries, and the former Soviet Union, fall into intermediate endemicity levels, with HBsAg prevalence of 2% to 7% and overall prevalence of infection of 20% to 55% (CDC 1990a; Hadler and Margolis 1989).

In the United States, an estimated 200,000 to 300,000 HBV infections occur each year, and about 18,000 to 30,000 (6% to 10%) of these persons become HBV chronic carriers. Some 75,000 infected persons develop symptomatic jaundice, and 15,000 of them are hospitalized. Currently, the United States contains an estimated pool of 1 to 1.25 million infectious carriers. Each year, an estimated 4,000 persons die from HBV-related cirrhosis, and more than 800 die from HBV related cancer (CDC 1990a, 1991a). HBV carriers have the potential to infect more contacts than HIV carriers because (1) HBV is easier to transmit than HIV, and (2) the life span of HBV carriers is usually far longer than that of HIV carriers, giving them a far larger possible network of contacts.

In Taiwan, infections with HBV are common. The prevalence of HBsAg is 15% to 20% in the general population, one of the highest rates in the world. HCC has been the leading cause of death from cancer, with an annual (1988) mortality rate of 18.5 per 100,000 population. Furthermore, cirrhosis is the seventh leading cause of death, with 17.8 deaths per 100,000 population in 1988 (R.O.C. Department of Health 1989). More than 80% of patients with cirrhosis of the liver or HCC are HBsAg positive (Chen et al. 1987). HBV infection has been an extremely important health issue in Taiwan.

## THE DEMOGRAPHIC CHARACTERISTICS OF HBV INFECTION

### United States

In the United States, reported cases of HBV infection steadily increased from 1966 to 1985. After reaching a peak in 1985, there have been only slight declines in the last several years. Until 1988, the western region experienced higher overall rates than other regions, while the Midwest consistently reported the lowest regional incidence rate. Since 1985, a general decrease has characterized all regions, with the sharpest decline occurring in the West (CDC 1992).

In 1978, 15,016 cases of clinical hepatitis B were reported to the Centers for Disease Control (CDC), an incidence rate of 6.9 per 100,000 people. At that time, CDC estimated that 200,000 HBV infections, including 50,000 clinical cases with jaundice, had occurred in 1978. The reported incidence of disease increased to 9.2 per 100,000 in 1981, the year before the hepatitis B vaccine became available, and it continued to increase during the first 4 years of vaccine availability, reaching a peak of 11.5 per 100,000 in 1985, with an estimated 300,000 new infections per year. After the steady increase of HBV infection, the reported incidence of hepatitis B declined 18% to 9.4 per 100,000 in 1989 (CDC 1992). Compared with the history of other vaccine-preventable diseases, the results of introducing hepatitis B vaccine to reduce HBV infection is disappointing. For example, the incidence of reported measles cases decreased rapidly after measles vaccine was licensed in 1963. By 1968, the number of measles cases had dropped to 5% of prevaccine levels (Markowitz et al. 1989).

In the United States, HBV infection is highly prevalent in certain groups. Most HBV infections occur among adolescents and adults. These infections are highly associated with risk behaviors, such as intravenous drug use, homosexual activity, and active heterosexual activity with multiple partners. Infections among people aged 15 to 39 account for about 80% of all cases. For children less than 10 years old, the infection rate is extremely low; they comprise less than 1% of all cases, which suggests little mother-infant vertical transmission or horizontal transmission among children in the United States (Table 9–1). However, infants often acquire the infection subclinically and may never be reported.

No gender difference exists in susceptibility to infection among children, and the risk of becoming an HBV chronic carrier among children is equal in boys and girls. However, there is a predominance of male chronic carriers among adults (Hadler 1989). The male-to-female ratio of hepatitis B cases is about 1.5:1 (Table 9–2), which may result from an overrepresentation of males in those groups at high risk of acquiring the HBV infection, such as intravenous drug abusers and homosexual men.

The rates of HBV infection differ significantly among various racial and ethnic groups (Table 9–3). In 1980, the reported rates of HBV infection were 74.5% in whites and 18.4% in blacks. In 1989, the rates changed to 62.4% and 21.6%, respectively. Generally, there is a declining trend among whites and an increasing trend among blacks. Hepatitis B is the predominant type of hepatitis among blacks, accounting for 53% of all cases (CDC 1992). In the Second National Health and Nutrition Examination Survey (NHANES II), serologic markers of HBV infection were found in 3.2% of white participants and 13.7% of black participants. In addition, the prevalence of HBV carriers per 1,000 was 1.9 for whites and 8.5 for blacks (CDC 1989b).

Looking at the factors of race, gender, and age among all HBV cases, we

**TABLE 9–1. Percentage Distribution of HBV Reported Cases by Age, United States, 1982–1989**

| *AGE* | *1982* | *1983* | *1985* | *1987* | *1988* | *1989* |
|---|---|---|---|---|---|---|
| <5 | 0.5 | 0.5 | 0.4 | 0.4 | 0.4 | 0.4 |
| 5–9 | 0.5 | 0.5 | 0.3 | 0.4 | 0.4 | 0.5 |
| 10–14 | 0.8 | 0.6 | 0.7 | 0.7 | 0.7 | 0.8 |
| 15–19 | 10.2 | 8.7 | 8.8 | 8.9 | 8.6 | 8.5 |
| 20–29 | 46.6 | 45.3 | 48.4 | 46.5 | 44.1 | 42.3 |
| 30–39 | 19.2 | 20.2 | 21.8 | 24.8 | 26.4 | 27.8 |
| 40–49 | 8.1 | 8.1 | 7.8 | 8.4 | 9.3 | 9.8 |
| 50–59 | 5.9 | 5.6 | 4.8 | 4.5 | 4.2 | 4.3 |
| 60+ | 6.6 | 6.5 | 5.8 | 4.7 | 4.9 | 4.4 |
| Unknown | 1.6 | 4.1 | 1.4 | 1.0 | 1.1 | 1.0 |
| TOTAL | 100.0 | 100.1 | 100.2 | 100.3 | 100.1 | 99.8 |

Note: Percentages may not exactly total 100 because of rounding.
Source: Centers for Disease Control, Hepatitis Surveillance, 1982–1989

find that blacks, males, and persons between the ages of 20 and 39 have the highest risk of acquiring HBV infection in the United States. In addition, persons born in areas of high HBV endemicity and their descendants also remain at high risk of infection. A screening for HBV infection among refugees arriving in the United States from 1979 to 1991 shows that the crude prevalence rates of HBsAg were highest among refugees from Southeast Asia, with prevalence rates of 15.5% among Laotians, 15.2% among Cambodians, 14.2% among Thais, and 13.8% among Vietnamese (CDC 1991b). Another study indicates that prevalence of HBsAg in pregnant Asian-American women is highest among Chinese, Taiwanese, and Hong Kong immigrants, and that there was an 11.4% prevalence rate among all Asian-American women (Stevens et al. 1985). HBV is highly endemic in other populations as well, such as Alaskan Natives and Pacific Islanders, with an 8% to 15% HBV prevalence rate (CDC 1990a).

**TABLE 9–2. Percentage of HBV Reported Cases by Gender, United States, 1980–1989**

| *SEX* | *1980* | *1982* | *1983* | *1985* | *1987* | *1988* | *1989* |
|---|---|---|---|---|---|---|---|
| Male | 62.4 | 62.1 | 61.1 | 60.7 | 59.7 | 59.0 | 57.5 |
| Female | 37.6 | 37.0 | 36.6 | 37.4 | 38.6 | 38.9 | 40.5 |
| Unknown | — | 0.9 | 2.3 | 1.9 | 1.7 | 2.1 | 2.0 |
| TOTAL | 100.0 | 100.0 | 100.0 | 100.0 | 100.0 | 100.0 | 100.0 |

Source of data: Centers for Disease Control, Hepatitis Surveillance, 1980–1989

**TABLE 9–3. Percentage of HBV Reported Cases by Race and Ethnic Group, United States, 1980–1989**

| *RACE* | *1980* | *1982* | *1983* | *1985* | *1987* | *1988* | *1989* |
|---|---|---|---|---|---|---|---|
| White | 74.5 | 64.6 | 65.4 | 66.1 | 62.4 | 62.0 | 62.4 |
| Black | 18.4 | 19.7 | 19.0 | 18.4 | 19.9 | 21.5 | 21.6 |
| Hispanic | — | 4.2 | 4.4 | 4.7 | 7.1 | 5.4 | 5.1 |
| Other and unknown | 7.1 | 11.6 | 11.2 | 10.8 | 10.6 | 11.1 | 10.9 |
| TOTAL | 100.0 | 100.1 | 100.0 | 100.0 | 100.0 | 100.0 | 100.0 |

Note: Percentages may not exactly total 100 because of rounding.
Source of data: Centers for Disease Control, Hepatitis Surveillance, 1980–1989

### Taiwan

In Taiwan, the prevalence of HBV infection (HBsAg) rises from birth and peaks between 8 and 12 years of age. The age-specific prevalence curve for antibody to HBsAg (anti-HBs indicates past infection with and immunity to HBV) also rises from birth, with a peak of 70% at about 10 years of age. It is clear that in Taiwan individuals are at high risk from a very early age. Prevention of HBV is important not only because of the high incidence of HBV infection in young children, but also because the probability of becoming a HBV carrier is inversely related to age. Moreover, carriers are at high risk of developing HCC (Beasley et al. 1981, 1982). There was no relation between the presence of HBV markers and gender. However, among those who had been infected with HBV, the frequency of HBsAg was higher in males than in females, although this difference was not statistically significant (Beasley et al. 1982). Additionally, there was a much higher incidence of liver-related diseases among males. The male-to-female ratios of HCC and cirrhosis were 4:1 and 3:1, respectively (R.O.C. Department of Health 1989).

## ROUTES OF HBV TRANSMISSION

### United States

Certain lifestyles result in acquisition of the HBV infection and high rates of infection. Intravenous drug use and contact with another person infected with HBV (primarily sexual and sometimes household contacts) have been the two most frequently reported risk factors since 1984 (Table 9–4). The percentage of HBV persons reporting intravenous drug use in 1989 (24%) was similar to that reported in 1987 and 1988 but represents a dramatic increase since 1983. Intravenous drug users have shown the highest HBV infection rates in the United States, with more than 65% positive for HBV markers (Piot et al. 1990).

**TABLE 9–4. Crude Frequency of HBV Reported Cases by Potential Sources, United States, 1982–1989**

| *RISK FACTORS* | *1982* | *1983* | *1985* | *1987* | *1988* | *1989* |
|---|---|---|---|---|---|---|
| Parenteral drug use | 13.5 | 12.7 | 19.5 | 24.6 | 24.6 | 24.2 |
| Personal contact with HBV patient | 14.6 | 14.8 | 19.7 | 20.6 | 19.4 | 19.6 |
| Homosexual activity | 7.8 | 8.7 | 9.7 | 7.8 | 7.0 | 6.6 |
| Medical employment | 8.1 | 6.9 | 6.5 | 4.9 | 4.6 | 4.5 |
| Blood transfusion | 3.9 | 3.5 | 3.2 | 1.4 | 1.6 | 1.6 |
| Dental work | 14.5 | 13.7 | 16.0 | 14.1 | 13.5 | 13.0 |
| Surgery | 7.0 | 6.7 | 8.7 | 6.7 | 6.7 | 6.2 |
| Prior hospitalization | 14.4 | 14.4 | 16.0 | 14.2 | 14.9 | 14.0 |
| Other percutaneous exposures | 16.6 | 15.3 | 18.7 | 16.1 | 14.9 | 15.0 |
| TOTAL | 100.4 | 96.7 | 118.0 | 110.4 | 107.2 | 104.7 |

Note: Risk factors are not mutually exclusive and hence may total more than 100%.
Source of data: Centers for Disease Control, Hepatitis Surveillance, 1982–1989

The percentage reporting personal contact with another infected person (mostly sexual contact) increased about 30% from 1983 to 1989, with about 20% of reported cases in 1989. Heterosexuals with multiple partners have replaced homosexual men in importance as a risk group. Risk of infection increases with number of sexual partners, number of years of sexual activity, and history of other sexually transmitted diseases (Alter et al. 1989; Margolis et al. 1991; Piot et al. 1990; Rosenblum et al. 1990). Although sex partners and household contacts of infected persons are known to be at increased risk of HBV, casual nonhousehold contact is not known to result in transmission (CDC 1992).

Declines in the other reported risk factors—homosexual activity, health care employment, and blood transfusion—continued in 1989. Homosexual activity, reported by 6.6% of cases, was at its lowest point since 1984. For homosexual men, the decline since 1985 continued a trend that has been attributed to behavioral changes in the face of increasing incidence of HIV infection. Health care employment declined from about 6% to 4.5% of all HBV cases between 1984 and 1989. The reduction in hepatitis B among health care workers appears to be attributable to the use of HBV vaccine and to greater precautions taken by health care workers to prevent the spread of HIV, such as greater use of masks and gloves, more care in the disposal of used syringes, and so on. Transfusion-associated HBV declined very slightly in 1989 from its 1988 level, continuing the slow, steady decline begun in 1983. This decrease provides evidence of continued success in improving the safety of the blood supply in the United States through serologic screening and exclusion of high-risk donors (CDC 1992).

Another trend that needs to be noted is that of medical-related events, such as prior hospitalization, dental work, and surgery. Some studies indicate that 10% to 30% of health care professionals or dental workers show serologic evidence of past or present HBV infection (CDC 1989a); however, studies also suggest that the proportion of HBV cases attributable to provider-to-patient HBV transmission is very low (Hadler 1990). The mechanism of how these events relate to HBV infection is still unclear and needs to be further explored.

Trends in the reported risk factors for hepatitis B differ in important respects between males and females. Among males, intravenous drug use, homosexual activity, and contact with another infected person have been the most common risk factors. After an approximately 50% increase from 1983 to 1988, the proportion of men reporting intravenous drug use decreased by 2% in 1989. The proportion of men reporting personal (including sexual and household) contact with another infected person increased almost 30% from 1983 to 1989. The percentages of male patients reporting each of the following risk factors declined between 1983 and 1988: homosexual activity, health care employment, and blood transfusion. Among females, intravenous drug use and personal contact with a HBV patient have been the most frequent risk factors, each accounting for as many as 19% of cases and showing approximately 63% and 33% increases, respectively, from 1983 to 1989. The decrease in the percentage of females reporting medical and dental employment is more pronounced than that for males (CDC 1992).

The same trends in both males and females have been observed in the Sentinel Counties Study. The Sentinel Counties Study concludes that for males, a decline in importance of homosexual activity and an increase in the importance of intravenous drug use and heterosexual exposure can be seen recently. For females, heterosexual contact with an HBV-infected person was the most common risk factor reported in all years, although intravenous drug use, which increased over time, was also an important risk factor. The decline in health care employment as a risk factor for HBV is most prominent among females (Alter et al. 1990).

HBV among children younger than 15 years is associated primarily with personal contact with another infected person. A small percentage of these children reported drug use as the primary risk factor (CDC 1992). During the mid-1980s, heterosexual exposure was the major risk factor for HBV infection for persons of either gender aged 45 or over. Intravenous drug use was uncommon in this group, but homosexual activity, health care employment, and transfusions accounted for substantial numbers of cases from 1982 through 1985. Declining numbers of cases were reported in these three risk groups after that time. Another important issue of HBV infection is that at least 30% of patients cannot be associated with an identifiable risk factor and therefore are difficult to reach in vaccination programs aimed at groups at high risk. These patients tend to belong to minority populations and have characteristics associate with low socioeconomic level. In the Sentinel Counties Study, blacks, Hispanics, and other groups who had no source for HBV infection were more likely than whites to be unemployed (Alter et al. 1990).

### Taiwan

In Taiwan, perinatal mother-to-child HBV infection (vertical transmission) plays a key role in maintaining chronic carriage of HBsAg from generation to generation. There is a strong relationship between the presence of HBV markers in the child and HBsAg positivity in the mother (Beasley 1982). It has been shown that 40% to 50% of infants born to HBsAg-carrier mothers will also become chronic carriers early in life (Hsu et al. 1988). In addition, a strong correlation was found between HBeAg positivity of the serum of HBsAg-carrier women in Taiwan and the subsequent development of surface antigenemia in their babies (Stevens et al. 1979). That is, the infants at highest risk are those born to HBsAg-carrier mothers who are also hepatitis B e-antigen (HBeAg) positive or who have a high titer of HBsAg. These infants have an 86% to 96% chance of becoming chronic HBV carriers (Beasely et al. 1977; Chen et al. 1987; Hsu et al. 1988).

One follow-up study indicates that besides vertical infection, there is a significant correlation between the frequency of injections of medicine and the incidence of HBV infections. This study suggests that injection equipment in local clinics might frequently be inadequately sterilized. Treatment by injection is popular in Asia, and Taiwan is no exception. As medical practice is frequently carried out in small clinics, some injections are given without adequate sterilization of the equipment between use, with a resulting high incidence of HBV infection (Beasley et al. 1982). However, the relationship between frequency of injections of medicine and HBV infection needs to be explored further.

## HEPATITIS B PREVENTION

### United States

In the United States, the HB vaccine has been available since 1982. No current medical treatment reliably eliminates chronic HBV infection and thus eliminates the source of new infections in susceptible persons. Therefore, new infections can be prevented only by immunizing susceptible persons. In the United States, most HBV infections occur among adults and adolescents, so the recommended strategy for preventing these infections has been the selective vaccination of persons with identified risk factors. However, this strategy has not lowered the incidence of HBV infection. Nationwide, the incidence of HBV infection increased by 67% from 1978 to 1985, with slight declines in the last several years. In 1990 the incidence of HBV infection was greater than that in the years just prior to licensure of the vaccine (AAP 1992a). The CDC claims that this selective strategy failed primarily because high-risk behaviors (intravenous drug abuse, multiple and active heterosexual activities, and homosexual activities) are not easily defined or detected, and those most likely to be in jeopardy may be least likely to receive preventive health care. It has been shown that intravenous drug abusers and active heterosexual persons are extremely difficult to reach, as is the delivery of the HBV vaccine to them (CDC 1990b). In addition, many infected persons have no identifiable source for their infections and thus cannot be targeted for vaccination (AAP 1992a; CDC 1991a).

Furthermore, health care providers are often not aware of groups at high risk of HBV infection and frequently do not identify candidates for vaccination during routine health care visits. In addition, studies show that there has been only limited vaccination of susceptible household and sexual contacts of HBsAg carriers identified in screening programs for blood donors (CDC 1991a). The major group using the vaccine has been health care workers, who account for less than 5% of reported cases. It apparently has had little effect on overall rates of HBV infection.

In 1984, the Immunization Practices Advisory Committee (ACIP) recommended that pregnant women in certain groups at high risk for HBV infection should be screened for HBsAg during a prenatal visit. If they were found to HBsAg-positive, their newborns should receive hepatitis B immune globulin (HBIG) and hepatitis B vaccine at birth. However, several studies and the experience of public health workers indicate that major problems have been encountered in implementing these recommendations. First, only 35% to 65% of HBsAg-positive mothers would have been identified by these ACIP guidelines. Second, many health care providers are too busy or may be reluctant to obtain the sexual and drug-use history necessary to identify high-risk patients for screening. In addition, persons providing health care to pregnant women often are not aware of the risks of perinatal transmission of HBV and of the recommended screening and treatment guidelines. One study shows that 40% of obstetricians could name no more than two groups at high risk for HBV infection, and only 28% knew the recommended treatment for infants born to HBV carrier mothers (CDC 1988).

Because screening selected pregnant women for HBsAg has failed to identify a high proportion of HBV-infected mothers, prenatal HBsAg testing of all pregnant women is now recommended (CDC 1988, 1990a, 1991a). More than 90% of prenatal infections can be prevented if HBsAg-positive mothers are identified so that their infants can receive the HBV vaccine and HBIG soon after birth. Annually, universal prenatal testing would identify an estimated 22,000 HBsAg-positive women and could prevent at least 6,000 chronic HBV infections (CDC 1991a).

Because of the failure of targeting high-risk adolescents and adults, the Immunization Practices Advisory Committee (ACIP) of the CDC and the American Academy of Pediatrics (AAP) Committee on Infectious Diseases recommend universal infant vaccination for controlling HBV infection recently.

The AAP and ACIP argue that the current feasibility of capturing all adolescents for three doses of vaccine over 6 months is low, and the least accessible adolescents may be those most at risk (AAP 1992a, 1992b). Besides, the probability of becoming an HBsAg carrier is inversely related to age; therefore, both AAP and ACIP conclude that the HBV prevention program requires a new approach. They insist that universal infant immunization is required and should include immunization of adolescents whenever resources permit. The AAP recognizes that in areas where resources are limited, universal infant immunization should be given priority (AAP 1992a).

### Taiwan

A nationwide HBV vaccination program was launched by Department of Health in Taiwan in 1984. In addition to the vaccination program, the Department of Health also supervised the screening of the blood supply for the HBV marker among hospitals and clinics to prevent HBV infection by transfusion (R.O.C. Department of Health 1984). The vaccination program started with newborns of HBsAg-carrier mothers. In July 1986, the program was extended to all newborns; in 1988 preschool children were included; and in 1990, school-age children and adolescents were also included. Vaccination among college students and adults became the focus of this program in 1992 (R.O.C. Department of Health 1992). During the early stage of the program, 352,721 of 450,585 pregnant women nationwide were screened for HBsAg, an overall rate of 78%. The prevalence of HBsAg pregnant women in all areas was 18%. Among the 62,359 pregnant HBV carriers identified, about 50% of them were classified as highly infectious (HBeAg). Of infants born to highly infectious carrier mothers, 77% received hepatitis B immune globulin within 24 hours after birth. The coverage of all susceptible infants receiving the first, second, third, and fourth booster doses of vaccine was 88%, 86%, 84%, and 71%, respectively. To evaluate the mass HBV vaccination program in Taiwan, the vaccine efficacy was measured in a serologic study (Hsu et al. 1988). Among infants who were born to highly infectious mothers and who received hepatitis B immune globulin and vaccine on schedule, the HBsAg positivity rate was 14%, far less than the HBsAg carrier rate of 86% to 96% in infants who were not immunized, indicating that the protective efficacy was about 85%. For immunized infants born to less infectious carrier mothers, the HBsAg positivity rate was 4%, compared with 10% to 21% of unvaccinated infants (Hsu et al. 1988; R.O.C. Department of Health 1987).

A follow-up seroepidemiologic study was conducted in 1989 in a Taipei district to study the impact of this ongoing vaccination program on HBV infection among children. A baseline seroepidemiologic study of HBV infection in children in Taipei was carried out in 1984, just before the mass vaccination program (Hsu et al. 1986). In 1989, 5 years after the beginning of that program, another study was conducted on children in the Taipei area to study seroepidemiologic changes. The results show that the prevalence of HBsAg in children under 5 years of age decreased from 9.3% in 1984 to approximately 2% in 1989. A significant decrease in HBsAg prevalence in 5- to 8-year-old children who were not immunized against HBV showed that horizontal infection among the older children had also decreased. These results demonstrate that the HBV vaccination program not only protected vaccinated subjects, but the reduction in numbers of highly infectious young HBV carriers also contributed to a lower prevalence of HBV infection and carrier rates in some older children (Tsen et al. 1991). In conclusion, this vaccination program is effective in protecting the majority of children in Taiwan from acquiring HBV perinatal and horizontal infections and from becoming chronic carriers. However, this program has not foreseen the problem of coverage of HBV vaccine booster later in the adulthood among these vaccinated children.

## SOME SOCIOLOGIC SPECULATIONS ON HBV PREVENTION PROGRAMS

### The United States

Although several studies show that the vaccine-induced antibody could persist at least 5 to 10 years in 80% to 90% of immunized infants and adults (Lo et al. 1988; Stevens et al. 1992; Wainwright et al. 1989), the long-term (at least 15 to 20 years) vaccine efficacy for infants and the feasibility of an HBV vaccine booster for adults are still unclear. Moreover, it is naive to expect that a large proportion of inner-city minority infants, who will be most at risk in adolescence and early adulthood, can be reached by a universal infant vaccination program. The failure of measles eradication programs demonstrates that additional strategies to reach inner-city populations are needed. The continuing outbreaks of measles among preschool-age children illustrates the difficulty of reaching inner-city populations (Markowitz et al. 1989). For example, surveys of children in Jersey City in 1981 and 1986 found that measles immunization levels of 2-year-old children were 56% and 65%, respectively (CDC 1986). In Miami, surveys of 2-year-old children indicated that between 49% and 65% had been vaccinated against measles (CDC 1987). Thus, although a universal infant vaccination program is recommended as a long-range solution for persistently high HBV incidence, it will probably suffer from a low coverage rate in the future, especially in central cities.

The results of general childhood vaccination in the Chicago area also suggest that persuading inner-city parents to get their children vaccinated is often a difficult task, particularly for the poor. Compared with the struggles for food and safety in daily life, immunization becomes a low priority for the inner-city poor (Thompson 1993). In addition, the unpleasant struggle with bureaucratic public health systems and a lack of state supervision of preschool children's full immunization requirement result in relatively low immunization rates among inner-city children.

The large-scale HBV prevention program among Alaskan Natives started in 1983 was the first and only successful attempt in the United States to immunize susceptible persons, including all newborn babies. Among Alaskan Natives, the proportion of HBsAg was significantly higher in children than in adults, and HBV infection was commonly transmitted within the home (Heyward et al. 1985). After complete immunization of 90% of the susceptible persons in this area, the annual incidence of acute symptomatic HBV infection decreased from 215 to 14 cases per 100,000 people (McMahon et al. 1987). However, generally speaking, it is much easier to gain access to HBV-susceptible children than to high-risk adolescents and adults. Moreover, a single, integrated health system in Alaska provided relatively close surveillance of HBV infection. This system is different from the diffuse public health system in the rest of the United States. In addition, the administration of HBV vaccine to families living in small, remote villages in Alaska was also easier than in crowded, more anonymous inner-city populations in the remaining states. Thus, simply transporting the Alaskan strategy to the lower 49 states may not work. We have found no studies of the level of effectiveness of HBV immunization programs in covering inner-city infants in the United States. In short, there is no scientific basis for claims that the universal infant vaccination program may work in the United States. Even if universal infant vaccination is carried out, we suspect that the coverage of HBV vaccine among the most susceptible infants and children will still be inadequate.

Black adolescents and adults have the highest risk of HBV infection in the United States; hence they need access to preventive services most. Ironically, they are the persons least likely to have access to preventive health resources, either because of their poverty or because of inconvenient and unpleasant experiences in public health clinics. Studies in medical sociology have shown that, in general, blacks tend to use health care services less often than whites (Cockerham 1989; National Center for Health Statistics 1992). Even when blacks do see a physician, they are more likely to use public sources, where health services are generally disease-oriented rather than preventive (Dutton 1978). The CDC claims that changing the HBV prevention policy to a universal immunization program for infants is an alternative to targeting high-risk groups, which mostly include black adolescents and adults. We suspect that this new approach is a political compromise. Historically, it has been shown that most policies that target low-income groups or racial minorities cannot generate sufficient political support to sustain themselves, especially when the national economy is in a period of little growth, no growth, or decline (Wilson 1987). Cross-national research on social expenditures also has found that universal programs such as universal infant immunization are more politically sustainable in democracies even if they are more expensive than targeted policies (Skocpol 1991). Because the highest risk groups for HBV infection are intravenous drug abusers and active heterosexual persons, who are mostly composed of socially disadvantaged and politically powerless minorities, it is not surprising that the CDC recommends a universal infant vaccination program instead of preserving targeted high-risk group programs. However, this topic requires further research.

### Taiwan

The success of the HBV prevention program in Taiwan can be attributed to meticulous public education, continued reiteration of the importance of this program to the medical profession, perseverance of health officers, full support from the government, and the careful and practical design of the program (Chen et al. 1987; R.O.C. Department of Health 1985).

In contrast to the decentralized federal government in the United States, the Taiwanese government plays an active and dominant role in implementing the HBV prevention program. To detect the ongoing pattern of HBV occurrence and to implement the HBV prevention program, a computerized registration program for HBV infection was set up in 1983, and an active surveillance network was developed in 1991 by the Department of Health. An extensive household registration system developed during the Japanese colonial period also made case-finding and the delivery of HBV vaccine much easier. In general, the full support by the state and the active surveillance by the Department of Health contributed to the great success of the HBV prevention program in Taiwan.

Historically, the destruction of the large landlord class during early 1950s provided the state with ample autonomy in development efforts. This state's autonomy further enhanced the government's ability to design and implement public policies more equitably, without the interference of the wealthier social strata. Following the state's active and sophisticated intervention in economic development from the 1950s on, Taiwan has enjoyed an outstanding record of economic growth and a relatively equitable distribution of wealth in society (Barrett and Whyte 1982; Deyo 1987). Because the Taiwanese government perceives economic development and improved social welfare for everyone as the best means of enhancing its political regime, it inevitably plays a dominant and active role in such domains as public health.

Some might argue that some cultural factors led to the success of the Taiwan program; perhaps an authoritarian state and a communally oriented population has more success at control of HBV than a democratic state attempting to reach an individualistic population. However, the success of the U.S. Public Health Service's HBV infant immunization program in Alaskan Eskimo, Aleut, and Native American villages suggests that the key variable here may not be culture, but rather the priority given to the program and the energy with which it is carried out.

## SUMMARY AND SUGGESTIONS

The infection rates and transmission patterns of HBV vary markedly in various parts of the world. Therefore, strategies for HBV prevention necessarily differ from area to area according to the severity of HBV-related liver diseases and prevalence of HBV infection, demographic and epidemiologic patterns of HBV infection, socioeconomic factors, and cultural background.

In Taiwan, perinatal mother-to-child HBV infection plays the most significant role in HBV infection cases. The infants at highest risk are those born to HBsAg-carrier mothers who are also hepatitis B e-antigen (HBeAg) positive. In Taiwan, the HBV vaccination program is efficacious in preventing perinatal HBV transmission and the development of the chronic carrier state. The prevention strategy of Taiwan may provide a practical model for other countries where the epidemiology of hepatitis B is similar to that of Taiwan. For future studies, researchers should also be aware that horizontal infections among adolescents and adults may become the major mode of HBV transmission in Taiwan. Recent studies showing a large increase in premarital sexual activity in Taiwan also suggests that other preventive efforts (such as the inclusion of information on sexual transmission of HBV in family planning classes in schools) may be needed as well. In the future, a broader and more comprehensive strategy of HBV prevention will probably be required.

In the United States, blacks, males, adolescents, and young adults have the highest risk of acquiring HBV infection. Intravenous drug use and contact with HBV-infected persons are the two major risk factors for acquiring HBV infection. Homosexual activity, health care employment, and blood transfusion have shown continued declines in incidence. Although the hepatitis B vaccine has been available since 1982, HBV incidence has declined only slightly.

The CDC claims that the failure of targeting high-risk groups, such as drug users and multiple and active heterosexual persons, shows the unsuccessful result of this kind of selective prevention of HBV infection. Recently, an infant universal vaccination program has been launched to control HBV infection. However, the difficulty of implementing a truly effective universal infant immunization program (i.e., a program that will reach infants with only a tenuous linkage to the health care system) is no less than for targeted high-risk group programs.[1] Some may argue that immunizing a very large proportion of middle-class infants against HBV may provide the protection of "herd immunity" to those who are immunized and hence is a worthwhile societal goal. However, the routes of transmission of measles are very different from those of HBV. Measles is acquired through direct contact with the secretions of infected persons or through airborne spread; it is highly communicable in schools and other public settings. Any immunization program for HBV will probably be least effective in reaching young people who are part of the same social milieu where HBV is already most common and where the largest proportion of carriers are found. Herd immunity will not protect these young people; instead, their social isolation will prevent their successful inclusion in such an immunization program and maintain their continued exposure to the major routes (unprotected sexual exposure to carriers and joint needle use) of transmission of the disease.

In addition, it may be a huge waste of money to immunize a group that has the lowest rate of HBV incidence (i.e., nonminority upper- and middle-class infants and children) with a vaccine that may well be less than 50% effective by the time they reach adolescence (unless an immunization booster program is also started). A comprehensive HBV vaccination program that targets susceptible infants and adolescents is needed. Although the CDC has suggested that susceptible groups continue to be targeted (CDC 1991a), their contention that such programs have largely failed and that universal immunization should be used has introduced a new competitor for scarce public health dollars. The addition of this latter strategy without the infusion of new appropriations will undoubtedly decrease the funds available for targeted programs.

We maintain that targeting key population groups is a more effective way to reduce high HBV incidence. Several strategies are suggested to improve the HBV prevention programs. One of major reasons for the previous failure of HBV prevention is that health care providers are unaware of the importance of HBV infection and have failed to recognize high-risk groups. Therefore, the importance of HBV infection and preventive guidelines should be stressed among health care professionals. Effective coordination among health care providers is indispensable to recognize HBV carriers and to prevent potential infections.

The feasibility of targeted programs is being demonstrated by a project in Zurich, where it was shown that intravenous drug users can be vaccinated with a high coverage rate, with 70% of them receiving at least a second vaccine injection. It also shows that intravenous drug users were reluctant to report to any official institution but more likely to assent to vaccination by volunteer health care workers in the street in downtown areas (Grob et al. 1985).

A study of a multiyear, community-wide hepatitis B/delta control program shows that HBV-susceptibles among intravenous drug users were accessed most efficiently from local jails and drug treatment centers, which suggests possible sites for targeting HBV infection in this group. Although this program indicates that only 39% of the susceptible drug users received at least two doses over 6 months, it was concluded that this control program was cost-saving, given the expenditures for the campaign versus estimated economic costs averted through the prevention activities (Shartz et al. 1990).

Heterosexuals with multiple sex partners comprise one category of persons at increased risk for HBV infection (CDC 1990a). Moreover, the prevalence of HBV infection among adolescents and adults has been shown to be associated with serologic evidence of previous infection with syphilis (CDC 1989b). In 1990, the CDC initiated a demonstration project to assess the feasibility of offering HBV vaccination in sexually transmitted diseases (STD) clinics to persons at high risk for sexually transmitted HBV infection (CDC 1991c). The findings suggest that STD clinics may be opportune sites to vaccinate persons in this risk group against HBV infection. However, such strategies need to be further elaborated to improve the completion rate of the HBV vaccine series.

Vertical transmission of HBV is a problem among Asian-Americans, especially among poor, less-educated immigrants. Greater awareness of the dangers of HBV infection is needed among these populations and among medical personnel who serve them. In addition, Asian language propaganda on HBV infection and Asian-American health care workers who understand their client's cultural background could have a rapid impact here because the problem is not usually motivation, but rather knowledge and access to vaccination. For example, some HBV-positive mothers may not understand that they must bring their infants back for the full series of three shots to achieve successful protection against vertical transmission of the disease.

From a social-ecologic point of view, we may first recognize high-risk areas of HBV infection and their social characteristics. (As far as we know, there has been little or no attempt to use the new computer-based geographic mapping technologies to map the incidence or prevalence rates of HBV within cities or metropolitan areas to guide the commitment of resources for its control.) Once these high-risk areas are identified, the HBV vaccine should be provided and educational programs should be enhanced for residents of these areas to make HBV prevention more accessible to them, especially to the poor. Strategies may include educating adults and parents who live in high-risk areas to get themselves and their children vaccinated, reducing inconvenient and unpleasant experiences in public health clinics, enhancing the state's regulation regarding childhood vaccination, and providing strong incentives such as extra welfare benefits to encourage residents in these areas to get vaccinated.

The present shift from targeting high-risk groups to a flawed strategy misleadingly called universal vaccination will probably lead to a massive waste of scarce medical resources and perhaps to an increase in HBV incidence throughout our society. As the Taiwan program shows, universal infant vaccination is a useful strategy when the primary route of HBV transmission is vertical and when there is a strong, committed, and well-coordinated public health effort to make it work. Because vertical transmission of HBV is not the major problem in the United States, because the legal and economic responsibility for providing vaccination is highly diffuse, and because the scope of the HBV problem is not recognized by doctors, political authorities, or the general public, we think that universal infant vaccination simply will not work in either the long or the short run.

## NOTE

1. For any HBV immunization program to be effective in major urban areas, there would have to be some form of implied or obvious coercion. For example, parents or guardians cannot register their children for school without evidence of certain immunizations. Including a new immunization for HBV would require changing many state laws. In order for many poor parents to be able to afford this immunization (which currently costs about $100 for the three-shot series), it would have to be distributed free or at very low cost, as is already done by many local health departments for other required immunizations. The CDC's failure to address these legislative and financial problems leads us to question whether the proposed program will ever cover a large proportion of urban infants.

## REFERENCES


ALTER, MIRIAM J., PATRICK J. COLEMAN, W. JAMES ALEXANDER et al. 1989. "Importance of Heterosexual Activity in the Transmission of Hepatitis B and Non-A, Non-B Hepatitis." *JAMA* 262:1201–05.

ALTER, MIRIAM J., STEPHEN C. HADLER, HAROLD S. MARGOLIS et al. 1990. "The Changing Epidemiology of Hepatitis B in the United States: Need for Alternative Vaccination Strategies." *JAMA* 263:1218–22.

AMERICAN ACADEMY OF PEDIATRICS (AAP). 1992a. "Control of Hepatitis B: To Be or Not to Be?" *Pediatrics* (commentaries):274–77.

______. 1992b. "Universal Hepatitis B Immunization." *Pediatrics* 89:795–99.

BARRETT, RICHARD E., and M. K. WHYTE. 1982. "Dependency Theory and Taiwan: Analysis of a Deviant Case." *American Journal of Sociology* 87:1064–89.

BEASLEY, R. 1988. "Hepatitis B Virus: The Major Etiology of Hepatocellular Carcinoma." *Cancer* 61:1942–56.

BEASLEY, R. PALMER, CHRISTAN TREPO, CLADD E. STEVENS, and WOLF SZMUNESS. 1977. "The e Antigen and Vertical Transmission of Hepatitis B Surface Antigen." *American Journal of Epidemiology* 105(4):94–98.

BEASLEY, R., LU-YU HWANG, CHIA-CHIN LIN, AND CHIA-SIANG CHIEN. 1981. "Hepatocellular Carcinoma and Hepatitis B Virus: A Prospective Study of 22,207 Men in Taiwan." *Lancet* 2:1129–33.

BEASLEY, R., LU-YU HWANG, M. L. LEU et al. 1982. "Incidence of Hepatitis B Virus Infection in Preschool Children in Taiwan." *Journal of Infectious Disease* 146(2):198–204.

CENTERS FOR DISEASE CONTROL (CDC). 1986. "Measles—New Jersey." *Morbidity and Mortality Weekly Report* 35:213–15.

______. 1987. "Measles—Dade County, Florida." *Morbidity and Mortality Weekly Report* 36:45–48.

______. 1988. "Prevention of Perinatal Transmission of Hepatitis B Virus: Prenatal Screening of all Pregnant Women for Hepatitis B Surface Antigen." *Morbidity and Mortality Weekly Report* 37(37):341–47.

______. 1989a. "Guidelines for Prevention of Transmission of Human Immunodeficiency Virus and Hepatitis B Virus to Health-Care and Public-Safety Workers." *Morbidity and Mortality Weekly Report* 38(S-6):1–37.

______. 1989b. "Racial Differences in Rates of Hepatitis B Virus Infection—United States, 1976–1980." *Morbidity and Mortality Weekly Report* 38(47):818–21.

______. 1990a. "Protection Against Viral Hepatitis." *Morbidity and Mortality Weekly Report* 39(RR-2):1–26.

______. 1990b. *Hepatitis Surveillance* 53:1–32.

______. 1991a. "Hepatitis B Virus: A Comprehensive Strategy for Eliminating Transmission in the United States Through Universal Childhood Vaccination." *Morbidity and Mortality Weekly Report* 40(RR-13):1–25.

______. 1991b. "Screening for Hepatitis B Virus Infection Among Refugees Arriving in the United States, 1979–1991." *Morbidity and Mortality Weekly Report* 40(45):784–86.

______. 1991c. "Successful Strategies in Adult Immunization." *Morbidity and Mortality Weekly Report* 40(41):700–709.

______. 1992. *Hepatitis Surveillance* 54:1–21.

CHEN, DING-SHINN, HSU-MEI HSU, JUEI-LOW SUNG et al. 1987. "A Mass Vaccination Program in Taiwan Against Hepatitis B Virus Infection in Infants of Hepatitis B Surface Antigen–Carrier Mothers." *JAMA* 257:2597–2603.

COCKERHAM, W. C. 1989. *Medical Sociology*. Englewood Cliffs, N.J.: Prentice Hall.

DEYO, F. C. (ed.). 1987. *The Political Economy of the New Asian Industrialism.* Ithaca, New York: Cornell University Press.

DUTTON, DIANA B. 1978. "Explaining the Low Use of Health Services by the Poor: Costs, Attitudes, or Delivery Systems?" *American Sociological Review* 43:348–68.

GROB, P. J., M. RICKENBACH, R. STEFFEN et al. 1985. "Hepatitis B Vaccination Campaign in a Low Endemicity Area." *European Journal of Clinical Microbiology* 4:408–11.

HADLER, STEPHEN C. 1990. "Hepatitis B Virus Infection and Health Care Workers." *Vaccine* 8(Supplement):S24–S28.

HADLER, STEPHEN C., and HAROLD S. MARGOLIS. 1989. "Viral Hepatitis." Pp. 351–90 in *Viral Infections of Humans,* edited by A. S. Evans. New York: Plenum Medical Book Company.

HEYWARD, WILLIAM L., THOMAS R. BENDER, BRIAN J. MCMAHON et al. 1985. "The Control of Hepatitis B Virus Infection with Vaccine in Yupik Eskimos." *American Journal of Epidemiology* 121:914–23.

HSU, HSU-MEI, DING-SHINN CHEN, CHENG-HUA CHUANG et al. 1988. "Efficacy of a Mass Hepatitis B Vaccination Program in Taiwan." *JAMA* 260:2231–35.

HSU, H. Y., M. H. CHANG, D. S. CHEN et al. 1986. "Baseline Seroepidemiology of Hepatitis B Virus Infection in Children in Taipei, 1984: A Study Just Before Mass Hepatitis B Vaccination Program in Taiwan." *Journal of Medical Virology* 18:301–07.

LO, KWANG-JUEI, SHOU-DONG LEE, YANG-TE TSAI et al. 1988. "Long-Term Immunogencity and Efficacy of Hepatitis B Vaccine in Infants Born to HBeAg-Positive HBsAg-Carrier Mothers." *Hepatology* 8:1647–50.

MARGOLIS, HAROLD S., MIRIAM J. ALTER and STEPHEN C. HADLER. 1991. "Hepatitis B: Evolving Epidemiology and Implications for Control." *Seminars in Liver Disease* 11(2):84–92.

MARKOWITZ, LAURI E., STEPHEN R. PREBLUD, WALTER A. ORENSTEIN et al. 1989. "Patterns of Transmission in Measles Outbreaks in the United States, 1985–1986." *New England Journal of Medicine* 320(2):75–81.

MAYNARD, J. E. 1990. "Hepatitis B: Global Importance and Need for Control." *Vaccine* 8(Supplement):S18–S20.

MCMAHON, BRIAN J., EVERETTE R. RHOADES, WILLIAM L. HEYWARD et al. 1987. "A Comprehensive Programme to Reduce the Incidence of Hepatitis B Virus Infection and Its Sequelae in Alaskan Natives." *Lancet* 2:1134–36.

NATIONAL CENTER FOR HEALTH STATISTICS. 1992. *Health, United States, 1991.* Hyattsville, MD: Public Health Service.

PASTOREK, JOSEPH G. II. 1989. "Hepatitis B." *Obstetrics and Gynecology Clinics of North America* 16:645–57.

PIOT, P. C., C. GOILAV AND E. KEGELS. 1990. "Hepatitis B: Transmission by Sexual Contact and Needle Sharing." *Vaccine* 8(Supplement):S37–S40.

R.O.C. DEPARTMENT OF HEALTH. 1984, 1985, 1987, and 1992. *The Prevention Program for Hepatitis B Virus Infection.* Taipei, Taiwan: The Executive Yuan (in Chinese).

______. 1989. *Health Statistics.* Taipei, Taiwan: The Executive Yuan.

ROSENBLUM, LISA S., STEPHEN C. HADLER, KENNETH G. CASTRO et al. 1990. "Heterosexual Transmission of Hepatitis B Virus in Belle Glade, Florida." *Journal of Infectious Diseases* 161:407–11.

SHARTZ, G., S. C. HADLER, J. MCCARTHEY, M. SMITH, and F. BIRCH. 1990. "Outbreak to Needle Users and Sexual Contacts: A Multi-Year, Community-Wide Hepatitis B/Delta Hepatitis Control Program in Worcester, Massachusetts." P. 533 in *Progress in Hepatitis B Immunization,* edited by P. Coursaget and M. J. Tong. France: INSERM/John Libbey Eurotext Ltd.

SHERLOCK, S. 1990. "Hepatitis B: The Disease." *Vaccine* 8(Supplement):S6–S9.

SKOCPOL, T. 1991. "Targeting Within Universalism: Politically Viable Policies to Combat Poverty in the United States." Pp. 411–36 in *The Urban Underclass,* edited by C. Jencks and P. E. Peterson. Washington, DC: The Brookings Institution.

STEVENS, CLADD E., ROBERT A. NEURATH, R. PALMER BEASLEY, and WOLF SZMUNESS. 1979. "HBeAg and Anti-HBe Detection by Radioimmunoassay: Correlation with Vertical Transmission of Hepatitis B Virus in Taiwan." *Journal of Medical Virology* 3:237–41.

STEVENS, CLADD E., PEARL T. TOY, MYRON J. TONG et al. 1985. "Perinatal Hepatitis B Virus Transmission in the United States." *JAMA* 253:1740–45.

STEVENS, CLADD E., PEARL T. TOY, PATRICIA E. TAYLAR et al. 1992. "Prospects for Control of Hepatitis B Virus Infection—Implications of Childhood Vaccination and Long-Term Protection." *Pediatrics* 90:170–73.

THOMPSON, CHERYL W. 1993. "Shots to Go." *Chicago Tribune* March 30.

TSEN, YEE-JENG, MEI-HWEI CHANG, HONG-YUAN HSU et al. 1991. "Seroprevalence of Hepatitis B Virus Infection in Children in Taipei, 1989: Five Years After a Mass Hepatitis B Vaccination Program." *Journal of Medical Virology* 34:96–99.

WAINWRIGHT, ROBERT B., BRIAN J. MCMAHON, LISA R. BULKOW et al. 1989. "Duration of Immunogenicity and Efficacy of Hepatitis B Vaccine in a Yupik Eskimo Population." *JAMA* 261:2362–66.

WILSON, WILLIAM J. 1987. *The Truly Disadvantaged: The Inner City, the Underclass, and Public Policy.* Chicago: University of Chicago Press.

Chapter 10

# Early Retirement and Normal Male Identity: Assessing an Aspect of Quality of Life after Coronary Artery Bypass Surgery*

*Uta Gerhardt*

Over the past decades, early retirement has become increasingly prominent (Conrad 1988; Jacobs and Kohli 1990). Germany is a special case and unique internationally because its social security system provides for medically certified incapacity as the main route to early retirement (Kohli et al. 1991). The statutory age for retirement is 65 years for males, with provisions to opt for an earlier exit at 63 years. However, with a temporary program offering "brought-forward-retirement" at 58 years in the 1980s, the mean age for men's exit from the workforce is below 58 years (Lehr and Niederfranke 1991; Verband der Rentenversicherungsträger 1991).

Early retirement on a disability pension occurs mostly on the grounds of medically certified incapacity to work (Schuntermann et al. 1990). Access to disability is regulated by social security legislation. It entails two steps. First, the person is granted the status of severe handicap, which involves a medical eval-

*For thorough criticism and most helpful comments of previous versions of this paper, I wish to thank Cathy Charmaz, Eva Kahana, Nico Stehr, and the editors of this volume. The research was funded by the German National Research Foundation (Deutsche Forschungsgemeinschaft), Grant No. Ge 313/1–5, between 1987 and 1993. For generous collaboration on the design of the study, particularly its medical aspects, and for granting access to the patients representing the study population, I wish to thank Friedrich-Wilhelm Hehrlein and Martin Schlepper, Justus Liebig University Medical School and Max-Planck Institute of Cardiovascular Diseases, Giessen and Bad Nauheim (Germany).

uation that judges him (or her) to have suffered a 50% reduction in ability to work. This is laid down in the "Law Securing Integration of the Severely Handicapped into Work, Occupation, and Society" (enacted 1974, revised 1986). Second, the "Federal Assistance Law" (enacted 1982) specifies that the severely handicapped are entitled to draw a disability pension irrespective of their age. This "Inability to Work Pension," which is its official name, makes those whose ability to work is reduced leave the labor force altogether. When they reach statutory retirement age, their early retirement pension is automatically converted into an old-age retirement pension (at age 65). However, the first of these steps need not necessarily lead to the second one. As an alternative to early retirement, persons with severe handicap status may refrain from applying for a disability pension while returning to work. Owing to their reduction of work capacity, they are then entitled to take old-age retirement on a full old-age pension at age 60 as a statutory right (Arbeitsgruppe Sozialpolitik 1988; Schmähl 1988).

The "Law Securing Integration etc." stipulates that patients undergoing major surgery are to be judged to have suffered a reduction of their ability to work of 50% or more, depending on their diagnosis. Therefore, these patients acquire the status of severe handicap. This status is granted for 3 years but can be made permanent subsequently if suitable employment is unavailable. Among the major surgical procedures included in this entitlement to severe handicap status is *open-heart surgery* (Weidemann 1984). Coronary artery bypass surgery (CABS), ameliorating the effects of coronary artery disease (CAD), is the most frequent type of open-heart surgery. The administrative guideline for attributing a specific degree of residual work capacity to various diagnoses stipulates for CABS: "After heart operations a period of improvement must be granted (usually three years). During this period, reduction of work capacity is at least fifty percent. Subsequently, the degree of reduction of work capacity depends crucially on the residual physical ability. . . . The eventual degree of reduction of work capacity should not be below fifty percent . . . for coronary surgery" (Bundesministerium für Arbeit und Sozialordnung 1977, p. 63).

Among German CABS patients, blue-collar workers use their severe handicap status to obtain early retirement on disability pensions more frequently than those in other occupational groups (Gerhardt 1992a). This is confirmed by the data gathered by cardiovascular surgery units. Their research finds that among the self-employed or those who are employed in white-collar jobs in industry or government, between 50% and 90% return to work after CABS, but only 20% to 40% of workers in blue-collar occupations resume employment postoperatively (Hacker et al. 1985; Schmitz and Welsch-Hetzel 1987; Walter et al. 1983). Moreover, semi-skilled and unskilled blue-collar workers have the lowest average age at the time of their exit from the labor force after CABS, and they are the only occupational status group whose average age does not differ significantly between those who return to work and those who retire early: it is approximately 50 years (Vetter et al. 1985, p. 35).

Early retirement has been analyzed as a shock (Stauder 1955) or as a boon (George and Maddox 1977). Recent German research distinguishes three styles of coping with early retirement: *active* structuring of one's past and present; *passive* acceptance of the externally induced change of one's life world; and *active-passive* rearrangement of one's commitments (Niederfranke 1989). Four types of competence characterize one's style of coping, as other German research shows: achievement-oriented, accepting, depressive, and desperate (Kruse 1986). A British study investigates styles of adjustment of male patients undergoing coronary graft surgery: it reports variation between active-denial (continuation of previous high activity level), accommodation, resignation, and secondary gain (experience of freedom through the illness and its consequences) (Radley 1988; Radley and Green 1985).

*Coping with early retirement* invokes the debate about *quality of life* after CABS (Caine et al. 1991; Killip 1988; Walter 1992). The issue is usually addressed from a psychological angle. German myocardial infarction patients (with or without subsequent CABS) who retire early on disability pensions are reported to find their quality of life poor. The reason is said to be that their idleness causes depression as well as feelings of inadequacy and dependency (Badura et al. 1987, 1988). A British study clarifies that "for a fifth of patients global quality of life was no better or worse than before surgery and this poor outcome was not closely related to physical state. Patients who described their psychological symptoms or had a 'passive' approach to their illness before operation were less likely to have a good outcome" (Mayou and Bryant 1987, p. 239). One interpretation of these findings suggests that usual quality-of-life measures are "likely to be misleading in men who are not working" because they fail to distinguish between "forced unemployment because of sickness" and unemployment caused otherwise (Oakley 1987, p. 182).

However, unemployment or retirement due to sickness need not necessarily be *forced.* In the German social security system, open-heart surgery entitles one to severe handicap status irrespective of the outcome of CABS. Severe handicap status, in turn, entitles one to early retirement under conditions frequently prevailing, such as unavailability of lighter work in the firm or lack of likelihood to find re-employment elsewhere. In this situation a certain freedom is granted the individual undergoing CABS, who may decide whether to take advantage of the available option(s). Whereas practically all patients apply for severe handicap status and acquire it, only a fraction of those who could apply for early retirement on disability pension do apply. Of those who do apply for early retirement, most are aware of the conditions that must be met to receive the retirement pension for which they apply. They must prove or make plausible to the physicians who evaluate their application that they are unable to do their previous jobs and that alternative or lighter work is unavailable in the same firm or elsewhere. Thus, a certain scope of discretion is opened up for the patients, who may use this latitude when making the transition to early retirement. That is, sickness-induced retirement is not forced upon the patient in Germany. A considerable number of patients, however, are nevertheless convinced that they experience a "no choice" situation that forces them into the subsequent course of events, and these patients often express dissatisfaction with their early retirement (Loose et al. 1982; Schott 1987). To use M. E. P. Seligman's terms (Seligman 1975), early retirement in Germany does not automatically convey helplessness, but it may nevertheless be deemed an externally imposed biographical turning-point that signifies to a person his lack of control over his life. At the same time, to be sure, early retirement may be experienced as welcome termination of the work-life. Inasmuch as early retirement permits participation in the decision making and/or some manipulation of physicians' decisions, it contains a certain chance for what Seligman calls *mastery*.

Such mastery, in sociologic terms, is a matter of coping; it has two aspects. One is *lifestyle,* that is, for male patients after early retirement, continuation or re-establishment of work-related biographical commitments typical for men. Male identity, in modern industrial society, is work related with special reference to employment (including self-employment). Men are compelled to follow the sole pattern of employment-focused "male normal biography" (Osterland 1990), and their gender identity is geared toward occupational achievement, whereas women may be both family-focused and/or employment-focused (Gerhardt 1991a). Therefore, men in the situation of CABS who want to retain their male-gender social identity have two options: Either they return to work and thus continue their lives of "normal work," or they retire early but must find ways to secure commitments that justify their claim to a "normal male identity" (Fooken 1989). Because early retirement "brings forward" the point in one's life where the transition is made from "working life" to "old age" (i.e., "premature" postemployment status), patients must restructure their life style to emulate normal male biographies representing normal male identities (Gerhardt 1992b). They may accomplish this by resuming more or less normal work, suitably adapted to old age (Kohli et al. 1993).

To be sure, the notions of normal identity and normal work epitomize the social meaning of gender. In individuals' own perspectives in everyday interactions, such social meaning is represented by idealized typified patterns (Gerhardt 1991b; Soeffner 1989). That these patterns are of ideal-type "purity" when used in individuals' orientations has been underestimated in most research dealing with gender identity. The image of how a man *should* be (i.e., the "pure" type) is what makes him consider himself a normal male (e.g., being a provider), and this shapes his identity as it is expressed in his interactions (McCall and Simmons 1966). Individuals use the ideal-type image as a guideline when they realign their lives after major surgery. They cope with the more or less dramatic rupture of their working identity that happens at the time of their early retirement, and subsequently they either match or deviate from what they or their significant others consider an activity level characteristic of men.

The second aspect of mastery concerns *feelings of independence;* they suggest freedom of the individual to make his own decisions and to have some control over what happens to him (Palmore et al. 1985). An important aspect of male identity in modern society is that a man is able to have some influence on his circumstances rather than having his decisions made for him by others (Vaillant and Vaillant 1981). This suggests that attitudes of activity and passivity characterize the outlook of patients after CABS who are more or less able to exert mastery, that is, to decide what they themselves want and act accordingly.

In text material on patients' experiences, activity or passivity is conveyed in the patient reports on crucial events of their sickness biographies, focusing particularly on CABS and early retirement. On the one side, patients may feel driven into their operation and pushed into their early retirement without being able to influence what happens to them; their attitude is that they are dependent on others, who choose which of the patient's options is enacted and who actively shape the course of events. On the other side, patients may find ways to actively exert influence on what happens, either deciding themselves, urging others along, or being given a choice between acceptable alternatives; they participate actively rather than simply follow others' wishes or decisions. These perspectives are related to male identity because they convey the presence or absence of a sense of independence.

I propose to assess patients' quality of life by examining their style of coping. Coping may be active or passive, and it has two dimensions related to the normal male identity. One dimension is *lifestyle,* or the extent to which the man's activities after retirement resemble a work-biography of a normal (i.e., actively employed) male life pattern. The other is *independence* of decision making, in particular availability of choices rather than being forced by others. The independence-dependence issue concerns the question of who—in the patient-couple's perspective—is responsible for the patients' CABS and early retirements.

## DESIGN OF THE STUDY

This study is based on a qualitative investigation of 60 patients and their spouses (patient-couples) and their physicians. The 60 patients, who were investigated on a case-by-case basis, were homogenous except that 30 of the patients had been operated on in the late 1970s and the other 30 in the late 1980s. Each patient met three criteria for maximum likelihood of postoperative return to work: age at operation not exceeding 55 years (in a few cases, however, age was 57 years), full employment status prior to CABS, and left ventricular ejection fraction (LVEF) of at least 50% preoperatively. Their CAD had to be diagnosed by angiography; furthermore, they had to be married or have lived with a partner for some time (Gerhardt and Thönnessen 1990). Age, employment, and LVEF have been shown to be preoperative predictors of maximum likelihood of postoperative resumption of work (Allen 1990; Almeida et al. 1983; Russell et al. 1986). The two study groups were also homogenous with regard to other criteria. The mean age of the 1970s cohort was 50.3 years and of the 1980s cohort 50.5 years; among the 1970s cohort sick leave averaged 4.3 months when patients returned to work and 7.9 months when they did not, whereas among the 1980s cohort average sick leave was 3.5 months when they returned to work and 7.3 months when they retired early. Thus, our study investigates two homogenous groups of patients with optimal preoperative chance of postoperative return to employment and whose date of operation differs by some 10 years (Gerhardt 1992c).

The two study groups of 30 were drawn from a somewhat larger interview sample of 40 cases; the extra 10 in each cohort allowed for drop-outs, deaths, and so forth, while 30 fully documented cases could be reached. The *prospective* interview population was recruited as consecutive cases meeting the three criteria and receiving CABS at University Hospital between April 1, 1987 and September 1988. The *retrospective* interview group was constituted in a two-step procedure. First, all names of patients fulfilling at least two of the criteria were drawn from the register of patients angiographed at the Max-Planck Cardiovascular Unit after January 1, 1976, and questionnaires were mailed to the physicians of the 147 suitable patients angiographed and operated on up to 1980. Of these, 115 were returned, 107 of which were analyzable, documenting that 92 patients were alive and could be contacted. Second, 40 patients were contacted and they and their spouses were interviewed at home, whereas their physicians were interviewed in their offices or on the telephone, using a conversational format. Table 10–1 outlines the two study populations in terms of their medical and social characteristics.

## DATA COLLECTION AND ANALYSIS

A total of 303 in-depth structured interviews were conducted; of these, 240 investigated the 60 cases of the retrospective and prospective study populations. In the retrospective study, patient-couples and their doctors were interviewed *once,* covering 7 to 11 years of postsurgery biography (total of 60 interviews). Those in the prospective study were interviewed three times, that is, preoperatively, postoperatively after 3 months, and after 18 months; the postoperative physician interview at 3 months was conducted with a member of the surgical team (total of 180 interviews). In addition, case data on preoperative and postoperative symptomatology were elicited from clinical records of the angiography hospital for the retrospective study population, and of the cardiovascular surgery unit and rehabilitation hospital for the prospective study population.

The interview schedule for patients and their spouses consisted of a 24-step guideline of topics covering medical history plus occupational and family biography over the entire period following onset of symptoms in chronologic

**TABLE 10–1. Some Medical and Social Characteristics of the Retrospective and Prospective Patient Populations**

| | *RETROSPECTIVE STUDY POPULATION* | *PROSPECTIVE STUDY POPULATION* |
|---|---|---|
| *Age at operation* | N = 30 | N = 30 |
| Up to 50 years | 17 (57%) | 15 (50%) |
| Over 50 years | 13 (43%) | 15 (50%) |
| *Disease status* | N = 30 | N = 30 |
| One-vessel disease | 3 (10%) | 3 (10%) |
| Two-vessel disease | 5 (17%) | 6 (20%) |
| Three-vessel disease | 20 (67%) | 21 (70%) |
| Mainstem stenosis | 1 (3%) | — |
| Multiple/unknown | 1 (3%) | — |
| *Gender* | N = 30 | N = 30 |
| Male | 29 (97%) | 28 (93%) |
| Female | 1 (3%) | 2 (7%) |
| *Socioeconomic status* | N = 30 | N = 30 |
| Professional/manager | 3 (10%) | — |
| Higher employee | 5 (17%) | 2 (7%) |
| Middle employee, self-employed | 7 (23%) | 3 (10%) |
| Higher-class status | 15 (50%) | 5 (17%) |
| Supervisor, low-level employee | 4 (13%) | 10 (33%) |
| Skilled worker | 5 (17%) | 3 (30%) |
| Semi-skilled, unskilled worker | 6 (20%) | 3 (20%) |
| Lower-class status | 15 (50%) | 25 (83%) |
| *Postoperative employment status* | N = 30 | N = 30 |
| Return to work | 22 (73%) | 14 (47%) |
| Retirement | 8 (27%) | 16 (53%) |

order. The tape-recorded interviews matched the schedule as closely as the conversation format permitted. The main topics had to be covered extensively (preoperative occupation and job; diagnosis and decision about operation; CABS; return to work and/or retirement). The guideline used to interview patient-couples is shown in Table 10–2. The interview schedule for physicians covered the issues in less depth and concentrated on medical history, medication, prognosis, and the physician's explanation of the patient's postoperative history regarding employment.

All physician interviews were transcribed (average length was 30 minutes); however, they are not used in this chapter. Of the patient-couple inter-

**TABLE 10–2. Biographical Interview Schedule (Medical-Occupational-Family)**

| |
|---|
| Past history occupation and family |
| *Occupation* |
| Explanation of illness ("cause") |
| Myocardial infarction, diagnosis |
| Family structure and situation |
| Marital division of labor re health management |
| Decision for surgery |
| *Operation* |
| Perioperative events and in-hospital stay |
| Rehabilitation hospital stay |
| Marital health management postoperatively |
| Marital decisions regarding spouses' occupation(s) |
| Decision to return to work |
| *Return to work* |
| Marital occupational division of labor |
| Decision to retire from work |
| *Retirement* |
| Consequences of retirement |
| Marital health (illness) management today |
| Marital occupational and domestic division of labor today |
| Explanation of illness today |
| Family structure today |
| Clinical state and health situation today |
| Family's (patient's) economic situation today |

views (average length 90 minutes), extended text passages were transcribed which covered the information dealing with each of the major stages of the case development (occupation; operation; return to work; retirement). Non-transcribed parts of the interviews were reconstructed in descriptive summaries of what was said about the various topics on the interview schedule. All excerpts, both transcribed and paraphrased, were given time markers to enable researchers to review the dialogue being reproduced or reconstructed.

Data analysis uses a special procedure of qualitative interpretation which has been developed in various analyses over the last 10 years (Gerhardt 1986b; Gerhardt and Kirchgässler 1987; Gerhardt et al. 1994). It consists of two main phases. At first, case dynamics are reconstructed in *profiles* covering the 24 stages of case development (shortened to a 12-stage version). These profiles contain the text of the summaries characterizing the case development. They allow for further comparative analysis on a case-by-case basis either on a longitudinal axis (biographical time-flow) or a latitudinal axis (by specific stages of cases).

The second phase of data interpretation searches for types to find structures in the material. Its first step is case reconstruction; they are taken from the profiles and document the flow of events and experiences in selected stages of the case. In a second step, case reconstructions are contrasted to find similar cases and group them together. This step must extend to the entire study population and should not be based on only one or a few paradigmatic cases, as is often done in qualitative data interpretation. In the context of this chapter, the relevant study population was the 28 cases of early retirement, of which 26 were men among the 60 cases investigated. The third step is the construction of empirical types. A fourth step of analysis explores ideal-type patterns and determines antecedent conditions that facilitate or inhibit certain case developments in the context of the empirical types or in the broader structures of case developments suggested by the empirical types (Gerhardt 1986b, 1993). This latter step, however, is not shown in this chapter.

The following analysis aims at types of coping with early retirement. In its initial part, it looks at *long-term* case developments. Therefore, the argument starts with analyzing retrospective cases. Their lifestyle and perceptions of control regarding the decisions to operate and to retire early are ascertained separately and then combined into types of coping. Subsequently, the findings from the retrospective case analysis are further clarified on the basis of the prospective cases, which represent *ongoing* coping at the time before and shortly after CABS. Eventually, the two groups of cases are compared with regard to typical coping, and conclusions are drawn regarding the impact of social class status on early retirement as well as the impact of date of operation (whether the patient belonged to the 1970s or the 1980s cohort).

## RESULTS

Among the 30 *retrospective* cases (29 males) with optimal preoperative chance of postoperative return to work, 7 retired early without resuming employment, and 4 retired early after 1.5 to 10 years of postoperative employment. Their style of social adjustment subsequent to early retirement varied considerably, as the following two cases document.

### CASE 05R

Occupation. The patient, born in 1922, was a semiskilled machine worker who moonlighted for his employer as a lorry driver on overnight trips.

Diagnosis and Decision to Operate. He had had angina pectoris for 5 years when, in 1977, he found himself unable to move and consulted his wife's physician, who referred him to angiography. Because of acute risk of myocardial infarction, he was hospitalized as an emergency measure and operated on immediately.

Operation (November 1977). Revascularization was successful, but during his postoperative hospitalization he fantasized himself into a life-and-death situation that he experienced as traumatic.
Retirement. After the operation, he did not return to work and refused to engage in any activity except walking. His local physician supported his application for early retirement, and he received a relatively low disability pension starting 3 months postoperatively. His income was so low that his wife had to take in his (disliked) stepmother, nursing her at home to be able to add her widow's pension to his disability pension. He remained completely idle, not even helping his wife with the housework or the care of his bedridden stepmother. He had no social contacts, read the newspaper all day, and left the house only to go on solitary walks. He slept about 12 hours daily.

CASE 13R

Occupation. The patient, born in 1928, was a foreman in the construction industry.
Diagnosis and Decision to Operate. Owing to chest pain at work, he visited an internist, who referred him to the cardiology unit of the angiography hospital where his CAD was diagnosed, and CABS was recommended. From this point in time, he went on sick leave, describing it with the slang expression, "Of course I celebrated sick" (A 03.45) (The time marker signifies the taped text: A = first side of tape, 03.45 = 3 minutes, 45 seconds). When his symptoms got worse, he insisted to his local physician that the operation be scheduled, which it was.
Operation (January 1980). "I must say, I did not go into hospital with bad feelings. Of course, I hadn't had a myocardial infarction; that was always my plus when I was in hospital" (A 05.30–05.35). Revascularization was satisfactory. He said, "Of course you have to have some courage and willpower to make it work" (A 31.00).
Retirement. Various physicians (rehabilitation hospital doctor, local physician) recommended early retirement. Nobody mentioned retraining. At the time, he was shocked but later came to think that return to work or occupational retraining might have been too much stress for him anyway. He postponed the date of application for his disability pension to maximize the time period receiving sick pay. His pension was low. It took a year for him to get accustomed to staying at home. Then—helped by his wife—he obtained work as a janitor, which yielded some extra income. He was aware that his wife would get only 60% of his pension if he were to die. Although he has by now adapted to life after retirement, he says, "Financially it could be a bit better" (A 15.50).

These two cases are similar in that both retired early without postoperative resumption of employment, and the amount of their disability pension was low. However, they represent different solutions with regard to *provider identity.*

Whereas in case 05R, the wife had to make good on the patient's loss of income, in case 13R the patient did it himself. Also, *lifestyle* varied. Whereas in case 05R the patient lost all social contacts and became isolated and passive, in case 13R after an adaptation period the patient resumed active participation in work-life as a retiree, taking on a part-time job as a janitor where the pay was such that it did not jeopardize his entitlement for disability pension.

Using three types of activities as criteria, namely, *hobbies* (e.g., woodwork, carpentry in one's own hobby room), membership in a *social club* (e.g., rifle club, choral society), and *extra work* (e.g., supervising a hunting ground, housework, gardening), the retrospective cases of early retirement whose postoperative coping has been observed over 7 to 11 years can be put on a continuum from most *passive* to most *active*. Table 10–3 gives details.

Table 10–3 documents for the 11 cases adoption of a passive or active lifestyle is only partly related to the outcome of the operation in individual cases. The 2 patients with *unsuccessful* operations are 03R and 15R, and only 15R had a passive lifestyle at the time of interview. The 7 patients with long-term *relief of angina pectoris* are 05R, 17R, 19R, 30R, 32R, 37R, and 40R; among them are 4 with eventual passive lifestyle (05R, 15R, 37R, and 40R) and three with an active lifestyle, including return to work for up to 10 years (17R, 19R, and 30R). The two patients experiencing postoperative *return of symptoms* (13R, 28R) have a rather active lifestyle.

Postoperative return to work, although later converted into early retirement (as in cases 03R, 17R, 19R, and 30R), is a good predictor of an active lifestyle 7 to 11 years postoperatively. All those who temporarily returned to work managed to maintain an active lifestyle after their subsequent early retirement. Among those who did not return to work (which includes 40R, who had a half-day of return to work), only 2 of 7—13R and 28R—were able to adopt an active work-related lifestyle.

The normal male identity pattern, I believe, is more closely matched after early retirement by those who accomplish active social adjustment. In the same vein, passive lifestyle appears more alienated from the normal male identity pattern. Such alienation expresses itself in a lesser degree of independence and a higher degree of dependence on others as perceived by the patient couples. The question is what they see as the reason for the decisions regarding CABS and early retirement, as reported in the interviews.

I assume that these interview reports are not necessarily factual. Rather, I venture that *from the present-day state of mind* patient couples retrospectively reconstruct in the interview dialogue what they remember to have happened at the time (Mishler 1986). This retrospective reconstruction befits mainly the patient couple's situation at the time of the interview. The course of events leading up to the present state of affairs is reconstructed from the vantage point of the (relative) end-stage of today, viewing the situation of the past through the lens of the present.

The assumption is that the activity level or lifestyle of today constitutes

**TABLE 10–3. Early Retirement Cases in Retrospective Sample, Ranging from Most Passive to Most Active Lifestyle**

| CASE NO. | ACTIVITIES | EARLY RETIREMENT | REVASCULARIZATION | OCCUPATION |
|---|---|---|---|---|
| 37R | No hobbies<br>No social clubs<br>No extra work | At age 52,<br>1 year postop.<br>without return<br>to work (RTW) | Successful | Foreman |
| 40R | No hobbies<br>No social clubs<br>No extra work | At age 54,<br>soon after op.<br>after 1/2 day<br>of RTW | Successful | Semiskilled worker |
| 05R | No hobbies<br>No social clubs<br>No extra work | At age 55,<br>1 year postop.<br>without RTW | Successful | Unskilled worker |
| 15R | No hobbies<br>No social clubs<br>No extra work | At age 49,<br>1 year postop.<br>without RTW | Unsuccessful | Semiskilled worker |
| 32R | No hobbies<br>No social clubs<br>No extra work<br>(some sharing of housework) | At age 52,<br>soon after op.<br>without RTW | Successful | Semiskilled worker |
| 19R | Does fair amount of housework<br>Daily sports with wife (swimming, hiking, etc.) | At age 59,<br>10 years postop.<br>after 10 years<br>of RTW | Successful | Manager of retail business |
| 03R | Hobby: woodwork<br>Works in the house and garden | At age 52,<br>5 years postop.<br>after 4 years<br>RTW | Unsuccessful | Skilled worker |
| 28R | Hobby: woodwork<br>Helps to supervise hunting<br>Does work in house and garden since wife had stroke 4 years postop. | At age 51,<br>1 year postop.<br>without RTW | Successful, but return of symptoms | Supervisor on construction sites |
| 13R | Takes up extra work as janitor 2 years | At age 51,<br>7 mos. postop.<br>without RTW | Successful, but return of symptoms | Foreman |

*(continued)*

**TABLE 10–3. *(continued)***

| CASE NO. | ACTIVITIES | EARLY RETIREMENT | REVASCULAR-IZATION | OCCUPATION |
|---|---|---|---|---|
| | postop. (with his wife) | | | |
| 17R | Continues his "second business" (farming) for another 6 years until age 59, then retains advisory function to younger farmer who bought patient's machines | At age 51, 2 years postop. after 1.5 years of RTW | Successful | Semiskilled worker |
| 30R | Takes up carpentry<br>Joins choral society<br>Finds himself job as sick-fund control-person | At age 58, 7 years postop. after 6.5 years of RTW in lower job in same firm | Successful | Supervisor in industry |

the present perspective under which the patient couple perceives and reports the past events. How they remember the degree of influence exerted on the two crucial transition periods of the patient's life is shaped by the degree of mastery contained in their present-day active or passive lifestyle.

Because male identity means *independence* from outside influence, I expect that patients with a passive lifestyle describe themselves as more dependent on others when they remember the decision to be operated on. Also, they do not see themselves involved in the decision to retire early. On the other hand, patients with an active lifestyle are expected to describe themselves as having influenced the decision to operate and as having themselves decided that they wanted to quit their jobs or exerted influence on the physician(s) who decided that they should retire when they did. Table 10–4 gives details from the intensive interviews documenting the data. Table 10–5 summarizes Table 10–4.

Tables 10–3 to 10–5 distinguish between three *types of coping* on a case basis.

**TABLE 10–4. Reports on Decisions to Operate and to Retire Early**

| *CASE NO.* | *DECISION TO OPERATE* | *DECISION OF EARLY RETIREMENT* |
|---|---|---|
| 37R | Was referred from one doctor to the next, several times being reproached for simulating while he had severe symptoms; eventually the diagnosis was made because one doctor let him have an angiography. | Retirement recommended by GP* and hospital physician, Professor XY. P* and PW* made an appointment with the sick-fund agency: "Somehow we told it all to the clerk at the sick-fund and got it right with him, and 4 weeks later the pension notice arrived" (A 40.00–40.05). |
| 40R | Refused to believe that his coronary artery disease was as severe as the doctors said it was. Could not do anything but agree to the operation suggested to him because "I had to believe it; I could not prove the opposite" (A 05.15). | Physician wanted him retired, and she insisted that he quit his job. "So I tried it once but with construction work part-time is difficult anyway and it went badly and then I stopped" (A 07.10–07.30) —after one half day. "It was a difficult year for me until I got used to it (laughs) that I could no more go to work, well there was no other way, I had to stay home then" (A 07.50–08.15). |
| 05R | "They told me if you are not operated on, you are dead in 3 months, you see, and so I had no choice" (A 01.00–01.20). | Two doctors (occupational medicine, pension fund) examined P's discharge papers from his rehabilitation hospital stay: "Then the one from the employment exchange said, 'Look at it, gentlemen, how can we make work for him? He must go on a pension, nothing else is possible'" (B 12.10–12.30). |
| 15R | P is given the choice between operation and early retirement. PW says that he had no choice but to be operated on because he was in tremendous pain. P felt deceived when he was reoperated on without knowing for what. | Physician in rehabilitation hospital recommended early retirement. (P had some difficulty getting his pension.) He found it difficult to adjust to retirement. But "if you give yourself up, then you are |

*(continued)*

**TABLE 10–4. *(continued)***

| CASE NO. | DECISION TO OPERATE | DECISION OF EARLY RETIREMENT |
|---|---|---|
| | | lost anyway, which I never did" (B 29.50–30.00). |
| 32R | "The physicians told me what was the matter with me and that I could now call my wife, which of course frightened me. I've never cried, you see, but there I started, I mean it is a hard blow if you hear something like that" (A 07.10–07.30). He was told that otherwise he would have another 6 months to live. | "Well, they could not use me anywhere; it came, I would say, quite naturally that they, even the GP etcetera, that they wrote me pensioner" (A 16.15–16.20). |
| 28R | P was suspicious when being told that he was urgently to be operated on. "Said I, 'Why is that now so urgent?' 'Yes, it is urgent; it must be done; we have checked it again.' Well, now, I don't know what is so urgent; maybe they happened by chance to have an opening to be filled, I can't see anything else" (A 07.00–07.15). | The sick-fund physician told him: "'You can write that on the moon that you could work again. That you go abroad for a further commission, to work in the condition in which you are now there is no chance'" (A 19.00–19.20). "Then also the firm they joined in immediately; they said to themselves, what shall we do with the guy? We don't need him anyway. Oh, yes, the moor has done his service, away with him, nothing but out" (A 19.50–20.00). |
| 19R | Physician(s) put the decision to P and PW; they decided that "it has to be done if he is to get well" (A 08.50). He did not want to give up at age 48. Could choose between two hospitals at different locations where he wanted his operation done. | Decided that he retire from work (after a diabetic shock) rather than risk his health. Decided to leave the remaining work connected with the firm's closing down to his colleagues. His physician supported his decision to quit after 10 years of postoperative employment. |
| 03R | Got angry when told by a physician that his symptoms had improved. Subsequently, the physician arranged for his angiography. The physician later apologized to him: "'If that hadn't happened, maybe I | His physician urged him to apply for early retirement. "Said the GP, 'If you want to remain my patient, you go to the agency tomorrow morning and apply for a retirement pension. I can't |

(*continued*)

**TABLE 10–4.** ***(continued)***

| CASE NO. | DECISION TO OPERATE | DECISION OF EARLY RETIREMENT |
| --- | --- | --- |
| | wouldn't be here any longer" I told him'; 'Maybe you are right,' he said" (A 16.20–16.40). | take the responsibility any longer that you want to continue to work; otherwise you must look for another doctor" (A 18.15–18.40). |
| 13R | Decided immediately after diagnosis to go on sick leave. Later saw his doctor, said: "Doctor, I just don't want to go on like this any longer'" (A 04.10), which triggered scheduling of the operation date. | Two doctors recommended early retirement. "It was a blow for me . . . I would have liked to do something but, on the other hand, I must say I'm glad" (A 15.20–15.30). Decided himself at what time to put in the application for early retirement because he wanted to get sick pay as long as possible. |
| 17R | At the hospital everybody was astonished that P was still working despite his severe CAD. "But I had a good heart, you see, I did a lot of sports and that was why I was lucky; the heart stood up to it although I was in pain, but it did not give in" (A 03.10–03.30). P consented to the suggestion to be operated on. "Nothing else I could do, they said in 6 months it's over otherwise" (B 07.50). | One physician suggested that he return to work for the time being. Another physician said he has the will power but lacks the strength. Supervisor wanted to put P on hourly pay. This would have lowered P's income and future pension. He decided to quit work in order to preserve his level of income. "It was a difficult struggle" (A 08.25) to retire from work. He managed to persuade his supervisor to take his son on his job in his stead. |
| 30R | Took initiative in getting a correct diagnosis and a date for his operation. "Everybody must himself with this whole illness from A to Z 100% be watchful; that's what I tried to make clear to the physicians" (A 30.30–31.05). | Took enough time after the operation to feel fit when returning to work. Came to regret it nevertheless because got removed to a lower job where he was incompetent. Became depressed. Took long sick leaves on several occasions. Eventually got recommended to retire early on the grounds of his vascular disease. |

*(continued)*

**TABLE 10–4.** ***(continued)***

| CASE NO. | DECISION TO OPERATE | DECISION OF EARLY RETIREMENT |
|---|---|---|
| | | "I smuggled myself into pension status" (A 20.00) —from which time on he became an active person in more than one respect. |

*P = patient; PW = patient's wife; GP = general practitioner

1. Passive. All five patients whose lifestyle is passive (see Table 10–3) do not remember having had a choice or deciding themselves regarding CABS and early retirement. The case numbers are 05R, 15R, 32R, 37R, and 40R.
2. Active. At the other extreme, in four of the cases of active lifestyle, patients remember taking a share in decision making or, in fact, deciding on their own altogether. The case numbers are 03R, 13R, 17R, and 30R.
3. Active-passive. Between these alternatives, case 28R has an active lifestyle but remembers having no choice in the decision for surgery or early retirement. Case 19R had a choice regarding CABS and early retirement, but his life shows little preservation of an actively male lifestyle.

Up to this point, only retrospective cases have been analyzed. They elucidate coping as a *long-term* accomplishment, looking back over 7 to 11 years.

**TABLE 10–5. Independence Versus Dependence in Two Crucial Decisions**

| CASE NO. | DECISION TO OPERATE | DECISION OF EARLY RETIREMENT |
|---|---|---|
| 37R | Physician decided | Two physicians recommended |
| 40R | Forced upon P* | GP* decided |
| 05R | No choice | Doctors decided |
| 15R | No choice | Physician recommended |
| 32R | Forced upon P | Physician decided |
| 28R | Forced upon P | No choice |
| 19R | Decision left to PW* | Decided by P |
| 03R | Urged the decision | Physician urged P |
| 13R | Pushed decision | Decision by physician, timing by P |
| 17R | Physicians' suggestion but P's strong heart | Decision by P |
| 30R | Took initiative | "Smuggled himself into" pension status |

*P = patient; PW = patient's wife; GP = general practitioner

What about coping, though, as the patient-couples go through the experience of CABS and subsequent early retirement? The early-retirement cases in the *prospective* study group must be looked at to understand better how coping works.

The following questions arise with regard to independence/dependence: Do patients in the prospective study who later retire early have an active or passive view of their CABS *preoperatively*? What is their postoperative view with respect to the decision about early retirement?

The prospective study group contains 13 cases of early retirement without return to work, and 2 cases of retirement after 1 month or 1 year of postoperative return to work. Table 10–6 documents their views on how the decision to operate was made (data from preoperative interviews), their views on how early retirement was decided upon (data from the two postoperative interviews), and their retirement age and occupation.

Table 10–6 elucidates two separate issues. First, preoperative views anticipate postoperative degree of activity/passivity to a considerable extent. The three cases of passivity (03R, 05R, and 11R) perceived no initiative for themselves regarding either CABS or early retirement. The five active-passive patients (02P, 06P, 09P, 22P, and 32P) either perceived some discretion for themselves in one of the two decisions, or their role was one of agreeing to what was suggested (note that they did not complain of having no choice but spelled out a role for themselves as one who accepted the physicians' suggestion). The seven active patients (08P, 14P, 16P, 17P, 23P, 28P, and 35P) took a distinctive part in the CABS decision, and they were actively involved in either pushing for their early retirement or trying to avoid it by determined attempts to return to work.

Second, one coping strategy mentioned in the prospective case material not found in the early retirement cases of the retrospective study group is the strategy of *seeking a second opinion,* that is, having the diagnosis and proposed treatment confirmed by another physician (or more than one other physician). Such lack of credulity vis-à-vis the medical profession is obvious in case 17P but also, to a lesser extent, in cases 14P and 16P. It represents an attitude toward medical work which is typical, not of the lower classes, who usually have a compliant relationship with medicine, but of the upper classes (Koos 1954); indeed, cases 14P and 17P belong to higher-status groups. Among the higher social strata, as is known from the literature on CABS, are frequently found patients who continue their employment despite unsuccessful revascularization (Borgetto and Gerhardt 1993; Niles et al. 1980; Sieber et al. 1986).

*Social class* is measured in our study using a scale developed for Germans in life-course analysis, geared to individuals born between 1920 and 1940 and based on the indicators of occupation, education, and type of residence (house ownership versus rented housing) (Handl 1977). Its 30 levels of socioeconomic status are grouped together into six class-status groups: I (professionals, managers), II (top employees, owners of a large or medium-size business), III (mid-

**TABLE 10–6. Retirement Cases in Prospective Sample, Ranging from Most Passive to Most Active Participation in Decision-making**

| *CASE NO.* | *DECISION OF OPERATION* | *DECISION OF EARLY RETIREMENT* | *EARLY RETIREMENT* | *OCCUPATION* |
|---|---|---|---|---|
| 03P | "They must know" (A 03.50). | Has not even a say when application was made by employer or rehabilitation hospital. | At age 57 | Skilled worker |
| 05P | Does not believe in operation; decision made by angiography physician. | Physicians decide, no choice. | At age 58 | Unskilled worker |
| 11P | Lets it happen, "must be done" (A 02.45). | Decision made by sick-fund; accepts it (firm does not want him back); disability pension for 2 years initial period. | At age 54 | Foreman (construction industry) |
| 32P | "I said operation here health" (A 25.10). | Follows advice of physicians (GP,* sick-fund, physician), is convinced that lighter work is unavailable. | At age 45 | Unskilled worker (lorry driver) |
| 09P | Is reluctant but accepts that it must be done. | Lets physicians decide, but sees himself no alternative because his supervisor wants him "out." | At age 54, after 1 year of RTW | Unskilled worker (industry) |
| 22P | Does not hesitate to agree to what physician suggests. | Physicians decide and P* agrees (gets pension of 99% of previous wage). | At age 55 | Ambulance driver |

| | | | | |
|---|---|---|---|---|
| 06P | Does not want to know, lets physicians get on with their work as afraid of blood, etc. | Glad about rehabilitation hospital physician's recommendation because has been fired by employer. | At age 42 | Supervisor in small firm |
| 02P | No choice, has to trust in medics. | Decision made to quit job preoperatively, for which he has prepared himself by taking out more than one life insurance over the last years. | At age 57 | Head of finance department in industrial firm |
| 08P | Lets physicians decide but trusts them and has no fears. | Applies himself, since deems lighter work unavailable. | At age 58 | Foreman (iron industry) |
| 23P | Agrees to operation suggested to him since otherwise no life expectance. | After recommendation by two physicians, puts in application when he runs out of sick leave (he wants to retire early). | At age 52 | Skilled worker |
| 28P | Accepts that it must be done, collects his medical data actively. | Postpones application as long as possible to get maximum sick pay. | At age 56 | Semiskilled worker |
| 35P | "Always thought it would happen one day" (A 31.25). | Employer makes application because P is unlikely to RTW*; P gets 2-year lower pension but wants disability pension and goes to court. | At age 44 | Skilled worker |

(continued)

**TABLE 10–6.** ***(continued)***

| *CASE NO.* | *DECISION OF OPERATION* | *DECISION OF EARLY RETIREMENT* | *EARLY RETIREMENT* | *OCCUPATION* |
|---|---|---|---|---|
| 16P | He gives his GP "go ahead" to have operation scheduled. | Discusses early retirement thoroughly with GP. | At age 54 | Worker in chemical plant |
| 14P | Himself recommends to GP to have angiography. | Employer applies, P is relieved and agrees. | At age 50 | Weather service employee |
| 17P | Consults another GP and a cardiologist before following advice. | Tries everything to go back to work before giving in to the fact that his symptoms are too severe. | At age 49, after 1 month unsuccessful RTW | Head of local branch of bank |

*P = patient; GP = general practitioner; RTW = return to work dle-level white-collar employees, owners of a small business), IV (low-level white-collar employees, farmers, supervisors in industry), V (foremen, skilled blue-collar workers), and VI (semiskilled and unskilled blue-collar workers). Table 10–1 above uses these to describe our data material. Table 10–7 indicates how frequent the various types of coping are in the different class-status groups.

Two findings emerge from Table 10–7. First, early retirement is much more frequent in the lower classes, that is, in status groups IV to VI than in status groups I to III. A comparison between the retrospective and the prospective study groups shows that although their date of operation was approximately one decade apart, about half of the working-class males (status groups IV to VI) in both groups took early retirement (without return to work) postoperatively (7 of 14 in the R group and 11 of 23 in the P group). Furthermore, in the lower classes, three retrospectively (03R, 17R, and 30R) and one prospectively (09P) returned to work but later retired early. Status groups I to III had four cases of early retirement, among whom the only retrospective one was also the only one who temporarily went back to work. At the same time, 13 of 15 higher-class retrospective patients were employed at the time of interview or had retired at statutory age and 1 was unemployed, whereas 2 of 5 higher-class prospective patients were in the same situation. At the same time, the retrospective study population, 7 to 11 years postoperatively, comprised 4 of 14 lower-class men who were still employed or had retired at statutory age (i.e., they had rejected early retirement), but the prospective study population, approximately 18 months postoperatively, contained 11 of 23 patients still employed.

**TABLE 10–7. Type of Coping by Status Group of Retrospective and Prospective Cases**

| *STATUS GROUP* | *COPING TYPE* | *RETROSPECTIVE CASES* | *PROSPECTIVE CASES* |
|---|---|---|---|
| II | Active | 19R | 17P |
| | Active-passive | — | 02P |
| | Passive | — | — |
| III | Active | — | 14P |
| | Active-passive | — | — |
| | Passive | — | — |
| IV | Active | 30R | — |
| | Active-passive | 28R | 06P, 22P |
| | Passive | — | — |
| V | Active | 03R, 13R | 08P, 23P, 35P |
| | Active-passive | — | — |
| | Passive | 37R | 03P, 11P |
| VI | Active | 17R | 16P, 28P |
| | Active-passive | — | 09P, 32P |
| | Passive | 05R, 15R, 32R, 40R | 05P |
| TOTAL NO. OF CASES | | 11 | 15 |

Second, coping style seems to have undergone a dramatic change in the lowest social strata (status groups V and VI). Although the number of cases of early retirement in status groups V and VI remains relatively stable (eight and ten, respectively), their coping styles differ markedly between the two samples. Among retrospective cases, five were passive and three were active copers (none was active/passive). Among prospective cases, however, only three were passive copers, whereas five were active and two were active-passive. That is, when percentages are used (which is only for illustration), in the lowest social strata, some 40% retrospectively but 70% prospectively assert some mastery in their style of coping. Among early-retirement patients in the prospective study population, 12 of 15 have a somewhat active coping style and only 3 do not. Therefore, patients in the 1980s cohort appear considerably more inclined than patients in the 1970s cohort to adopt a more active coping style.

## DISCUSSION

The cases in this qualitative study are homogenous on three criteria known to correlate with high likelihood of postoperative return to work. The selection criteria for the entire study group ensure that each case has high preoperative probability of postoperative employment. These homogenous cases are investigated to clarify the conditions and biographical dynamics under which CABS patients return to work or retire early. Previous medical research has clarified already that the blue-collar workforce has a generally higher tendency to retire early than the white-collar workforce, and the highest likelihood is among workers in the lowest jobs. These findings are replicated in our sociologic study despite its specific methodologic approach.

Germany is unique among Western countries because its social security system makes it possible for every CABS patient, irrespective of age and quality of revascularization, to retire early.

The two issues favor contradictory tendencies in the cases. The three selection criteria stand for preoperative "resistance" to postoperative early retirement, but the social security system facilitates early retirement. In a way, "push" and "pull" forces regarding return to work are present at the same time, and early retirement constitutes an individual resolution of these forces.

From this vantage point, early retirement is investigated on a case basis as an outcome of biographical dynamics. It emerges that between the late 1970s and the late 1980s, the proportion of the blue-collar workforce that retired early among those most likely to return to work remained fairly constant. About half of the workers in the retrospective and prospective groups of predictably high postoperative chance of return to work took early retirement in the immediate postoperative period.

What has changed in the last decade is the coping style typically adopted by those who retire early. Three coping styles are distinguished—active, passive, and active-passive. They are defined by two dimensions: (1) postretirement lifestyle that comprises or lacks activities emulating "normal male identity" and (2) presence or absence of control by the patient-couple regarding the decisions of CABS and early retirement, as documented in the tape-recorded interview.

Active or active-passive coping was seen with half of the early retirement patients whose operation took place in the late 1970s. However, a more active coping style was adopted by some four fifths of those operated on in the late 1980s. About half of the early retirement patients in the retrospective sample had a passive style of coping. However, only one fifth of those in the prospective sample adopted a passive coping style.

In my view, an active coping style allows for a male gender identity and facilitates an approximately normal male biography after early retirement. To be sure, the typically more-active coping style of the patients in the 1980s cohort is achieved despite the fact that, with two exceptions, those patients lacked one favorable condition for an active coping style among retrospective cases; namely, they typically retired without return to work. This makes the finding more salient that early retirement patients in the 1980s cohort are highly likely to be active copers. It means that they overwhelmingly manage to preserve their work-related and independent-prone gender identity and better achieve a quality of life engendering a normal male biography after their early retirement.

The question arises as to how this change of typical coping style could have happened between the late 1970s and the late 1980s. I will venture three tentative answers to this question and then return briefly to the issue of quality of life.

1. *Changes in the diagnostic criteria.* In the early 1980s, percutaneous transluminal coronary angioplasty (PTCA) was introduced as an alternative treatment for CAD. Subsequently, upper-class patients appear to have been preferably referred for PTCA rather than CABS. Consequently, the proportion of lower-class patients has increased for the CABS clientele. Therefore, among recipients of CABS who are now predominantly working class (and, typically, older than PTCA patients), a mentality of more activity-prone coping may have come to prevail. Owing to their having had a choice (or, for that matter, their physicians having had the choice between referring them for CABS or PTCA), a more active approach to life after CABS may have emerged.
2. *Changes in the labor market.* Among patients with higher-class status (status groups I to III), the prospective study group contains three cases of early retirement without postoperative return to work but the retrospective sample contains none. That is, whereas all upper-class patients with optimal preoperative chances of postoperative employment in the 1970s group did, in fact, return to their jobs, higher-class patients in the 1980s

group seem far less prone to do so. It is true that the numbers are small and there is a decline of higher-class patients having CABS among those with optimal preoperative likelihood of postoperative job return—presumably due to the availability of choice since the early 1980s between CABS and PTCA. That three of the five higher-class patients in the prospective sample choose early retirement might reflect the worldwide trend to higher unemployment generally and the danger of unemployment in older age groups for the higher classes during the 1980s. In this situation, a biographically rational move for higher-class patient is to avoid unemployment by choosing early retirement, which may be attained through severe handicap status. The tendency of higher-class patients to join the ranks of the early retired after CABS may have an indirect effect on lower-class patients whose tendency has remained stably high. They may now be less apprehensive about their postretirement lifestyle and attitudes. They may also emulate more active higher-class coping styles by adopting or preserving their own active coping style.

3. *Changes in male self-image.* An alternative interpretation could focus on cultural values defining male identity. As an aftereffect of the "revolution of the 1960s," achievement-mindedness and belief in hard work have waned in Germany. However, the younger cohorts have been more affected by the change of work values than the older cohorts, who tended to retain their appreciation of occupational work and employment-achievement. Whereas both study groups were somewhat over 50 years at the time of their operation, most patients in the retrospective group were in their forties when the "revolution of the 1960s" occurred, whereas those in the prospective group were only in their thirties. Therefore, the younger men might have experienced more dramatic erosion of the "work-at-any-price" ethic connected with the "traditional" outlook of the German man and adopted a more flexible self-image and identity. In this vein, the typically more active coping style of the patients in the 1980s cohort signifies change of the pattern of normal male identity from books such as *Staying the Course* (Weiss 1990) to *Men in Families* (Lewis and Salt 1986).

*Quality of life* of a man who retires, I assume, is higher for those who retain their male gender identity. Those who find ways to continue rather than abandon their pattern of normal male identity are thought to be better off, preserving or attaining the quality of life that comes with self-esteem as a man. Of course, all patients eventually retire, as do, in fact, practically all those in the labor force. The point, however, is that "premature" entry into the old age status of retirement could jeopardize a CABS patient's gender identity. Comparison of the cases in our retrospective and prospective samples makes it plausible that patients today are better able to maintain the quality of life conducive to a functioning gender identity than were those a decade or more ago. When interviewed in the late 1980s, patients in the 1970s cohort typically had a lower postretirement sense of mastery after 7 to 11 years of retirement than patients in the 1980s cohort. Coping was frequently passive; that is, those patients felt driven into retirement against their will and they often pursued few activities emulating a normal male's duties. In contrast, patients in the later cohort typically managed to have a higher quality of life. Their coping appears overwhelmingly more active, giving them an opportunity to see themselves as agents of their own biographies who also engage in many activities making them "feel like a man."

## REFERENCES


ALLEN, JERILYN K. 1990. "Physical and Psychosocial Outcomes After Coronary Artery Graft Surgery: Review of the Literature." *Heart and Lung* 19:49–55.

ALMEIDA, DEYANIRA, JAMES M. BRADFORD, NANETT K. WENGER, et al. 1983. "Return to Work After Coronary Artery Surgery." *Circulation* 68 (Sup. II):295–313.

ARBEITSGRUPPE SOZIALPOLITIK. 1988. "Alter und Sozialpolitik." Pp. 132–56 in *Alter und Alltag,* edited by G. Göckenjan and H.-J. von Kontratowitz. Frankfurt, Germany: Suhrkamp.

BADURA, BERNHARD, JOSEPH BAUER, GERHARD KAUFHOLD, et al. 1987. *Leben mit dem Herzinfarkt. Eine sozialepidemiologische Studie.* Berlin: Springer.

BADURA, BERNHARD, GERHARD KAUFHOLD, HARALD LEHMANN, et al. 1988. "Soziale Unterstützung und Krankheitsbewältigung—Neue Ergebnisse aus der Oldenburger Longitudinalstudie 4 Jahre nach Erstinfarkt." *Psychosomatik Medizinische Psychologie* 38:48–58.

BORGETTO, BERNHARD and UTA GERHARDT. 1993. "Gesellschaftliches Altern und Operationserfolg nach koronarer Bypassoperation. Eine verstehende Typenanalyse." Pp. 224–27 in *Konflikte und Strukturen im neuen Europa,* edited by H. Meulemann and A. Elting-Camus. Frankfurt, Germany: Campus.

BUNDESMINISTERIUM FÜR ARBEIT UND SOZIALORDNUNG (ed.). 1977. *Anhaltspunkte für die ärztliche Begutachtung Behinderter nach dem Schwerbehindertengesetz.* Bonn, Germany: BMA.

CAINE, N., S. C. W. HARRISON, L. D. SHARPLES, and J. WALLWORK. 1991. "Prospective Study of Quality of Life Before and After Coronary Artery Bypass Grafting." *British Medical Journal* 302:511–16.

CONRAD, CHRISTOPH. 1988. "Die Entstehung des modernen Ruhestandes. Deutschland im internationalen Vergleich 1850–1960." *Geschichte und Gesellschaft* 14:417–47.

FOOKEN, INSA. 1989. "Kompetenz im Alter—ein Beitrag zur Psychologie des Mannes." Pp. 245–70 in *Kompetenz im Alter,* edited by C. Rott and F. Oswald. Vaduz, Liechtenstein: Peutinger Collegium Liechtenstein Verlag.

GEORGE, LINDA and GEORGE L. MADDOX. 1977. "Subjective Adaptation to Loss of the Work Role: A Longitudinal Study." *Journal of Gerontology* 32:456–62.

GERHARDT, UTA. 1986a. *Patientenkarrieren. Eine medizinsoziologische Studie.* Frankfurt, Germany: Suhrkamp.

______. 1986b. "Verstehende Strukturanalyse: Die Konstruktion von Idealtypen als Analyseschritt bei der Auswertung qualitativer Forschungsmaterialien." Pp. 31–83 in *Sozialstruktur und soziale Typik,* edited by H. G. Soeffner. Frankfurt, Germany: Campus.

______. 1991a. "Women's Role and Role Theory: A View from the Federal Republic of

Germany." Pp. 249–77 in *Research in the Sociology of Health Care,* Vol. 9, edited by Dorothy Wertz. Greenwich, CT: JAI Press.

______. 1991b. "Chronische Erkrankung: Handlungsrationalität und das Problem der sozialen Pathologie." Pp. 61–87 in *Gesellschaft und Gesundheit: Essays by Uta Gerhardt.* Frankfurt, Germany: Suhrkamp.

______. 1992a. "Frühberentung und Handlungsrationalität: Zur Statusdynamik der Rehabilitation von Arbeitern nach koronarer Bypassoperation." *Soziale Welt* 43:422–48.

______. 1992b. "Alternsdynamik und Rehabilitation nach koronarer Bypassoperation." *Zeitschrift für Gerontologie* 25:243–54.

______. 1992c. "The Relationship Between Medical and Occupational Rehabilitation in Two Cohorts of Coronary Artery Bypass Patients Ten Years Apart." Pp. 215–26 in *Quality of Life After Open Heart Surgery.* Dordrecht, the Netherlands: Kluwer Academic Publishers.

______. 1993. "Case-Type-Structure Analysis: The Use of Weberian Ideal-Type Methodology in Qualitative Data Interpretation." Unpublished manuscript.

GERHARDT, UTA and KLAUS KIRCHGÄSSLER. 1987. "Analyse idealtypique de carrières de patients." *Sciences Sociales et Santé* 5:41–91.

GERHARDT, UTA and JOACHIM THÖNESSEN. 1990. "Aortokoronarer Venenbypass und Rückkehr zur Arbeit." Interim Report. German National Science Foundation (Deutsche Forschungsgemeinschaft), Grant No. Ge 313/1–5. Bonn and Giessen, Germany: Justus Liebig University Medical School.

GERHARDT, UTA, BERNHARD BORGETTO, and BEATE ROCKENBAUCH. 1994. *Kranke Gesunde: Analyse von Verlaufstypen der Biographien der Berufsrückkehr und Frühberentung nach koronarer Bypassoperation.* End-of-grant-report. German National Science Foundation. (Deutsche Forschungsgemeinschaft) Grant No. Ge 313/1–5.

HACKER, R. W., H. RIEDL, I. GUGGENMOOS-HOLZMANN, and M. TORKA. 1985. "Employment Status of Patients after Coronary Artery Bypass Surgery." Pp. 38–45 in *Return to Work After Coronary Artery Bypass Surgery,* edited by P. J Walter. Berlin: Springer.

HANDL, JOHANN. 1977. "Sozioökonomischer Status und der Prozeß der Statuszuweisung—Entwicklung und Anwendung einer Skala." Pp. 101–53 and 247–63 in *Klassenlagen und Sozialstruktur,* edited by J. Handl, K. U. Mayer, and W. Müller. Frankfurt, Germany: Campus.

JACOBS, KLAUS und MARTIN KOHLI. 1990. "Der Trend zum frühen Ruhestand." *WSI-Mitteilungen* 43:498–509.

KILLIP, T. 1988. "Twenty Years of Coronary Bypass Surgery." *New England Journal of Medicine* 319:366–68.

KOHLI, MARTIN, MARTIN REIN, ANNE-MARIE GUILLEMARD, and HERMAN VON GUNSTEREN (eds.). 1991. *Time for Retirement. Comparative Studies of Early Exit from the Labor Force.* Cambridge, UK: Cambridge University Press.

KOHLI, MARTIN, HANS-JÜRGEN FRETER, MANFRED LANGEHENNING, et al. 1993. *Engagement im Ruhestand. Rentner zwischen Erwerb, Ehrenamt und Hobby.* Opladen, Germany: Leske und Budrich.

KOOS, EARL. 1954. *The Health of Regionville: What People Thought and Did About It.* New York: Columbia University Press.

KRUSE, ANDREAS. 1986. "Kompetenz bei chronischer Krankheit im Alter." *Zeitschrift für Gerontologie* 20:355–66.

LEHR, URSULA M. and ANNETTE NIEDERFRANKE. 1991. "Pensionierung." Pp. 377–88 in *Gerontolog. Medizinische, psychologische und sozialwissensschaftliche Grundbegriffe,* 2nd revised and enlarged edition, edited by W. D. Oswald, W. H. Herrmann, S. Kanowsky, et al. Stuttgart, Germany: Kohlhammer.

LEWIS, ROBERT A. and ROBERT E. SALT (eds.). 1986. *Men in Families.* Beverly Hills, CA: Sage Publishers.

LOOSE, D. A., CHR. VON FERBER, L. VON FERBER, et al. 1982. *Rehabilitation serfolgnach gefäßchirurgischen Eingriffen.* Reinbek, Germany: Einhorn.

MAYOU, RICHARD and BRIDGET BRYANT. 1987. "Quality of Life After Coronary Artery Surgery." *Quarterly Journal of Medicine* (new series) 62:239–48.

McCALL, GEORGE and JOHN L. SIMMONS. 1966. *Identity and Interaction.* Chicago: Chicago University Press.

MISHLER, ELLIOTT. 1986. "The Analysis of Interview-Narratives." Pp. 233–55 in *Narrative Psychology: The Storied Nature of Human Conduct,* edited by T. R. Sarbin. New York: Praeger.

NIEDERFRANKE, ANNETTE. 1989. "Bewältigung der vorzeitigen Berufsaufgabe bei Männern." *Zeitschrift für Gerontologie* 22:143–50.

NILES, N. W., T. H. VAN DER SALM and B. S. CUTLER. 1980. "Return to Work After Coronary Artery Bypass Operation." *Journal of Thoracic and Cardiovascular Surgery* 79:916–21.

OAKLEY, CELIA M. 1987. "Is There Life After Coronary Artery Surgery?" *Quarterly Journal of Medicine* (new series) 62:181–82.

OSTERLAND, MARTIN. 1990. "'Normalbiographie' und 'Normalarbeitsverhältnis.'" Pp. 351–62, in *Lebenslagen, Lebensläufe, Lebensstile,* edited by P. A. Berger and S. Hradil. Göttingen, Germany: Otto Schwartz.

PALMORE, ERDMAN B., BRUCE S. M. BURACHETT, GERDA G. FILLENBAUM, et al. 1985. *Retirement: Causes and Consequences.* New York: Springer.

RADLEY, ALAN. 1988. *Prospects of Heart Surgery: Psychological Adjustment to Coronary Bypass Grafting.* New York: Springer.

RADLEY, ALAN and RUTH GREEN. 1985. "Styles of Adjustment to Coronary Graft Surgery." *Social Science and Medicine* 20:461–72.

RUSSEL, RICHARD O., PIERRE ABI-MANSOUR, and NANETTE K. WENGER. 1986. "Return to Work After Coronary Bypass Surgery and Percutaneous Transluminal Angioplasty: Issues and Potential Solutions." *Cardiology* 73:306–22.

SCHMÄHL, WINFRIED. 1988. *Verkürzung oder Verlängerung der Erwerbsphase?* Tübingen, Germany: Mohr (Siebeck).

SCHMITZ, W. and M. WELSCH-HETZEL. 1987. "Wiederaufnahme der beruflichen Tätigkeit nach aortokoronaraer Bypassoperation." *Langenbecks Archiv für Chirurgie* 371:149–59.

SCHOTT, THOMAS. 1987. "Ursachen und Folgen von Erwerbsunfähigkeit nach Herzinfarkt." *Zeitschrift für Sozialreform* 33:732–43.

SCHUNTERMANN, MICHAEL F., HANS E. LÖFFLER, WALTER MÜLLER-FAHRNOW, and RICHARD BRAUN. 1990. "Die Rehabilitations-Verlaufsstatistik-Ergebnisse eines Forschungsprojektes zur Epidemiologie in der medizinischen Rehabilitation—Teil III: 'Die Reha-Anamnese.'" *Deutsche Rentenversicherung* (No. 2/1990):66–100.

SELIGMAN, MARTIN E. P. 1975. *Helplessness: On Depression, Development, and Death.* New York: Freeman.

SIEBER, R., M. E. ROTHLIN, and A. SENNING. 1986. "Berufliche Rehabilitation nach aortokoronarer Bypass-Operation." *Schweizerische Medizinische Wochenschrift* 116:838–45.

SOEFFNER, HANS-GEORG. 1989. *Auslegung des Alltags—Alltag der Auslegung.* Frankfurt, Germany: Suhrkamp.

STAUDER, K. H. 1955. "Über den Pensionierungsschock." *Psyche* 481–91.

VAILLANT, GEORGE E. and CAROLINE D. VAILLANT. 1981. "Natural History of Male Psychological Health: X. Work as a Predictor of Positive Mental Health." *American Journal of Psychiatry* 138:1433–40.

VERBAND DER RENTENVERSICHERUNGSTRÄGER (ed.). 1991. *Rentenversicherung in Zahlen und Zeitreihen.* Frankfurt, Germany: VDR.

VETTER, H. O., H. HOFMANN, K. GLONNER, et al. 1985. "Employment Status of Patients After Coronary Artery Bypass Surgery." Pp. 30–37 in *Return to Work After Coronary Artery Bypass Surgery,* edited by P. J. Walter. Berlin: Springer.

WALTER, P. J. (ed.). 1992. *Quality of Life After Open Heart Surgery.* Dordrecht, the Netherlands: Kluwer Academic Publishers.

WALTER, PAUL J., BLANCHE THIES, and UTA GERHARDT. 1983. "Wieviele Patienten nehmen nach einer Koronaroperation ihre Arbeit wieder auf?" *Medizinische Klinik und Praxis* 78(8):46–57.

WEIDEMANN, HERMANN. 1984. *Leitfaden zur beruflichen Wiedereingliederung und Berentung des Koronarkranken.* Darmstadt, Germany: Steinkopff.

WEISS, ROBERT S. 1990. *Staying the Course: The Emotional and Social Lives of Men Who Do Well at Work.* New York: Fawcett Columbine.

Chapter 11

# Oil Wells on Fire: A Study of Stress in Kuwait

*Naheel S. Al-Nafisi, Rashed J. Al-Hamdan, Hayfa H. Ali, Philip M. Moody, and Jaafar Behbehani*

As defined by Lazarus and Cohen (1977), cataclysmic phenomena are sudden, powerful events that severely tax the adaptive abilities of those who are exposed. These phenomena may be acute or chronic in that natural disasters usually pass quickly, whereas effects of war or imprisonment may be more prolonged. When events are of brief duration, psychological disturbances subside as the event ends and social cohesiveness and effective coping increase. When more prolonged, these events are associated with longer disturbances (Baum et al. 1983; Giel 1991).

The events of the Iraqi invasion of Kuwait provided a sudden and powerful stressor that had both acute and chronic components. In February 1991, 731 oil wells were set afire in Kuwait (Figure 11–1) by the Iraqi army as it precipitously evacuated Kuwait after its occupation for 6 months. The smoke and pollutants from these fires continued for about 8 months until the last fire was extinguished on November 6, 1991. The immediate effect of the fires was striking. The daytime sky was dark. Layer upon layer of oily particles and dust descended and coated all exposed surfaces. The air was thick and malodorous; persons with respiratory problems had added difficulty in breathing.

The long-term effect of this smoke upon the health of the people in Kuwait and nearby Gulf states is not yet known. However, some preliminary health-related data have been revealed. The Environmental Protection De-

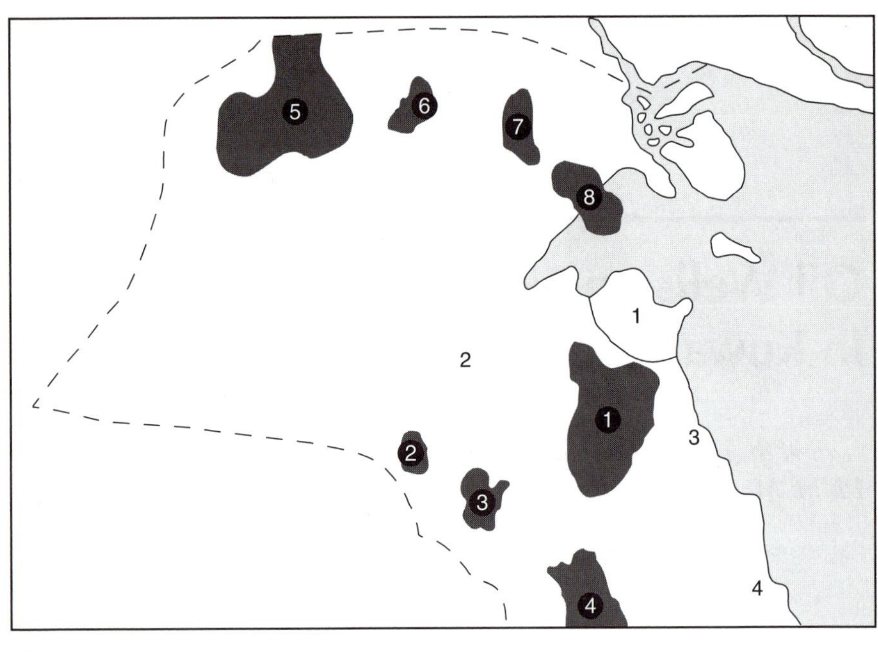

**FIGURE 11–1.** Locations of the burning oil fields and the residental areas in Kuwait City.

partment of the Kuwait Ministry of Public Health studied the data taken from the Medical Casualty of Adan Hospital, the nearest general hospital to the burning oil wells. From March to July 1991, the data available showed that 6% of the cases were bronchitis, 29.5% chest infections, and 12.5% heart problems. A comparison of these findings with the year 1990 showed no percentage of increase (Al-Awadi 1991). Many studies measuring the effects of air pollution on physical health are currently being conducted in Kuwait. The purpose of this chapter, however, is to explore the air pollution as a form of stress upon persons living in Kuwait during that period. This aspect of psychological effects is as important as the physical effects of pollution, yet it has not been studied.

A body of literature has focused on environmental disasters and their effects upon the psychological well-being of the persons who experience those disasters. For example, in 1979, following the Three Mile Island (TMI) power plant incident near Harrisburg, Pennsylvania, several investigators reported heightened somatic and psychological symptoms, as well as attitudinal concern among persons living in the immediate vicinity of the plant (Houts et al. 1980).

Other research at TMI reported evidence of psychological stress and mental health problems, including demoralization, fear, and emotional disturbances (Dohrewend et al. 1979). Other studies reported on the continuing effects, including increased risk for depression, anxiety, and heightened symptoms up to 9 months after the TMI accident (Bromet 1980a, 1980b).

Noxious physical conditions and fears over future consequences disrupt victims who are already experiencing social stress from everyday life experiences (Edelstein 1988). Furthermore, once a threat is recognized, it is appraised by individuals to ascertain its potential health implications. A decision must be reached about whether the threat can be ignored or further attention is needed (Edelstein 1988). Because appraisal of the threat of noxious physical conditions is subjective, varied interpretations and behaviors are likely. Some may take the threat seriously and either avoid the noxious condition or modify their personal behavior to lessen the effect from the condition. Other persons may not perceive the condition as serious and thus continue their personal everyday behavior as if the noxious physical condition were not there at all.

In examining socioeconomic variables and reactions to the TMI incident, it was found that persons closer to the reactor, younger people, women, and married people were more likely to react to the TMI incident (Cleary and Houts 1984).

Behavioral responses to air pollution have also been reported. For example, laboratory studies show that secondary or "passive" cigarette smoke as well as malodorous pollutants cause annoyance, irritation, fatigue, and negative affect, plus lead to dislike and avoidance of others. Furthermore, air pollution has been shown under some circumstances to increase aggression and reduce altruism. Clinical case studies suggest associations of indoor air pollutants with various behavioral abnormalities, including somnolence, irritability, psychomotor dysfunction, and depression. Correlations have been found between ambient pollutants and psychiatric admissions (Evans et al. 1987). A study by Giel (1991) in the Netherlands looked at the psychosocial reaction of two major disasters in the former Soviet Union: the Chernobyl nuclear accident and the earthquake in Armenia. Giel's research was based on observations and interviews. The purpose was to look at the contextual differences of the two disasters and the sequences for the victims trying to cope with the traumatic events. The impact in Armenia was overwhelming and tangibly evident. In Chernobyl, however, there was no real impact other than the growing awareness of a disastrous yet insidious threat from radioactivity. Post-traumatic stress disorders and outright depression were expected in Armenia, whereas in the contaminated areas of Chernobyl the health care system faced increased morbidity and use of health care services. Evans and colleagues (1987) investigated the effects of air pollution on the ability of subjects to cope with a recent life event and found poorer mental health in those subjects exposed to pollution than in their counterparts.

The heavily polluted air in Kuwait, a direct consequence of the oil wells set afire by the retreating Iraqi troops, was assumed to be a cause of stress for the people of Kuwait. However, the origin and context of the air pollution were directly related to the invasion and occupation of Kuwait by Iraq. This study assesses the stress caused by the air pollution. Related to that, it also ascertains any differences in stress between persons who were in Kuwait during the occupation and those who returned or came for the first time following the occupation's end. A second, related objective was to control for length of exposure to the air pollution and place of residence in ascertaining any differences in stress scores. The following are the specific objectives:

1. To compare the subjective stress scores related to the air pollution from the burning oil wells of adults who were in Kuwait during the whole period of the Iraqi invasion with those who arrived in Kuwait after the liberation. We hypothesized, partly on personal experience,[1] that the degree of stress regarding air pollution is higher for those who stayed outside the country during the invasion than for those who were in Kuwait under military occupation for 7 months. We also made these assumptions based on general interviews and informal meetings with others prior to the study. For the latter group, the liberation of Kuwait was, we thought, primary and the air pollution secondary.
2. To compare the subjective stress scores of persons with a long period of exposure to the pollution with that of those with a short period of exposure. It was hypothesized that those with short exposure would have higher stress scores than those with long exposure for the same reasons as in the previous hypothesis. For the latter group, liberation of Kuwait was of great value, no matter the consequences.
3. To compare the subjective stress scores of persons living in relatively lightly polluted areas with that of persons living in heavily polluted areas. We expected residents of the heavily polluted areas to express more subjective stress than residents of less polluted areas.
4. To compare the subjective stress scores of those who changed their ordinary daily behaviors such as outdoor activities and drinking tap water with those subjects who did not change.

Subjective stress from the air pollution was measured by the Impact of Event Scale (Horowitz et al. 1979), which is a scale based on a list of items describing episodes of intrusion and avoidance as the two major reactions to stressful life events. For the present study the impact of the air pollution from the oil well fires was used as the stressful life event. An example of items detecting intrusion is "I had dreams about air pollution"; an example of items detecting avoidance is "I tried not to talk about the air pollution." Thus, the questions were directed specifically to the issue of air pollution.

## METHODOLOGY

The data were collected from patients and escorts attending the outpatient clinic departments (OPDs) of three major hospitals in two areas: a highly polluted area, which is the Ahmadi area, and a less polluted area, Farwania, during a 4-day period, November 16 to 20, 1991. (The last oil well fire was extinguished in November 1991.)

The sample (N = 511) was collected from every individual attending the OPDs, whether they were patients or the escorts of the patients. Thirty individuals refused to complete the questionnaire because of illiteracy or related problems. Thus, we obtained a response rate of 94%.

The questionnaire consisted of three subdivisions. The first included demographic data: gender, age, nationality, area of residence, and education. The exposure to air pollution was determined by asking about the presence of the individual during the invasion, whether he or she had left during the invasion, the date of return to Kuwait, and if he or she had left the country again. This enabled us to calculate the number of months each respondent was exposed to the air pollution resulting from the fires of the oil wells.

The second part of the questionnaire contained the Impact of Event Scale, which consisted of 15 items, 8 of which described episodes of intrusion and 7 described episodes of avoidance. The subscores of intrusion and avoidance were added to give a total subjective stress score.

The scale was first administered by Horowitz as reported in 1979 to 66 adults who sought psychotherapy as a result from serious life events ranging from bereavements to accidents to surgery. Each subject completed the Impact of Event Scale after the initial interview, which averaged 25 weeks after the occurrence of the event. The results showed that all items were endorsed frequently. The scale was then given to a new sample: 25 physical therapy students starting to dissect a cadaver for the first time. The students completed the Impact of Event Scale twice and the test-retest reliability found to be 0.87 for the total stress scores (Horowitz et al. 1979).

The Impact of Event Scale was translated from English to Arabic, and the wording was modified to suit the normal layperson in Kuwait. The task was not difficult. However, one of the 15 statements proved difficult to render in Arabic, as the responses subsequently revealed. We decided to delete it from the results.

The third part of the questionnaire dealt with changes in behavior in response to the air pollution. These included changing habits like outdoor activities, drinking tap water, time spent in outdoor activities, allowing children to play outdoors, and waiting for clear days for outside activities.

On the basis of data obtained from the Kuwait Environment Protection Council, which measured pollution in Kuwait, we divided the residential areas into lightly and heavily polluted areas and then selected hospitals accordingly. The Kuwait Oil Company Hospital and Adan Hospital were chosen to represent the highly polluted areas, whereas Farwainia Hospital was chosen to reflect the relatively less polluted area (Fig. 11–2 and 11–3). We surveyed subjects from the three above hospitals on four successive days from 8.00 A.M. to 1:00 P.M. in November 1991.

The residential areas were divided into two groups: highly polluted areas (N = 264) and less polluted areas (N = 237) (nonrespondents N = 10) and the duration of exposure, which was calculated in months, with the short exposure group (N = 123) those individuals who were exposed to the pollution for 4 months or less and the prolonged exposure group (N = 388) those individuals exposed for more than 4 months. The maximum exposure period was 8 months, from February to November 1991. The exact area of residence was obtained from each respondent, who was then coded into a heavily or lightly polluted area.

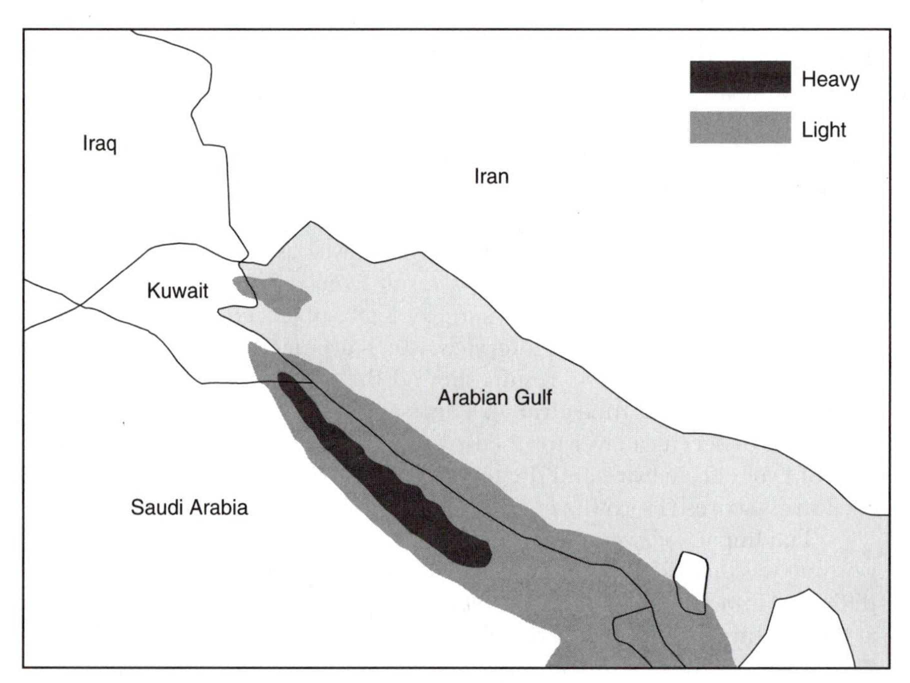


NOAA Satellite Derived
Plume Distribution
09 July 1991 10:54Z

**FIGURE 11–2.** The location of the smoke from the north and south burning oil wells.

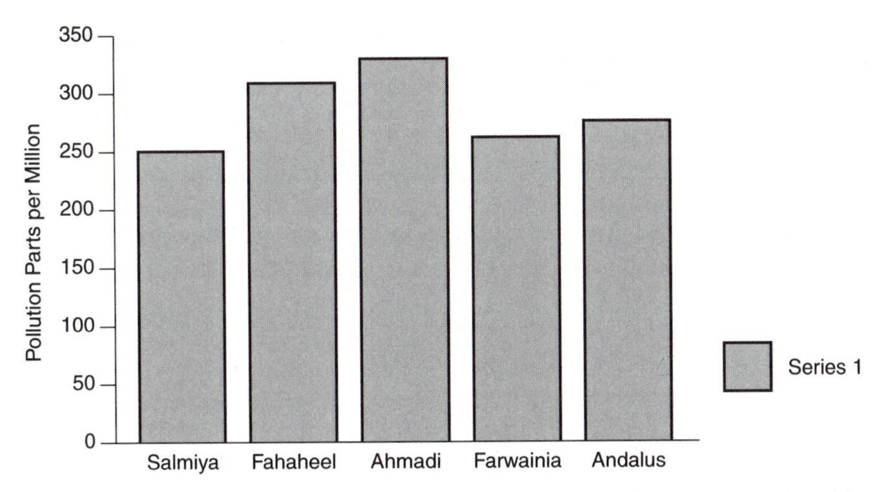


**FIGURE 11–3.** Concentration of pollutants (parts per million) by neighborhood location.

The responses to the Impact of Event Scale included not at all (0), rarely (1), sometimes (3), and frequently (5). These responses were added, giving a total stress score. The present sample had a mean stress score of 36.9, compared with Horowitz's (1979) sample of 66 stress clinic patients, which had a mean of 35.3 for male patients and 42.1 for female patients.[2]

The sample was 62.2% male and 37.8% female. Kuwaitis made up 75% of the sample; 25% were non-Kuwaiti. Ages ranged from 18 to 65, with a mean of 28.5 years. Seven percent of the sample had a university degree, 66.5% had a high school certificate, and 20.9% had less than a high school certificate. Missing data on education accounted for 6.3% of the total sample.

The behavior questions dealt with changes in drinking of water, staying outdoors, allowing children to play outdoors, sports, and other outdoor activities. The t-test was used to analyze the results.

## RESULTS

As seen in Table 11–1, older patients had a higher stress score ($\overline{X}$ = 37.9) than younger subjects ($\overline{X}$ = 36.3), although it was not statistically significant. Females had a higher stress score ($\overline{X}$ = 37.4) than males ($\overline{X}$ = 36.6), which is not statistically significant. Married subjects had lower stress scores ($\overline{X}$ = 36.7) than single persons ($\overline{X}$ = 37.3), which is also not statistically significant.

There were no differences in stress scores between subjects who stayed in Kuwait the entire time of the Iraqi occupation of Kuwait ($\overline{X}$ = 36.7) and those who were not present the entire time ($\overline{X}$ = 37.0) (Table 11–1). However, there

**TABLE 11–1. Comparison Between Mean Stress Scores of Sample (N = 511) Dichotomized by Selected Independent Variables**

| VARIABLE | STRESS SCORE $\overline{X}$ | SD | *t* | *P* |
|---|---|---|---|---|
| Age | | | | |
| Younger (< 28 yrs)(N = 231) | 36.3 | 10.4 | | |
| Older (28+ yrs)(N = 280) | 37.9 | 11.5 | 1.50 | NS |
| Gender | | | | |
| Female (N = 193) | 37.4 | 9.8 | | |
| Male (N = 318) | 36.6 | 11.7 | 0.85 | NS |
| Marital status | | | | |
| Married (N = 369) | 36.7 | 9.6 | | |
| Not married (N = 138) | 37.3 | 11.5 | 0.68 | NS |
| Present during Iraqi occupation | | | | |
| Yes (N = 246) | 36.7 | 11.0 | 0.28 | NS |
| No (N = 265) | 37.0 | 11.2 | | |
| Duration of exposure | | | | |
| Short (N = 123) | 38.6 | 10.8 | 1.96 | < 0.05 |
| Long (N = 388) | 36.3 | 11.1 | | |
| Residential area | | | | |
| High pollution (N = 264) | 38.0 | 11.0 | 2.54 | <0.01 |
| Low pollution (N = 237) | 35.5 | 11.1 | | |

$\overline{X}$ = mean; SD = standard deviation; *t* = t test; *P* = probability.

was a significant difference ($P = 0.05$) in stress scores between subjects who had low exposure ($\overline{X} = 38.6$) to pollution and those who had high exposure ($\overline{X} = 36.3$) (Table 11–1). Furthermore, subjects from highly polluted areas had a significantly higher stress score ($\overline{X} = 38.0$) than persons from less polluted areas ($\overline{X} = 35.5$) (Table 11–1).

Finally, we were interested in the effect of the air pollution on behavior. We wanted to find the differences in stress scores between those persons who changed their behavior because of the air pollution and those who did not change their behavior.

Table 11–2 shows that 48.5% did not stop drinking tap water but 51.5% did so. Those who stopped drinking tap water had a mean stress score of 38.8 and those who did not stop drinking tap water had a lower mean stress score of 34.8, which was significantly different ($P < 0.01$).

Examining the second item, "staying outdoors less," we found that 36.4% of subjects did not change their habits whereas the remaining 63.6% limited their outdoor exposure. However, the difference in stress scores between the two groups was not significant.

**TABLE 11–2. Effect of Air Pollution: Comparison Between Mean Stress Scores of Those Who Changed Their Behavior and Those Who Did Not**

| | YES | | | NO | | | |
|---|---|---|---|---|---|---|---|
| | | STRESS SCORE | | | STRESS SCORE | | |
| *BEHAVIOR CHANGE* | *%* | $\overline{X}$ | *SD* | *%* | $\overline{X}$ | *SD* | *P* |
| I stopped drinking tap water because of air pollution. | 51.5 | 38.8 | 10.2 | 48.5 | 34.8 | 11.6 | 0.0001 |
| I spend less time outdoors because of air pollution. | 63.6 | 37.4 | 11.1 | 36.4 | 35.9 | 10.9 | NS |
| Because of air pollution I minimized the time children stay outdoors. | 81.2 | 37.3 | 0.8 | 18.8 | 34.2 | 11.7 | 0.05 |
| My outdoor sports activity was reduced. | 67.1 | 37.4 | 10.7 | 32.9 | 35.8 | 11.7 | NS |
| I waited for clear and sunny days to spend time outdoors with friends or family. | 81.2 | 37.4 | 0.7 | 18.8 | 34.7 | 12.2 | 0.05 |

$\overline{X}$ = mean; SD = standard deviation; *P* = probability.

Children were a major worry for their parents; the great majority, 81.2%, limited the outdoor time, whereas only 18.8% did not prevent their children from spending time outdoors. Moreover, parents who reduced the time for their children to stay outdoors had higher stress scores (X = 37.2) than those who did not (X = 34.2); this difference was significant ($P < 0.05$).

Outdoor sports activities were changed in 67.1% because of the pollution compared with the 32.9% who were not affected by the polluted air. The latter group had less subjective stress than the former, but the difference was not significant.

Only 18.8% did not stop going out with friends and family members, whereas 81.2% changed their habits and went out only when the atmosphere was relatively clear. Those who were not deterred by the pollution had a significantly lower degree of subjective stress than those who were deterred by the pollution.

## DISCUSSION

The heavily polluted air in Kuwait, caused by the oil wells ignited by the retreating Iraqi troops, was a stressful event for people in Kuwait. However, the ultimate origin of the air pollution was the invasion of Kuwait, which itself was a major cause of stress. Thus, it is difficult to separate people's feelings toward these two negative events.

In our study we concentrated on air pollution and examined the degree of subjective stress resulting from it. We used the Impact of Event Scale (Horowitz et al. 1979) to study the stressful effect of air pollution, isolated as much as possible from other associated stressing factors.

We found that the stress scores obtained from responses to the questions on the scale were similar to those obtained by Horowitz's stress clinic patients (Horowitz et al. 1979). We did not find any differences in stress scores between younger and older subjects, men and women, and married and single people. These data do not conform to the results found by Cleary et al. (1984) on TMI.

In our first assumption, we anticipated a lower degree of subjective stress in persons who stayed inside Kuwait during the invasion than in those who were outside the country during the time of occupation. We hypothesized that for those who stayed inside Kuwait, the main goal was to end the occupation, no matter what it might cost. We assumed that for them the air pollution was a secondary concern resulting in a lower degree of subjective stress. However, the air pollution itself was also a major source of stress. We determined this from general interviews and informal meetings with others prior to carrying out this study. The results obtained, however, revealed a nonsignificant difference between the two groups. Air pollution had caused subjective stress in those who were outside the country as well as in those who were inside Kuwait during the Iraqi occupation. Both groups of subjects reported high stress scores from the air pollution, and thus no significant differences were found. Furthermore, it is difficult to know the effects of the Iraqi occupation on those persons outside of Kuwait because they could have experienced great stress from concern about friends and family who were inside Kuwait.

The results of the study confirmed our second expectation—that those who lived in highly polluted areas encountered more stress than subjects living in less polluted areas. A study conducted in New York by Howe (1988) and Cleary et al. (1984) noted a positive association between actual residential distance and concern about radioactive leakage into the air and water (TMI accident). The closer the people lived to TMI, the stronger was the perceived threat to them (Cleary et al. 1984). This was further confirmed by a study done by Lindin et al. (1989) in Sweden. The study showed that people in the high-risk zone (heavy fallout) had stronger negative reactions to the Chernobyl accident and higher frequencies of changed habits than people in the country as a whole (Weisaeth 1991). The duration of exposure was also an important factor affecting the degree of subjective stress. The results showed a significant relationship between the two parameters in that those who were exposed for a shorter period of time to air pollution had a higher mean of subjective stress than those who were exposed for a prolonged period of time. Subjects who were exposed for a longer period of time adapted—they developed a coping mechanism. The relationship between coping and stress reactivity has been studied in a handful of general population studies. Such studies show that people who demonstrate a coping strategy generally have better physical and emotional health outcomes (Mullen and Suls 1982). This explains the lower scores of subjective stress in those who were exposed to longer duration of pollution. Finally, those who made behavioral changes in not drinking tap water, reducing the time their children played outside, and waiting for sunny clear days for outdoor activities due to the air pollution had higher subjective stress scores than their counterparts.

What were the limitations of this study? Reliability and sensitivity tests for the Arabic translation of the Impact of Event Scale were not conducted because of time constraints. Furthermore, data were collected 10 to 14 days after all the oil well fires were put out. Stress scores might have been different if the fires had been burning at the time the data were collected.

Although many studies have focused on stress and environmental disasters caused by humans (Edelstein 1988), our study on the oil well fires in Kuwait is one of the few that discusses the effect of human-made disasters, on such a large scale, on the psychological health and the behavior of the public, especially since this disaster followed the encompassing stressful events of war itself.

In sum, more studies are needed to analyze the psychological effects of disasters such as the one experienced in Kuwait. It is anticipated that research now underway on post-traumatic stress in Kuwait will help resolve some of the issues raised here. We believe this study will contribute to the mounting effort of sociologists and other social scientists and public health specialists to assess the stressful impact of human-made and natural environmental degradation.

## NOTES

1. This applies to the first three authors of this research, who were present in Kuwait during the Iraqi occupation.
2. Horowitz et al. (1979) also found the mean stress scores of a control sample of medical students to be 6.9 for males and 12.7 for females.

## REFERENCES

Al-Awadi, Abdulrahman A. 1991. "Environmental Pollution Resulting from the Iraqi Invasion Of Kuwait." From a lecture given to the National Guard in Kuwait, October 1991.

Baum, Andrew, Robert J. Gatchel, and Marc A. Schaeffer. 1983. "Emotional, behavioral and physiological effects of chronic stress at Three Mile Island." *Journal of Consulting and Clinical Psychology* 51:565–72.

Bromet, Evelyn J. 1980a. *Preliminary Report on the Mental Health of Three Mile Island Residents.* Pittsburgh, PA: Westerns Psychiatric Institute.

______. 1980b. *Three Mile Island: Mental Health Findings.* Pittsburgh, PA: Westerns Psychiatric Institute and Clinic and the University of Pittsburgh.

CLEARY, PAUL D. and PETER S. HOUTS. 1984. "The Psychological Impact of the Three Mile Island Incident." *Journal of Human Stress* Spring:28–34.

DOHREWEND, BRUCE P., BARBARA S. DOHREWEND, S. V. KASL, and G. J. WARHEIT. 1979. *Report of the Task Group on Behavioral Effects to the President's Commission on the Accident at the Three Mile Island.* Washington, DC: US Government Printing Office.

EDELSTEIN, MICHAEL R. 1988. *Contaminated Communities: The Social and Psychological Import of Residental Toxic Exposure.* Boulder, CO: Westview Press.

EVANS, GARY W., STEPHEN V. JACOBS, DAVID DOOLEY, and RALPH CATALANO. 1987. "The Interaction of Stressful Life Events and Chronic Strains on Community Mental Health." *American Journal of Community Psychology* 15:23–34.

GIEL, R. 1991. "The Psychosocial Aftermath of Two Major Disasters in the Soviet Union." *Journal of Traumatic Stress* 4:381–92.

HOROWITZ, MARDI, NANCY WILNER, and WILLIAM ALVAREZ. 1979. "Impact of Event Scale: A Measure of Subjective Stress." *Psychosomatic Medicine* 41:209–18.

HOUTS, PETER, R. W. MILLER, G. K. TOKUHATA, and K. S. HAM. 1980. *Health-related Behavioral Impact of the Three Mile Island Nuclear Accident (Report submitted to the TMI Advisory Panel on Health-related Studies).* Hershey, PA: Pennsylvania Department of Health.

HOWE, HOLLY L. 1988. "A Comparison of Actual and Perceived Residential Proximity to Toxic Waste Sites." *Archives of Environmental Health* 43:415–19.

LAZARUS, RICHARD S. and FRANCES COHEN. 1977. "Environmental Stress." Pp. 90–127 in *Human Behavior and Environment, vol. 2,* edited by J. F. Wohlwill and I. Altmann. New York: Plenum Press.

LINDIN, T., B. MARDBERG, and U. OTTO. 1989. "The Chernobyl Disaster: Psychological and Psychiatric Effects in Sweden." Unpublished.

MULLEN, BRIAN and I. SULS. 1982. "The Effectiveness of Attention and Rejection as Coping Style: A Meta Analysis of Temporal Differences." *Journal of Psychosomatic Research* 26:43–49.

WEISAETH, LARS. 1991. "Psychological Reaction in Norway to Nuclear Fallout from the Chernobyl Disaster." Pp. 53–80 in *Communities At Risk: Collective Responses to Technological Hazards,* edited by S. R. Couch and J. S. Kroll-Smith. New York: Peter Long Publishing.

Chapter 12

# The Medical Dignity of the Individual: A Cultural Exploration

*Eugene B. Gallagher*

In teaching undergraduate medical sociology courses, I have recently used a video entitled "Traditional Healing in Mexico" (Toledo 1989). It shows that health care can be given by professionals who function very differently from the doctors with which my students are familiar, and in physical premises quite different from the accustomed medical suites and clinics.

One especially provocative part of the video portrays an 80-year-old male herbalist at work. He is a very busy healer, seeing some 200 patients daily. He discourages patients from giving narrative accounts of symptoms; for diagnosis he relies on his own rapid manual and visual inspection. However, there is more to it than simply saving time. He believes that he has divinely given diagnostic powers, as do his patients. They, like him, are poor, uneducated rural folk. Most of them live in the vicinity; some, however, travel many miles to see him. His family assists him in gathering, cutting, grinding, drying, and mixing the locally available plants that form the material base of his healing activity.

His practice setting is rustic and unadorned. It consists of a sparsely furnished examination and treatment room and a waiting room full of patients and accompanying family members. Much of what goes on in one room is visible from the other.

One scene shows the herbalist emerge from the treatment room with a patient to whom he is administering an inhalant medication—perhaps camphor or ammonia. Then he proceeds to walk around the waiting room, prompting the people there also to inhale the healing vapor. The film shows many of them inhaling, coughing, and then breaking into smiles and laughter. No doubt they are conscious of the filmmaker's camera, but perhaps they are also slightly embarrassed at being socially exposed to each other in a moment of physiologic dishabille.

I ask students to critique the video: How does the health care depicted in it differ from what you are personally familiar with? I receive many responses that focus disapprovingly on the patient's *lack of privacy:* "It's really awful the way people in the waiting room can look right in on the doctor and the patient." Often added to this response are other negative comments about the casual, communal treatment in the waiting room. "Why does the doctor come out of the treatment room like that?" "What sort of medicine could it be that's good for everyone?" "A place like that and a doctor like that may be all right for those people, but for myself, I want something better!"

These are the judgments of middle-class undergraduate students in a state university. Their critiques reveal important truths about the expectations that patients in the individualistic societies of the contemporary West typically carry with them into medical situations—about the patient's sense of self and his or her claims to dignity in meeting with the doctor and other health personnel.

Some students used this classroom situation as a forum to complain about the casual impersonal treatment that they feel they get at the university health service. They said that the doctors have just two or three different prescriptions that they give to everyone, close to the notion that "one size fits all." Without denying the students' sense of grievance, it still seems to me that the university doctors differ in one important respect from the Mexican herbalist: The herbalist transformed a clinical occasion into a communal one, but the university doctors adhered to norms of privacy and confidentiality.

The Mexican video episode and my students' reactions to it are the background and stage for the main thesis of this chapter: *Medical care in modern society is an important avenue for recognizing the dignity of the individual,* for lifting him or her out of the ascriptive forces of class and ethnicity that are the hallmark of tradition, and for counteracting the brisk impersonality of urban life. Medical care has *surplus meaning* beyond its instrumental value (which is of demonstrable benefit to the individual and/or which is part of professionally accepted treatment/care protocols). That surplus meaning is the "medical dignity of the individual," to be elucidated after I examine a series of related concepts: the expanding scope of medical care, the medicalized self, medicalization, and medical care as a human right.

## THE EXPANDING SCOPE OF MEDICAL CARE

The point is frequently made by medical sociologists and other social observers that the role of medicine in society has grown remarkably within recent decades. Medical sociologists have frequently averred that the scope of medicine in society has increased tremendously within recent decades.[2] This is a general trend that can be documented in virtually every nation of the world, both industrialized and developing.

Empirical indicators of the trend include features such as the following: The number of workers in the labor force who provide medical care has risen greatly. This change is an important component of the broad sociohistorical movement of economies from rural-agricultural to urban-industrial and thence to service economies; medical services are a sizable fraction of the gainful services delivered in modern economies. Paralleling labor force changes are fiscal changes, such as shifts in the relative share of components of the annual gross national product (GNP). In the United States, for example, each of the past four decades has seen at least a 1% increase in the relative share of the GNP devoted to health care; in the 1990s, however, the current is swelling into a deluge, such that the 1990 figure of 12% may jump to 15% by the year 2000. Current efforts at health care cost containment in the United States must be tempered by the realization that a shrinking of the medical care system could well put many people out of work—an increase in a stubborn structural unemployment of highly specialized workers whose skills are not easily transferable into other kinds of work (Purdom 1994).[3]

The foregoing figures refer to the production of services. Medical work is labor-intensive—one unit of service, such as an appendectomy, drawing on diverse coordinated professional skills plus background maintenance services such as room and food services in a hospital. One might say that health services require more and more to produce less and less. However, on the side of consumption of services, the curve of utilization is rising. There are, to be sure, some particular niches of reduction. In the United States, the average length of hospitalization dropped after the introduction 10 years ago of the diagnosis-related group (DRG) or flat-rate principle of reimbursement. Also, on a worldwide scale the past 20 years have seen a marked drop in mental hospitalization for dealing with severe mental illness.

Even in such instances, however, the specific reductions may well have led to offsetting compensatory increases in the provision of other services, such as less hospitalization but more counseling in the community and more use of psychoactive medication. It would be difficult to chart empirically such compensations, but it is expected that, given the upward curve of the health care system as a whole, specific "local" and categorical reductions will be tempered by increases in other directions. Furthermore, the fluid dynamism of the system can be seen in the fact that new forms of service and organization are being continuously created, which make it difficult to track the full ramifications of any single change in services.

## THE MEDICALIZED SELF WITHIN THE EXPANDING HEALTH CARE SYSTEM

Through the foregoing discussion of the increasing weight and complexity of medical care in society, I have set forth the societal context within which important moral and socioeconomic changes are occurring in the significance of medical care for the individual and in the growing importance attached to sheer *access* to medical care.

My argument is that the technologic powers of medicine are, in their ever-widening arc of employment, not simply the practical application of new remedies to the ancient human problems of pain, disability, and suffering, but rather that they develop in an interactive counterplay with a modern (some might say "postmodern") sense of the social self.

This social self is, in the ways in which social scientists have analyzed modernity, a strongly individualized entity. In its multiple aspects, the modern self is ideally capable of formulating and acting in its economic self-interest and of actualizing its legal and political rights, self-reflective and responsible to its own conscience, free and unconstrained in its spiritual aspirations and religious affiliations, able to form affectionate, sexual, and family commitments, and able in concert with chosen others to advance the interests of a larger community.

To this conception of the modern self, as it has been formed within the crucible of industrial, demographic, and political change that has enveloped the world during the past four centuries, must now be added the notion of the self as the object, beneficiary, and consciously reflective user of medical services. This "health service user" is not yet as fully formed as "economic man," but even at the present point it is more than an incidental aspect of the modern self.

For convenience, I call this entity the "medicalized self." It is related to the related term *medicalization,* a concept that has achieved wide usage within the past 15 or 20 years. Medicalization designates the widespread tendency in contemporary societies to expand the meaning of medical diagnosis and the relevance of medical care.

I will briefly review how other scholars have discussed medicalization. According to Conrad (1975), medicalization is "defining behavior as a medical problem or illness and mandating or licensing the medical profession to provide some type of treatment for it." In Conrad's thinking, medicalization signifies the growing tendency to relabel behaviors formerly regarded as bad, wicked, or weak (such as alcoholic excesses); under the new label, these behaviors are regarded as naturally exigent rather than intentional, as "illness" rather than "badness," and social acceptance and treatment are urged rather than rejection or punishment for those who exhibit such behaviors. As specific examples, he offers the medical treatment of alcoholism and drug addiction and also the diagnosis of violent behavior as a genetic trait or brain disorder.[4]

Fox's conception of medicalization is less pointedly analytical than Conrad's but it is laid out on a broader historical and cultural plane. Thus she writes: "Accompanying the increasingly comprehensive idea of what constitutes health and what is appropriate for medical professionals to deal with is the growing conviction that health and health care are rights rather than privileges, signs of grace, or lucky, chance happenings. In turn, these developments are connected with higher expectations on the part of the public about what medicine ideally ought to be able to accomplish and to prevent" (Fox 1977, p. 10).

Although Fox does embrace Conrad's notion of "the medicalization of deviance," she adds to it the idea that the scope of medical intervention has been enlarged to address all manner of personal shortcomings, frustrations, and problems—such as short stature, infertility, excess fertility, learning difficulties, and sexual dysfunction. Included also are the unambiguously somatic crises, such as cancer, tuberculosis, stroke-induced paralysis, and sensory impairments that can sometimes be cured by the biomedical "miracles" such as the antibiotics or at least alleviated by halfway interventions such as hemodialysis and insulin. Fox also includes in her conception of medicalization the enormous increase in social and legal status that has overtaken the medical profession, particularly in the United States: "The great 'power' that the American medical profession, particularly the physician, is assumed to possess and jealously and effectively to guard is another component of the society's medicalization" (Fox 1977, p. 12).

The most far-reaching, and on that account controversial, conception of medicalization comes from Illich. Instead of seeing it merely as one element in contemporary life, co-existing with other, possibly countervailing trends, Illich sees it as a unilaterally dominating and—from his Marxist-Catholic (liberation theology) perspective—corrupting force (Illich 1976, 1994).[5] He believes that the exaltation of biomedicine diminishes the capacity of human beings to deal with anxiety, suffering, and death. Their autonomy is overwhelmed by the encroachments of the health professions and undermined at a cultural level by claims about biomedical discoveries.

Although medicalization constitutes a powerful, complex, and admittedly not entirely benign trend in modern society, Illich's dark vision of it strikes me as hysterical and overblown. With the characteristic provocativeness of scholastic logic and flamboyant rhetoric, he pushes medicalization beyond its empirical reach, in order to condemn it.

The notion of the medicalized self, as I intend it, does not stretch to include the abject dependence on medicine, the iatrogenic damage, and the addictive propensities that deeply color Illich's picture of what modern medicine has done to modern man.[6] This caveat is the reason why I speak of the medicalized self with some trepidation. Well short of Illich's picture, I wish instead to formulate the medicalized self as a strong emergent side of the total modern self who may become the demoralized wretch that Illich depicts but who, alternatively, may master his or her relationship to medicine to personal advantage, with enhanced rather than diminished personal autonomy. I do not reject, however, Illich's picture as a totally impossible outcome of the medicalization process. The concept of the medicalized self has an elastic quality to it, envisioning Illich's wretch as a plausible but not inexorable, and certainly not currently realized, outcome.

To the medicalized self, illness is not a fated aspect of human existence but rather an empirically caused, frequently remediable state for which medical care is a valuable resource. In the medicalized society, the reigning presumption is that sick or ailing people seek medical services and use them in keeping with the character of the available technology, in accordance with their personal tastes and values, and in the light of their autonomous reflective assessment of the benefits and hazards of alternative types of intervention. Although the foregoing is an idealized statement of how medical care would be available in a nondominating mode, the Illich position is a more stringent model in its assumption that medical culture sweeps away individual judgment and autonomy.

In the foregoing statement, the phrase "reigning presumption" indicates that, in contrast with earlier times when individuals were less prone to seek medical care, in the modern era of medicalization the medicalized self, as a rule, opts for medical care. Whether any particular individual does so, given a certain level of symptoms or distress, depends upon factors that are familiar in sociologic analysis—the power of prevailing norms, the influence of social networks, available information, economic expense, and situational convenience. The phenomenon of medicalization indicates a major historical change but it is nonetheless an intermediate position, less extreme than the Illich vision of a society cowed and subjugated by health values and medical imperatives.

## HEALTH CARE AS A HUMAN RIGHT

It is no accident that the formation of the concept of health care as a human right has occurred in the period of great growth in the effectiveness of biomedicine, the process of medicalization, and the emergence of the medicalized self.

One of the earliest statements dealing with health care as a human right appears in the Universal Declaration of Human Rights, adopted by the United Nations General Assembly in 1948. It states: "Everyone has the right to a standard of living adequate for the health and well-being of himself and of his family including food, clothing, housing and medical care and necessary social services, and the right to security in the event of unemployment, sickness, disability, widowhood, old age or other lack of livelihood in circumstances beyond his control" (United Nations General Assembly 1948, p. 105).

A more recent and much-debated statement is the formulation coming from the 1978 WHO conference at Alma-Ata: "The Conference strongly reaffirms that health, which is a state of complete physical, mental and social well-being, and not merely the absence of disease or infirmity, is a fundamental human right and that the attainment of the highest possible level of health is a most important world-wide goal whose realization requires the action of many other social and economic sectors in addition to the health sector" (World Health Organization 1978, p. 2).

The right to health care is a relatively recent entrant into the gallery of human rights. It can be better comprehended if placed in historical sequence with other, earlier enunciated types of human rights.

All statements concerning human rights envisage an abstract human being who stands for the mass of humanity. This abstraction rises directly out of the trend of Western humanist-rationalist thinking that has since the Enlightenment progressively refined concepts of the individual (or the "person"). The individual is the bearer of human rights; "society" or "government" is conceived of as the counterpoised opposite entity, upon which falls the duty of recognizing and implementing the rights of the individual.

In the political sphere, the applicable rights embrace the whole fabric of representative government—the government's mandate resting upon the consent of the governed; and the individual's juridical rights "against" even a representative government, as expressed in the Bill of Rights, the first 10 amendments to the U.S. Constitution. These legal-political rights are probably nowhere obtainable in full measure, not even in the liberal democracies; they are, however, only grudgingly conceded in authoritarian Third World nations. The opponents of these rights usually emphasize the embeddedness of the individual within various ascriptive solidarity groups. Typically they assert the need and right of the "community" to define, guide, and control the interests of the individual (An-Na'im 1992).

Economic rights followed political rights. They were first formulated as "property rights" that guarantee to the individual means of reaping and retaining economic advantage from his enterprise, safe from both private thievery and arbitrary confiscation by the government. With the spread of the Industrial Revolution, mass production, and large-scale corporate organization, an important new economic right was added to property rights, namely the right to employment; and modern governments find themselves obligated to shape an economy that sustains full employment or, for the unemployed, a redistribution of income to provide a minimal base of sustenance. The individual's right to employment does not fall upon any specific grantor, nor is it an enforceable right that the individual can lay upon the government; in this respect it resembles the right to health care. The right to employment is, instead, a "policy right"—a goal that the government seeks to achieve through economic strategies. In many developing countries, where industry is not yet well developed but millions of people have left subsistence agriculture behind and migrated to metropolitan areas, governments attempt to shore up employment by themselves hiring the otherwise unemployed.

Western liberal thinkers have traditionally emphasized political-legal rights. They have had much less to say about economic rights, their conceptual tools and predilections being much weaker for dealing with the latter. Marxist and socialist thinkers have had the opposite weakness; they champion economic rights but cannot imagine why individuals who are employed, well-fed, clothed, and housed would want political rights and why a government able to sustain a full-employment economy should also be politically accountable to the governed.

Considered as a basic, universal human right, the right to health care has not yet taken its place within overarching philosophies of human nature and society to the same extent as have political and economic rights.[7] Neither Western liberalism nor socialism, for example, offers a distinctive view of the health needs or predispositions of the individual. This philosophical quietude reflects the fact that in the nineteenth century and earlier, medical care had not yet gained the effectiveness and assumed the social magnitude that it has attained during the twentieth century. In the period when the core ideas of political democracy, capitalism, and socialism were being laid down, the premodern technologies and social institutions for health care, passive in outlook, had not yet generated concerns about access to treatment, effectiveness of medical procedures, and equity in paying for it.

The nineteenth-century predecessors of today's articulate advocates of health care as a human right formulated intermediate positions. Thus, the English sanitary movement scrutinized the health-aversive conditions of industrialization and urbanization in England and concluded that poor health was a major cause of inability to work and thus of poverty and related social ills (Rosen 1958; Susser 1993).

Friedrich Engels put the reverse interpretation on the poverty-illness linkage. He argued that poverty caused disease and other sufferings that were not merely to be eased through health reforms but were instead to be eradicated by an uprising of the oppressed class. That is, he did not see health as a merely instrumental value in promoting a more prosperous, politically settled laboring class; rather, he viewed poor health, dangerous working conditions, child labor, wretched housing, and other hardships of the era as moral evils and their opposites—among them, health—as social values in their own right.

Aside from the reformist-versus-revolutionary debates over the causes of widespread disease in the England of that era, a broadly epidemiologic focus brought to light the extent of health problems and contributed to the process whereby "health took on force as a general social value" (Susser 1993, p. 419).

The tone of contemporary thinking about health as a human right, including that reflected in the United Nations' declarations quoted above, has become more absolute. The individual viewed as the recipient of health care is more detached from his or her social surroundings. The alone, possibly lonely, patient being slid into a computed axial tomography (CAT) scanner might be taken as a visual metaphor for the way in which social, psychological, and cultural attributes of the bearer of rights have been rendered irrelevant in health care.

The situational privacy and the biomedical uniqueness of the patient resonate with various sociologic images of modernity. Thus Berger notes: "It is important to understand that it is precisely this solitary self that modern consciousness has perceived as the bearer of human dignity and of inalienable human rights. . . . Dignity . . . always relates to the intrinsic humanity divested of all socially imposed roles or norms. It pertains to the self as such, to the individual regardless of his position in society" (Berger et al. 1973, pp. 88–89).

Given the cultural and historical presuppositions that shape contemporary thinking, it is not difficult to draw upon the stock of cultural icons to form images of the dignity of the political man, deliberating, perhaps discussing with peers, how he will cast his ballot or what legislative priorities will best serve the common weal. In regard to economic rights, the dignity of the laborer has been anciently symbolized by the sweat of his brow; now that nonhuman energy is a very substantial substitute for human physical effort, less graphic concepts have arisen, recognizing the value of work qualities such as responsibility, reliability, teamwork, and professional skill.

## THE MEDICAL DIGNITY HYPOTHESIS

Does a comparable dignity form in the individual who receives health care? That question embodies the "dignity hypothesis," which is tentatively explored here. If such dignity can be found, it would help to explain the growing moral conviction that health care is a basic human right and that to be denied health care places a person on a subhuman plane and simultaneously degrades the community that denies him.

One way to examine this hypothesis is to look into the medical care accorded to low-status or marginal members of society—criminals, deviants, or derelicts.

Fox and Swazey, long-time students of patients and treatment for end-stage renal disease, dealt with this situation in their analysis of the case of Ernie Crowfeather (Fox and Swazey 1978). Before resources for renal dialysis became widely available in the 1970s, Ernie was taken into hemodialysis at University Hospital in Seattle, Washington. He had a record of robbery and petty thievery that continued after he became a patient. Issues connected with minority racial status also arose because Ernie was a Native American. Once in the role of patient, he engaged in new forms of deviance by his frequent transgressions of the treatment requirements. Despite his many failings, his doctors continued with his treatment until he died, some 30 months after he started dialysis.

Other factors were at work in his case besides the notion that treatment sustains human dignity. As an identified patient, Ernie became the object of the staff's sympathy. Furthermore, it is emotionally straining for treatment providers to "give up" on a patient whom they have come to know well; if the patient dies or otherwise stops treatment, it appears to the staff to be their own failure. Even these subsidiary factors, however, work together to uphold the general idea that the patient deserves the treatment and that his worth is enhanced by receiving it.

A still more stringent confirmation of the "dignity hypothesis" comes from the fact that convicted criminals who are serving time in prison have a right to health care (Dubler 1979). Courts have held, however, that this is a limited right (*New York Times* 1992). Recent publicity about the plight of a federal prisoner, DeWayne Murphy, who has severe cardiomyopathy, has brought to light the limits of federal provision of medical care, but it may well turn out subsequently that there are limits to the limits (Kolata 1994). Murphy is in a deteriorating state at the time of this writing. Without a heart transplant, doctors expect him to die within several months, but under federal policy, the Bureau of Corrections does not ordinarily pay for transplants. However, if the patient dies without one, could that be construed as "cruel and unusual punishment," prohibited by the Eighth Amendment to the U.S. Constitution? A number of experts—bioethicists, lawyers, and social scientists—believe that Murphy should be able to have any treatment that doctors recommend; essentially, they view health care as an unconditional human right. They are unwilling to qualify it according to the civil status of the patient (prisoner versus ordinary citizen) or the expense of the treatment.

A third example supports the dignity hypothesis, but from a different direction. In this case, the recipient of treatment was, as a child, a morally innocent member of society. The issue in the case of Amos Mast, an Amish boy with advanced abdominal cancer, is not the worthiness of the patient but the purpose and effectiveness—the "worthiness"—of the treatment. The fact that the treatment was legally mandated is a telling exemplification of the connection between health care and human dignity (Mead 1989).

The facts of the case were stark. Amos was 6 years old when, in October 1988, he was diagnosed with the cancer; his family belonged to a small Amish community that had recently established itself in central Kentucky. The family's ambivalent response to biomedical treatment was entirely typical of the Amish subculture (Kraybill 1989). The Amish reject as "worldly" many features of modern material culture such as telephones and automobiles, and they exercise a selective discerning judgment concerning others, such as modern medicine.

In the Mast case, Amos's parents took him to a children's hospital in

Louisville, Kentucky, for the recommended chemotherapy. However, after several weeks they stopped taking him because it left him "just about lifeless"—a far from unusual side effect of cancer chemotherapy. A district judge, Janet Coleman, in the county where the Masts lived issued a court order for Danny Mast, Amos's father, to continue taking his son to the Louisville hospital for the chemotherapy. When Danny refused, she jailed him for contempt of her order. He entered the jail voluntarily; after 3 days the judge relented and ordered his release, although she did not rescind the order. She also took the unusual step of reading, at a press conference, a statement that justified it. It read, in part: "The most important concern of this court is the welfare of the child involved. I have done my best to convey to Mr. Mast the seriousness of his legal position, in the hope that he might relent and not allow his child to die untreated. . . . The court still has a very grave concern that this child is being treated for terminal cancer with vitamins." (In speaking of treatment with vitamins, the judge was referring to reports that Danny had taken his son to a clinic in Mexico where he received such treatment.)

The illustrative value of the Mast case here rests first on the judge's strongly expressed conviction that a terminally ill child should not die untreated, and second that she by implication saw the herbal-vitamin regime as "nontreatment."[8]

The judge's sentiment that the father should "not allow his child to die untreated" has, for purposes of exploring the dignity hypothesis, an instructive analogue in the Catholic doctrinal insistence on the anointing of the sick (formerly called "extreme unction") for dying persons—that a person should not be permitted to die unshriven.

In the Mast case the requisite cultural form was not a religious ministration but a legally mandated medical treatment. Religious ritual has its own sufficient dignity and transcendent efficacy within the community of the faithful. Medical treatment is obviously quite different; as part of biomedical science, it rests upon a worldly, empirical base.

However, beyond the ever-skeptical, rational realm of biomedical research a larger "societal community" exists, where sentiment is mounting that medical care falls within a canon of human dignity. In this canon, medical care is judged more by its symbolic fittingness than by its empirical efficacy. The judge spoke as a representative of the societal community. What gives her sentiment a powerful relevance to the dignity hypothesis is the fact that the patient was terminally ill—she was not expecting him to receive therapeutic benefit from the treatment.[9] Judge Coleman imputed to him a need to be cared for by modern medicine; it was not a felt need of the individual but a need of the community to set standards for its members. Judges, of course, have unique power to impute such needs and to lay penalties upon those who obstruct them.

Judge Coleman did not shrink from her power and her responsibility, but in releasing the Amish father after a few days of detention she nodded toward non-Amish community members, sympathetic to the Amish, who petitioned for his release. She came to a posture of persuasion rather than coercion vis-à-vis a defendant who, though stubborn and uncompromising, belonged to the judicially noncombatant, politically meek and unskilled, pacifist Amish subculture. In my interpretation, the judge's softened stance said much about judicial politics in a multicultural community but left untouched its positive implication for the medical dignity of the individual.

## MEDICAL DIGNITY AND WESTERN INDIVIDUALISM

Another, very different side to the phenomena of medicalization is the emergence of the medicalized self and medical dignity. Let me pose the question: Is medical dignity simply another aspect of the rootless, anomic individual who has, through the vast social changes inherent in urbanization and industrialization, been cast out from the earlier security of belonging within a place, a community, and a value habitus? Is medical dignity a byproduct of a civilization that requires more radical communal restructuring than simply making medical care more abundant?

To examine these questions, it is valuable to consider certain basic features of medical care that predate scientific medicine. Medical care is always addressed clinically to individuals in the uniqueness of what is, or may be, wrong with them. It has an inherent caring component that is of course often obscured by the bureaucratic processes of "care delivery," the intense specialization of technologic medicine, and the economic nexus of reimbursement for services rendered. Despite these blemishes, what modalities outside of close family and other intimate relationships could be more caring, more solicitous, and more gratifying to the basic emotional needs of the individual than the biomedically identifying attention to his body in the phenotypic uniqueness that marks it as different from all other bodies? Not even the earlier cosmogonies that placed humans' securely at the center of an anthropomorphic universe or zodiac created for human enjoyment and dominion actually depicted the uniqueness, both of heredity and subsequent impinging life events, of the individual person *qua soma*.

The critics of medicine, some of them in the ranks of medical sociology, seek to humanize medicine, to smooth off its impersonal edges, and to invigorate its "burnt-out" deliverers, too often depersonalized themselves, with a sustainable career and rewarding sense of caring and compassion. However, is this vision a quest that, although not unworthy or false, seeks a lesser good? Has medical care come to be a symbol of caring that implies more than it can ever deliver?

To return to the Mexican herbal healer, could it be that my students who object to the collectiveness and lack of privacy of his treatment speak as minions of a culture that has injured their ability to think and to feel as members of a group? Observers of non-Western societies frequently observe that members of those societies typically hold a self-concept and a view of human relationships that emphasize the connectedness of the individual to others and his rootedness in a social context—in contrast to the detached, sometimes heroic, but always isolated individual of Western thought and sensibility.

This difference shows up in many ways. Doctors and nurses who deal frequently with Asian and African immigrant patients in American hospitals have sometimes remarked on it. It even penetrates into intellectual discourse, sometimes reflected there in the incommensurability of key concepts between languages. Thus Pomerantz (1991, p. 8), reports that the Chinese term for *individualism,* "geren juyt," means something akin to *selfishness* in Chinese thinking. Fox reports that the field of bioethics, when transformed by Chinese values, leads to a concern for self- and group improvement in the practicalities of providing good patient care; it manifestly shuns the Western analytic passion for spelling out the implications of varying concepts of conception, birth, dying, and death (Fox and Swazey 1984).[10]

DeCraemer, in his analysis of personhood, offers a particularly penetrating statement of the basic Western position. He says that non-Western cultures "not only share, but they *emphasize* the contextual, relational nature of personhood, its inseparability from social solidarity, its body-and-psyche, as well as self-and-other holism, and its 'inner,' emotive, symbolic, and ritual aspects. This way of looking at and understanding the person, on the one hand, and our own individual-oriented, rational and analytic, positivistic and legalistic perspective on the person, on the other, carry with them different sets of meanings, fulfillments, and strains for the individuals and groups who live within these frameworks" (DeCraemer 1983, p. 32).

## SUMMARY

The United States is in the throes of health reform that focuses on bringing about universal coverage and on containing costs. Other Western societies have solved the first problem but are increasingly troubled by the second. The ongoing knowledge explosion in biomedicine, combined with the "technologic imperative" to use everything possible in health care, promise endless trouble with cost and resource containment. Pre-existing and enlarging conceptions of health care as a human right militate against "market rationing" of health care according to the economic capacity of the individual citizen or family. If community norms regarding appropriate, not technologically unbridled health care could be fashioned—not necessarily the same for all communities—then health care could be given economic guidance or restraint within a moral fabric. There is urgent and challenging work here for medical sociologists and many other scholars engaged in the analysis of medical care and health policy.

## NOTES

1. Geographically, rural Mexico is of course "West." However, culturally and medically, it is considered part of the Third World, where the concept of the individualized, autonomous self free of the press of ascriptive solidarities has not taken strong root. Furthermore, the difference between this peasant medical setting and those that the middle-class students know cannot be reduced to a matter of socioeconomic status. In other words, it is not simply the case that poor people endure being herded together medically while more affluent people get more commodious, individualized treatment. In the thoroughly middle-class, affluent, technologically advanced culture of Japan, Japanese patients probably have a stronger sense of collective membership than do comparably middle-class patients in the West (Doi 1986).
2. The emergence of medical sociology and its strength as a subspecialty within society are in themselves indications of the growth of medicine. Although medical sociology is, in terms of personnel, publications, and research, a respectable slice of the total pie of sociology, it is of course only a small sliver in the vast domain of medicine in society.
3. Purdom's *New York Times* article discusses the threat to the economy of New York City posed by possible cutbacks in the staffing of teaching hospitals and medical research laboratories. Such cutbacks are likely to occur, although their actual magnitude may be small, as part of various health care reform proposals. The restructuring would place greater emphasis upon primary care, but within the overall context of a shrinking health sector. Institutions such as teaching hospitals and research laboratories, in the forefront of health progress, are staffed by the skilled and renowned physicians and biomedical scientists—hard to replace when they are needed, and hard to place when the demand for them declines. In general, however, in all nations, the entire health sector of the economy—not just the teaching hospitals and the laboratories—contains a very large proportion of highly skilled individuals, concentrated in urban-metropolitan areas. The combination of skill and urbanity in health service is one reason why it has a distinctively "modern" ambience in the minds of many people.
4. For a recent review essay on medicalization, see Conrad (1992). In contrast to Conrad's, my own view of medicalization detaches it from notions of social control. I believe that medicalization might well, on the whole, enhance individual dignity, rather than impose social restraints. Social control as an oppressive process falls, as sociologists usually see it, most heavily on persons with little economic or political power. Medicalization, in contrast, often raises the status of the dispossessed by giving them access to clinically individualized medical attention and services. I do not deny that there is frequently a link between medicalization and social control, but there are other ways of looking at medicalization.
5. Illich acknowledges that health care is "costly and unevenly distributed" (Illich 1975, p. 80) but because he views it as morally corrupting, he is no advocate for a more equal distribution of it. Measures to promote patients' better understanding of medical procedures he dismisses as "consumer protection for addicts" (Illich 1975, p. 67). He also argues that great harm is done by doctors through the proliferation of the side effects of medical interventions, and thus he writes: "Limited medical benefits also mean limited iatrogenic by-products. If outputs were to be increased, goals more rationally controlled, and distribution of access more equitable, the present system could deepen its sickening effect. . ." (Illich 1975, p. 80).
6. Elsewhere I have used the terms "biomedical transcendence" and "health absolutism" to designate component trends in the medicalization process, but they do not imply the hypertrophied distortion of society conveyed in Illich's dogmatic fantasy (Gallagher and Ferrante 1987).

7. The right to health care is not as unqualified as the right, for example, to the security of one's person against assault and arbitrary arrest. A substantial critical debate goes on about how far the right to health care extends and what constitutes its legal/philosophical basis (Hayes 1992). The debate is not entirely academic. There have been, in the United States, numerous court decisions concerning the limits of the right; frequently they center on whether a given provider—usually a hospital—is obligated to provide emergency care and what, if anything, beyond that.
8. Did Amos Mast have a *duty* to receive the treatment? That question is moot; because he was a minor, he was not a legal actor to whom rights and duties apply. If he had been an adult, he would have been autonomously free to accept or reject the treatment. It is generally settled that a legally competent adult is free to reject "doctor's orders" unless there is a public health issue, as with contagious diseases. Regarding children and other legally dependent persons, courts have not taken a consistent line concerning the duties of their caretakers. Parents are not always obliged to follow doctor's recommendations for their children, although the predominant tendency does lie in that direction. My purpose here is not to analyze the nuances of legal and bioethical opinion, important as they may be in other contexts, but rather to point out the relevance of the Mast case for the concept of medical dignity.
9. Under the rubric of "medical futility," bioethicists have recently begun to question the ethicality and, in a broader sense, the policy justification of physicians' carrying out treatments, particularly when they are expensive, of patients who are certain to die within days or weeks (Callahan 1991). These analyses are relevant to debates about rationing and rationalizing of the distribution of medical resources. Economic data about resources expended and money spent on medical care during the last days of a person's life are opportune grist for this type of argument. Are the "futility thinkers" medical Luddites who are out to demedicalize modern society? Probably not. Some argue that their objective is to avoid prolonged dying rather than to save money or to shorten life, even life of poor quality. Others argue that resources devoted to high technology–based measures to stave off impending death should be shifted to primary care. In general, even if only implicitly, they support the general advance of medical care in society; however, they stand mute concerning the issue of social equity in medical care. "Should wealthy patients be allowed to seek out, and pay for, 'futile' care while poor patients cannot?" is a question that they do not take up within their realm of discourse.
10. From this, one might infer that the Western analytical mentality has an acute, disembodied concern with the beginning and end of life and relatively little unconcern with what happens in between. The Chinese practical mentality is in contrast this-worldly, directing its attention and energy to what happens between the moments of birth and death. This hiatus in the Western bioethical mind may explain why bioethicists do not demonstrate similar analytic passion when they touch upon issues of rationing medical care, which are in the main concerned with mundane, non–life-saving uses of medicine.

## REFERENCES

AN-NA'IM, ABDULLAHI AHMED (ed.). 1992. *Human Rights in Cross-Cultural Perspectives.* Philadelphia, PA: University of Pennsylvania Press.

BERGER, PETER, BRIGITTE BERGER, and HANSFRIED KELLNER. 1973. *The Homeless Mind.* New York: Random House.

CALLAHAN, DANIEL. 1991. "Medical Futility, Medical Necessity: The Problem-Without-A-Name." *Hastings Center Report* 21(4):30–35.

CONRAD, PETER. 1992. "Medicalization and Social Control." *Annual Review of Sociology,* 209–32.

CONRAD, PETER. 1975. "The Discovery of Hyperkinesis: Notes on the Medicalization of Deviant Behavior." *Social Problems* 23:12–21.

DE CRAEMER, WILLY. 1983. "A Cross-Cultural Perspective on Personhood." *Milbank Memorial Fund Quarterly/Health and Society* 61:19–34.

DOI, TAKEO. 1986. *The Anatomy of Self—The Individual Versus Society.* Tokyo: Kodansha International.

DUBLER, NANCY. 1979. "Depriving Prisoners of Medical Care: A 'Cruel and Unusual' Punishment." *Hastings Center Report,* 7–10.

FOX, RENEE C. 1977. "The Medicalization and Demedicalization of American Society." *Daedalus—Journal of the American Academy of Arts and Sciences* 106:9–22.

FOX, RENEE C. and JUDITH P. SWAZEY. 1978. *The Courage to Fail.* Chicago: University of Chicago Press.

______. 1984. "Medical Morality Is Not Bioethics: Medical Ethics in China and the United States." Pp. 645–71 in *Essays in Medical Sociology,* 2nd ed., edited by Renee C. Fox. New Brunswick, NJ: Transaction Books.

GALLAGHER, EUGENE B. and JOAN FERRANTE. 1987. "Medicalization and Social Justice." *Social Justice Research* 1:377–92.

HAYES, JOHN A. 1992. "Health Care as a Natural Right." *Medicine and Law* 11:405–16.

ILICH, IVAN. 1975. *Medical Nemesis—The Expropriation of Health.* London: Marion Boyars.

______. 1994. "Brave New Biocracy: Health Care from Womb to Tomb." *New Perspectives Quarterly* 11:4–12.

KOLATA, GINA. 1994. "U.S. Refuses to Finance Prison Heart Transplant." *New York Times,* February 5, p. A6.

KRAYBILL, DONALD B. 1989. *The Riddle of Amish Culture.* Baltimore, MD: The Johns Hopkins University Press.

MEAD, ANDY. 1989. "Amish Man Freed; Sick Son in Hiding." Lexington Kentucky *Herald-Leader,* January 31, pp. A1 and A5.

NEW YORK TIMES. 1992. "Excerpts from High Court Ruling on Rights of Prison Inmates," February 26, p. A6.

POMERANTZ, MARSHA. 1991. "Chinese [Non-] Individualism." *Harvard Magazine* 94.

PURDOM, TODD S. 1994. "Teaching Hospitals Fear Harm in Plan to Reduce Specialization." *New York Times,* January 24, pp. A1 and A9.

ROSEN, GEORGE. 1958. *A History of Public Health.* New York: MD Publications.

SUSSER, MERVYN. 1993. "Health as a Human Right: An Epidemiologist's Perspective on the Public Health." *American Journal of Public Health* 83:418–26.

TOLEDO, J. R. 1989. Video. *Traditional Healing in Mexico* (60 minutes). Denton, TX: Department of Psychology, University of North Texas.

UNITED NATIONS GENERAL ASSEMBLY. 1948. *Universal Declaration of Human Rights,* Article 25. Brussels, Belgium: Amnesty International.

WORLD HEALTH ORGANIZATION. 1978. *Primary Health Care.* Geneva, Switzerland: WHO.

Chapter 13

# AIDS as a Globalizing Panic

*John O'Neill*

In the present context of HIV/AIDS knowledge, marked as it is by the absence of a vaccine discovery, it falls to the social and health sciences broadly conceived to devise institutional responses to AIDS that will contain both the illness and our social responses to it. Here, of course, 'containment' is sought on two levels and it may be that a considerable fiction is involved in hoping that the HIV virus is, so to speak, *virus sociologicus*. While it is doubtful that the virus can learn sociology, it is certainly true that sociology cannot remain ideologically ignorant of virology. But this in turn means that the social sciences in general are obliged to rethink themselves before they can be adapted ready-made to the new limitations which HIV/AIDS imposes not only upon our sexual conduct but upon a range of professional behavior where contact with AIDS is involved. This is especially the case since the professionalization of the social sciences, like that of the medical sciences, has proceeded in terms of an ideological demarcation between factual knowledge and moral knowledge that, while honored by hardline scientists of either ilk, is in fact breached by developments in the bio-technological sciences that have reopened the frontier of ethico-legal enquiry. The social sciences no longer have any neutral

*Reprinted with permission from *Theory, Culture & Society* (SAGE, London, Newbury Park and New Delhi), Vol. 7 (1990), 329–42.

ground in these matters, and this is particularly the case with those who suffer from AIDS since they oblige us to reconceive our social policies and our moral values regarding trust and community.

Although AIDS is a relatively recent phenomenon, and despite the complexity of the virological and epidemiological dimensions of the HIV virus, it may be said that we have acquired a considerable knowledge of it in the short span of little over five years research (Royal Society of Canada, 1988; Spurgeon, 1988; Fee and Fox, 1988; Altman, 1987; *Daedalus,* 1989; New England Journal of Public Policy, 1988; *The Milbank Quarterly,* 1986; Ornstein 1989). Indeed, AIDS has moved quickly through a cycle of first stage of relative ignorance, followed by intensive research and discovery, to a plateau where we are waiting for the breakthrough which would permit us to counteract the HIV virus by means of a vaccine. This state of affairs has only been achieved through a considerable pace of biomedical research (*Scientific American,* 1988; *Daedalus,* 1989) and the involvement of governmental health agencies from the federal to municipal level, including hospitals, clinics, gay community organizations, AIDS workshops, hotlines and pamphleteering, in addition to a constant reportage of AIDS information in newspapers and on television. AIDS has even generated its own art forms in theatre, film and folk art (Crim, 1988; Watney, 1987). All these activities, then, have combated social ignorance with social awareness. As a new stage of conscious-raising, AIDS awareness is now projected to recruit even pre-adolescent children. The cardinal virtues of contemporary sexual citizenship are exemplified in our awareness of the practices of contraception and abortion, as well as the achievement of copulation and the avoidance of AIDS. It should be observed that by the same token a great deal of secular faith is involved in the assumption that 'awareness'—which varies from sect-like membership to glancing through myriad minor pamphlets—will alter sexual conduct to any great extent. 'Safe' sex is not so easily institutionalized if only because the concept of 'sex' is itself not to be understood outside of any extraordinary range of social behavior where 'excitement' may preclude 'safety' in any form.

I want to argue that, despite what we already know about HIV and AIDS, any further development in our knowledge and the pedagogies to be devised in public education programs is confronted with the phenomenon I shall call *socially structured carnal ignorance.* Here, what I have in mind is a number of factors that determine bodily conducts as necessarily, wilfully and desirably matters of 'unknowing', of 'spontaneity', of 'passion', of 'desire', or of 'fun', 'phantasy'. In short, we use our clothing, eating, drinking and sexual behavior to achieve relationships and end-experiences that may be considered moral or immoral, rational or nonrational, competitive or communal, safe or risky. It is not our task to pursue the cultural, class, and gender and age variations that operate here, although these operate upon the social structure of carnal knowledge and ignorance (O'Neill, 1985a). Nor have we to recount the historical and ideological shifts in the codes that dress our bodily conduct, provided we do not overlook them. It must suffice to articulate with regard to AIDS the following elements that condition a structure of ignorance which in turn generates the fear of AIDS upon which so much public energy is expended:

1. the carrier may not be known to him/herself due to the latency period of up to eight years;
2. the range of risk behaviors may not be known to potential victims;
3. the HIV carrier may not be known to him/herself;
4. the pursuit of epidemiological knowledge regarding the HIV virus may conflict with the civil rights affording non-knowledge of persons' behavior and associations; and
5. the code of civil rights may guarantee non-knowledge of persons or ways that prevent or conflict with medical, police, educational, employment practices of testing and identification of 'AIDS persons'.

In turn, within the general population carnal ignorance may be valued in such experiences and settings as: (a) sex; (b) drugs; (c)alcohol; (d) at parties; (e) at concerts, clubs; and (f) on the street, in alleys, in cars. The specific behavioral codes defining these experiences where reason 'goes on holiday', so to speak, will vary according to membership in a variety of settings and practices shaped by: (a) age group; (b) sexual ideology, e.g., consumptive rather than reproductive sex; (c) sexual identification, i.e., homosexual, lesbian, bisexual and/or heterosexual; (d) religious beliefs; (e) ethnicity; and (f) socio-economic class, i.e., level of education, income and professional ideology.

There exists an enormous bias in the social sciences against the study of the ways in which our ignorance, misinformation and deception is socially structured. For this reason our enlightenment with regard to sexual behavior proceeds much more slowly than the deliverance promised to us by our present rationalist bias towards knowledge. If we are to make any progress in devising sexual pedagogies to respond to sexually transmitted diseases (STD), specific empirical and ethnographic data on the social structure of carnal ignorance, as I have outlined it, must be gathered (Rubin, 1984; Crawford, 1977). In part, such information is already available in material collected from the standpoint of the sociology of attitudes, beliefs and opinions. What can be said, however, is that those who are least educated and most socio-economically underprivileged in virtue of class, racial and colonial status, will bear the brunt of prostitution, drugs and HIV-infected births in the urban areas of the world which constitute a 'fourth world' of social problems wherever they are situated.

With these remarks in mind, I shall turn now to the development of a framework for the study of AIDS which sets national and local concerns in the context of the global political economy (Law and Gill, 1988). From this standpoint, AIDS must be considered as one of a number of panics of a political, economic, financial and 'natural' sort to which the global order responds with varying strategies of crusade, sentimentality or force. By a *globalizing panic* I understand any practice that traverses the world to reduce the world and its cultural diversity to the generics of coca-cola, tourism, foreign aid, medical aid, military defense posts, tourism, fashion and the international money markets (O'Neill, 1988a). Since these practices are never quite stabilized, their dynamics include deglobalizing tendencies which will be reinscribed by the global system as threats to the 'world order'. Some nations may consider themselves to be the prime agents in this world order, while others can only maintain an aligned status, or else are allowed to enjoy a toy nationality, like that of Canada, which can be appealed to in order to supply neutrality functions on behalf of the world order. The globalizing panics that confirm the world order rely heavily upon the media and television, newspapers, magazines, films and documentaries to specularize the incorporation of all societies in a single global system designed to overcome all internal division, if not to expand into an intergalactic empire. Such a vision is confirmed, for example, by the performance of chemical experiments under the gravity-free conditions of space flight which may enhance the future discovery of an AIDS vaccine. Thus sexual practices that would not be tolerated within the social system of the space capsule nevertheless provide ideological justification for global medicine's quest for a perfect experimental environment. Furthermore, the relatively ghettoized sexuality of gays and black and Hispanic IV drug users finds its projection in the starry heaven of the heroes of all-American science, war and medicine. Meantime, this medicine is largely unavailable to the poor in the United States and the so-called Third World whose infants are ravaged by disease and death amidst populations that are continuously uprooted by famine, flood and warfare. By the same token, media images from this part of the world are exploited on behalf of the promise of the global order whose own political economy is largely responsible for the natural disasters that ravage the third world.

The sexual economy, which must be treated as the framework for any grasp of the political economy of AIDS, is subject to every other sub-system of the global economy and national political economy. It is so when it appears most disengaged because its disengagement celebrates the processes of disenfranchisement elsewhere in the society, i.e. the degradation of gendered economies, of family and of church authority, as well as of any politics grounded in these communities. When the general will is sexualized, politics is privatized; when politics is privatized, the general will is idiotized. The politics of desire is the desire politics of a global economy which entirely escapes articulation in the speechlessness of sexualized desire. Meantime in the West, the postmodern insistence on cultural fragmentation implodes all differences and reduces everything to shifts in fashion and its constant revision of the spatio-temporal order of global capitalism which itself remains class and colonial in nature and cannot be thought in terms of the shibboleths of sexism, racism or anti-humanism which it has outlawed at the same time that it is the principle source of these very phenomena because reformism on these issues is anything but revolutionary.

It might be argued that postmodernism celebrates a phantasmatic economy of sex and power while remaining tied to the market for global rock, drugs and fashion and to the concert politics whose evanescent sentimentality reflects and deepens the global exploitation (O'Neill, 1988b). From this standpoint, postmodernism is the 'classless' culture of a globalizing economy that exports its industrial basis whenever labor is cheapest while dividing its internal economy into rich and poor service sectors. In these sectors activities are neither community nor self-building. Here the political economy of the signifier without sign (family, class, race, gender) is operative. Since there is nothing at the center of a doughnut or of a dress, variety is everything. Since money has no absolute value, variety is the only norm. In this culture, those who look for signs are traditionalists, semantic fools, or semiotic idiotics—they are out of style, out of touch. Nothing looks worse on television than nationalism, fundamentalism and anti-colonialism with their murders, their starving children, their destruction and immolation. The same is true of the images of domestic poverty, urban decay, illiteracy and alienation that are floated without any attempt to implicate the class system. To be 'it' is to be 'out' in the game of global circulation.

The global economy is concerned equally with the promotion of individualism and its sexualized erasure. Its primary politics are those of corporate identity which, in turn, conscripts an aggressive individuality pitted against his-or-her own nature and community. The active, young, calculating, realistic, and hedonistic recruits to corporate capitalism and its cosmopolitan culture are the idols of global media culture. They move like gods and goddesses amidst the debris of urban crime and desolation, cocaine colonialism and the life and death struggles of high-tech medicine, war and 'communication'. To this end, global culture is perfectly 'unisexual', i.e., it is a same-sex-culture whose technological infrastructure is indifferent, benign or emancipated with respect, to its male and female protagonists. (O'Neill, 1985a: ch. 4). In turn, this monoculture refigurates itself as 'difference' by means of its agonistic pursuits of profit, sex, drugs, peace, health, justice and progress. Here winners are 'hypermen', a caste which includes 'executive' women who have proven they can be winners within the agonistic culture of global high technology and corporate capitalism. That is why it is important that females not be excluded from the business and social science professions and especially that they not be excluded from the police and military forces. Global capitalism is 'unisexual' and it offers every prosthetic and therapeutic aid to the monobodies required to service its way of life. Against this promise, AIDS may be understood to constitute a potential global panic on two fronts; namely (a) a *crisis of legitimation* at the level of global unisexual culture; and (b) a *crisis of opportunity* in the therapeutic apparatus of the welfare state and the international medical order. AIDS threatens to produce a *crisis of cultural legitimation* because it tempts highly committed individuals to withdraw from the unisexual culture of global capitalism and to renounce its specific ideologies that (a) sex is the most intimate expression of freedom and choice in the market society; (b) sex is consumptive and not necessarily productive; (c) sex is genderless, unfamilied, classless and homeless; (d) sexual repairs are available through the biomedical and psychiatric services of the therapeutic state; and (e) all high risk behavior on behalf of global capitalism will be supported by its prophylactic and prosthetic technologies whose ultimate aim is to immunize its members against the environment of their own risk behavior.

The experience of AIDS panics the sexual culture of global capitalism in several ways. In the first place, it has 'disappointed' those who were most committed to its ideology of sexual freedom. To its credit, the gay community has learned that its sexuality cannot be played out in the anonymous intimacy and extraordinarily high rates of casual contact which were enjoyed in the bath houses. This re-evaluation has taken effect precisely because gays in fact constituted a quasi-community marked by levels of literacy and organizational skills beyond what can be found in the IV drug alleys (Brandt, 1988; Altman, 1988). However, heterosexuals have been tempted to turn against the gay community in a number of ways that threaten to degrade the civil rights achievable in capitalist democracies. Business, educational and medical institutions have all been strained by the fear of AIDS. At the heart of these delegitimizing strains in the social order is the immediate lack of any vaccine against HIV which would, as it were, immunize the society against its responses to what I shall call *AFRAIDS*. Short of a vaccine, AIDS constitutes a panic both on the individual life level and on a collective level where AFRAIDS threatens to undermine the order of civil liberties. To the extent that panic spreads, especially where AFRAIDS or the fear of AIDS, generates secondary fundamentalist and revisionist panics, the sexual economy of global capitalism is threatened with a crisis of legitimation. The AIDS panic, however, strikes most deeply into the legitimation process when it prompts the general population in a rationalized industrial society to question the probability value of scientific knowledge with demands for absolute certainty or for the immediate availability of drugs such as AZT where the experimental controls and clinical tests properly required may be short-circuited by the clamor for immediate reduction of suffering, 'fast-tracking' hope despite the necessarily cautious pace of research. Here modern medical knowledge is particularly exposed since rational experiment, placebo practices, and the ethico-legal issues in patient consent reveal the costs as well as the benefits of our commitment to the industrial order. This order is threatened less by proposals to ghettoize AIDS patients, however politically crude such a suggestion may be, than by any loss of commitment to the protocols of the medicalization of health and happiness (O'Neill, 1986). As things stand, there is a considerable need to attempt some realignment between community based medicine, corporate research and national medical research.

At the very worst, the AIDS panic threatens the liberal order of global capitalism with a 'rebarbarization' of its social bond. Hitherto, it was possible to sustain the global phantasy of a social order without deep commitment, as in the figure of the American Express man whose creditability lies in his credit and whose faith lies in the fiction of a card that would make him at home in the homeless world of global capitalism. Will the American Express Card guarantee immunity against foreign HIV tests, and even if it did, can we be sure that American Express will issue its precious cards at home to persons without a prior HIV test? Or will those who carry the American Express Card, having passed an HIV test, constitute a new biological order of eligible capitalists? However bizarre such questions may seem, they already have their counterpart in the experiment with AIDS-free singles clubs. What is extraordinary in such responses is that they threaten to return the capitalist order to a *purity rule,* that is, to return us to a social order founded upon a contagion model of social relations rather than on the present contract model of society that has been the engine of our extraordinarily globalizing history. If this were the ultimate consequence of the AIDS panic, global capitalism would have succeeded in rebarbarizing itself because of an unfortunate contingency in its sexual culture, rather than because of its other phantasied threats of interstellar barbarism.

AIDS presents *a crisis of opportunity* in the global culture of late capitalism precisely because its immediate features, namely: (a) autotoxicity; (b) fatality; and (c) absence of vaccine renew demands upon the therapeutic state and its biomedical apparatus to provide interim care, socio-legal immunity and a vaccine. To do this, the social and health sciences have already been recruited to furnish ethical, economistic and pedagogical discourses, conferences, pamphlets, multi-disciplinary research and media treatments to the public. Here, the supply of AIDS 'knowledge' and pedagogy to the public whose fears demand it creates a perfect symbiosis between state power as knowledge, on the one hand, and knowledge as individual power/powerlessness, on the other hand. Individuals attempt to learn that only they can stop AIDS, or drinking/driving or waste, whereas these are cultural complexes produced by and (re)productive of the ideological and therapeutic culture in which they live. In this process individuals learn that

1. The state is the ultimate producer of knowledge/science.
2. The state is the ultimate producer of health, education and employment.
3. The state is the ultimate guarantor of civil liberties.
4. The state is the ultimate guarantor of all ideologies.
5. The state is the ultimate producer of the state and of society and of the individual.

It is important to see that whatever ways we devise to speak about our sexuality, sexual disease, sexual discrimination, sexual liberation, they are shaped by a pre-existing field of institutionalized discourses which have been devised by the church, the state and the socio-medical sciences with a concern for public and private welfare. These discourses contain both prescriptive and descriptive technologies to which different professional groups claim legitimate access and application in the complex of power-knowledge-pleasure that may be called the 'therapeutic state'. Thus the HIV/AIDS phenomenon enters into a highly structured field of discourse upon social policy, health and moral ideology that is contested by church, state, family, school and secular countercultural groups with varying degrees of progressive and fundamentalist beliefs in the possibility of social control of youth sexuality, drugs and family breakdown (Treichler, 1988a, 1988b). The danger exists that 'AIDS' will function as a pretext for a social backlash against the civil rights of gays, lesbians and the achievement of gender equality to the extent they are seen as the source of troubles plaguing groups marginalized by the larger global economy in which these movements function. For want of a comparable pedagogic effort from the national center, these marginalized groups will be educated by televangelism which itself adopts an extraordinary global mimetics in reporting and commenting upon the world sources of spiritual trouble (Luke, 1989; chapter 3). Social critics will be quick to pounce upon such degraded versions of the cultural hegemony of the family and religious values, as well as pointing to the danger of rightist political regression. However, some moral and cultural weight must be reassigned to the primary institutions upon which modern societies continue to depend unless they can envisage a social order whose fundamental bond is entirely an effect of secondary institutions. The pedagogical challenge this would involve quite exceeds anything we can reasonably expect in a postmodern age of collapsed narratives. At the same time, emancipatory ideologies of the absolute autonomy of the individual in all matters of sexuality and reproduction cannot be pursued outside of a framework of institution, law and morality which in turn require large allocations of public energy. They thereby raise the question—which we cannot consider here—of their own allocative position within the political economy of nation states. At this level, we must surely ask how this individualized sexual economy functions within the new global political economy.

The crises of global culture are at once extraordinarily nation state-building, at least with respect to the levels of the therapeutic apparatus of the state—and transnational on the economic and political level, depending upon shifts in the multinational corporate agenda. Of course, these two levels interact, so that global capitalism responds to its own trans-state activities through the nation state and even through a layer of 'international' agencies. Seen in this context, AIDS is again simultaneously a globalizing panic and a national state epidemic, mobilizing government health institutions from the municipal level all the way to the World Health Organization (Christakis, 1986, 1989). As a global panic, AIDS becomes a further charge upon the Third World, whereas US AIDS is principally an advanced economy, urban male (age 20–40 years), anal partner hazard, with drug users and bisexual males as secondary transmitters. US AIDS has benifited from the same trade routes as other sexually transmitted diseases. But gay subculture has been a highly articulate ideological element in North American society. The imperial dominance of American capitalism within the global system, of course, diffuses American 'life-style' ideologies through global mass culture, tourism, commercial and military travel.

Thus the global health system is only the promissory side of a world disease system. Each generates the other. Here, once again, there is a potential for a rebarbarization of the global order through quarantine orders, immunization control and racism—witness the construct of Afro-AIDS. The concept of Afro-AIDS is marvelously suited to project on to 'world history' so to speak, an Afro-origin for AIDS whereas the socio-economic conditions of blacks and Hispanics in the United States and its dependencies are clearly the principal source of American disease, crime and poverty. Similarly in Africa, where AIDS is a widespread heterosexual trouble, one must take into account shifts in marriage practices due to urban migration, poverty and a fragile medical infrastructure, before 'racializing' the disease (Fortin, 1987; Christakis, 1988). Yet the search for a Simian-based HIV, endorsed by the *Scientific American* (Essex and Kanki, 1988) inspires hopes of naturalizing a colonial and class history whose overwhelming dimensions cannot possibly be reduced by the bio-medical sciences. Since America's internal black population is the immediate source of virtually inorganizable and ineducable IV drug users, who are in turn viewed as the principal transmitters in the heterosexualization of AIDS, a third crisis looms within the US medical system inasmuch as so many millions of Americans are without any medical coverage but could hardly continue to be ignored should their deaths be attributable to AIDS. As we have said, AIDS as a global pandemic puts considerable stress on the international (world) health order.

The United States and Africa are the two epicenters of the AIDS pandemic, with respectively 204 and 150 cases per million, despite huge differences in socio-economic and socio-medical infrastructures. Yet these two centers cannot be treated in the same way, as though the one were the shadow of the other, nor can they be allowed to drift apart. In the meantime, the world medical order will have to reappraise its foundations built upon Western biomedicine and the colonial power of its corporate pharmacological institutions (Hunt, 1988; Ehrenreich and Ehrenreich, 1971; Navarro, 1976). National states will vary in their capacity to sustain the costs of AIDS where these are predicated upon a purely medical strategy that presupposes no state intervention with respect to high risk sexual and narcotic behavior. These countries may also take different stances upon American efforts to medicalize AIDS just as they may or may not co-operate with American efforts to 'police' the international order on such other issues as immigration or environmental pollution. Similarly, it may not be possible to impose allegedly international standards of medical and social science research across cultures whose definition of illness, community and knowledge are known to vary. To do so, embroils such research in counter charges of a medical imperialism with which colonial countries are already familiar (Christakis, 1986, 1989).

It is a conceit of the American political order that beyond its borders life is everywhere short, nasty and brutish—despite the fact that its own urban scene answers at least as well to such description as any foreign culture to which it is thought to apply. US AIDS intensifies the lethal content of American culture in unprecedented ways because it threatens to spill over the class wall which separates the rich from the poor, the suburbs from the inner city and family life from individual lifestyles that challenge it. By the same token, since this spillage has largely been a construct of the media coverage of AIDS, the state therapeutic complex has simultaneously achieved a considerable 'containment' of the epidemic as one that is by and large responsive to its administrative institutions without raising revolutionary changes to our fundamental ethical and political constitution. So long as we are able to muddle along in this fashion, we avoid the most catastrophic scenarios envisaged as an effect of the global ravage of AIDS. Here, of course, the ultimate breakdown would be in *the class system* as an immunological order and the destruction of the medical system predicated upon such an order. Short of such a conflagration, we may expect class politics to slide into caste politics in the hope of preserving the health of society by sacrificing its principle of charity to group preservation. To the extent that this scenario develops, the global order will have collapsed into a barbarous conflict of national biological elites each seeking to preserve its own purity whilst trying to eliminate the other as a possible contaminant (O'Neill, 1985).

## NOTE

This paper has benefited from earlier presentations at the Tenth International Summer Institute for Semiotics and Structural Studies, University of British Columbia, Vancouver, 13 August 1988, and the Theory Culture & Society Conference on Global Futures, The Burn, Aberdeen, 14 September 1988, as well as the Public Access series Counter-Talk: The Body, 25 October 1988.

## REFERENCES

Altman, Dennis. 1987. *AIDS in the Mind of America.* New York: Anchor Press.

Altman, Dennis. 1988. 'Legitimation through Disaster: AIDS and the Gay Movement', pp. 301–15 in Elizabeth Fee and Daniel M. Fox (eds), *AIDS: the Burdens of History.* Berkeley: California University Press.

Brandt, Allen M. 1988. 'AIDS: From Social History to Social Policy', pp. 147–71 in Elizabeth Fee and Daniel M. Fox (eds), *AIDS: The Burdens of History.* Berkeley: California University Press.

Christakis, Nicholas A. 1986. 'International Aspects of AIDS and HIV infection' in *Confronting AIDS: Directions for Public Health, Health Care and Research.* Washington: National Academy Press.

Christakis, Nicholas A. 1988. 'The Ethical Design of an AIDS Vaccine Trial in Africa, *Hastings Center Report* 18(3):31–7.

CHRISTAKIS, NICHOLAS A. 1989. 'Responding to a Pandemic: International Interest in AIDS Control', *Daedalus* (spring): 113–34.

CRAWFORD, ROBERT. 1977. 'You are Dangerous to Your Health: the Ideology and Politics of Victim Blaming', *International Journal of Health Services* 7(4):663–80.

CRIM, DOUGLAS (ed.). 1988. *AIDS: Cultural Analysis, Cultural Activism.* Cambridge, MA: MIT Press.

*DAEDALUS.* 1989. Special issue 'Living with AIDS' (spring).

EHRENREICH, B. and EHRENREICH, J. 1971. *The American Health Empire: Power, Projects and Politics.* New York: Random House.

ESSEX, MAX and KANKI, PHYLLIS J. 1988. The Origins of the AIDS Virus', *Scientific American* (October): 64–71.

FEE, ELIZABETH and FOX, DANIEL, M. 1988. *AIDS: The Burdens of History.* Berkeley: California University Press.

FORTIN, ALFRED, J. 1987. 'The Politics of AIDS in Kenya'. *Third World Quarterly* 9(3):907–19.

HUNT, CHARLES 1988. 'AIDS and Capitalist Medicine'. *Monthly Review* (January):11–25.

LAW, DAVID and GILL, STEPHEN (eds). 1988. *The Global Political Economy: Perspectives Problems and Policies.* New York: Harvester Press.

LUKE, TIMOTHY W. 1989. *Screens of Power: Ideology, Domination and Resistance in Informational Society.* Urbana: University of Illinois Press.

*THE MILLBANK QUARTERLY.* 1986. Special issue on 'AIDS: The Public Context of an Epidemic', 64 (supplement 1).

NAVARRO, VINCENTE. 1976. *Medicine Under Capitalism.* New York: Prodist.

*NEW ENGLAND JOURNAL OF PUBLIC POLICY.* 1988. Special issue on AIDS, 4(1).

O'NEILL, JOHN. 1985a. *Five Bodies: The Human Shape of Modern Society.* Ithaca: Cornell University Press.

O'NEILL, JOHN. 1985b. 'To Kill the Future?', *Bulletin of the Graduate School of International Relations* No. 3. Nigigata: International University of Japan.

O'NEILL, JOHN. 1986. 'The Medicalization of Social Control', *Canadian Review of Sociology and Anthropology* 23(3):350–64.

O'NEILL, JOHN. 1988a. 'Techno-culture and the Specular Functions of Ethnicity', pp. 17–35 in I.H. Angus (ed.), *Ethnicity in a Technological Age.* Edmonton: University of Alberta.

O'NEILL, JOHN. 1988b. 'Religion and Postmodernism: the Durkheimian Bond in Bell and Jameson', *Theory, Culture & Society* 5(2–3):493–508.

ORNSTEIN, MICHAEL. 1989. *AIDS in Canada: Knowledge, Behaviour and Attitudes of Adults.* Toronto: University of Toronto Press.

ROYAL SOCIETY OF CANADA. 1988. *AIDS: A Perspective for Canadians.* Ottawa: Royal Society of Canada.

RUBIN, GAYLE. 1984. 'Thinking Sex: Notes on For a Radical Theory of Politics of Sexuality', pp. 267–319 in Carole S. Vance (ed.), *Pleasure and Danger: Exploring Female Sexuality.* London: Routledge.

SCIENTIFIC AMERICAN. 1988. 'What Science Knows about AIDS', 259 (4/October).

SPURGEON, DAVID. 1988. *Understanding AIDS: A Canadian Strategy.* Toronto: Key Porter Books.

TREICHLER, PAUL A. 1988a. 'AIDS, Gender, and Biomedical Discourse: Current Contests for Meanings', in pp. 190–266 Elizabeth Fee and Daniel M. Fox (eds.), *AIDS: The Burdens of History.* Berkeley: California University Press.

TREICHLER, PAUL A. 1988b. 'Biomedical Discourse: an Epidemic of Signification', in D. Crim (ed.), *AIDS: Cultural Analysis, Cultural Activism.* Cambridge, MA: MIT Press.

WATNEY, SIMON. 1987. *Policing Desire: Pornography, AIDS and the Media.* Minneapolis: University of Minnesota Press.

Chapter 14

# Social Factors and Knowledge of HIV/AIDS in Vietnam

*Nhung Le and David R. Williams*

AIDS/HIV is a worldwide pandemic that is expected to become even more prevalent in the coming decade. In many Third World countries the advent of the HIV/AIDS epidemic has had a major adverse effect on the economic, social, and health progress only recently attained. The newest wave of the HIV epidemic is in Latin America and Asia (World Health Organization 1993). The three Asian countries with the most cases are India, the Philippines, and Thailand. Vecchi (1992) provides data on the growing threat of AIDS in Asia. There are more than 1 million cases of HIV infection in India. Thirty percent of Bombay's 100,000 prostitutes, who serve a combined average of 400,000 clients per day, are HIV positive. Thirty percent of Thailand's 800,000 prostitutes are infected with HIV, and the number of HIV cases there (currently 500,000) is expected to be between 1 million and 3 million by the year 2000.

Given the growing problem of AIDS/HIV in Asia, it is likely that AIDS soon will be a significant public health problem in Vietnam. According to the surveillance report of the World Health Organization (WHO) Global Program on AIDS, as of June 30, 1993, there were no cases of AIDS in Vietnam. However, between April and July 1993, local newspaper reports claimed that there were 10 cases of AIDS and 617 cases of HIV infection (Reuter News Agency 1993). Dr. Ngo Thi Khanh, Director of the National AIDS Committee, predicted a total of 20 AIDS cases by the end of 1993 (Vecchi 1992). As of July 28,

1994 there were 1,484 cases of HIV infection and 155 cases of AIDS (Pasteur Institute 1994).

The majority of the literature on AIDS fails to adequately identify the social context in which HIV is transmitted. High levels of preventable disease, inadequate health resources, and a background of poverty, rapid urbanization, commercial sex, social upheaval, and community marginalization are factors that may affect the spread of the AIDS epidemic (Zwi and Cabral 1991). Research that advances our understanding of factors amenable to change by public health intervention, as well as of population subgroups that are likely to be affected by the rapid spread of HIV infection, can inform policy initiatives that seek to combat the AIDS epidemic. Information of this kind can also help clarify the appropriate role of health services, research, and culturally relevant AIDS intervention efforts.

At the present time empirical data on AIDS in Vietnam is very limited. We are largely unaware of the beliefs, values, and attitudes toward AIDS and the levels of knowledge of HIV infection which characterize some of the groups that may be most vulnerable to the disease. Controlling the spread of AIDS in Vietnam is likely to be a major challenge to public health officials in that country. It is generally assumed that AIDS education and information can eliminate misconceptions and promote behaviors that reduce the spread of AIDS. Accordingly, many governments have initiated educational efforts to inform their citizens about the risk, transmission, and prevention of AIDS.

A baseline survey that provides levels of knowledge and beliefs regarding HIV can be useful in identifying knowledge gaps and particular beliefs and attitudes regarding HIV that may facilitate the spread of the disease. This chapter reports on the findings of a survey that explored levels of knowledge regarding modes of transmission of the AIDS virus among women of childbearing age in Vietnam. Because the spread of HIV/AIDS in Vietnam and many Third World countries is primarily through heterosexual contact, women of childbearing age may be a particularly vulnerable group who are also at risk of passing on HIV to their children. Within Vietnamese culture, women also play a major role in the dissemination of health information.

We first consider the sociopolitical and health conditions that are likely to intensify the impact of AIDS in Vietnam. Then we present findings from a survey of women regarding their attitudes and beliefs about AIDS. Finally, we explore the levels of knowledge regarding the transmission of HIV in our research population and identify social factors associated with variations in AIDS information.

## SOCIOPOLITICAL CONTEXT OF AIDS IN VIETNAM

### Political Context of Vietnam

The present political infrastructure of Vietnam is probably best viewed as a transitional one with many uncertainties. A traditional Vietnamese folksong summarizes the political situation of Vietnam with great accuracy: "A thousand years of Chinese reign, a hundred years of French domain, and 20 years of fighting among ourselves." Vietnam has not been at peace for a long time. Domestic politics did not play an important role until recent years. Vietnam was not open to the Western world for over a decade after 1975, and during that period of isolation, widespread political violence and crime intensified within the country.

April 1975 marked the end of U.S. military involvement in Vietnam. Shortly after the withdrawal of American troops, the Republic of South Vietnam was defeated by the regime of the current socialist government. The aftermath of the war resulted in major social, political, and economic setbacks that give Vietnam the dubious distinction of being one of the five poorest countries in the world. The withdrawal of U.S. troops in 1975 also marked the discontinuation of aid from the U.S. government and the initiation of a trade embargo against Vietnam. Among other things, these actions blocked Vietnam from receiving financial support from both the International Monetary Fund and the World Bank. In 1982, Vietnam's Foreign Minister, Nguyen Co Thach, summed up the economic condition of Vietnam as : "Very bad, but not worse." Since then, Vietnam's economy has worsened, with inflation in 1989 exceeding 700% (Cohen 1991).

During the past few decades, military defense has been a major priority of the government. At the end of 1989, Vietnam had the world's fourth-largest standing military force, the largest in Asia outside of China, and the highest military-to-civilian ratio in the world (Cohen 1991). The demise of the Soviet Union marked the loss of a major source of economic assistance to Vietnam. However, living conditions appear to be improving as the government concentrates more on domestic development and is actively pursuing economic ties to other Western countries.

### Social Conditions and Health Problems

As noted earlier, given the spread of HIV infection in Asia, Vietnam is probably vulnerable to the AIDS epidemic. We now consider a number of factors that can affect the nature of the official response to AIDS in Vietnam and could exacerbate its impact.

***Youthful, urban population*** During the 1970s and early 1980s, many Vietnamese fled to other countries for political asylum. In recent years, Vietnam has been characterized by rapid internal movements of people as many individuals seek better economic opportunity by migrating to large metropolitan areas. This massive migration to urban centers has led to considerable overpopulation, housing shortages, and unemployment within Vietnam's largest cities. Vietnam's population is also disproportionately youthful: 68% are under age 30, with 39% under age 15, and 29% between 15 and 29 years old (*Britannica Book of the Year* 1993).

***Inadequate health information system*** The health information system in Vietnam is weak and available statistics are not always precise (United Nations Development Program 1991). This affects our overall level of knowledge of health in Vietnam. A report submitted to the WHO indicates that the infant mortality per 1,000 live births was between 34 and 36 during the 1975 to 1986 period. This report also indicates that death rates for children under 1 year of age was 65 per 1,000 (United Nations Development Program 1991). There is some variation between sources, which suggests the need to improve reporting. Vietnam's vital registration system is also incomplete, and most birth and death rates are approximate. Official recognition of the potential problem the country faces with AIDS and of the need for accurate reporting is essential for identifying the magnitude of the problem and developing effective efforts to address it.

***Malnutrition*** Malnutrition is a major health problem in Vietnam. It is estimated that 50% of children under 5 years of age suffer from some nutritional problem (Cohen 1991). At puberty, children are 6 to 8 inches shorter and weigh 20 to 30 pounds less than children in neighboring countries (United Nations Development Program 1991). Cohen (1991) indicates that deficiencies of vitamin A, iodine, and iron are also common. Vitamin A deficiency is evident for 78% of the population. As a result, there is a prevalence rate of 8% for active forms of corneal lesions and 13% for xerophthalmic scars. Iodine deficiency affects about 7 million people, mainly in mountainous areas, and the prevalence of iron deficiency is estimated at 50% in pregnant women. Half of the infants in Vietnam are breastfed for 3 months because working mothers receive only 3 months maternity leave. After the infants are weaned, they receive a thin rice soup that does not provide all of the nutrients necessary for growth and development.

***Effects of war*** The effects of the last several decades of war are present in Vietnam and contribute to the ailing health condition of the Vietnamese people (Bonacci 1990). This can be seen in both the high number of war-disabled individuals and the readily evident long-term effects of dioxin (agent orange). The shortage of prosthetic limbs is a concern because of the large numbers of individuals wounded in the war who had their legs, arms, or other parts of their bodies amputated during or since the war. Unexploded ammunition is still a problem, and the accidental exposure of artillery shells and landmines in rice paddies or on sandy beaches ensures that a need for more prosthetic limbs will persist.

***Medical consequences of the embargo*** The trade embargo of Vietnam has reduced the availability of both medicines and food to the Vietnamese. Modern western medical and pharmaceutical supplies are scarce in Vietnam. The Vietnamese currency is not acknowledged on the international monetary market. The available drugs and medical supplies that are imported are purchased at outrageous cost (Bonacci 1990). The U.S. government also continues to oppose humanitarian aid to Vietnam. On the floor of the United Nations, the United States has voiced its discontent with the Dutch and Swedish programs of medical aid to Vietnam (Bonacci 1990). In large urban hospitals in Vietnam, only the most pressing surgeries are performed because of the shortage of catgut.

***Tourism*** Tourism is another factor that may facilitate the spread of AIDS in Vietnam. The tourism industry contributes significantly to the economy of the country, but it also fosters a high incidence of sexually transmitted diseases. In 1991 Vietnam's Office of Tourism estimated that more than 300,000 persons, including Vietnamese living abroad, had visited Vietnam in the previous 2 years. More than two thirds of those visitors came from Australia, Europe, and America, where AIDS is increasingly prevalent. Although these visitors contribute to the economy of the country, the advent of tourism is also encouraging the resurgence of prostitution. Although prostitution is officially illegal in Vietnam, it is estimated that there are over 400,000 prostitutes. Many of these are young unmarried women who view prostitution as their only means of economic support. However, a number of prostitutes in Vietnam are married, and use prostitution to supplement their family income.

The rate of unemployment and underemployment among women is high in Vietnam. This, combined with poverty and inflation, have propelled many of these women to provide sex in exchange for money. These women earn from US $10 to US $50 per visit, while physicians who work at prestigious medical institutions earn approximately US $30 to US $50 per month. Consequently, the number of women engaged in prostitution has increased dramatically as the influx of tourists has expanded opportunities. The social conditions in Vietnam are thus very similar to Thailand before the rapid spread of AIDS in that country.

The first case of HIV infection reported by the Vietnamese was in December 1990. There was massive media coverage about the patient and the disease. The patient was a Vietnamese woman in her 30s who is believed to have acquired the disease from an overseas individual through sexual intercourse. She was diagnosed as HIV positive in the process of having a physical screening done before her emigration to Australia. If she were not planning to leave the country, it is not likely that she would have been screened for exposure to HIV. Screening for AIDS is expensive, and in a country where many people have problems knowing where their next meal is coming from, AIDS screening is not a priority on their agenda.

## BELIEFS AND ATTITUDES REGARDING AIDS

This chapter reports on the first attempt to assess levels of knowledge about AIDS in a sample of women of childbearing age in the Vietnamese population. Even in industrialized countries, women have been a neglected topic in studies of the

AIDS epidemic (Ickovics and Rodin 1992). In the United States, the National Research Council, noting that AIDS is one of the 10 leading causes of death among women aged 15 to 44, declared that women and AIDS must be a research priority for the decade of the 1990s (Miller et al. 1990). In many parts of the world, relatively little baseline information is available regarding awareness, attitudes, and behavior related to AIDS before the country is stricken by the epidemic. In countries where AIDS prevalence is low, this is especially true. Southeast Asian countries are a good example of a region of the world where AIDS awareness may be low. Only 3% of the cumulative global AIDS cases are in Asia (WHO Global Program on AIDS 1993). However, given reports of potentially skyrocketing rates there, Asia may be the "sleeping giant" of the AIDS epidemic.

### The Research Site

The Tu Du Hospital is a large urban hospital in Saigon and is regarded as one of the most highly advanced hospitals for women in Vietnam. In 1990 it provided services to 43,511 inpatients and 34,032 outpatients. It operates three outpatient clinics: family planning, obstetrics, and gynecology. The data reported here were collected from 376 women who attended the Tu Du Hospital outpatient clinics between June and August 1991. Sixty percent of the respondents were from the family planning clinic, 20% from the obstetric clinic, and the remaining 20% from the gynecologic clinic. A random sample of women registering at the outpatient clinics was selected to participate in the interview, which was based on a structured questionnaire adapted from the WHO's global program and other AIDS surveys in the United States. It was translated into Vietnamese and back-translated to check for accuracy. All respondents were interviewed by one of the authors in Vietnamese. Three hundred eighty-eight women were selected to participate in the study and 376 (97%) agreed to be interviewed.

Table 14–1 provides the sociodemographic characteristics of the women in this study. The women ranged in age from 18 to 45, with a mean age of 28 years. The majority (66%) of the women were employed at the time of the study, and almost all (92%) were married. Seventy percent of the women had completed a high school education or more, with only six of the interviewed women being unable to read or write in their native language of Vietnamese. Sixty-seven percent of the respondents had no children or only one child. This is reflective of the trend of having fewer children in Vietnam. Prior to 1975, Vietnamese women had several children. The change in the number of children may be a result of both the family planning initiatives implemented by the government and the economic situations of families.

***AIDS awareness*** Overall, the respondents manifested high levels of awareness of AIDS. Almost everyone (98%) indicated that they had heard of AIDS, and 81% responded affirmatively to the question, "Do you think there

**TABLE 14–1. Demographic Characteristics**

| *CHARACTERISTICS* | *(N = 376)* |
|---|---|
| Age (in years) | |
| M (mean) | 28 |
| R (range) | 18–45 |
| Employment | |
| Unemployed | 128 |
| Employed | 248 |
| Marital status | |
| Not married | 31 |
| Married | 338 |
| Education | |
| No/primary education | 112 |
| Secondary education | 225 |
| Higher education | 39 |
| Number of children | |
| No children | 99 |
| One child | 151 |
| Two children | 81 |
| More than three children | 42 |
| Residence | |
| Saigon | 200 |
| Outside of Saigon | 170 |

is anyone with AIDS in Vietnam?" Fourteen percent provided a "don't know" response to the latter question. When asked to indicate the most serious disease or health problem facing the world today, 73% of the sample spontaneously mentioned AIDS. The next most-frequently mentioned problem was cancer (17%).

***Sources of information*** When respondents were asked where they had received most of their information about AIDS, the three most frequently mentioned sources were newspapers and magazines (50%), television (23%), and radio (10%). Instructively, only 3% mentioned friends or colleagues as a source of AIDS information and hospitals and medical personnel did not emerge as an important source.

Respondents were also specifically asked about information received and discussions held regarding AIDS within the previous 2 months. Table 14–2 presents responses to these questions. The role of the social network emerges as more important on this question. Sixty-three percent of the respondents indicated that they had discussed AIDS with family/relatives/close friends, and

**TABLE 14–2. Percent of Respondents Discussing or Receiving Information Regarding AIDS in the Last Two Months**

| | *FREQUENCY* | | | |
|---|---|---|---|---|
| *DISCUSSION/INFORMATION* | *NEVER* | *ONCE OR TWICE* | *MANY* | *DON'T KNOW* |
| Within the last two months, how many times would you say you have: | | | | |
| 1. Discussed AIDS with family/relatives/ close friends? | 28 | 44 | 19 | 9 |
| 2. Heard or seen something about AIDS in mass media? | 7 | 51 | 33 | 9 |
| 3. Discussed AIDS with friends/peers/ neighbors? | 24 | 48 | 19 | 9 |

67% indicated that they discussed AIDS at least once with friends/peers/ neighbors. The media again emerge as important information sources, with 51% of the sample indicating that they had received information from the mass media regarding AIDS once or twice in the previous 2 months, and an additional 33% reported that they had received information from the mass media many times.

### Attitudes and Beliefs

***Beliefs about people with AIDS*** Table 14–3 indicates the levels of support for various strategies toward patients with AIDS. Most respondents believed that AIDS patients should be treated kindly (82%) and should be provided treatment and all needed amenities (90%). In contrast to these initially com-

**TABLE 14–3. Attitudes Toward AIDS Patients**

| | *PERCENT SAYING* | | |
|---|---|---|---|
| *STRATEGY* | *YES* | *NO* | *DON'T KNOW* |
| 1. Kill all people with AIDS | 13 | 79 | 8 |
| 2. Isolate in institution | 42 | 49 | 9 |
| 3. Force to live separately from family | 55 | 36 | 9 |
| 4. Treat kindly | 82 | 11 | 7 |
| 5. Be careful so that no one touches them | 48 | 41 | 11 |
| 6. Provide treatment and needed items | 90 | 5 | 5 |

passionate views, some 13% would support killing all people with AIDS, 42% believe that AIDS patients should be isolated in an institution, 55% believe that they should be forced to live separately from their families, and 48% believe that care should be exercised so that no one touches an AIDS patient.

***Perceived severity*** There does not appear to be a clear recognition on the part of most respondents that AIDS is a fatal disease. Eighteen percent of the sample believed that a person who has AIDS can be cured, 45% believed that no cure was available, and 37% were unsure. Similarly, when asked how many of the people who get AIDS will die of the disease, only 20% reported "everyone." Three percent reported "no one," 10% reported "a few," 30% reported "a large number," and 37% were unsure.

***Perceived risk*** Only a relatively small percentage of the respondents believed that they were at risk of getting AIDS. In response to the question, "What are the chances that *you* might catch AIDS?" 46% of the sample responded "not very likely" or "never" and an additional 33% were unsure. Fifteen percent believed their chances of getting AIDS was "somewhat likely" and 6% said "very likely." The respondents' perception of the likelihood of getting AIDS might be linked to their beliefs that they do not belong to the risk groups of likely AIDS patients. When asked what kind of people are likely to get AIDS, 50% of the sample spontaneously reported prostitutes, and an additional 25% indicated those who engage in promiscuous behavior.

***Efficacy*** A majority of respondents believed that people can do something to protect themselves from AIDS. Sixty-two percent of the sample indicated that a person can avoid getting AIDS by changing his or her behavior. Thirteen percent believed that behavior change would not reduce one's risk, and 25% were unsure. Fifty-seven percent of the respondents indicated that they were planning to make changes in their own behavior as a result of what they had heard about AIDS, 24% anticipated not making any changes, and 19% were unsure.

Respondents who indicated that they intended to make changes in their behavior as a result of the AIDS epidemic were asked a follow-up question about what they had actually done or were planning to do. Table 14–4 presents the respondents' responses to the question of what kinds of changes they had made or intended to make in response to their knowledge about AIDS. The most common spontaneously reported strategy is that of a woman telling her entire family to be more careful and to lead a clean life (32%). Other frequently reported strategies were engaging in only monogamous relationships (13%) and changing attitudes in general with regard to sex (15%). It is instructive that the use of condoms was not mentioned as a strategy for avoiding AIDS.

**TABLE 14–4. Strategies Used by Respondents to Reduce the Risk of Getting AIDS**

| *STRATEGY* | *PERCENT REPORTING* |
|---|---|
| 1. Telling husband not to fool around | 5 |
| 2. Telling entire family to be careful and lead a clean life | 32 |
| 3. Engage in monogamous relationships | 13 |
| 4. Fewer visits to nightclubs and bars | 2 |
| 5. Change attitudes with regard to sex | 15 |
| 6. More caution regarding sexual partners | 3 |
| 7. More cuation regarding social interaction | 5 |
| 8. Other | 11 |
| 9. Don't know | 14 |

## AIDS KNOWLEDGE IN VIETNAM

The most widely used model for understanding health behavior, the Health Belief Model, assumes that an individual's level of knowledge is an important prerequisite for effective prevention efforts (Rosenstock 1974). Given a level of knowledge, this model focuses on cues to action that may be important in initiating or maintaining particular health behaviors. This approach has been widely used in research on attitudes, beliefs, and behavior with regard to AIDS. Identifying the factors predictive of variations in AIDS knowledge can also facilitate efforts to focus prevention strategies on the most vulnerable subgroups.

Some evidence from studies in the United States suggests that knowledge about AIDS can be an important determinant of change in behavior related to AIDS transmission. Data from several large surveys that have examined changes in sexual behavior in gay men since the start of the AIDS epidemic indicate that there have been reductions in high-risk behaviors (Lawrence et al. 1989). A combination of knowledge about HIV transmission obtained through intensive and credible educational efforts and the sense of personal vulnerability created when an individual's close friends died of AIDS have contributed to the reduction in high-risk behavior (Winklestein et al. 1989; McKusick et al. 1985).

***Knowledge about AIDS transmission*** Table 14–5 presents responses to the 15 questions that were used to measure knowledge about the modes of transmission of the AIDS virus. The structure of responses shows considerable diversity. The distribution of responses is skewed on some items but evenly bal-

**TABLE 14–5. Distribution of Responses to the AIDS Knowledge Questions**

| KNOWLEDGE ITEM | % YES | % NO | % DON'T KNOW |
|---|---|---|---|
| Do you think: | | | |
| 1. A person can be infected and have the virus that causes AIDS but not have any symptoms? | 49.0 | 16.6 | 34.3 |
| 2. A person can catch AIDS from someone who has this disease? | 85.8 | 5.2 | 9.0 |
| 3. Someone who looks healthy but who has the AIDS virus can pass it to other people? | 79.6 | 4.4 | 16.1 |
| 4. One can get AIDS by touching the body of a person who has the disease? | 16.1 | 60.5 | 23.4 |
| 5. One can get AIDS by kissing a person who has the disease? | 30.0 | 51.5 | 18.5 |
| 6. One can get AIDS by sharing cups or dishes with a person who has the disease? | 35.4 | 48.0 | 16.6 |
| 7. One can get AIDS by using the same needle that an infected person used beforehand? | 80.7 | 9.0 | 10.4 |
| 8. One can get AIDS by having sex with prostitutes? | 89.4 | 4.4 | 6.3 |
| 9. One can get AIDS by having sex with many people? | 80.1 | 8.4 | 11.4 |
| 10. One can get AIDS by being bitten by mosquitoes or other bloodsucking insects? | 39.5 | 38.1 | 22.3 |
| 11. One can get AIDS by having sex with a man who has the disease? | 87.7 | 3.3 | 9.0 |
| 12. One can get AIDS by a blood transfusion/receiving blood from a person who has AIDS? | 85.0 | 4.9 | 10.1 |
| 13. One can get AIDS by wearing clothes used by a person who has the disease? | 48.2 | 31.6 | 20.2 |
| 14. One can get AIDS by having sex with a woman who has the disease? | 89.4 | 2.2 | 8.4 |
| 15. A woman who has AIDS can pass it on to her baby? | 74.1 | 6.5 | 19.3 |

anced on others. For example, 86% of the respondents believe that a person can catch AIDS from someone who has the disease, and 88% believe that someone can catch AIDS from having sex with an infected man. On the other hand, fully 30% believe that AIDS can be transmitted by kissing, and 35% believe sharing cups or dishes is a potential source of infection.

The pattern of "don't know" responses also varies across the range of questions. Thirty-four percent did not know whether someone can be infected but not have any symptoms, and 23% indicated they did not know whether or not a person could get AIDS by touching an infected person's body. These were the two highest percentages from the don't know category. At the low end, 6% indicated that they did not know whether someone can get AIDS by having sex with a prostitute, and 8% had no idea whether having sex with a woman who has AIDS can increase one's chances of getting the disease.

Exploratory factor analysis was performed with the 15 AIDS knowledge questions to identify the extent to which there was an underlying pattern to the items. Principal components factor analysis with varimax rotation resulted in the emergence of two well-defined factors. The first factor consists of the questions that deal with whether AIDS can be transmitted by casual contact, with the exception being the questions that deal with the transmission of AIDS through mosquitoes or other bloodsucking insects and those that deal with the perinatal transmission of AIDS. The second factor consists primarily of questions that address the transmission of AIDS through sexual contact. A question dealing with the transmission of the AIDS virus through sharing needles and another dealing with getting AIDS from blood transfusions cluster with the sexual contact items.

Table 14–6 presents the distribution of correct responses to each of the knowledge questions grouped by the two major categories: casual and sexual contact. Although the level of knowledge is high for some items, for other measures of knowledge regarding the transmission of AIDS the majority of respondents did not provide the correct answer. There were relatively low correct percentages on the transmission of HIV by wearing clothes (32%—the lowest correct percentage on the casual knowledge items), by being bitten by a mosquito (38%), and by sharing utensils with an infected person (48%). Misinformation, false beliefs, and uncertainty about the transmission of HIV are clearly shown on these items.

On several other items, the percentages of correct responses were only slightly better. Only 49% had the correct response to the question of whether it is possible for a person to be infected with the AIDS virus and not have any symptoms. This suggests that a substantial proportion of the respondents would rely on symptoms for the identification of an individual who has been exposed to the AIDS virus. Similarly, only 52% had the correct answer to the question about AIDS transmission via kissing someone who has the disease, and 60% responded correctly to the question of whether one can get AIDS by touching the body of an infected person. In contrast to the casual transmission items, Table 14–6 reveals that the majority of respondents offered the correct responses to the questions regarding sexual transmission. For example, the lowest percentage of correct responses on the six sexual transmission items was 80% (the question with regard to whether one can get AIDS by having sex with many people). These data nonetheless indicate that although the majority of

**TABLE 14–6. Percentages of Correct Responses to Questions Measuring Knowledge of AIDS**

| *KNOWLEDGE ITEMS* | *% CORRECT* |
|---|---|
| *Casual Contact Items* | |
| 1. Do you think a person can be infected and have the virus that causes AIDS but not have any symptoms? | 49.0 |
| 2. Do you think a person can catch AIDS from someone who has this disease? | 85.8 |
| 3. Do you think someone who looks healthy but who has the AIDS virus can pass it to other people? | 79.6 |
| 4. Do you think that one can get AIDS by touching the body of a person who has the disease? | 60.5 |
| 5. Do you think that one can get AIDS by kissing a person who has the disease? | 51.5 |
| 6. Do you think that one can get AIDS by sharing cups or dishes with a person who has the disease? | 48.0 |
| 7. Do you think that one can get AIDS by wearing clothes used by a person who has the disease? | 31.6 |
| 8. Do you think that one can get AIDS by being bitten by mosquitoes or other bloodsucking insects? | 38.1 |
| 9. Do you think that a woman who has AIDS can pass it on to her baby? | 74.1 |
| *Sexual Contact Items* | |
| 1. Do you think that one can get AIDS by using the same needle that an infected person used beforehand? | 80.7 |
| 2. Do you think that one can get AIDS by having sex with prostitutes? | 89.4 |
| 3. Do you think that one can get AIDS by having sex with many people? | 80.1 |
| 4. Do you think that one can get AIDS by a blood transfusion/receiving blood from a person with AIDS? | 85.0 |
| 5. Do you think that one can get AIDS by having sex with a man who has the disease? | 87.7 |
| 6. Do you think that one can get AIDS by having sex with a woman who has the disease? | 89.4 |

N = 367

women are not misinformed on the major modes of AIDS transmission, 10% to 20% of them are misinformed or unsure about the correct response.

The overall pattern that emerges here suggests that Vietnamese women are fairly well informed on the major means by which AIDS is actually transmitted. However, they also demonstrate high levels of belief in, or uncertainty about, the transmission of AIDS in ways it is not actually transmitted (the casual transmission items).

### Sociodemographic Factors and AIDS Knowledge

***Bivariate analyses*** It is likely that levels of AIDS knowledge are not randomly distributed in the population. It is thus important to identify the sociodemographic characteristics that predict variation in levels of AIDS knowledge. Table 14–7 presents the association between six sociodemographic characteristics and AIDS knowledge. Two summary measures of AIDS knowledge were created. The casual AIDS knowledge measure was created by summing the number of correct responses to the nine items that deal with casual AIDS knowledge. Similarly, the sexual AIDS knowledge measure was created by summing the number of correct responses to the six items dealing with sexual AIDS knowledge. Statistical significance of differences between mean levels of AIDS knowledge was assessed by t-test differences using the least square means procedure in the Statistical Analysis System (SAS) program package.

Table 14–7 reveals that place of residence was an important predictor of knowledge of both the casual and sexual transmission of AIDS. Women who lived in Saigon had more correct information regarding AIDS than those who lived outside the city. The association between AIDS knowledge and residence may be due to the differential access to health information and health care in urban versus rural settings. Literature from other Third World countries indicates that access and information regarding health are less adequate in rural than urban areas. These studies also reveal that the rural population, on average, has a lower knowledge level (Wilson et al. 1989). People who live in rural areas also tend to have lower levels of formal education. Therefore, it is not surprising that average levels of AIDS knowledge are slightly higher for persons who live in Saigon than for their more rural peers.

Knowledge about AIDS transmission did not vary by employment or marital status. However, a strong relationship exists between formal education and AIDS knowledge. Education is positively related to knowledge about the transmission of HIV. Age was also significantly related to the casual measure and manifested a marginally significant ($P < 0.10$) association with the sexual AIDS transmission measure. Older women tended to have higher levels of AIDS knowledge than younger women. There was also a relationship between parity and AIDS knowledge. Respondents who had one child were more knowledgeable about the casual transmission of AIDS than those with no children. In con-

**TABLE 14–7. Association Between Sociodemographic Factors and AIDS Knowledge**

| SOCIODEMOGRAPHIC CHARACTERISTIC | MEAN OF CORRECT RESPONSES | |
|---|---|---|
| | CASUAL AIDS KNOWLEDGE | SEXUAL AIDS KNOWLEDGE |
| Employment | | |
| Unemployed | 4.89 | 4.80 |
| Employed | 5.15 | 5.10 |
| Residence | | |
| Outside Saigon | 4.75‡ | 4.70‡ |
| In Saigon | 5.33 | 5.30 |
| Marital Status | | |
| Not married | 4.55 | 4.80 |
| Married | 5.10 | 5.05 |
| Age | | |
| 18–24 years (R) | 4.55 | 4.68 |
| 25–29 years | 4.96 | 5.13† |
| 30–34 years | 5.41* | 5.03 |
| 35+ years | 5.40* | 5.15 |
| Education | | |
| No/primary education (R) | 4.33 | 4.60 |
| Secondary education | 5.20‡ | 5.10* |
| Higher education | 6.33‡ | 5.60* |
| Number of children | | |
| No children (R) | 4.60 | 4.68 |
| One child | 5.42* | 5.13 |
| Two children | 5.22 | 5.03 |
| Three children | 4.50 | 5.14* |

† = $P<0.10$; * $P<0.05$; ‡ = $P<0.01$

R = Reference category for the significance tests

trast, only women with three or more children were more knowledgeable about the sexual transmission of AIDS than those with no children.

***Multivariate analyses*** Multivariate analyses using ordinary least squares regression were performed to assess the relative contribution of the sociodemographic variables to levels of knowledge about AIDS. These analyses revealed that the earlier reported association between casual knowledge about AIDS and both place of residence and formal education remained significant in the multivariate analyses when all six sociodemographic variables were entered together. The association between number of children and casual knowledge was reduced to marginal significance ($P< 0.10$), and the relationship between age and casual knowledge disappeared in the multivariate model. However, most of the bivariate associations between sociodemographic variables and sexual knowledge of AIDS remained robust in the multivariate analyses. The association between place of residence and formal education remained statistically significant, whereas the association between age and sexual knowledge of AIDS was reduced to marginal significance ($P < 0.10$). In the multiple regression analyses, the relationship between the number of children and sexual knowledge of AIDS is not significant.

In sum, education and residence have emerged as predictors of the level of the knowledge about AIDS among women at the outpatient clinics of Tu Du Hospital. Women who live in Saigon clearly manifest higher levels of knowledge of HIV transmission than women who live in more rural areas. Similarly, the more education a woman has, the greater is her level of knowledge about AIDS. These findings suggest the importance of making special efforts to target AIDS educational programs to rural residents and less educated persons in Vietnam because these two groups may be more vulnerable to contracting the AIDS virus due to their lack of adequate knowledge.

## SUMMARY

The attitudes, beliefs, and knowledge of a sample of women of childbearing age in Vietnam provide reason for optimism, as well as reason for concern. On the one hand, the overall level of knowledge about AIDS is high. Both the USAID and the WHO have suggested using the percentage of people in a given country knowing two correct transmission routes as an indicator of AIDS knowledge within that country. Using this criterion, more than 8 of 10 of the sampled women would be classified as knowledgeable about AIDS transmission. At the same time, although the major AIDS transmission routes are correctly identified, a relatively large number of respondents also have misconceptions about the ways in which AIDS can be transmitted. It is noteworthy that almost 70% of Vietnamese women believe that a person can get AIDS by wearing clothes used by a person who has the disease and by insect bites.

Another area of concern is that a substantial proportion of respondents did not perceive themselves as personally at risk. However, studies of other Third World populations suggest that perceived risk is not directly linked either to knowledge of AIDS or the performance of risky behaviors (Fishbein et al. 1993). Joseph et al. (1987), using data from the United States, also questioned the centrality of perceived risk in the health belief model. That is, persons who perceive themselves at risk are not as likely to engage in preventive actions as the health belief model would predict.

There appears to be a problem of underreporting and underrecognition of HIV infection from the official health infrastructure in Vietnam. The need for accurate and reliable surveillance is imperative and essential to effective efforts to arrest the spread of HIV infection. The present study provides useful baseline information on knowledge, attitudes, and beliefs related to AIDS in Vietnam. The findings of this study can facilitate efforts to address the threat of the AIDS epidemic in a society where that threat is high. This study provides a basis for effective targeting of interventions to particular subgroups and for targeting the information gaps that were unearthed.

The need for more AIDS educational programs to provide the Vietnamese people with accurate information concerning transmission is clear. These programs should incorporate information that pertains to safer sexual behaviors. Culturally, Vietnamese women are very timid in discussing sexual practices. They tend to comply with their mates' sexual desires and to have little input when it comes to their sexual pleasures. Compounding this problem is a lack of knowledge about condom usage. It is instructive that when women were asked what kinds of changes they had made or intended to make in their behavior as a result of the AIDS epidemic, condom usage was not mentioned. Because condoms are neither readily available nor inexpensive in Vietnam, regular usage is not widespread there. This is a particular problem among young women involved in prostitution. Several conversations that one of the authors had with male European tourists in Saigon suggests that as many as 7 of every 10 prostitutes did not know what a condom was when it was shown to them. The depressed economic situation in Vietnam leads many of these women to engage in risky sexual behaviors with no knowledge of their risk. Aggressive outreach efforts to inform these women about condoms may be an effective strategy for reducing the spread of AIDS in Vietnam. The Vietnamese government should inform and educate the Vietnamese people about HIV infection and AIDS transmission and promote safe-sex behavior.

Although this study contributes to a better understanding of the health knowledge possessed by women of childbearing age in Vietnam, its generalizability is limited because the sample was restricted to women using outpatient clinics at one major hospital in one Vietnamese city. The respondents may have been predisposed to health information because they were inclined to seek health care services. More research is needed to understand the threat of AIDS in Vietnam. Vietnam is ripe for public health interventions regarding AIDS, but these prevention initiatives must be guided by a clear, well-designed focus.

## REFERENCES

BONACCI, MARK A. 1990. Pp. 34–39 in *The Legacy of Colonialism: Health Care in Southeast Asia.* Washington, DC: Asia Resource Center.

BRITANNICA BOOK OF THE YEAR. 1993. Chicago: Encyclopedia Britannica, p. 749.

COHEN, BARBARA. 1991. Pp. 2–7 in *Vietnam Guidebook.* Boston: Houghton Mifflin.

FISHBEIN, MARTIN, DAVID TRAFIMOW, CLAUDETTE FRANCIS, et al. 1993. "AIDS Knowledge, Attitudes, Beliefs, and Practices (KABP) in Two Caribbean Countries: A Comparative Analysis." *Journal of Applied Social Psychology* 23:687–702.

Ickovics, Jeanette R. and Judith Rodin. 1992. "Women and AIDS in the United States: Epidemiology, Natural History, and Mediating Mechanisms." *Health Psychology* 11:1–16.

Joseph, Jill G., Susanne B. Mongtomery, Carol-Ann Emmons, et al. 1987. "Perceived Risk of AIDS: Assessing the Behavioral and Psychosocial Consequences in a Cohort of Gay Men." *Journal of Applied Social Psychology* 17:231–50.

Lawrence, Jeanette, Harold V. Hood, and Ted L. Brasfield. 1989. "Differences in Gay Men's AIDS Risk Knowledge and Behavior Patterns in High and Low AIDS Prevalence Cities." *Atlantic Information Services,* September:1–5.

McKusick, Leon, William Horstman, and Thomas Coates. 1985. "AIDS and Sexual Behavior Reported by Gay Men in San Francisco." *American Journal of Public Health* 75:493–96.

Miller, Heather G., Charles F. Turner, and Lincoln Moses (eds.). 1990. P. 55 in *AIDS: The Second Decade.* Washington, DC: National Academy Press.

Pasteur Institute in Ho Chi Min City. 1994.

Reuter News Agency. 1993. "HIV Cases Rising Among Vietnamese." July 30, p. 3.

Rosenstock, Irwin. 1963. "The Health Belief Model and Preventive Health Behavior." Pp. 98–99 in *The Health Belief Model and Personal Health Behavior,* edited by Marshall Becker. Thorofare, NJ: Slack.

United Nations Development Program. 1991. "Report on the Economy of Vietnam." Hanoi, Vietnam.

Vecchi, Nicole. 1992. "Vietnam HIV: The New Epidemic." *Vietnam Generation* 34:4.

Wilson, David C. 1989. "Towards an AIDS Information Strategy for Zimbabwe." *AIDS Education and Prevention* 1:96–104.

Winkelstein, Warren Jr., Nancy S. Padian, George Rutherford, and Harold W. Jaffe. 1989. "Homosexual Men." Pp. 117–35 in *The Epidemiology of AIDS: Expression, Occurrence, and Control of Human Immunodeficiency Virus Type 1 Infection,* edited by R. A. Kaslow and D. P. Francis. New York: Oxford University Press.

World Health Organization (WHO) Global Program on AIDS. 1993. AIDS Cases Reported to Surveillance, Forecasting and Impact Assessment Unit (SFI). Washington, DC: World Health Organization Office of Research, August 30.

Zwi, Anthony and Anthony Cabral. 1991. "Identifying 'High Risk Situations' for Preventing AIDS." *British Medical Journal* 303:1527–29.

Chapter 15

# Sex, Condoms, and Risk of AIDS in Bangladesh*

*Steven Folmar and S. M. Nurul Alam*

In the short time since AIDS was identified as a disease, it has grown into a major epidemic in many countries. Owing to its insidious, lethal, and incurable status, AIDS is one of the most feared diseases in the world. The ease with which AIDS is transmitted has led to explosive incidence rates in many regions of the world. Infection patterns are closely linked to specific behaviors such as sexual contact and intravenous (IV) drug use. Without a medical breakthrough, the greatest chances for slowing the spread of this disease rest in modifying such behaviors. In a world besieged by the ravages of this killer disease, any country with low rates of this disease should be cause for great hope, assuming that it has effective mechanisms for detecting and reporting AIDS.

Unfortunately, beneath many countries' claims to have virtually no problem with AIDS, Bangladesh included, are more equivocal realities. Any survey of research and policy statements about AIDS in Bangladesh would suggest that there should be little concern to Bangladeshis. To date there has been an extremely low reported incidence of the disease and the virus that causes it (HIV).

*The Condom Use Project was funded by a grant from the United States Agency for International Development, through Family Health International. Drs. Mridul Chowdhury, Sharon Jackson, and Janardan Subedi made useful comments on earlier drafts, and we thank them. The views expressed in this chapter are solely our own.

In fact, only one case of AIDS from Bangladesh has thusfar been officially reported to the World Health Organization (WHO 1993). Consistent with this statistic is the lack of published evidence that many people engage in the major risk behaviors for AIDS, such as liberal sexual practice or IV drug use.

Epidemiologically, Bangladesh may well be following a course of HIV transmission similar to other Asian countries like India. Until recently, observers recognized three basic patterns for AIDS transmissions (Mann and Chin 1988; Mann et al. 1988). Asia, the Middle East, and Eastern Europe shared a type characterized by two features: (1) minuscule numbers of reported cases, and (2) belief that cases originated via sexual contact with foreigners. However, just a few years after these patterns were first described, some of the Asian countries began reporting alarming numbers of cases of HIV infection and/or AIDS. For example, India had not reported five cases of AIDS by 1988 (Mann et al. 1988) but now recognizes that it has 1 million or more people infected with HIV.

Such a steep increase in prevalence calls into serious question the validity of the Mann and Chin model (1988). Although AIDS has spread extremely quickly in these countries, one must seriously question the baseline prevalence rates that were reported in the mid 1980s in many of these countries. In India's case, for example, it appears that the problem was initially underestimated because AIDS was perceived to be a foreign problem with little potential to threaten the public health of a country in which few people engage in risky sexual or drug-use behavior. In such a seemingly safe environment, there was believed to be little need to screen blood for HIV infection, thus making officials slow to recognize how large a problem AIDS actually was. In the absence of screening, prevalence was underestimated and spread of HIV infection was facilitated by ignorance of the magnitude of the problem. By the time screening was introduced, AIDS had already become an epidemic.

Like India before it, Bangladesh now reports an extremely low prevalence of AIDS. As of December 1992, newspapers had reported only the tenth case of AIDS nationwide. These 10 cases were identified by a screening program sponsored by the Government of Bangladesh (GOB). However, this program is recent in origin and has been targeted at vaguely defined high-risk groups. Details of the program, such as what groups are being targeted and how many people have been screened, have not been released, making it impossible to interpret what level of problem these cases represent. In mirror image to the sluggish initiation of screening is the virtual absence of any educational efforts to inform the public about AIDS or programming to promote safe lifestyle habits.

Why official response to the spread of AIDS has been so listless is rather a complex situation. First, it is believable that AIDS would be introduced to Bangladesh very slowly. Although not landlocked, Bangladesh is among the poorest nations on Earth, with few exportable resources and a history of capitalizing on a labor force willing to toil for meager wages to manufacture cheap goods for export. Coupled with its poor economic position, Bangladesh is not a favorite spot on Asian tourist trails. In short, Bangladesh is not a magnet to outsiders, some of whom might carry HIV. A second and more important factor is that avenues for the spread of HIV among Bangladeshis, especially via sexual pathways, are not recognized. Bangladesh is believed by outsiders and by the Bangladeshis themselves to be a highly sexual conservative society whose sexual mores provide something of a cultural immunity to the spread of HIV. It is in this light that the GOB's response to AIDS must be evaluated. Officials in the GOB, like many professional researchers and development workers in Bangladesh, believe that transmission of AIDS would be exceedingly difficult and therefore felt no urgency to screen for AIDS or to educate the public about its dangers.

Underpinning the image of invulnerability to HIV infection is the predominant religious affiliation of Bangladesh's people, Islam, which upholds a sexually conservative doctrine. Thus Bangladeshis are assumed to have low rates of prostitution, relatively few sexual partners per person, and a low incidence of risky sexual practices such as homosexuality, anal intercourse, and extramarital or premarital sex.

A salient feature of Islam is the practice of *purdah,* or the strict segregation of women from men resulting from male dominance over female sexuality. Men, too, are believed to be sexually conservative, with sex being sanctioned only in marriage for purposes of procreation and marital harmony. It should, therefore, not be surprising that a major preventive measure for AIDS, the condom, has been associated almost exclusively with family planning, and its promotion has not been aimed at prevention of HIV infection.

The official view of a sexually conservative Bangladesh is so entrenched that AIDS is not regarded as a problem, condom use is not considered necessary to prevent its spread, and low rates of condom use (in the vicinity of 2.5% of married couples under age 50, [Mitra et al. 1992]) are of little concern. Research on family planning rarely incorporates questions about sexual practices because it is feared that such inquiry will yield little information and might insult the respondents. Thus, popular beliefs abut sexuality go unchallenged more because of a lack of any contradictory data than because of a body of evidence that actually supports this viewpoint. Finally, the sensitive nature of sex and related topics (like condom use) hinders the open exchange of accurate information about sex. This has led professionals to misconstrue the range and extent of various sexual practices and the public to misunderstand a variety of sexual and contraceptive matters.

The purpose of this chapter is to examine the implications of findings from the Condom Use Project (CUP) for AIDS prevention in Bangladesh. Although the research for CUP was designed to examine condom use in the context of family planning issues (Folmar et al. 1992), the findings are important for AIDS research because the condom represents the point of intersection for research and programming on both family planning and AIDS. It is the only device recognized as an effective contraceptive and prophylactic. The recommended method of use for both purposes is identical.

## METHODS

CUP was a family planning–driven project oriented toward elucidating a more precise understanding of the effectiveness of condoms by studying how they are used by men. The investigators began with a simple premise rarely employed in surveys: We did not know how condoms were used; condom users did (Folmar et al.). Therefore, although our ultimate goal was to administer a standard questionnaire to condom users, we constructed the questionnaire only after we had interviewed condom users in open-ended format so that they could identify for us what the relevant questions ought to be. The ethnographic approach has been instrumental in identifying the range of sexual behaviors found in everyday life in rural Bangladesh (Aziz and Maloney 1985) and more recently in identifying behaviors that put people at risk of HIV infection in a variety of social situations. Combining ethnographic with survey methods has proven useful in other investigations of the effect of culture on fertility and family planning (Folmar 1992) and on health behavior (Friedenberg et al. 1993).

We began our project by conducting in-depth interviews with a variety of people involved with condom use at various levels, from condom distributors to condom users. From 25 such people, we elicited as much detail about their experience with condoms as possible. We asked personal and uncomfortable questions that explored the details of their sexual lives. The candor of the subjects in responding to these questions convinced us that it was feasible to obtain highly confidential information without violating the integrity of personal privacy.

From the information these interviews yielded, we constructed an hour-long questionnaire that was field-tested with several pilot-test subjects and then revised accordingly. As our original objective focused on identifying the range of uses of condoms in Bangladesh and determining how those practices varied among subgroups of users, the survey focused exclusively on condom users. In all, there were 403 subjects, equally divided into three groups (one group was oversampled by one respondent, see Figure 15–1). All subjects came from the city of Khulna and surrounding rural and semiurban communities. This area reports condom-use rates representative of national rates (Mitra et al. 1992) but has a higher concentration of Hindus, which is reflected in our sample.

In this sample all but five respondents, who are excluded from further analysis, were currently married. The mean ages of the respondents and their

**FIGURE 15–1.** Survey sample.

| Place of Residence | Rural | Semi-Urban | Urban |
|---|---|---|---|
| Number in Survey | 135 | 134 | 134 |

wives were 36 and 27 years, respectively. The respondents had married at an average age of 25 years and now had about two living children, one of whom was a son. Most of the sample also lived with other family members, in a household of nearly six persons, crowded into less than three rooms. Occupation varied by place of residence. Agriculture was the primary occupation in the rural subsample (which also had a substantial number of professionals), whereas the urban and semiurban subsamples had more diverse occupations in the services, businesses, and the professions. More than half the sample (58.3%) reported that their average household monthly expenditures were less than 3,001 Taka (US $1.00 = 38 Taka).

The final questionnaire we used to survey the above sample contained many detailed questions on condom use and also several items on various sexual practices and three questions related to AIDS. For two reasons, we felt encouraged to pursue a degree of detail that would generally be considered too explicit and embarrassing in Bangladesh. The first was that other ethnographic reports (Maloney et al. 1981; Khan and Arefeen 1982) indicated that there was greater license for sexual behavior than one would believe from everyday conversation with most people, even with professionals working in the field of family planning in Bangladesh. The second reason was that the ethnographic portion of our fieldwork strongly confirmed the first reason and demonstrated that we could get at this uncomfortable topic by using same-sex (male) interviewers, treating the topic with sensitivity, assuring confidentiality, and emphasizing the "professional" nature of the encounter. In short, we strove to create an atmosphere of trust in which people could appropriately discuss a topic for which there are few other conversational outlets.

Our analytic methods consist of a combination of ethnographic and quantitative techniques. Because the goal of this chapter is to bring to light relatively unknown practices and to interpret these in light of AIDS prevention, the aim of our analysis is to describe some relevant cultural beliefs and behaviors. It is not intended to produce precise parametric estimates.

## FINDINGS

The following presentation interweaves ethnographic and survey findings into a narrative on how men view, practice, and talk about their sexual experiences. It also discusses how the rules regarding communicating about sex affect condom use and ultimately the potential impact of sexual practices and condom use on the risk for AIDS.

### Communicating About Sex

The image of a sexually prudish Bangladesh derives more from how sex is talked about than how it is practiced. A more accurate assessment of Bangladeshi sexuality can be achieved by appreciating the gap that exists between actual sexual practices and styles of reporting on that behavior (Folmar et al.). As a starting point, we must revisit the practice of *purdah* briefly.

The most visible aspect of *purdah* is the segregation of women from men, but the practice relates more generally to social boundary maintenance. It may more properly be considered the separation of the public from the private domain, in a system in which more individual freedom is expressed privately than is acknowledged publicly. Anthropologic investigation of Bangladeshi culture has supported this interpretation, demonstrating that more sexual license exists than public discourse about it recognizes (Aziz and Maloney 1985; Maloney 1974; Maloney et al. 1981). Understanding this, the difference between what people do and what they say they do, especially with regard to sexual behavior, is critical to applied demography in general and family planning in particular in Bangladesh. Misunderstanding the gap between peoples' behavior and how they recount that behavior has led many policy makers to take at face value what Bangladeshis say about sex as an accurate reflection of their sexual behavior, when, in fact, their style of talking about sex maintains a level of privacy they consider essential.

The word for privacy in Bangla, *goponiyata,* refers to personal information that cannot be discussed with or disclosed to others except where and when it is absolutely necessary. *Goponiyata* describes a culturally defined personal boundary surrounding sensitive information such as sex. This boundary is maintained by a set of mainly emotional but also cognitive and behavioral orientations to matters of sexuality in Bangladesh. These include embarrassment, modesty, shame, and the attempt to maintain decorum and to prevent individual (private) sexuality from becoming a matter of public record (Folmar et al.).

The principal psychological mechanism for regulating privacy is the expression of shyness, the Bangla equivalent of which is *lozza.* In Bengali culture, *lozza* is a quality that people internalize through the process of childhood socialization. Parents model *lozza* to their children by refraining from discussions about sex and by demonstrating embarrassment if conversation turns to sexual matters. Displays of *lozza* are inherent in any situation with sexual overtones, and people attempt to avoid such situations by regulating the flow of sexual information across appropriate boundaries.

The opposite of *lozza* is *nirlozza,* a term often used to portray a person who does not observe decorum relating to private matters. *Nirlozza* can also refer to qualities inherent in things or in actions. Anything relating to sex, including discussions about sexuality, sexual acts, problems relating to sex, contraceptive use, and women's physiology, are considered shameful or *nirlozza.* In the area of sexual matters, the exposure of information about sex rather than the sexual acts themselves bring on shame and embarrassment. Although any discussion of sex has the potential to induce such feelings, the degree of impropriety is proportional to how conspicuous the information is about personal sexual behavior.

In other words, it is possible for people to speak about sex at multiple levels, ranging from one extreme of general and abstract to the opposite extreme of specific and personal. At the same time, it is necessary to recognize that different degrees of explicitness correspond to how wide an audience has access to this information. For example, discussions of sexual intercourse can range from the conceptual, "Sexual intercourse is necessary for reproduction," to the concrete, "I had sexual intercourse last night." Because the first statement is not linked to the behavior of any recognizable individual, it can be said to a much wider audience than the second. The social boundaries that limit the flow of such sensitive information include, but are not limited to, gender, familial relationship, social status, age, and familiarity. In other words, relatively explicit sexual conversation cannot pass between men and women, generations within the family, or people of obvious age differences. The more immodest the information, the more clearly defined and the more restricted are the social circles to whom one can convey this information. One example that helps illustrate how sexual information is controlled is found in a woman's visit to her gynecologist. This situation sanctions a frank exchange about specific sexual information between a woman and her doctor, but her husband is normally excluded from the interview. Although he is her regular sexual partner, a woman would still be embarrassed to discuss matters of her own physiology with her husband because of his gender.

Among all the contraceptive devices available, the condom is particularly imbued with *nirlozza* because of its potential to spread shame or embarrassment. So, examination of its use can help us to understand the relationship between behavior and claims more precisely. In Bangladesh, marital sex is expected, appreciated, condoned, and even encouraged. Nonetheless, it is immodest and embarrassing, or *nirlozza,* to bring sexual performance out into the open. Therefore, great pains are taken to conceal that specific acts of coitus occur between couples even though it is assumed that they do have sex. The timing, frequency, and other details are unknown outside the couple's relationship. The purchase and especially the disposal of a condom provide concrete evidence that a specific act of sex will occur or has occurred.

### Sexual Behavior

Contrasted with the highly discreet style of public expression about sex is the rich set of positive values Bangladeshis hold for sex. For example, sexual intercourse is believed to enhance health and psychological well-being. Embedded in the sexual/health belief system of Bangladesh are notions that sexual intercourse is good and healthy, that the mixing of male and female semen is beneficial, and that a man's semen is something of a health-promoting tonic for a woman (Aziz and Maloney 1985).

Equally important to both men and women in Bangladesh is the psychological gratification that sex offers. Responsibility for sexual satisfaction is a reciprocal obligation between husband and wife. One factor a woman uses to measure her worth as a wife is whether or not she satisfies her husband's sexual desires. Men hold similar feelings of responsibility about their wives' sexual satisfaction. It is important to men that their wives are satisfied through sex and view it as their duty to fulfill that satisfaction.

Ideally, sex should occur only within marriage, but sexual outlets do exist for people who are not married. Other research, for example, has illuminated the importance of prostitutes (Khan and Arefeen 1982) and other types of partners for married and unmarried men (Aziz and Maloney 1985). Information from both of our data collection strategies, the ethnographic interviews and the survey questionnaires, bear out other research that finds nonmarital sexual activity to be important in Bangladesh. Table 15–1 shows that in our survey, nearly 30% of men reported experience with premarital sex.

Because our project was not based on a large random survey of sexual practices in Bangladesh, we face the potential criticism that these data do not indicate cultural reality in Bangladesh, but that they reflect the greater amount of sexual permissiveness expressed by educated urbanites, who represent only a small proportion of the population. But our results suggest that, if anything, we are making a *conservative* estimate of the degree of sexual license in Bangladesh. One reason we make that claim is that our informants were unlikely to have overresponded to this inquiry because their culture does not sanction expressions of sexual bravado. We believe the data are of high quality in this regard. Secondly, we found higher rates of premarital sex reported in rural areas than in urban or semiurban areas. In fact, the rate for premarital sex in rural areas is twice as high as in semiurban or urban areas. Furthermore, we found no statistical association between level of education and experience with premarital sex, as can be seen in Table 15–2, below. Finally, we found no difference in the proportion of Hindus and Muslims who had reported having sex before they married (Folmar et al.).

One particularly relevant finding is the association between premarital and extramarital sex. According to the self-reported sexual experiences of the men in our sample, premarital sexual activity acts as the gateway to extramarital activity. As Table 15–3 shows, virtually no one who denied premarital sex admitted to extramarital sex, whereas a substantial number of those admitting to

**TABLE 15–1. Experience with Premarital and Extramarital Sex**

| | *URBAN* | *SEMIURBAN* | *RURAL* | *TOTAL* |
|---|---|---|---|---|
| Premarital intercourse | 29/134 (21.6) | 29/129 (22.5) | 59/135 (43.7) | 117/398 (29.4) |
| Extramarital intercourse | 7/134 (5.2) | 10/129 (7.8) | 12/135 (8.9) | 29/398 (7.3) |

The numerator represents the number of condom users who responded affirmatively to having engaged in these sexual encounters. The denominator equals the number of men who were asked the question. Figures in parentheses are percentages.

**TABLE 15–2. Education and Nonmarital Sex**

| | *NONE* | *PRIMARY* | *SECONDARY* | *COLLEGE* | *TOTAL* |
|---|---|---|---|---|---|
| Premarital intercourse | 12/39 (30.8) | 22/60 (36.7) | 36/129 (27.9) | 45/168 (26.8) | 115/396 (29.0) |
| Extramarital intercourse | 4/39 (10.3) | 9/60 (15.0) | 9/129 (7.0) | 7/168 (4.2) | 29/396 (7.3) |

The numerator represents the number of condom users who responded affirmatively to having engaged in these sexual encounters. The denominator equals the number of men who were asked the question. Figures in parentheses are percentages.

premarital sex confessed to having extramarital affairs as well. The pertinent point here is that this evidence suggests that multiple-partner sexuality is concentrated in a subgroup that enjoys several partners over a number of years, thus exposing themselves and their partners to increased risk of HIV infection over prolonged periods of time.

The most important of our findings is that Bangladeshi culture does not inhibit sexuality to the degree that many officials suppose. The more noticeable effect of culture on sexuality is the restriction of information about sex. Although the many sanctions that restrict the flow of sexually related information do not prevent risky sexual practices, they do restrict accurate information that may help to reduce those risks, such as the proper use of condoms, one of the major foci in most strategies to prevent AIDS transmission (Potts et al. 1991).

### Condom Use

Few men in Bangladesh use condoms. The most recent (1991) Contraceptive Prevalence Survey (CPS) of Bangladesh shows that only 2.5% of the husbands of married women under age 50 currently use them and only 13.4% have ever used them (Mitra et al. 1992). Although women tend to underreport condom use (Mitra and Kamal 1984), it is unlikely that current use rates are double the rate estimated by the CPS. Discrepancies between the number of

**TABLE 15–3. The Association Between Premarital and Extramarital Sex**

| | *REPORTS EXTRAMARITAL SEX* | |
|---|---|---|
| | *NO* | *YES* |
| Reports Premarital Sex | | |
| No | 280 | 1 |
| Yes | 89 | 29 |

condoms used and the number of coition reported by our sample suggests that at least 10% of sexual acts among condom users occur without condoms. The number of unprotected sexual acts within marriage is probably even higher than that because some men report the practice of using two condoms in one act of sex (Folmar et al. 1992). When men have sex outside marriage, they are even less likely to use a condom. Only 30% of the men who admitted to premarital sex claimed to have used condoms at those times. Although more men (67%) who had extramarital sex used condoms for those acts, fully one third did not.

The relatively low rates of condom use are not surprising, given the potential for condoms to reveal specific acts of sex, thus causing shame and embarrassment, especially for those acts not sanctioned by marriage. Of all the possible contraceptive devices, the condom bears the closest direct relationship to sexual intercourse. For example, a course of birth control pills must be taken daily for 1 month regardless of the number of sexual acts that occur within that month. It is not even certain that the pill is being taken by a woman for contraceptive purposes, in that it may be used for "menstrual regulation" as well. Conversely, a condom is used for a specific act of sex and so its purchase and especially its disposal can be assumed to signal that sexual activity will occur or has occurred.

Because condoms are so closely connected to specific sexual events and are especially imbued with *nirlozza,* it is not surprising that accurate information about how to use condoms is difficult for men to get. Until 1992, written and pictorial instructions did not accompany any condom packaging in Bangladesh (and then only in *English*) and field workers and family-planning professionals gave little direct instruction in their actual use. In the intensive phase of our field work, we talked with family-planning workers who described their embarrassment in instructing people in the proper techniques of applying a condom. One family-planning officer, for example, told us that in one monthly meeting of Family Planning Assistants (FPAs), he was describing with the help of a plastic model the steps involved in putting on a condom properly. His vivid description caused discomfort among the participants. During the presentation the officer was approached by an FPA who urged him politely not to be so graphic because there were some women at the meeting. The family planning officer said that afterward he became very careful about his descriptions.

Problems with getting accurate information have significant implications for how men use condoms. The information may be as basic as the application of the condom to a man's penis. One in ten men do not know how to put them on. They report that they unroll the condom first, before placing it over the penis. Other forms of misapplication occur for similar reasons. For example, a few men reuse condoms, giving the explanation that such repeated usage "causes no harm." By all accounts, men who misuse condoms in this way appear uninformed about and unaware of information that discourages such use because it increases the risk of breakage. This, like the application of an unrolled condom, results from the tightly restricted system of information about sex and condom use.

Because access to formal educational materials and knowledge about condom use is so tightly controlled, many men turn to informal networks of information exchange such as friends and acquaintances. In these networks important messages are conveyed through tales of condom failure. Virtually every man knows of someone whose wife got pregnant because of condom breakage, but few actually have direct evidence of such failure. The indirect nature of this information does little to diminish the power of the message that condoms can fail the user. In order to decrease such risk, 13% of the men in our sample reported using two condoms, one unrolled over the other, during sexual intercourse.

Condoms are also used in conjunction with other methods of birth control, sometimes in ways that increase the likelihood that the condom will fail to provide complete protection. One such use is with the withdrawal method. To balance considerations of sensual pleasure with contraception, slightly over 40% of the men in this study reported that they at least sometimes begin intercourse without using a condom, but when they approach climax, withdraw and put on a condom to finish!

Attitudes toward condoms in Bangladesh present a mixture of positive and negative views. Because condoms have been promoted only in the context of contraception, most of the attitudes people have developed toward them pertain to family planning or more directly to sexuality. For example, when asked whether they used condoms for contraceptive or prophylactic purposes, more than 87% said that they used them only to prevent pregnancy, even though 62% of the sample had heard of AIDS.[1] Generally speaking, condoms are viewed as a good, reliable method of contraception. A substantial majority of people in Bangladesh recognize condoms as a reliable means of contraception and view them as having certain assets compared with other methods. Condoms are considered to be more reliable than either rhythm or withdrawal. They are a temporary method that many people favor over permanent methods. Condoms are inexpensive and easy to obtain. They also are viewed as having the considerable advantage of causing few and minor side effects for the wife, whose health is viewed as essential not only for the work she performs but also for the "peace of the family."

On the other hand, the fact that the condom prevents a woman from having direct contact with a man's semen is considered undesirable, a value that may present a major obstacle to future AIDS prevention programming. The barrier the condom poses to the exchange of sexual fluids is seen as unhealthy to a woman's physical health because semen is believed to be something of a tonic for women. The complaint that a condom interferes with a man's sexual pleasure is by no means unique to Bangladesh, but the relationship of condom use and the wife's role in her husband's pleasure is a point that merits discussion. Women in Bangladesh believe that it is their duty to satisfy their husbands' sexual desires, and the knowledge that a condom interferes with this duty makes many women reluctant to use condoms. Wifely duty certainly compounds the problem of eliciting accurate statements about condom use because women believe that it erodes their esteem as a good wife. Men widely believe that the condom decreases erotic sensations for women just as it does for themselves and makes it difficult for women to achieve climax.

One of the most difficult problems people report with respect to condoms is associated with disposing of it after it is used. Again, the need to be discreet is paramount. People take pains to conceal a used condom by flushing it into a modern toilet if available. Otherwise, they can throw it into a trash bin, bury it in a field, or dispose of it in another way. No matter how much care is taken, however, some condoms are left exposed, a few to be reused by children who rinse them out and make toys or balloons from them, most to assault the dignity of modest people who prefer their sex to be a matter of privacy.

## SUMMARY

This chapter does not attempt to portray Bangladesh as a promiscuous culture. It is far from that. However, to say that it is more sexually conservative than a society like the United States should not imply that Bangladesh is prudish. It is essential to recognize that sexual behavior is more complex than represented by public discussion about sex.

Perhaps the most descriptive metaphor for sexuality in Bangladesh can be found in one of the primary symbols of *purdah*, the *burqa*. The *burqa* is the shroud worn by women who strictly follow *purdah*. It conceals all the details about the woman wearing it from men not in her family, revealing only that the wearer is indeed a woman. Similarly, everyday conversation in Bangladesh admits only to the fact that sex exists, but the true character of Bangladeshi sexuality is revealed only by removing the veil, through direct and systematic inquiry.

The Condom Use Project suggests that men practice premarital and extramarital sex much more commonly than many Bangladeshis suppose. The rates of these practices in CUP may not be representative of the rates found in the general population; but if anything, our estimates are probably conservative. Our findings have not been supported by previous survey research only because surveyors have not yet ventured far into this territory.

However, we are supported by prior anthropologic investigation of sexuality in Bangladesh (Aziz and Maloney 1985), which has estimated that as many as half of all young people in Bangladesh engage in premarital sex. Many have also had extramarital sexual experiences. Aziz and Maloney (1985) included women in their study, which we did not. They found the situation on sex outside of marriage to be largely comparable between the genders, but men appeared to be more sexually active. Neither gender has a cultural immunity to AIDS.

Because of its emphasis on family planning, we did not apply CUP to other highly risky sexual practices. However, Aziz and Maloney included homosexual behavior in their investigation and found a surprising degree of homosexual experimentation to exist among both men and women. For those who wish to follow exclusive homosexual lifestyles, homosexual communities are known to exist in large urban areas such as Dhaka. Unfortunately, however, bulletins on risk of AIDS, safe sexual practices, and screening of HIV do not yet exist, leaving such communities extremely vulnerable to infection by the AIDS virus. Other easily identifiable high-risk populations exist as well. Large populations of prostitutes are known to inhabit the cities and coasts of Bangladesh, where their exposure to men from Bangladesh and from many foreign countries facilitates the spread of AIDS.

The time for complacency is over. If Bangladesh intends to prevent or slow the spread of AIDS, initial actions should be geared toward screening and education programs. Condoms, which are already successfully marketed in Bangladesh, can be promoted as an effective preventive measure, but cultural barriers to communication about condoms must first be overcome through a sensitive understanding of how to communicate appropriately about them. Finally, we must attempt to understand more about the sexual risk factors that exist in Bangladesh. This calls for a more vigorous research agenda focused on the sexual practices of both men and women and from other areas of the country. Especially important will be research that specifically addresses the sexual behaviors of groups that have a high risk of HIV transmission, such as prostitutes and homosexuals.

## NOTE

1. We know nothing about how the respondents perceived AIDS because we did not probe for this information.

## REFERENCES

AZIZ, K., M. ASHRAFUL, and CLARENCE MALONEY. 1985. *Life Stages, Gender and Fertility in Bangladesh.* Dhaka, Bangladesh: International Center for Diarrheal Disease Research.

FOLMAR, STEVEN. 1992. "Variation and Change in Fertility in West Central Nepal." *Human Ecology* 20:225–48.

FOLMAR, STEVEN, S. M. NURUL ALAM, and A. H. M. RAIHAN SHARIF. 1992. *Condom Use in Bangladesh: Final Report.* Dhaka, Bangladesh: United States Agency for International Development.

FOLMAR, STEVEN, S. M. NURUL ALAM, and A. H. M. RAIHAN SHARIF. "Culture and Condom Use in Bangladesh." Unpublished manuscript.

FRIEDENBERG, JUDITH, MICHAEL MULVIHILL, and LOUIS R. CARABALLO. 1993. "From Ethnography to Survey: Some Methodological Issues in Research on Health Seeking in East Harlem." *Human Organization* 52:151–61.

KHAN, ZAREEN R. and H. K. AREFEEN. 1982. "Prostitution in Bangladesh: A Study." *The Journal of Social Studies* 41:1–28.

MALONEY, CLARENCE. 1974. *Peoples of South Asia.* New York: Holt, Rinehart and Winston.

MALONEY, CLARENCE, K. M. ASHRAFUL AZIZ, and PROFULLA C. SARKER. 1981. *Beliefs and Fertility in Bangladesh.* Dhaka, Bangladesh: International Center for Diarrheal Disease Research.

MANN, JONATHAN and JAMES CHIN. 1988. "AIDS: A Global Perspective." *New England Journal of Medicine* 319:302–303.

MANN, JONATHAN, JAMES CHIN, PETER PIOT, and THOMAS QUINN. 1988. "The International Epidemiology of AIDS." *Scientific American* 259(4):82–89.

MITRA, S. N. and G. M. KAMAL. 1984. *Bangladesh Contraceptive Prevalence Survey 1983: Key Results.* Dhaka, Bangladesh: Mitra and Associates.

MITRA, S. N., CHARLES LERMAN, and SHAHIDUL ISLAM. 1992. *Bangladesh Contraceptive Prevalence Survey 1991: Key Findings.* Dhaka, Bangladesh: Mitra and Associates.

POTTS, MALCOM, ROY ANDERSON, and MARIE-CLAUDE BOILY. 1991. "Slowing the Spread of Human Immunodeficiency Virus in Developing Countries." *Lancet* 338:608–13.

WORLD HEALTH ORGANIZATION (WHO). 1993. "The Current Global Situation of the HIV/AIDS Pandemic." WHO Report.

Chapter 16

# Women and AIDS in Africa: A Critical Review

*Dana Lear*

Acquired immune deficiency syndrome (AIDS) is caused by a retrovirus, the human immunodeficiency virus (HIV). Infection with HIV eventually causes immune suppression, resulting in an increased susceptibility to a spectrum of illnesses, sometimes referred to as HIV disease, but better known as AIDS. Those affected in Africa die not of the virus itself, but of the wasting syndrome generally known as "slim," or from a variety of opportunistic infections that vary somewhat according to population. Most AIDS patients in Africa die of their first opportunistic infections.

AIDS is not yet the most common nor the most serious disease facing most of sub-Saharan Africa; malaria and malnutrition are both objectively and subjectively more important factors in adult morbidity, despite the focus on HIV in the Western media. Yet AIDS appeals to the imagination of those in the West in a way that malaria does not. On a prosaic level, it concerns sex, something in which almost everyone is interested. However, AIDS also emphasizes that we live in a single global ecology (Mann 1991) and has challenged our understanding of health and our approach to providing care. The epidemic has forced us to examine the ways in which sexuality, health, and behavior relate to cultural, political, and economic reality (Krieger and Margo 1991). According to Mann (1991), AIDS has the potential to foster global solidarity at a time when Africa has much to lose or gain from the epidemic. This chapter reviews and analyzes the epidemiologic and social research on HIV in Africa, beginning with its epidemiologic background. It addresses cultural and economic issues as they affect sexuality and African health care systems, focusing specifically on AIDS as it affects women. Finally, it discusses ethical issues relating to women and AIDS and approaches to prevention as they relate to Africa.

## SIGNIFICANCE

AIDS has the potential to create extreme demographic changes in Africa. It is estimated that over 6 million people, or 2.5% of the adult population, was infected with HIV by the end of 1992 (Hunter 1993). The dependency ratio in sub-Saharan Africa is already 30:70 and may change drastically for the worse in some places. AIDS has already become the leading cause of death for women aged 20 to 40 in cities from Abidjan and Brazzaville to Kigali and Djibouti (DeCock et al. 1990; Lallemant et al. 1992; Lindan et al. 1991; Rodier et al. 1993). In places where the prevalence rate among pregnant women is 20%, the infant mortality rate can be expected to increase by 30% more than would otherwise have been expected. UNICEF predicts that the average infant mortality rate in 10 East and Central African countries will rise from a current rate of 164 deaths per 1,000 to 185 by the year 2000. Prior to the epidemic, these rates had been projected to fall to 130 per 1,000. AIDS will arrest any progress which has been made in child health in the past few decades (Carovano 1991; Chin 1990; Widy-Wirski 1989) and will reverse population growth rates, which currently average 3% per year (> 4% in Kenya) (Anderson et al. 1988, 1992).

The impact of the expected cases of AIDS on health care systems will be enormous, a burden added to the already heavy load from other endemic diseases. African countries, whose health budgets normally range from the equivalent of US $3–$15 per person per year, will become more dependent on Western aid programs for food and medicine. If global solidarity can extend to military "peacekeeping" amounting to millions of dollars per day, surely it can extend to the fight against HIV.

There is a sociopolitical dilemma beyond the economic: The epidemic initially took hold and remains severe among the better educated and those employed in supervisory positions, and where urban women are more likely to work outside the home (Allen et al. 1991; Ankrah 1989), creating a threat to stability where a large proportion of community leaders are affected. In countries where the military is severely affected—in Zambia, for example, more than 20% of the army is HIV+—there is the possibility for political destabilization (Miller et al. 1989). As the ill return to rural homes to be nursed, the impact on subsistence production in the rural areas will be felt, placing an enormously increased burden on rural women, who may be ill themselves and unable to produce and whose duties include not only cultivation and nursing, but also time away from work to receive mourners (Obbo 1989).

## EPIDEMIOLOGIC OVERVIEW

### The Origin of AIDS

Essex and Kanki (1988), veterinarians from the Harvard School of Public Health, proposed that HIV was related to a similar retrovirus in African green monkeys. In other words, "their origins were inextricably linked," particularly HIV-2, which is considered genetically closer to the simian immunodeficiency virus (SIV) (Gao et al. 1992; Markovitz 1993). The conclusion that HIV therefore began in Africa was supported by Gallo of the National Cancer Institute in the United States and Montagnier, discoverer of HIV at the Pasteur Institute in France (Gallo and Montagnier 1989). Nonetheless, the origin of HIV has not yet been conclusively proved nor disproved; positive HIV-1 specimens have been traced to the late fifties in Zaire (Editors 1990; Fleming 1988), HIV-2 infection has been observed in West Africa since the 1960s (Remy 1993), and an AIDS death in 1969 has been retrospectively identified in the United States (Garry 1990; Katner 1989). Examination of sera obtained between 1964 and 1975 from Uganda, where HIV infection is most prevalent, showed no evidence of HIV antibodies (Levy et al. 1986), but 38 Africans with AIDS were treated in Belgium between 1979 and 1984 (Clumeck et al. 1984), suggesting that the disease emerged at about the same time in both Europe and Africa.

Knowing the origin of a virus is important to understand viruses generally and may reveal ways to control HIV disease or to develop a vaccine against it. However, the reaction to the presence of AIDS throughout the world has been one of denial, scapegoating, and blame, and African governments reacted defensively, fearing racist reprisal and averring any association with a disease known to be transmitted homosexually (Lear 1990). There was a racist slant to Western media reports, which reinforced images of Africa as "the dark continent," full of primitive savages who ate and maybe also mated with monkeys. Some governments, notably Kenya's, feared the loss of tourist and investment revenues, which had increased after the filming of the movie *Out of Africa.* The debate over the origin set AIDS education back by a couple of years in individual and collective African countries. Most countries began to form national AIDS committees between 1986 and 1988, with actual government attention begun, on average, 2 years later.

### Population Affected

It has been enormously difficult to assess the impact of HIV on such a huge heterogeneous continent, hence there has been some tendency to over generalize. The first cases of HIV-1 in Africa have been retrospectively identified in Zaire from the mid-1970s, with cases following in Uganda and Zambia in the early 1980s (Biggar 1987). The African countries most affected thus far by the epidemic have been Uganda, Zaire, Malawi, Tanzania, Kenya, Burundi,

Zambia, Zimbabwe, Rwanda, Congo, and the Central African Republic, all in Central and East Africa, together accounting for nearly 90% of AIDS cases to date. A second and distinct locus of AIDS, retrospectively observed in West Africa since the 1960s (Remy 1993), first identified in Guinea, and largely caused by HIV-2 or mixed HIV-1 and HIV-2 infections, emerged in Senegal, Ivory Coast, Ghana, Burkina Faso, Mali, Niger, Guinea-Bissau, Cameroon, Togo, Gabon, and Nigeria, and accounted for approximately 10% of cumulative reported cases in Africa (Felman 1990).

### Prevalence

It is difficult to know what the true prevalence is in sub-Saharan Africa, but the situation is regarded as extremely serious in most countries. Although seroprevalence rates of up to 90% are found among prostitutes in Nairobi, Butare and Kampala (Moses et al. 1991), incidence of HIV infection in sub-Saharan Africa generally ranges from 19% to 35% of sexually active adults, depending on location and population selected for study (Allen et al. 1991; Barongo et al. 1992; Gnaore et al. 1993; Harry et al. 1992; Müller et al. 1992; O'Farrell et al. 1992; Rodier et al. 1993; Wannan 1992). Prevalence rates among sexually transmitted disease (STD) clinic attenders in Kampala in 1991 were 24% for men and 35% for women, with similar rates among women giving birth (Müller et al. 1992). According to the World Health Organization (WHO), the minister of health for Rwanda, one of the more assiduous countries in its reporting, acknowledged that the country had underestimated cases by 100% (Müller et al. 1989). A national prevalence survey conducted in Rwanda in 1986 found rural prevalence of 1% and 18% among urban residents, but 30% among 26 to 40 year olds (Van de Perre et al. 1987). Informal reports cite HIV prevalence rates approaching 45% to 50% among adults aged 25 to 44 in cities such as Kampala and Kigali. In Cite D'Ivoire, prevalence is approximately 13% among women giving birth in hospital and 78% among those hospitalized for other conditions (Brattegaard et al. 1993).

Most epidemiologic surveys were largely confined to urban areas, and few were conducted in rural areas where most Africans lived (Quinn et al. 1986). Obetsebe-Lamptey predicted in 1988 that given a lag time of perhaps 5 years and African patterns of migration, rural areas would be expected to develop epidemiologic patterns found in urban areas if prevention did not soon become a greater priority. Prevalence had reached 45% by 1991 among women in the Ugandan rural district of Rakai, but again, popular reports cite current prevalence rates of up to 80% among young adults. WHO announced in 1990 that prevalence had indeed risen in many rural areas. Its estimates for prevalence of those infected with HIV in sub-Saharan Africa increased from 2.5 million in 1987 to about 5 million in 1990 and to 6 million in 1992. In 1987 most infected people were found in urban centers, but by 1990 extensive spread was being documented in rural areas in most sub-Saharan countries. As a result,

WHO concluded that about 1 in 40 adults was infected, compared to a prior estimate of 1 in 50 (WHO 1990a). Its estimates were based on a detailed review of seroprevalence data collected in 1988 and 1989. The report does not specify whether the increase was due solely to increased prevalence, or whether there was also an increase in reporting and better analysis, particularly in the rural areas. Underreporting is due to lack of time on the part of health workers, absence of an appropriate infrastructure, and the tendency of patients and physicians to avoid the diagnosis of AIDS (Müller and Abbas 1990).

***AIDS in women and children*** African women and children comprise 90% of HIV infections among women and children worldwide. WHO projected 4 million cumulative women and 1 million children infected with HIV in Africa in 1992. UNICEF has estimated that in East and Central Africa, as many as 5 million children will have lost their parents to AIDS by the end of the decade (Carovano 1991). For women and children, as for most patients in Africa, diagnosis of AIDS is usually followed by death within 1 year, given the later diagnosis, lack of treatment, and poorer health status of the population (Chin 1990).

#### Transmission

In the first few years of the epidemic, three relatively distinct epidemiologic patterns were identified. Cases in North America and Western Europe, labeled Pattern I, emerged in the late 1970s and early 1980s, and infection focused on homosexual and drug injecting behavior, only secondarily spreading to heterosexual partners, especially among minorities.

In Asia, the Pacific, and Eastern Europe, labeled Pattern III, the epidemic began relatively late and incidence was initially linked to contact with individuals from high-prevalence countries. Sub-Saharan Africa, with the exception of the Republic of South Africa, which has mixed patterns, was labeled Pattern II by WHO. AIDS cases began appearing in noticeable numbers in the late 1970s and early 1980s; transmission in this pattern is largely via heterosexual intercourse. Transmission has roughly followed a pattern of infection beginning among a small number of female sex workers, particularly low-wage ones, followed by STD patients and a large number of their clients, especially higher income men, truck drivers, and other migrant workers, and finally their wives and children, that is, the general population (Allen et al. 1991; Berkley 1990). In Ghana, for example, owing to the economic hardships of the last decade, many women went to work in Abidjan, Cite d'Ivoire. Returning home for holidays, and finally, ill, their numbers created an unusual gender ratio: 11:1 in 1986, 7.6:1 in 1987, and more recently, 5:1, but this rate now approximates the normal 1:1 as more Ghanaian men have become infected. There is thought to be a 1% chance of transmission per sex act, but transmission is not equal between genders: Per relationship, risk is 20% for women but only 11% for men

(Anderson et al. 1991) because transmission occurs more efficiently from male to female than the reverse (Allen et al. 1992). For this reason, the gender ratio will settle at somewhat more than 1:1.

Pregnant women are viewed as a reliable indicator of general prevalence, and rates among women attending antenatal or well-baby clinics approach 40% to 45% in the capital cities of Rwanda, Malawi, and Uganda. This figure may actually underestimate prevalence because it does not account for couples suffering from STD-related infertility. Current estimates of the proportion of infected babies born to infected women in Africa vary, but it is commonly recognized that 25% to 45% of babies will be infected (CDC 1991a; MacNaughton 1992). Vertical transmission occurs during pregnancy, delivery, and breastfeeding. The WHO has nonetheless recommended breastfeeding over formula feeding in Africa because of the known risk of morbidity and mortality associated with the latter (Choto 1990).

Transmission by mosquitoes or other insects is thought not to be possible because of the low rates of infection among those aged 5 to 15 and over 60. Transfusions have accounted for some cases of pediatric AIDS because children are often given blood transfusions to treat malaria-induced anemia or sickle cell anemia (Delaporte et al. 1993), although this practice is beginning to change among those aware of the association (Hedberg et al. 1993).

### Risk Categories for Transmission

Even though the epidemic is now so widespread, reaching as it does even into the rural areas, the literature still identifies transmission by risk group rather than behavior and mores. This type of categorization is due to the medical and medicomoral frameworks of those setting the research agenda (Seidel 1993). Such identification without political context has contributed to denial and blame in the handling of the epidemic in Africa, as in the United States, and has resulted in delay in facing the epidemic (Lear 1990; Watney 1989). This chapter reviews risk categories as they are treated in the literature.

***Prostitution*** As noted above, colonial governments encouraged migration of men but not women to the cities, a situation that continues under postindependent governments (Schoepf et al. 1988). In cities such as Kinshasa and Kampala, where gender ratios are nearly equal, jobs are stratified by gender and education, which is itself stratified. Various forms of multiple partner relationships have proliferated in response to historical and economic crises (Schoepf 1988), often labeled prostitution by Western writers. The exchange of sex for money or support covers a broad range of arrangements (Basset and Mhloyi 1991; Day 1988; Larson 1989; Parkin 1966; Vandersypen 1977). These may include sex with teachers to pay school fees, sex in exchange for gifts to supplement meager salary (Schapera 1971; Schoepf 1988), or noncommercial multiple relationships among single women (Obbo 1980). In Wilson's 1989 study, two thirds of the women engaged in commercial sex were divorced, and another quarter never married, a situation typical throughout Africa (Barongo et al. 1992). Most prostitutes in African cities (with the exception of Kampala) are immigrants (Kanki et al. 1992; Rodier et al. 1993), an indication of the economic hardships for women in Africa. The social implications of the lack of opportunity for schoolgirls and unmarried women must be addressed in structural approaches to the epidemic (Caldwell et al. 1989).

Certainly commercial sex exists as one category of multiple relationships, and women engaged in this type of monetary transaction may be interpreted as prostitutes from the literature. In the early years of the epidemic, a small number of prostitutes located in urban areas and along truck routes in rural southwestern Uganda and northeastern Tanzania became infected. In Nairobi, the infection rate was documented to rise from no infections in 1981 to nearly 80% by 1987 (Berkley 1990). Infection remained below 90% only because of deaths of those infected and in-migration of uninfected women (Ngugi, personal communication 1989). Between 1980 and 1985 infection was localized among these women and their clients, both identified through STD clinics.

***Sexually transmitted disease*** Sexually transmitted diseases have been present for over a century in many countries of Central and East Africa, creating an "infertility belt" across the continent reaching from Cameroon to Kenya. One third of women have had no children by the age of 30 among the Baganda, and the average number of children among women over the age of 45 was only 1.77, suggesting widespread secondary infertility. Half of women reported histories of gonorrhea or syphilis (Davies 1956; Hrdy 1987; Richards and Reining 1954; WHO 1987; and many others). Similar rates existed for the Bahaya of Tanzania, who also now have high rates of AIDS (Reining, personal communication 1989). A high correlation exists between STDs, including AIDS, infertility, and noncircumcision of males in Africa, according to some studies (Bongaarts et al. 1989). Infections with genital ulcerative disease are fairly common; those such as chancroid and syphilis create more efficient paths of transmission, and tissues inflamed by chlamydia and gonorrhea may also contribute to high rates (Lamoureux et al. 1987; Miotti et al. 1992; O'Farrell et al. 1992; Pepin et al. 1989). STDs are not confined to urban areas, and rural prevalence may have been a consequence of such cultural practices as lengthy postpartum abstinence, during which men were expected to seek sexual satisfaction elsewhere.

Men are generally expected to be non-monogamous in Africa. Men whose work demands migration between urban and rural areas have more partners and consequently higher rates of HIV (Abdool Karim et al. 1992; O'Farrell et al. 1992). Piot et al. noted in Kinshasa that 50% of AIDS patients and 14% of controls had histories of STDs (in Padian et al. 1990). Among two unidentified Nilotic warrior groups in East Africa, men estimated 11.8 partners per year (Konings et al. 1989). Custom among these groups encourages sharing sexual partners among age mates, a practice that encourages the spread of STDs. According to a study presented at the VII International Conference on AIDS in June 1991, a majority of men seeking treatment at a Nairobi STD clinic apparently feel invulnerable to AIDS; attempts to limit their high-risk sexual activities have had little impact (CDC 1991c). Allen et al. (1991) have reported that risk factors among men are more predictive of HIV infection among women than risk factors of the women themselves. Men who visit prostitutes, drink alcohol, and have incomes higher than US $100 per month have higher rates of HIV and other STDs and pose greater risks to their wives, and it is they who transmit the infection to women in the general population (Hunter 1993).

***Migrant work*** Migrant workers are separated from their families, and many seek casual sex near their place of work. Long-distance truck drivers in East Africa were recognized early on as a risk group; HIV seroprevalence among them averages nearly 25% (Mohammed et al. 1990). The epidemic followed trade routes from Zaire to Uganda and Zambia to Kenya and Tanzania, then to Zimbabwe and Malawi. In the Ugandan trading town of Kasensero, at the crossroads between Uganda, Tanzania, and Rwanda, over half of all deaths had been attributed to AIDS by 1987 (Hooper 1987). In some areas, male labor migration in search of wages which began in the colonial period has intensified in the past decade (Schoepf 1988, p. 626).

***Iatrogenic infection*** The greatest risk in this category has been to women and children who have received untested transfusions for malaria-induced anemia (Delaporte et al. 1993; Hedberg et al. 1993). There has been no important association between HIV transmission, traditional medicine, and practices such as scarification or female circumcision (Schmutzhard 1987), although they certainly pose a theoretical risk (O'Farrell 1987).

### Factors Contributing to Transmission in Africa

***Africa and colonialism*** African development was affected by colonization by (roughly) the English in eastern Africa, the French in western Africa, Belgians in central Africa, and the Portuguese, English, and Dutch in southern Africa. The colonial pattern of development, especially in eastern, central, and southern Africa, was based on migrant labor, in which men were recruited to work great distances from their families. The resulting depletion of males from the rural villages caused a deterioration in women's ability to provide for their families. Women thus began to change crops; for example, the easy-to-grow, high-yield, but nutritionally deficient cassava was substituted for established grains with higher levels of protein, such as millet and sorghum. Unmarried rural women who saw no means of adequate support for a family emigrated to the city, where there was little wage labor available to them. The unequal gender ratio of the cities made it difficult to sustain long-distance marriages and encouraged prostitution. Most urban prostitutes are divorced or single, indicating the economic consequences of the dissolution of traditional family structures and the difficulty for women of supporting themselves adequately. These changes led to a serious problem with sexually transmitted disease, providing easy entrée for HIV. Populations whose immune systems were compromised by disease resulting from the collapse of local food production and the dependency development pattern and whose health was continually challenged were not equipped to resist HIV.

The spread of HIV in Africa moves from areas of labor concentration to rural reserves and outward to the general population (Watney 1989; CDC 1991a). Transmission is enhanced in unstable countries by the military and by long-distance truck drivers who are the foundation of the black market: by 1986 more than half the truckers in Kampala were seropositive (Larson 1989).

Economies that depend on migrant labor do not provide for the health of their workers, so those who can no longer work return to their villages, carrying urban disease home. In the case of South Africa, migrant miners from countries of high prevalence, notably Malawi and Zambia, are subject to mandatory testing and have simply been refused further employment when seropositive, exacerbating the economic difficulties in those countries. Until the problem of migrant labor for men and divided families is confronted, unsafe sexual behavior will continue (Jochelson et al. 1991).

Despite the fact that the world's most impoverished region has potentially the greatest number of infected people, little attention has been paid to the associations between poverty and AIDS. Lack of access to health care and poor nutrition make people more susceptible to opportunistic infection. The most effective measure to reduce transmission of HIV would probably be to treat existing STDs, but at best this has been looked at as a side benefit of participating in research studies (Moses et al. 1991). Research is directed by the interests of Western epidemiologists, when for most of those affected by AIDS, the greatest need is for social services such as fare for transport to clinics, soap, extra sheets for night sweats and diarrhea, nutritious high-calorie food, and help with gardens when women are ill (Keogh et al. 1989; Obbo 1989). Deaths from AIDS may be expected to further break down social networks and destroy leadership needed to sustain or reorganize society so that indigenous channels of assistance can continue. In the context of increasing economic and social decline, the nature of African family structure can be expected to further decline. AIDS prevention campaigns that target prostitutes as a high-risk group to be avoided risk missing women who do not identify themselves as such and further marginalizing those who may, but who have little economic alternative. Until the problem of girls' inferior education and women's low wage labor is rectified, the social conditions that pose greater risk for women will continue.

Further compounding the difficulty in discussing AIDS in Africa, Africa is often referred to as if it were one homogenous country. In fact, it is a huge continent with 800 cultural set societies within 52 countries (Airhihenbuwa

1989). Different groups vary in terms of risk, but data on ethnic differences are scarce. Sometimes the myopia of researchers contributes to lack of differentiation, and sometimes it is the result of political sensibility. In Rwanda and Nigeria, for example, it is forbidden to collect data by ethnic group because of these countries' respective histories of civil war. Questions remain which may be best explained culturally, however; for example, why are there fewer cases in Niger than in neighboring Mali? Why has prevalence among 15 to 44 years olds stabilized at around 5% to 7% in Kinshasa, but continued to rise above 35% in Kampala (Müller et al. 1992; Wannan et al. 1992)? Studying cultural differences is a means of addressing this gap.

***Sociocultural factors*** Generally, several cultural factors contribute to the pattern of AIDS found in Africa. They include factors such as polygynous marriage, demands of the levirate, access to women's sexual favors by a husband's brothers and age-mates (Obbo 1986), and the age difference in formation of sexual partnerships, in which older men form relationships with younger women (CDC 1991b). Some parts of tropical Africa have extremely high rates of STDs such as syphilis, herpes, and chancroid disease which cause genital ulcers, thus offering more direct routes of entry for HIV (O'Farrell 1992; Pepin et al. 1989). Chlamydia, which remained largely undiagnosed until recently, appears to make women more susceptible to infection (Widy-Wirsky 1989). Lack of male circumcision has been highly correlated with infection in some studies (Bongaarts et al. 1989; Miotti et al. 1992; Reining, personal communication, 1989), but not others (Allen et al. 1991; Barongo et al. 1992), even among different ethnic groups within the same country. For a variety of reasons, methods of family planning are not well accepted in Africa, and there is nearly universal distaste for condom use, compounded by their general unavailability. People resist condoms (Irwin et al. 1991; McCombie 1990; Schoepf et al. 1988) because of beliefs about the contribution of a vital factor in semen to women's health and reproduction (Taylor 1988, 1990), fear that condoms may injure women (Lindan et al. 1991), get stuck, and even cause sterility; suspicion and hostility are believed likely to result from proposing condom usage to a partner and difficulties with in-laws over their use (McGrath et al. 1990).

Sexual mores contribute to transmission: Throughout Africa both men and women are inclined to accept male sexual freedom (McGrath et al. 1990). Where the colonial patterns of male migration led to a much greater number of men in cities than women, whose women who did migrate were viewed as suspect in the villages, were limited in their choices of occupation, and were subject to sexual coercion in many jobs (Little 1973). Women in towns may be financially supported in an informal way by one or more men or may accept gifts to supplement their income (Ulin 1992). Women in rural areas risk exposure when their husbands come to visit. These factors and others contribute to the high prevalence rates among young adults and predict a serious problem with vertical transmission.

## SOCIAL AND BEHAVIORAL RESEARCH ON AIDS IN AFRICA

### Knowledge, Attitude, and Practice (KAP) Studies

Discourse on AIDS has thus far been largely informed by biomedical research. Knowledge, attitude, and practice (KAP) surveys are a quantitative method that is the closest researchers have come to approaching behavioral issues. A review article on knowledge about condoms found that "knowledge of condoms is poor virtually throughout sub-Saharan Africa, where a majority of respondents in only 3 of 16 populations reported having heard of AIDS" (Goldberg et al. 1989). A KAP survey of Ugandans was conducted in rural Uganda in 1987. Eight-eight percent knew that AIDS could be acquired from other people and that having multiple sexual partners constituted high-risk behavior. Simultaneously, however, many people believed AIDS to be transmitted by insect bites, witchcraft, and casual contact, ideas that must also be addressed by prevention programs if people with AIDS are to be cared for by their families. A 1988 study in Uganda found only those in Kampala considered AIDS a threat, even though AIDS was already a serious problem in rural southern Uganda (Forster and Furley 1989). The majority of Ugandans surveyed by another 1988 study consider socioeconomic pressure a greater problem than AIDS. More than 90% of the first sample knew mutual monogamy to be the best way to avoid HIV, yet 68% of men in one of the rural areas surveyed nevertheless acknowledged contact with prostitutes. Only a minority (1.5% to 19%, depending on location) suggested condoms as a way to prevent AIDS. A survey of 4,000 Ugandan adults presented in June 1989 at the V International Conference on AIDS found a wide range of beliefs about transmission common. A survey among urban men in Zimbabwe found that most men had heard of AIDS, but knowledge decreased with age. Here also a range of beliefs prevailed about mode of transmission (Wilson 1989). More than 40% of high school students in Zimbabwe believed most Africans with AIDS to be homosexual, did not know that HIV+ people could look healthy, and thought AIDS could be contracted from toilet seats. An extensive 1988 survey in Zaire found that although most had heard of AIDS and knew its main modes of transmission, people still feared casual contact, sharing personal items, and mosquitoes. A survey of high school students presented at the V International AIDS conference, conversely, found that 80% of students could correctly identify HIV-associated risk factors. Bertrand's (1989) survey found that although virtually all Kinshasa adults had heard of AIDS and 90% knew the main modes of transmission, knowledge of the specific facts relating to AIDS was not associated with perceived risk.

A survey of the abstracts concerning Zaire from the VI International Conference of AIDS revealed contradictory results in studies of condom utilization, which included monitoring of use, "sex habits," martial status, and HIV serostatus. One found condom utilization successful (Jingu 1990), but two others found reticence to continue condom use, with desire for children the greatest predictor of "recidivism" among discordant couples (Batter 1990). A study of fertility of HIV+ women found fertility rates similar to those of HIV− women, indicating that risky behavior continues among couples when at least one member is seropositive (Badi 1990). Social marketing programs have included KAP surveys (Spilsbury 1990) but do not indicate whether any ethnographic research was conducted. In fact, this report noted that researchers found it difficult to find female residents willing to be interviewed but did not indicate the gender of the researcher or what methods were used to gain entry.

A 1985 survey in Rwanda found that most respondents had only recently heard of AIDS and considered it to be a stigmatized disease, although they did not know why. Not surprisingly, women were found to be less informed than men. Carael directed a KAP survey sponsored by the Norwegian Red Cross in 1986; he found 71% of respondents very afraid of AIDS, 66% of men knew what a condom was, and 8% had used one, although none recently or to reduce risk of HIV infection. Surveys in Zimbabwe and Botswana have found that fewer than 1% of women have reported use of condoms as a measure to prevent AIDS (Sheon et al. 1989). Surveys are planned in 22 sub-Saharan countries by the Demographic and Health Surveys Institute for Resource Development, a USAID-funded agency.

Although Kinsey and Masters and Johnson have proved it possible to elicit detailed sexual information through the use of surveys, they present several important weaknesses. Their highly structured questionnaire or fixed-choice interview format leaves little room for maneuvering into areas of social life about which respondents are unwilling or unable to report accurately, or that have a structure as yet unknown to the investigator. Many Rwandans do not know why AIDS is considered to be a stigmatized disease. Maxine Ankrah in Uganda and Brooke Schoepf in Zaire have been the primary proponents of sociocultural approaches to the study of HIV.

Earickson (1990) notes quite aptly that the AIDS situation in Africa is complicated by cultural struggle, "for the message of AIDS is derived from the West, a foreign concept in a foreign language that is dependent on the West for its meaning and continued development." The critical question, according to him, is what would an AIDS prevention program look like from the sociopolitical and cultural world view of those directly affected? He considers it impossible to address that question with the Western research model because of its conventional origins and limited perspectives. He suggests creative strategies such as the use of strong peer pressure and traditional social networks within specific target groups, and to that one might add the use of proverbs, drumming, and other forms of communication that are salient in many communities.

### Community-Based Approaches

Wilson noted in 1989 that "interventions have been commenced without ethnographic, psychosocial or sexological studies of sex worker or client samples. It is commendable that such interventions have been initiated, but their effectiveness is likely to be vitiated by the absence of relevant behavioral research." One notable exception is the work of Elizabeth Ngugi and colleagues, who have taken a community organizing approach with Nairobi prostitutes since 1985. Condom use among these women increased from less than 10% to 50% to 90% in only a couple of years. One reason for success in this group is that organizing occurred in a recognizable prostitute's quarter in Nairobi; it might be difficult to replicate among women less identifiable and among the majority who engage in multiple relationships but do not regard themselves as prostitutes. Finally, it must be emphasized that although the women described above comprise a sentinel group, the vast majority of women infected in Africa are (mostly) monogamous, for whom the only risk factor is intercourse with their husbands (Allen 1989; Desmond 1991, personal communications). Allen et al. (1991) report the prevalence of infection among women who report only one lifetime partner with whom they were currently in a monogamous union to be 21%. Clearly, monogamy does not offer much protection for these women.

Also in Kenya, the Personal Growth Services Centre emphasizes finding ways to speak more openly about sex in a language that people will accept and comprehend, understanding the social context in which unsafe sex occurs, helping individuals to recognize risk, and identifying the most acceptable safer sex behavior for couples and societies (Kimani 1991). They are conducting community discussion groups on safer sex, believing that through greater social communication about sex, better interpersonal communication will be encouraged.

The AIDS Support Organisation (TASO) was founded by Noerine Kaleeba, a woman whose husband died of AIDS in 1987, and is staffed by volunteer Ugandans who are personally, in one way or another, concerned about AIDS (WHO 1990b). Its work in Uganda is an attempt to bridge the gap between the community-based African approach to disease and the Western hospital-based approach. The result is a service providing home and community-based care to those affected by AIDS and HIV, which they find more culturally appropriate (Kalibala and Kaleeba 1989). Community-based care is becoming increasingly important in Uganda in particular, as AIDS exhausts the economic and emotional resources of the extended family (Ankrah 1993; Seeley et al. 1993).

Some encouraging work by mission programs was reported at the VII International Conference on AIDS. One home-care program in Zambia was started in 1987 in a rural district and featured a team of physicians and counselors visiting AIDS patients at their homes three times per week. This approach was found more effective than inpatient programs in meeting physical, psychological, social, and spiritual needs and reduced families' financial burden and the social stigma attached to AIDS at the same time (CDC 1991d; Chaava 1990). Family AIDS Caring Trust (FACT) is a Christian-based AIDS counseling and education service established in Zimbabwe in 1988. They have printed a newsletter, pamphlets, and a series of flashcards meant for storytelling that can be adapted for different target groups (WHO 1990c). These community-based approaches may offer more hope than individual counseling: According to Wilkins et al. (1989), individual counseling among asymptomatic seropositive individuals resulted in little improved understanding or behavior change. Although they note that community interventions may pose problems of confidentiality, African norms about family and community suggest that individual counseling alone does not offer the support needed to sustain behavior change.

## SOCIAL AND CULTURAL ISSUES FOR PREVENTION

### Women, Gender Roles, and AIDS

Considerations of types of prevention approaches practiced today illuminate the need for intervention that considers what is unique about African societies. A fundamental problem concerning women and HIV in an African context is the view on the part of prevention programs, research, and society at large that the concern is not with women themselves, but more the risk of transmission to their male partners and unborn children. Problems in reporting cases result from factors as varied as women's lack of access to health care, the exclusion of gynecologic symptoms from diagnostic criteria, and a "persistent attitude on the part of physicians that nice women don't get AIDS" (Carovano 1991).

Women's lack of social power is the cornerstone of their risk for AIDS because their position is honored largely through their contributions to the lineage—that is, the social benefits of joining their families of origin to that of their husbands', and their ability to produce children (Basset and Mhloyi 1991). In many cultures there is no place for a woman who is unable to bear children (Obbo 1980; Schoepf et al. 1988), increasing women's risk by leaving them fewer options to refuse sex. Refusing sex is grounds for divorce in most cultures, ultimately placing women at greater risk because of the economic precariousness of being unmarried. Yet to avoid transmission, they must protect themselves using methods that also prevent conception and must often depend on the cooperation of their partners. Furthermore, women feel they have no control over their husbands' behavior (McGrath et al. 1990). Women are aware that "babies and condoms don't go together, nonpenetrative sex is no sex at all for a man, and it is a woman's responsibility to bear a child," according to Noreen Kaleeba of The AIDS Support Organisation in Uganda. To provide them with HIV prevention without a change in status and fertility norms is to deny them effective protection (Carovano 1991).

### Sociosexual Context

Discussion about AIDS prevention cannot occur in the absence of cultural context. Culture, as it affects AIDS, includes the social, economic, and political history, as discussed above. On a more micro level, it includes the interrelationships of marriage and family systems, sexual norms and behavior, and the health care systems. These are addressed below.

Among the Baganda, children do not even directly greet their parents, for the literal meaning of one of the most common Luganda greetings is "How have you spent the night?" Because the question may have sexual connotations, it is considered inappropriate (Semwogerere, personal communication, 1991). Sexual matters are generally not discussed openly but are usually conveyed indirectly through proverbs and riddles, as are other matters of importance in Baganda social life. The sexual education of young girls is traditionally the responsibility of the father's sister, although other female relatives also play a role.

Norms about sexuality reflect ambivalence in Africa, as they do elsewhere. Whether a culture is restrictive or permissive with regard to sexuality does not prevent it from holding incompatible attitudes, nor with having elaborated rules about what is permitted, when, and with whom. Virginity for girls among the Baganda is traditionally valued, but punishment is not severe for its absence (Obbo 1987; Southall 1960). According to Southwold (1965), extramarital relations are not permitted for women because the husband would not be considered the father of any children not conceived with him. Ganda men's image of marital relations includes a dominating husband and submissive wife, and the men resent it when women do not cooperate with this view (Cassidy et al. 1989). McGrath et al. (1990) found that women considered it acceptable to have partners outside of marriage for economic reasons, for revenge against a husband's philandering, and for greater sexual satisfaction. Women in Rwanda and Uganda are supposed to take an active role in intercourse, and full sexual satisfaction, including orgasm, is expected; the lubrication may provide some protection against transmission. In many other Central African cultures, including some in Zaire, Zimbabwe, and Malawi, conversely, tightness and dryness are valued, and some women apply astringent herbs to achieve this effect, a practice that encourages excoriations that facilitate transmission (Cassidy et al. 1989; Runganga et al. 1992; Schoepf 1988).

Historically in Uganda there were times when women might be expected to have sex with men other than their husbands. These included rituals surrounding the birth of twins; funerals, especially that of a husband, where the wife might have sex with his brother; and weddings, where the parents of the bride might have sex with each other regardless of whether they were currently married, or the bride's paternal aunt might have sex with the groom. These practices are largely ignored in Kampala today (McGrath et al. 1990), although not necessarily in the rural areas. In Zambia, ritual cleansing among the Tonga is being replaced by having a suitable partner jump over the legs of the prone wife, passing a hoe under the bereaved's bent knees, sitting naked in each other's laps, or jumping over a cow that is later eaten by mourners, all excellent examples of African-initiated adaptations to the AIDS crisis (Chaava 1990). Traditional practices that regulate sexuality include initiation ceremonies, arranged marriage, proof of virginity, punishment for adultery, and polygyny (Banda 1991). Sanctions against polygyny by Christian churches have resulted in less stable outside relationships than previously existed.

Similarly, the notion of nonpenetrative sex as safer sex is a Western notion. All societies contain notions of taboo and pollution, and safer sex in African culture may more often involve avoiding breast milk and menstrual blood than semen and vaginal fluid. Ugandan women in McGrath's study of postpartum women, for example, revealed that one reason women had had only one partner in the previous year was because they believed that intercourse with a man other than the baby's father would pollute the breast milk and cause death to the infant. Cultural constructions of fatherhood include the notion of semen as vital to fetal development and even cultural survival, although customs that demand continued exposure to seminal fluid are being reinterpreted in the face of risk to mean that a man should support his pregnant wife and "not run around while she awaits the child" (Schoepf 1988). In Rwanda, three quarters of the women in Allen's study engaged in intercourse both on the day of delivery and within 1 week of childbirth, as part of the naming ritual (Allen et al. 1991). Menstrual taboos, according to Taylor, are also adhered to less consistently than before in urban Rwanda, and this may contribute to transmission. Still there is evidence that nonpenetrative sex practices exist and are widely practiced in Africa (Cassidy et al. 1989). In studies with prostitutes, the women and their clients report both fellatio and cunnilingus, and anal intercourse to a lesser extent (Wilson 1989). The extent of the practice is unknown outside of these groups. Most nonpenetrative practices are regarded by Baganda as preliminary or immature (Semwogerere, personal communication, 1991), practiced by adolescents, but perhaps could form some part of a prevention program, perhaps especially among adolescents. Those countries with elaborated sexual codes can incorporate AIDS prevention into whatever training normally occurs in the area of sexuality. Research must not neglect approaching those responsible for such training, usually older men and women who would not normally be targeted for AIDS education.

Condom use has been widely promoted in the fight against AIDS. However, condoms are no panacea: Ugandan officials were reluctant to support them until recently, partly because of their religious beliefs but also because they inevitably force reliance on foreign aid, which is too often fickle and subject to political will. Many people see them as genocidal, and people in some of the countries worst affected have already suffered from infertility for decades, so asking people to use condoms when they do not have all the children they want presents a dilemma. Furthermore, because condoms have been long regarded as unreliable to block sperm for even the few fertile days of a woman's cycle, many people wonder how they can be trusted to prevent passage of something as small as HIV every day of the month (Bell 1989).

Women have been encouraged to "use" condoms, as if they can in fact use them at all; such efforts ignore the power inequity in male-female relations, even for use of the "female condom" (Allen et al. 1992; Kanki et al. 1992; Lindan et al. 1991). For a woman to suggest condoms anywhere, but particularly in Africa, implies that she does not trust her partner, that she may be unfaithful and HIV positive, and that she has more money and power than she actually has. Yet the issue is even more complex, for the reverse is also true—when a man suggests condoms, women react the same way. In Cameroon, women refuse to allow men to wear condoms, both because of their desire for children and because to agree to have men use them would imply that they were prostitutes. Where women engaged in commercial sex have organized to demand condoms, as in Nairobi, they cannot always afford to refuse men who eschew their use, nor might they always want them with their romantic partners. One problem in critiques of condoms and advocacy for nonpenetrative sex, particularly among Western feminists, is an assumption that only men desire intercourse, that women could easily do without it, and only men loathe condoms, whereas women find them completely acceptable. Yet women have expressed concerns about how condoms feel and what it means symbolically to have a barrier (McGrath et al. 1990). Neither condoms nor nonpenetrative sex should be ignored as partial solutions, for it would be racist to suggest that Africans are somehow less capable than Westerners to adapt in this way to the AIDS crisis. However, the full complexity of the problem must not be ignored by prevention programs.

### AIDS and African Health Care Systems

AIDS in Uganda was originally believed to be caused by retribution for unfair black market trading practices between Ugandans and Tanzanians (Hooper 1987; Lwihula 1988). In 1988, 25% of Ugandans in three rural areas and Kampala believed that AIDS was caused by witchcraft. Generally, AIDS was perceived as a disease with an indigenous rather than a foreign origin. Traditional healers regarded it as a transgression of sexual taboos, a perception compatible with Western views. AIDS is therefore seen to be accessible to traditional treatment; however, traditional healers had all received patients who believed that the healer could *cure* them (Konde-Lule et al. 1989). Only three healers among 20 had received any AIDS education. Although 19 of 20 healers had treated AIDS patients and 18 had sent them to hospital, none had ever received referrals from allopathic physicians, despite the lack of available Western medicine in Africa. Referral systems do exist between traditional healers and the modern health care system in Botswana and Zimbabwe, however (Staugaard 1991).

Traditional healers provide important psychological and spiritual treatment in addition to herbal remedies for diarrhea and thrush (Ankrah 1991). They also may provide herbs, which increase the ability of the gut to absorb nutrients, probably the primary cause of "slim," or wasting (AHRTAG 1990). They can provide information on community sexual behavior and can serve as community health educators, particularly in rural areas. They also provide a "central role in the maintenance of social stability in local communities" (Staugaard 1991). They are perceived by the community as accessible, affordable, and acceptable in ways allopathic doctors are not (Green 1988). Midwives, particularly, are keys to women's networks in rural communities, especially in Moslem countries.

Recognizing this, WHO held a meeting in Botswana in 1990 to identify ways in which traditional healers might contribute to AIDS prevention and control. Botswana, Uganda, Tanzania, Kenya, Ethiopia, Zambia, and Zimbabwe had already defined areas such as community-based care and some forms of symptomatic treatment as being appropriate areas for their involvement and have included traditional healers in their medium-term plans for AIDS control (Staugaard 1991).

## ETHICAL ISSUES

### Africa and Racism

As noted above, the history of writing on AIDS has not been exempt from racism, with the debate on origin a particularly unfortunate example. The origin of HIV has not been settled, nor is it important for educational purposes. The debate reinforced the image of Africa as a "problem to be solved rather than a voice to be heard" (Watney 1989). African-led research efforts, which have resulted in the treatments MM-1 in Zaire and Egypt and Kemron (interferon-alpha) in Kenya were not taken seriously in the West (Koech and Obel 1990; Oliech 1990). Papers published in Western scientific journals repeatedly referred to "promiscuous" African behavior. In turn, African responses to racism have been categorized by denial, scapegoating, and blame, particularly in Kenya, which relies on tourism for much of its foreign exchange. Those who attempted to defend Africans' responses (Sabatier 1987) have been rejected along with those who had constructive criticism (e.g., Caldwell's critique of Miller in Caldwell et al. 1989).

### Reproduction

HIV is vertically transmitted from a women to her child in some 25% to 45% of cases (Berkley 1990). The studies on condom utilization and fertility reviewed above demonstrate that whether to counsel HIV+ women against becoming pregnant is a difficult issue for those committed to freedom of choice. Many women see childbearing as a life-affirming act in the face of death. Having even a 60% chance of bearing an uninfected child is perceived as odds worth risking in countries where 20% of children die anyway before their fifth birthday of malaria, measles, diarrhea, and malnutrition. Having healthy children fulfills women's duty to their lineage and leaves descendants by whom they will be remembered after death (Schoepf et al. 1988).

### Research

Research efforts are also subject to ethical concerns. Conflict occurs over the distribution of power among researchers, and struggles among scientists over credit for their work (Allen, personal communication, 1989; Earickson 1990). For example, in Africa issues such as informed consent and rights of the individual may not be understood in their Western context in cultures where societal good is more important. Economic difficulties may discourage free choice, even where compensation is not monetary but rather includes free health care and medicines. Violations of common ethical standards are not rare: in 1991, for example, it was disclosed that vaccine trials in Zaire conducted by the French researcher Daniel Zagury resulted in several deaths. It did not escape notice that vaccine trials were conducted in Zaire because "it was easier to get official permission than in France" (Christakis 1988, p. 31; Earickson 1990).

Western-directed AIDS research abounds in Africa, yet drugs such as AZT and ddI are unobtainable for people who are lucky to obtain palliatives to treat candidiasis and diarrhea, usually in return for research participation. Vaccines may be tested on Africans, but there is no assurance that a successful vaccine will be made available to those upon whom it was tested.

Most projects have been aimed at women, viewing them as little more than reservoirs (Lallemant et al. 1992) and assuming they have greater power to insist on change than actually exists. A project in Rwanda found that women found spermicide-containing nonoxynol-9 more acceptable than condoms because they could control it, often without their partners' knowledge. Yet when researchers received preliminary results suggesting that use of spermicide actually encouraged transmission (probably because it was irritating or allergenic), they decided to withhold the information to avoid biasing results. In this project, women were normally personally contacted by courier to remind them of their appointments. Yet the same project did not seek to personally inform women of a positive HIV test result if they missed an appointment, again in order not to bias results.

These are not isolated incidents but serve merely to illustrate the tension between the scientific model and participatory research. Ethical research must be culturally relevant and sensitive and express concern for the well-being of those who participate. Research has done little thus far to address the structural economic needs of those at risk and consequently must be viewed as somewhat self-serving. A research agenda that explores how women themselves perceive AIDS transmission and the strategies they use to prevent it is critical. Intervention strategies that recognize men's greater power and thus incorporate them directly in prevention efforts will go a long way toward reducing the incidence of AIDS in women and children.

## SUMMARY

As is evident from much of the foregoing discussion, many of those concerned with the social side of AIDS have justifiably taken a macroperspective, examining colonial and political history, social institutions, systems of marriage and descent, long-distance trade, settlement patterns, and migration to see how they might influence the speed and direction of HIV transmission (Ankrah 1991; Carovano 1991; Krieger and Margo 1991). Although some work does consider social factors that lead to multiple sexual partners and frequent partner change (Larson 1989), it seldom investigates what people actually do when they have sex, the meaning of safer sex, and how it is negotiated. Research that examines the microdeterminants of transmission and prevention can add to the cultural relevance and sensitivity of prevention efforts (Ulin 1992). Sexuality is subject to a number of powerful influences, some of them more powerful than fear of AIDS. Changing sexual behavior is complex and arduous even when there is threat to health or life. Qualitative methods such as those offered by ethnography or symbolic interactionism can be adapted to public health and offer a viable perspective that transfers across culture. Because AIDS is transmitted as a result of behavior at an interpersonal level, education efforts must not ignore the potential of approaches that seek a better understanding of the interaction and negotiation that takes place with regard to sex.

The fact that historically produced social conditions have created situations that promote behavior that puts people at risk for HIV should not be taken to mean that this behavior is inevitable, nor that only a complete social transformation will permit meaningful interventions to reduce transmission of HIV. Response to the war in Uganda, for example, has left Ugandans with the resolve not to let their country face devastation again, and with a sense of optimism in the rebuilding of the country. People in Zambia have altered traditional practices concerning the levirate which no longer place them at risk for contracting HIV. Grassroots efforts are underway on much of the continent to fight AIDS, and most governments are now also supportive. If the commitment to fight the epidemic has the potential to serve as a reminder of our global solidarity, it may also serve to redress the effects of colonialism and sexism. As Jonathan Mann said, there is hope that the importance of this mission can overcome self-interest.

## REFERENCES


ABDOOL KARIM Q., S. S. ABDOOL KARIM, B. SINGH, et al. 1992. "Seroprevalence of HIV Infection in Rural South Africa." *AIDS* 6:1535–39.

AHRTAG. 1990. "AIDS and the Traditional Healer." *AIDS Action* 12:7.

AIRHIHENBUWA, COLLINS. 1989. "Perspectives on AIDS in Africa: Strategies for Prevention and Control." *AIDS Education and Prevention* 1:57–69.

ALLEN SUSAN, JEFF TICE, PIERRE VAN DE PERRE, et al. 1992. "Effect of Serotesting with Counselling on Condom Use and Seroconversion Among HIV Discordant Couples in Africa." *British Medical Journal* 304:1605–09.

ALLEN SUSAN, CHRISTINA LINDAN, ANTOINE SERUFILIRA, et al. 1991. "Human Immunodeficiency Virus Infection in Urban Rwanda: Demographic and Behavioral Correlates in a Representative Sample of Childbearing Women." *Journal of the American Medical Association* 266:1657–63.

ANDERSON, R. M., R. M. MAY, M. C. BOILY, et al. 1992. Dynamics of HIV in Sub-Saharan Africa." *Philosophical Transactions of the Royal Society of London.* Series B: Biological Sciences, 336:135–55.

ANDERSON, R. M., R. M. MAY, M. C. BOILY, et al. 1991. "The Spread of HIV-1 in Africa: Sexual Contact Patterns and the Predicted Demographic Impact of AIDS." *Nature* 352:581–89.

ANDERSON, R. M., R. M. MAY, and A. R. MCLEAN. 1988. "Possible Demographic Consequences of AIDS in Developing Countries." *Nature* 332(6161):228–34.

ANKRAH, E. MAXINE. 1989. "AIDS: Methodological Problems in Studying Its Prevention and Spread." *Social Science and Medicine* 29:265–76.

______. 1991. "AIDS and the Social Side of Health." *Social Science and Medicine* 32:967–80.

______. 1993. "The Impact of HIV/AIDS on the Family and Other Significant Relationships: The African Clan Revisited." *AIDS Care* 5:5–22.

BADI, N. 1990. "Poor Sustainability of Birth Control Utilization and Consequent High Fertility Rates in a Cohort of 249 HIV+ Zairian Women Aware of Their Serostatus and Followed for 30 Months Post Partum." VI International Conference on AIDS, San Francisco, 20–24 June, Abstract presentation Th.D.121, p. 87.

BANDA, MAZUWE. 1991. "Faith, Hope, and Chastity." *AIDS Action* 13:4–5.

BARONGO, L. R., M. W. BORGDORFF, F. F. MOSHA, et al. 1992. "The Epidemiology of HIV-1 Infection in Urban Areas, Roadside Settlements and Rural Villages in Mwanza Region, Tanzania." *AIDS* 6:1521–28.

BASSET, MARY and MARVELLOUS MHLOYI. 1991. "Women and AIDS in Zimbabwe: The Making of an Epidemic." *International Journal of Health Services* 21:143–56.

BATTER, V. 1990. "Fertility Rates in HIV + Women in Zaire." VI International Conference on AIDS, San Francisco, 20–24 June, Poster F.B.459, p. 192.

BELL, NORA. 1989. "AIDS and Women: Remaining Ethical Issues." *AIDS Prevention and Education* 1:22–30.

BERKLEY, SETH. 1990. "AIDS in Africa: A Personal Perspective." *Rhode Island Medical Journal* 73:309–15.

BIGGAR, ROBERT J. 1987. "AIDS in Sub-Saharan Africa." *Cancer Detection and Prevention* S1:487–91.

BIZIMUNGU C., A. NTILIVAMUNDA, M. TAHIMANA, et al. (Rwandan HIV Seroprevalence Study Group). 1989. "Nationwide Community Based Serological Survey of HIV-1 and Other Human Retrovirus Infections in a Central African Country." *Lancet:* 941–42.

BONGAARTS, JOHN, PRISCILLA REINING, P. WAY, et al. 1989. "The Relationship Between Male Circumcision and HIV Infection in African Populations." *AIDS* 3:373–77.

Brattegaard K., J. Kouadio, M. L. Adom, et al. 1993. "Rapid and Simple Screening and Supplemental Testing for HIV-1 and HIV-2 Infections in West Africa." *AIDS* 7:883–85.

Caldwell, John, Pat Caldwell, and Pat Quiggin. 1989. "The Social Context of AIDS in Sub-Saharan Africa." *Population and Development Review,* 15.

Carovano, Kathryn. 1991. "More Than Mothers and Whores: Redefining the AIDS Prevention Needs of Women." *International Journal of Health Services* 21:131–42.

Cassidy, Claire, Robert Porter, and Doug Feldman. 1989. "Ethnographic Survey of Nonpenetrative Sexual Behavior." Unpublished manuscript.

Centers for Disease Control (CDC). 1991a. "Development Specialist Discusses Demographic AIDS Trap for Women in Africa." *CDC AIDS Weekly,* 15 July, pp. 9–10.

______. 1991b. "High Risk Sexual Practices Continue among Nairobi Men." *CDC AIDS Weekly,* 15 July, p. 10.

______. 1991c. "Seropositive Mothers Pose High Risk for Infant." *CDC AIDS Weekly,* 15 July, p. 11.

______. 1991d. "Home Care for Aids Patients: A Positive Experiment." *CDC AIDS Weekly,* 15 July, p. 12.

Chaava, T. 1990. "Approaches to HIV Counselling in a Zambian Rural Community." *AIDS Care* 2:81–87.

Chin, James. 1990. "Current and Future Dimensions of the HIV/AIDS Pandemic in Women and Children." *Lancet* 336:221–24.

Choto, R. G. 1990. "Breastfeeding: Breast Milk Banks and Human Immunodeficiency Virus." *Central African Journal of Medicine* 36:296–300.

Christakis, Nicholas. 1988. "The Ethical Design of an AIDS Vaccine Trial in Africa." *Hastings Center Report,* 31–37.

Clumeck N., J. Sonnet, H. Taelman, et al. 1984. "Acquired Immune Deficiency Syndrome in Belgium and Its Relation to Central Africa." *Annals of the New York Academy of Sciences* 437:264–69.

Davies, J. N. P. 1956. "The History of Syphilis in Uganda." *Bulletin of the World Health Organization* 15:1041–55.

Day, Sophie. 1988. "Prostitute Women and AIDS: Anthropology." *AIDS* 2:421–28.

DeCock, Kevin M., B. Barrere, L. Daiby, et al. 1990. "AIDS—The Leading Cause of Adult Death in the West African City of Abidjan, Ivory Coast." *Science* 249:793–96.

Delaporte E., M. Peeters, J. L. Bardy, et al. 1993. "Blood Transfusion as a Major Risk Factor for HTLV-1 Infection Among Hospitalized Children in Gabon (Equatorial Africa)." *Journal of Acquired Immune Deficiency Syndromes* 6:424–28.

Earickson, Robert J. 1990. "International Behavioral Responses to a Health Hazard: AIDS." *Social Science and Medicine* 31:951–62.

Essex, Max and Phyllis Kanki. 1988. "The Origins of the AIDS Virus." *Scientific American,* 64:71.

Felman, Yehudi. 1990. "Recent Developments in Sexually Transmitted Diseases." *Cutis* 46:204–6.

Fleming, A. F. 1988. "Seroepidemiology of Human Immunodeficiency Viruses in Africa." *Biomedicine and Pharmacotherapy* 42:309–20.

Forster, Sarah and Kemlin Furley. 1989. "1988 Public Awareness Survey on AIDS and Condoms in Uganda." *AIDS* 3:147–54.

Gallo, Robert and Luc Montagnier. 1989. "Response to M. Mulera" [letter]. *Scientific American* June, p. 11.

Gao, F., L. Yue, A. T. White, et al. 1992. "Human Infection by Genetically Diverse SIVSM–Related HIV-2 in West Africa." *Nature* 358(6386):495–99.

Garry, R. F. 1990. "Early Case of AIDS in the USA." *Nature* 347:509.

Gnaore, E., M. Sassan-Morokro, S. S. Kassim, et al. 1993. "A Comparison of Clinical Features in Tuberculosis Associated with Infection with Human Immunodeficiency Viruses 1 and 2." *Transactions of the Royal Society of Tropical Medicine and Hygiene* 87:57–59.

GOLDBERG, H. I., N. C. LEE, M. W. OBERLE, and H. B. PETERSON. 1989. "Knowledge About Condoms and Their Use in Less Developed Countries During a Period of Rising AIDS Prevalence." *Bulletin of the World Health Organization* 67:85–91.

GREEN, EDWARD. 1988. "Can Collaborative Programs Between Biomedical and African Indigenous Health Practitioners Succeed?" *Social Science and Medicine* 27:1125–30.

HARRY, T. O., O. KYARI, and I. MOHAMMED. 1992. "Prevalence of Human Immunodeficiency Virus Infection Among Pregnant Women Attending Ante-natal Clinic in Maiduguri, North Eastern Nigeria." *Tropical and Geographical Medicine* 44:238–41.

HEDBERG, K., N. SHAFFER, F., DAVACHI, et al. 1993. "*Plasmodium falciparum*—Associated Anemia in Children at a Large Urban Hospital in Zaire." *American Journal of Tropical Medicine and Hygiene* 48:365–71.

HOOPER, ED. 1987. "AIDS in Uganda." *African Affairs* 86:469–77.

HRDY, DANIEL B. 1987. "Cultural Practices Contributing to the Transmission of the Human Immunodeficiency Virus in Africa." *Review of Infectious Diseases* 9:1109–19.

HUNT, C. W. 1989. "Migrant Labor and Sexually Transmitted Disease: AIDS in Africa." *Journal of Health and Social Behavior* 30:353–73.

HUNTER, D. J. 1993. "AIDS in Sub-Saharan Africa: The Epidemiology of Heterosexual Transmission and the Prospects for Prevention." *Epidemiology* 4:63–72.

IRWIN, KATHLEEN, JANE BERTRAND, NDILU MIBANDUMBA, et al. 1991. "Knowledge, Attitudes and Beliefs About HIV Infection and AIDS Among Healthy Factory Workers and Their Wives in Kinshasa, Zaire." *Social Science and Medicine* 32:917–30.

JINGU, M. 1990. "High Condom Utilization and Low Seroconversion Rates Successfully Sustained in 175 Married Couples in Zaire with Discordant HIV Serology." VI International Conference on AIDS, San Francisco, 20–24 June, Poster S.C.695, p. 262.

JOCHELSON, KAREN, MONYAOLA MOTHIBELI, and JEAN-PATRICK LEGER. 1991. "HIV and Migrant Labor in South Africa." *International Journal of Health Services* 21:157–73.

KALIBALA, S. and NOREEN KALEEBA. 1989. "AIDS and Community Based Care in Uganda: The AIDS Support Organisation, TASO." *AIDS Care* 1:173–75.

KANKI, PHYLLIS, SOULEMANE M'BOUP, R. MARLINK, et al. 1992. "Prevalence and Risk Determinants of Human Immunodeficiency Virus Type 2 (HIV-2) and Human Immunodeficiency Virus Type 1 (HIV-1) in West African Female Prostitutes." *American Journal of Epidemiology* 136:895–907.

KATNER, HAROLD P. 1989. "Origin of AIDS." *Journal of the National Medical Association* 80:262.

KEOGH, PAULINE, CALLE ALMEDAL, SUSAN ALLEN, et al. 1989. "Evaluation of the Social Services Needs of HIV+ Women Enrolled in a Cohort Study in Kigali, Rwanda." V International Conference on AIDS, San Francisco, 6 June.

KIMANI, LILLIAN. 1991. "Preparing for That 'Big Day.'" *AIDS Action* 13:5.

KOECH, D. K., and A. O. OBEL. 1990. "Efficacy of Kemron (Low Dose Oral Natural Human Interferon Alpha) in the Management of HIV1 Infection and Acquired Immune Deficiency Syndrome." *East African Medical Journal* SS64–70.

KONDE-LULE, JOSEPH, SETH BERKLEY, and ROBERT DOWNING. 1989. "Knowledge Attitudes and Practices Concerning AIDS in Ugandans." *AIDS* 3:513–18.

KONINGS, E., R. M. ANDERSON, D. MORLEY, et al. 1989. "Rates of Sexual Partner Change among Two Pastoralist Southern Nilotic Groups in East Africa." [letter]. *AIDS* 3:4.

KRIEGER, NANCY and GLEN MARGO. 1991. "Women and AIDS: Introduction." *International Journal of Health Services* 21:127–30.

LALLEMANT, M., S. LALLEMANT-LECOEUR, D. CHEYNIER, et al. 1992. "Characteristics Associated with HIV-1 Infection in Pregnant Women in Brazzaville, Congo." *Journal of Acquired Immune Deficiency Syndromes* 5:279–85.

LAMOUREUX, G., L. DAVIGNON, R. TURCOTTE, et al. 1987. "Is Prior Mycobacterial Infection a Common Predisposing Factor to AIDS in Haitians and Africans?" *Annales de l'Institute Pasteur* 138:521–29.

LARSON, ANN. 1989. "Social Context of Human Immunodeficiency Virus Transmission in Africa." *Review of Infectious Diseases* 2:716–31.

LEAR, DANA. 1990. "AIDS in the African Press." *International Quarterly of Community Health Education* 10:253–64.

LEVY, JAY A., L. Z. PAN, E. BETH-GIRALDO, et al. 1986. "Absence of Antibodies to the Human Immunodeficiency Virus in Sera from Africa Prior to 1975." *Proceedings of the National Academy of Sciences of the United States of America* 83:7935–37.

LINDAN, CHRISTINA, SUSAN ALLEN, MICHEL CARAEL, et al. 1991. "Knowledge, Attitudes, and Perceived Risk of AIDS Among Urban Rwandan Women: Relationship to HIV Infection and Behavior Change." *AIDS* 5:993–1002.

LITTLE, KENNETH. 1973. *African Women in Towns.* Cambridge: Cambridge Press.

LWIHULA, GEORGE. 1988. "Social Cultural Factors Associated with the Transmission of HIV Virus in Tanzania." Presented at workshop on counseling of AIDS patients, Sokoine University, Tanzania, 31 October–4 November.

MACNAUGHTON, M. 1992. "HIV in Women." *Early Human Development* 29:217–20.

MANN, JONATHAN. 1991. "Global AIDS: Critical Issues for Prevention in the 1990s." *International Journal of Health Services* 21:553–59.

MARKOVITZ, D. M. 1993. "Infection with the Human Immunodeficiency Virus Type 2." *Annals of Internal Medicine* 118:211–18.

MCCOMBIE, SUSAN. 1990. "Beliefs About AIDS Prevention in Uganda." Presented at the American Anthropological Association Meetings, Philadelphia, November.

MCGRATH, JANET, CHARLES RWABUKWALI, and DEBRA SCHUMANN. 1990. "Cultural Determinants of Sexual Risk Behavior Among Baganda Women." Presented at the American Anthropological Association Meetings, Philadelphia, November.

MIOTTI, P. G., G. A. DALLABETTA, J. D. CHIPHANGWI, et al. 1992. "A Retrospective Study of Childhood Mortality and Spontaneous Abortion in HIV-1 Infected Women in Urban Malawi." *International Journal of Epidemiology* 21:792–99.

MOHAMMED, ALI, J. J. BWAYO, A. N. MUTERE, et al. 1990. "Sexual Behavior of Long-Distance Truck Drivers and Their Contribution to the Spread of Sexually Transmitted Diseases and HIV Infection in East Africa." Abstract FC729 (2):263, VI International Conference on AIDS, San Francisco, 22 June.

MOSES, STEPHEN, FRANCIS PLUMMER, ELIZABETH NGUGI, et al. 1991. "Controlling HIV in Africa: Effectiveness and Cost of an Intervention in a High Frequency STD Transmitter Core Group." *AIDS* 5:407–11.

MÜLLER, O., L. BARUGAHARE, B. SCHWARTLANDER, et al. 1992. "HIV Prevalence, Attitudes and Behaviour in Clients of a Confidential HIV Testing and Counselling Centre in Uganda." *AIDS* 6:869–74.

MÜLLER, O. and N. ABBAS. 1990. "The Impact of AIDS Mortality on Children's Education in Kampala (Uganda)." *AIDS Care* 2:77–79.

MÜLLER, O., J. LUBEGA, and J. SENOG. 1989. "The Impact of the AIDS Education Programme on Ugandan Schoolchildren." *AIDS Care* 1:135–36.

*Nature.* 1990. "How Did AIDS Begin?" 346:92.

OBBO, CHRISTINE. 1980. *African Women.* London: Zed Press.

______. 1986. "Some East African Widows." In: *Widows in African Societies,* edited by B. Potash. Stanford, CA: Stanford University Press.

______. 1987. "The Old and New in East African Elite Marriages." In: *Transformations of African Marriage,* edited by D. Parkin and D. Nyamways. Manchester University Press.

______. 1989. "Women, Production and AIDS." Presentation at AIDS and Society in Africa Conference, University of California at Berkeley, 11 March.

O'Farrell, N. 1987. "AIDS and the Witch Doctor" [letter]. *Lancet* 2(8551):166–67.

______, A. A. Hoosen, K. D. Coetzee, and J. van den Ende. 1992. "Sexual Behavior in Zulu Men and Women with Genital Ulcer Disease." *Genitourinary Medicine* 68:245–48.

Oliech, Joseph. 1990. "The AIDS Situation and Its Containment." *East African Medical Journal* SS29–30.

Padian, Nancy, P. J. Hitchcock, Robert E. Fullilove, et al. 1990. "Issues in Defining Behavioral Risk Factors and Their Distribution." Part I, Report of the NIAID Study Group on Integrated Behavioral Research for Prevention and Control of Sexually Transmitted Diseases. *Sexually Transmitted Diseases* 17:200–4.

Parkin, David. 1966. "Types of Urban African Marriage in Kampala." *Uganda Journal* 36:3.

Pepin, Jacques, Francis Plummer, Robert Brunham, et al. 1989. "The Interaction of HIV Infection and Other Sexually Transmitted Diseases: An Opportunity for Intervention." *AIDS* 3:3–9.

Quinn, T. C., Jonathan M. Mann, James W. Curran, and Peter Piot. 1986. "AIDS in Africa: An Epidemiologic Paradigm. *Science* 234(4779):955–63.

Remy, G. 1993. "Ancient Serological Traces of Infections by the Human Immunodeficiency Virus HIV-1 and HIV-2 in Sub-Saharan Africa: A Different Geography." *Medecine Tropicale* 53:33–43.

Richards, Audrey I. and Priscilla Reining. 1954. "Report on Fertility Surveys in Buganda and Buhaya." In: *Culture and Human Fertility,* edited by F. Lorimer. Paris: UNESCO.

Rodier, G., B. Couzineau, S. Salah, et al. 1993. "Infection by the Human Immunodeficiency Virus in the Republic of Djibouti: Literature Review and Regional Data." *Medecine Tropicale* 53:61–67.

Runganga, A., M. Pitts, and J. McMaster. 1992. "The Use of Herbal and Other Agents to Enhance Sexual Experience." *Social Science and Medicine* 35:1037–42.

Sabatier, Renée. 1987. *AIDS and the Third World.* London: Panos Institute.

Schapera, Isaac. 1971 [1940]. *Married Life in an African Tribe.* Harmondsworth, UK: Penguin.

Schumtzhard, Erich. 1987. "AIDS and the African Traditional Healer." *Lancet* 2:459.

Schoepf, Brooke. 1988. "Women, AIDS, and Economic Crisis in Central Africa." *Canadian Journal of African Studies* 22:625–44.

Schoepf, Brooke, Rukarangira wa Nkara, Claude Schoepf, et al. 1988. "AIDS and Society in Central Africa: The View from Zaire." In: *AIDS in Africa,* edited by Norman Miller and Richard Rockwell. Lewiston, ME: Edward Mellen.

Seeley, J., E. Kajura, C. Bachengana, et al. 1993. "The Extended Family and Support for People with AIDS in a Rural Population in South West Uganda: A Safety Net with Holes?" *AIDS Care* 5:117–22.

Seidel, G. 1993. "The Competing Discourses of HIV/AIDS in Sub-Saharan Africa: Discourses of Rights and Empowerment vs. Discourses of Control and Exclusion." *Social Science and Medicine* 36:175–94.

Sheon, Amy, C. N. Parirenyatwa, Ann Way, and W. Mapeta. 1989. "A National Level Survey of AIDS Awareness in Zimbabwe and Botswana and Uses of Demographic and Health Survey Data for AIDS Program Planning." Presented to the IVth International Conference on AIDS and Associated Cancers, Marseille, France, 18–20 October.

Sonnet, J., J. L. Michaux, F. Zech, et al. 1987. "Early AIDS Cases Originating in Zaire and Burundi (1962–1976)." *Scandinavian Journal of Infectious Disease* 19:511–17.

Southall, A. W. 1960. "On Chastity in Africa." *Uganda Journal* 24:2.

Southwold, Martin. 1965. "The Ganda of Uganda." In: *Peoples of Africa,* edited by J. Gibbs. New York: Holt, Reinhart.

Spilsbury, J. 1990. "Social Marketing of Condoms to Persons Practicing High-Risk Behavior in Zaire." VI International Conference on AIDS. San Francisco, 20–24 June. Poster S.C., 696(3):263.

Staugaard, F. 1991. "Role of Traditional Health Workers in Prevention and Control of AIDS in Africa." *Tropical Doctor* 21:22–24.

Taylor, Christopher C. 1988. "The Concept of Flow in Rwandan Popular Medicine." *Social Science and Medicine* 27:1343–48.

______. 1990. "Condoms and Cosmology: The 'Fractal' Person and Sexual Risk in Rwanda." *Social Science and Medicine* 31:1023–28.

Ulin, Patricia R. 1992. "African Women and AIDS: Negotiating Behavioral Change." *Social Science and Medicine* 34:63–73.

Van de Perre, Pierre, Bernard le Polain, Michel Carael, et al. 1987. "HIV Antibodies in a Remote Rural Area in Rwanda, Central Africa." *AIDS* 1:213–15.

Vandersypen, Marijke. 1977. "Femmes Libres de Kigali." *Cahiers d'Etudes Africaines* 65:95–120.

Wannan G. J., M. J. Cranefield, W. A. Cutting, et al. 1992. "How Many Bloods Will a 'HIVCHEK' check? Multiple Tests for HIV Antibody for a Single Screening Kit." *Tropical Doctor* 22:151–54.

Watney, Simon. 1989. "Missionary Positions: AIDS, 'Africa,' and Race." *Critical Quarterly* 31:45–77.

Widy-Wirski, R. 1989. "Epidemiologie du SIDA en Afrique." *Annales de Medecine Interne* 140:205–9.

Wilkins, H. A., P. Alonso, S. Baldeh, et al. 1989. "Knowledge of AIDS, Use of Condoms and Results of Counselling with Asymptomatic HIV-2 Infection in the Gambia." *AIDS Care* 1:247–56.

Wilson, D. 1989. "African Contributions on AIDS/HIV." *AIDS Care* 1:195–98.

Wilson, D., and S. Lavelle. 1990. "HIV/AIDS in Africa." *AIDS Care* 2:371–75.

Wilson, D., P. Chiroro, S. Lavelle, and C. Mutero. 1989. "Sex Worker, Client Sex Behaviour and Condom Use in Harare, Zimbabwe." *AIDS Care* 1:269–80.

World Health Organization (WHO). 1987. "Infections, Pregnancies, and Infertility: Perspectives on Prevention." *Fertility and Sterility* 47:964–68.

______. 1990a. "WHO Revises Global Estimates of HIV Infection." Geneva: WHO Press.

______. 1990b. "AIDS and the Status of Women: Challenges and Perspectives for the 1990s." *WHO Features,* 149, October.

______. 1990c. "Country Watch: Zimbabwe." *AIDS Health Promotion Exchange* 2.

Chapter 17

# A Role for Genetic Epidemiology in the Development of International Health Care Programs for Soil-Transmitted Helminthiases

*Sarah Williams-Blangero, John Blangero, and Janardan Subedi*

International health care programs require effective delivery strategies for infectious disease treatments. A strategy that has been used in a wide variety of situations is targeting the most susceptible segment of the population for treatment. For example, in the United States children in young age classes are targeted for measles vaccination, and nurses are targeted for hepatitis B vaccination owing to occupational hazards. It has been established for a number of age, occupational, and cultural criteria that not everyone in a population is equally susceptible to or equally exposed to infectious disease. Genetic factors may also influence susceptibility to disease, although targeting on the basis of genetic susceptibility has not received much previous attention.

## GENETIC EPIDEMIOLOGY

The field of genetic epidemiology covers a wide range of statistical techniques used to address questions concerning the relationships between genetics and disease. This rapidly growing area of genetic research has undergone an interesting development. Initially, genetic epidemiologists focused almost exclusively on the epidemiology of genetically determined diseases such as phenylketonuria, cystic fibrosis, and Tay-Sachs disease. These focal diseases generally had a simple, clear-cut inheritance due to a dominant (requiring only one copy of a gene from either parent for disease expression) or recessive (requiring one copy of the gene from each parent for disease expression) gene. As genetic epidemiology progressed, genetic techniques were applied to determine the genetic bases of complex multifactorial diseases such as atherosclerosis, diabetes, and cancer. The focus on complex diseases has resulted in utilization of a wide range of techniques for assessing quantitative and qualitative disease or disease-precursor phenotypes.

Data for genetic epidemiologic analyses must be gathered in family groups. Information on a wide range of relationships can be used. Simply determining father's and mother's identification for each individual in a population sample allows construction of a pedigree for genetic analysis by building up links generation by generation. Software (e.g., PEDSYS [Dyke 1989]) is available for pedigree reconstruction from such data.

Genetic epidemiologic methods test for the statistical effects of genes on disease-associated traits. The underlying model in genetic epidemiologic studies is that disease phenotypes are a function of both genetic and environmental influences. The statistical techniques of genetic epidemiology allow investigators to quantify the relative importance of genes, environment, and genotype by environmental interactions for determining a given phenotype. In the past decade, rapid advances have been made in the statistical analysis of quantitative phenotypes (reviewed by MacCluer 1989). Methods have been developed that allow the observation variation in quantitative physiologic traits to be partitioned among environmental components and genetic components attributable to unknown major loci, known candidate loci, and unknown polygenes having significant cumulative effects. Major genes are particularly important because their detection can lead to a better understanding of the pathways involved in the maintenance of variation. Once a major gene is detected, subsequent research can focus on identification of the gene and its effect on related traits, potentially leading to improved treatment interventions.

Two general methodologies can be used to assess the genetic determinants of disease phenotypes. These two approaches reflect two extreme models of the genetic determinants of disease. Quantitative genetic approaches use models in which the disease phenotype is determined by a large number of genes with small additive effects, which are known as polygenes. Classical segregation analysis approaches assume that the disease phenotype is determined by a single or small number of genes having large statistically quantifiable effects; these genes are called major genes. Of course, in practice these two statistical models are generally combined simultaneously to include the combined effects of major genes, polygenes, and minor genes (single genes with small but detectable effects).

The multifactorial or polygenic models (Falconer 1981) of quantitative genetics have been successfully used in animal breeding for decades and represent the important first exploratory steps in the examination of genetic variation in quantitative traits in man. The quantitative phenotype may be a quantitative disease trait such as blood pressure or the underlying quantitative liability for a discrete disease outcome such as breast cancer. The central parameter estimated in these analyses is the heritability, that is, the proportion of the total trait variance attributable to genetic factors.

Quantitative genetic analyses can be performed using maximum likelihood variance decomposition methods (Hopper and Mathews 1982; Lange and Boehnke 1983). These analyses provide information regarding the relative importance of additive genetic, shared environmental, and random environmental effects. The effects of potential covariates (such as age, sex, and socioeconomic variables) can be simultaneously estimated in these quantitive genetic analyses. If desired, these models can be used to predict an individual's underlying genotypic value, which can then be used as an index of genetic susceptibility.

The primary tool of modern genetic epidemiology is complex segregation analysis (Elston and Stewart 1971), which is used to find the effects of single genes in the presence of other genetic factors and can be performed on both disease states and related biologic response traits. This powerful statistical technique compares the ability of several different genetic and nongenetic statistical models to explain the observed distribution of disease in families. The detection of the effects of a single gene is dependent upon the observed pattern of transmission of the trait from parents to offspring. If the observed transmission probabilities are not significantly different from their Mendelian expectations and all other considered nongenetic transmission models can be rejected, there is evidence that a major gene influences the trait in question. Therefore, this approach is used to detect the statistical effects of unobserved and unknown genes on biologic characters. Once evidence of a major locus is established, the most likely major locus genotype of any individual can be predicted, given information on his and his relatives' phenotypes. Segregation analysis also can be used in conjunction with a technique known as linkage analysis, in which the unknown major gene is mapped to a specific chromosome by assessing its cosegregation with known genetic markers. When a marker is found that is tightly linked to the major locus, the precise genetic alteration leading to the observed aberrant phenotype can be searched for. Available information on a linked marker locus can also be used to better assess the underlying major genotype of any individual. Thus, these methods provide a framework that allows the prediction of an individual's genetic risk of disease.

A very limited number of applications of statistical genetics have been made to the problem of differential susceptibility to infectious disease. Genetic epidemiologic techniques remain to be fully exploited in refining our understanding of the myriad factors determining population distributions of infectious disease. Such knowledge will allow refinement of targeting strategies for infectious disease treatments and preventions. For example, there has been limited success in eradicating helminthic infections in developing countries.

Helminthic infections have a number of characteristics that make them well suited to genetic analysis, and they may provide a good potential application area for the use of genetic epidemiology in formulating international health care programs.

## THE POTENTIAL APPLICATION OF GENETIC EPIDEMIOLOGY TO DEVELOPING HEALTH CARE PLANS FOR SOIL-TRANSMITTED HELMINTHIASES

Assessment of helminthic infection in humans is generally a quantitative endeavor. The diagnosis of a pathologic condition is made by the evaluation of quantitative measurements of worm burden or of traits related to parasite-induced immunoresponse. Therefore, it is important to understand the underlying determinants of the observed variation in these quantitative indicators. The methods of statistical genetics can be used to assess the extent of genetic variation in such complex phenotypes.

Most statistical genetic models ignore the interaction between genotypes and the environments that they encounter. Because the assessment of susceptibility to and the resultant response to helminthic infection is inherently a problem of genotype × environment interaction, methods of genetic analysis that explicitly incorporate such interactions will be more informative and powerful than standard methods. New approaches for the detailed analysis of interactions between genotypes and environments have recently been developed (Blangero 1993; Blangero et al. 1990; Konigsberg et al. 1991; Perusse et al. 1991). Given the generality and power provided by statistical genetic analysis, application and adaptation of these and related methods is likely to facilitate greatly our understanding of the underlying genetic determinants of susceptibility to helminthic infections.

Roundworm, hookworm, and whipworm infections are major health concerns in both tropical and temperate areas of the world. Research on these helminthic infections may have important implications for international health programs. They are major causes of morbidity in the developing nations (Warren and Mahmoud 1990) and are known to contribute mortality in areas with limited health care delivery (WHO 1987). Approximately 25% of the world's population is affected by one of these three major helminthic infections (Pawlowski 1990; WHO 1987). Research on the patterns of infection and susceptibility components for helminths can provide important information for the development of health care strategies in areas of the world that have limited health care and delivery resources. The increasing urbanization of many areas in developing countries has resulted in ever-increasing rates of intestinal parasitic infections (Crompton and Savioli 1993). Many of the epidemiologic characteristics of intestinal helminths, including predisposition of individuals to infection and overdispersion, are also common to other parasitic infections of international health concern such as schistosomiasis and filariasis.

## EPIDEMIOLOGY AND HEALTH CONSEQUENCES OF HELMINTHIC INFECTIONS

The most common soil-transmitted helminthic infections include ascariasis, trichuriasis, and hookworm infection, with ascariasis being the most prevalent of the three. These infections often occur in combination with each other. There is no clear evidence for acquired immunity to roundworm (*Ascaris lumbricoides*), whipworm (*Trichuris trichiura*), or hookworm (*Ancylostoma duodenale* and *Necator americanus*), indicating that all individuals may be subject to reinfection after treatment (Bundy and Cooper 1990; Pawlowski 1990; Schad and Banwell 1990). Because these helminths are incapable of multiplying within the human host, parasite control mechanisms are focused on the transmission and death of the helminths (Anderson and May 1985).

**Ascaris lumbricoides** As noted above, ascariasis is the most prevalent of helminthic infections worldwide. Heavy roundworm infections cause serious morbidity and mortality due to intestinal blockage and related complications (Crompton et al. 1985; Mpairwe 1991; Savioli et al. 1992). For example, in one study of admissions to a pediatric surgical ward in Burma, 55% of abdominal patients were admitted because of ascariasis (Crompton et al. 1985). Of course, the majority of roundworm infections are not so severe that they require hospitalization (Pawlowski 1990), but the impact of ascariasis on community health should not be underestimated (Saviola et al. 1992). Chronic ascariasis also has been implicated in contributing to malnutrition in children (Crompton 1992; Gupta 1990; Thein-Hlaing et al. 1991b). Ascariasis may affect appetite and consequent food intake, digestion, absorption of nutrients, and metabolism, leading to growth deficits and developmental problems, especially in very young children (Crompton 1992).

**Trichuris trichiura** Trichuriasis exhibits a similar geographic pattern to ascariasis (Bundy and Cooper 1990). In contrast to roundworm infection, children affected with whipworm may exhibit chronic diarrhea (Bundy and Cooper 1989; Genta 1993). Because this diarrhea is often confused with bacterial or amoebic dysentary, the prevalence of trichuriasis may be underestimated (Bundy 1986; Nokes et al. 1992). In severest infections, trichuriasis can result in an ulcerative colitis (Bundy and Cooper 1990). However, even in lighter infections trichuriasis can have significant health consequences, especially for young children. Whipworm infection can result in malnutrition, stunting of growth, and iron deficiency anemia (Bundy and Cooper 1989, 1990; Cooper et al. 1990; Robertson et al. 1992). An association between trichuriasis and impairment of cognitive development has been demonstrated in a Caribbean population (Nokes et al. 1992), suggesting that this health problem has broad health consequences affecting children's ability to learn.

**Ancylostoma duodenale *and* Necator americanus** Hookworm infection is widely considered to be one of the most serious helminthic infections owing to its debilitating association with anemia due to blood loss from the intestines (Bundy and Cooper 1989; Bulto et al. 1992; Schad and Banwell 1990). Close to a billion people throughout the world are infected with hookworm (Warren 1988). This disease can lead to severe anemia via depletion of the body's iron stores (Pritchard et al. 1991), especially when local foods are low in iron content (Bulto et al. 1992). Additionally, hookworm infection may greatly impair work capacity in affected individuals (WHO 1987).

## OVERDISPERSION AND PREDISPOSITION IN THE DISTRIBUTION OF HELMINTHIC INFECTIONS

***Population distributions of helminthic infections*** The three major helminthic infections discussed above have a common characteristic which has been used in developing general mathematical models for assessing the potential impact of various treatment programs on the population distributions of parasite loads. Anderson and May (1985) have demonstrated that the distribution of parasitic infections in a population generally follows a negative binomial distribution. Parasites tend to be aggregated in a relatively small proportion of the population (Anderson and Medley 1985). For example, in a study of hookworm, whipworm, and roundworm in an Iranian population, Croll and Gharidian (1981) determined that 1% to 3% of the individuals in the population carried between 11% and 84% of the worms. Other reports have suggested that more than 70% of the parasites present are frequently found in less than 10% of the available hosts (Anderson 1982; Anderson and May 1982, 1985; Anderson and Medley 1985). This aggregation of helminthic infections in a small fraction of the population has been found repeatedly in studies of hookworm (Bradley et al. 1992; Schad and Anderson 1985), roundworm (Elkins et al. 1986; Forrester et al. 1988; Thein-Hlaing 1985; Thein-Hlaing et al. 1987), and whipworm (Bundy et al. 1987; Forrester et al. 1988).

***Predisposition of individuals to infection*** Many investigators have interpreted this overdispersion of parasites (i.e., the aggregation of most parasites in a relatively small proportion of potential hosts) to reflect predisposition of certain individuals to infection. As noted by McCallum (1990), if there are significant correlations between pre- and post-treatment parasite loads, then the involvement of innate host factors is suggested. Several investigators have addressed this point. For hookworm, roundworm, and whipworm, evidence suggests that individuals showing high parasite loads prior to treatment demonstrate the highest loads after a period of reinfection (Bundy 1986; Bundy and

Medley 1992; Forrester et al. 1990; Haswell-Elkins et al. 1987; Schad and Anderson 1985). However, Hall et al. (1992) studied the population distribution of helminthic infections after three rounds of treatment and found that, although there was overdispersion at each time point, there was no evidence for predisposition to reinfection. Predisposition to multispecies parasite loads has also been suggested (Bundy et al. 1987; Haswell-Elkins et al. 1987).

Observations on the predisposition of segments of populations to infection have implications for the development of treatment programs. Because human populations are not isolated, eradication of parasites is not a realistic goal (Anderson and Medley 1985). However, helminthic infections result in disease only when carried at higher loads. As reviewed by Anderson and May (1985), researchers suggested as early as 1924 that a cost-effective approach to diminishing the disease impact of helminthic infections on a population might be to target heavily infected individuals. Recent work addressing the possible predisposition of certain individuals to parasitic infection has also suggested targeting particularly susceptible individuals for treatment (Anderson and May 1982, 1985; Anderson and Medley 1985; Forrester et al. 1990; Haswell-Elkins et al. 1987; Medley et al. 1993; Schad and Anderson 1985; Tingley et al. 1988). An alternative strategy of selectively treating age groups within the population has been suggested (Saviola et al. 1992; Thein-Hlaing et al. 1991a) but the simulation studies of Anderson and Medley (1985) have shown that this approach has a low probability of affecting overall control of parasite transmission.

If targeting predisposed individuals is to be an effective disease-control strategy, then it is vital to understand the determinants and extent of predisposition to helminthic infections (Keymer and Pagel 1990). Simulation studies show that selectively treating predisposed individuals is effective if the predisposition is due to long-term innate factors rather than temporally variable factors such as heterogeneity of environmental exposure (Anderson and May 1982; Anderson and Medley 1985). The possibility of predisposition being a function of genetic susceptibility to parasitic infection has been raised by a number of authors (Anderson and Medley 1985; Schad and Anderson 1985). Although statistical genetic study of human susceptibility to helminthic infections has been done, the presence of significant household or family effects on patterns of helminthic infection has been identified in studies of ascariasis (Chai et al. 1983; Forrester et al. 1988; Williams et al. 1974), trichuriasis (Forrester et al. 1988), and filariasis (Walter 1974).

## GENETIC STUDIES OF SUSCEPTIBILITY TO HELMINTHIC INFECTIONS

The genetic characteristics of parasitic worms have been the subject of much study, as reviewed by Hammond and Bianco (1992). However, the specific genetic determinants of host response to helminthic infection have been inadequately explored, especially in humans. Extensive evidence exists that genetic factors are involved in host immune responses to infection, but only limited study has been done of the specific mode of transmission of these factors (Wakelin 1985, 1991).

***Genetic studies of helminthic infections in animal models*** The majority of research on the genetics of susceptibility and immunologic response to helminths has been conducted with animal models such as inbred strains of mice, as reviewed by Wakelin (1985, 1986, 1991). Much of this work has been devoted to simply determining presence or absence of a genetic component to the trait without further refinement of the genetic architecture of the traits. For example, several studies have compared inbred strains of mice to infer genetic influences on a variety of immune response parameters (reviewed by Wakelin 1985). Inbred strains of mice show significant differences in resistance and abilities to mount an antibody response to infection with the cestode *Taenia taeniaeformis* (Conchedda and Ferretti 1984; Mitchell et al. 1980). Additionally, different strains of inbred mice have been shown to have distinct eosinophil responses to infection with *Trichinella spiralis* (Lamas et al. 1989) and to clear resulting worm burdens at different rates (Bolas-Fernandez and Wakelin 1989).

The inflammatory response to helminthic infection is T-cell mediated, and several studies have suggested the involvement of genetic components in this response. There are differences in mast cell development upon helminthic infection between strains of inbred mice (Reed et al. 1988) and strain-specific patterns of T-cell response to infection with *Trichinella spiralis* have been demonstrated repeatedly (Pond et al. 1989; Zhu and Bell 1989). Because of the importance of T-cell mediated response to helminthic infection, the major histocompatability complex (MHC) has been a natural focus of investigations attempting to identify more directly the genetic components involved in response. Wassom et al. (1983) determined that two interacting MHC-related genes could account for much of the observed variation among strains in immune response to infection with *Trichinella spiralis*. Additionally, Wassom et al. (1984) found evidence for MHC gene effects on fecundity and expulsion of worms. The involvement of MHC genes in response to helminthic infections shows that major genes are important for regulating these parasitic diseases. However, the MHC cannot account for all the variation, and it is possible that additional unidentified major genes are involved. For example, Vadas (1982) has found evidence for a dominant gene controlling eosinophilia in response to helminthic infection in mice, but the gene involved remains unknown. Wakelin (1991) has suggested that genes other than those associated with MHC may be more important for determining response to helminthic infection.

Studies of pedigrees of larger mammals have provided further evidence for significant genetic influences on helminthic infections. Dargie (1982) has shown that sheep may be selected for resistance to gastrointestinal nematodes. Quantitative genetic studies in cattle have shown that helminthic worm counts and egg counts are significantly heritable, with heritabilities ranging as high as 0.93 (Barlow and Piper 1985; Leighton 1988; Mackinnon et al. 1991; Siefert 1977).

***Human genetic studies of helminthic infections*** Studies of the genetic components of response to helminthic infection in humans are limited. Findings from animal studies suggest that significant genetic influences on variation in response to infection are expected, and the detection and characterization of these genetic components may help refine the understanding of consistently observed patterns of overdispersion in parasitic diseases. A familial patterning to helminth-induced eosinophilia has been demonstrated (Moro-Furlani and Krieger 1992). This study implicitly assumed a polygenic mode of inheritance for immune-response parameters. A study of *Strongyloides fulleborni* infection in humans evaluated a number of transmission models for the diagnostic measure of egg counts (Smith et al. 1991). These authors were unable to identify any genetic components to egg count variation, but the pedigrees were far from optimal for analysis. Only 177 individuals distributed among 47 pedigrees were used, indicating that pedigree size and depth were extremely limited.

The results of previous epidemiologic studies of soil-transmitted helminthiases provide clear evidence of individual differences in both susceptibility to infection and severity of disease outcome. Results of analyses of human and animal data indicate the important role that genetic factors may play in determining individual susceptibility. Given the recent revolution in both statistical and molecular genetics, techniques are now available to potentially identify people who show increased susceptibility to infection due to their genotypes. Targeting treatments to individuals known (from the results of genetic epidemiologic analysis) to have a highly susceptible genotype can provide additional information for planning health care delivery strategies.

## PLANNING AND DEVELOPMENT

The literature review presented above indicates that genetic epidemiology can play a role in the development and planning of health care intervention and treatment delivery strategies. In combination with demographic, cultural, and behavioral information, genetic epidemiologic data can provide information for refining targeting of highly susceptible individuals. Genetic epidemiologic studies may indicate that no genetic factors are involved and that targeting should be based on other factors. Conversely, if genetic factors are identified, their relative importance can be determined, providing another avenue for directing limited resources to provide maximal health benefit to the population.

One genetic concept that is likely to be highly useful in health care intervention schemes is that of genotype-environment interaction. It is highly probable that different genotypes respond in different ways to various environmental factors or exposures. For example, genotype-specific patterns of the relationship of helminth burden with age may exist. In such a case, age may mark some changing aspect of either the endogenous biologic environment or the exogenous social environment of an individual. For this reason, it will be important to include quantification of relevant environmental and behavioral variables in genetic studies of susceptibility to infection.

Infectious diseases that are characterized by overdispersion, such as the soil-transmitted helminthiases, exhibit the inherent population patterning of diseases with genetic components. Thus it will be most profitable to initially focus genetic epidemiologic studies on such diseases. Population-based information with an intrinsic pedigree structure is necessary to perform such studies. Fortunately, many of the long-term epidemiologic studies of infectious disease in developing countries have been sampled by households, and thus probably by families. This historical information provides a rich database for use in future genetic epidemiologic studies of a wide variety of infectious diseases. Because of the apparent complexity of risk determinants for these diseases, it is imperative that future studies use a multidisciplinary approach with attention given to social, cultural, environmental, and genetic factors and their potential interactions.

## REFERENCES

ANDERSON, R. M. 1982. "The Population Dynamics and Control of Hookworm and Roundworm Infections." Pp. 67–106 in *Population Dynamics of Infectious Diseases,* edited by R. M. Anderson. London: Chapman and Hall.

ANDERSON, R. M. and R. M. MAY. 1982. "Population Dynamics of Human Helminth Infections: Control by Chemotherapy." *Nature* 297:557–63.

______. 1985. "Helminth Infections of Humans: Mathematical Models, Population Dynamics, and Control." *Advances in Parasitology* 24:1–101.

ANDERSON, R. M. and G. F. MEDLEY. 1985. "Community Control of Helminth Infections of Man by Mass and Selective Chemotherapy." *Parasitology* 90:629–60.

BARLOW, R. and L. R. PIPER. 1985. "Genetic Analyses of Nematode Egg Counts in Hereford and Crossbred Hereford Cattle in the Subtropics of New South Wales." *Livestock Production Science* 12:79–84.

BLANGERO, J. 1993. "Statistical Genetic Approaches to Human Adaptability." *Human Biology* 65:941–66.

BLANGERO, J., J. W. MACCLUER, C. M., KAMMERER, et al. 1990. "Genetic Analysis of Apolipoprotein A-I in Two Environments." *American Journal of Human Genetics* 47:414–28.

BOLAS-FERNANDEZ, F. and D. WAKELIN. 1989. "Infectivity of Trichinella Isolates in Mice is Determined by Host Immune Responsiveness." *Parasitology* 99:83–88.

BRADLEY, M., S. K. CHANDIWAANA, D. A. P. BUNDY, and G. F. MEDLEY. 1992. "The Epidemiology and Population Biology of *Necator Americanus* Infection in a Rural

Community in Zimbabwe." *Transactions of the Royal Society of Tropical Medicine and Hygiene* 86:73–76.

BULTO, T., F. H. MESKAL, T. ENDESHAW, and A. DEJENE. 1992. "Prevalence of Hookworm Infection and Its Associations with Low Haematocrit Among Resettlers in Gambela, Ethiopia." *Transactions of the Royal Society of Tropical Medicine and Hygiene* 86:184–86.

BUNDY, D. A. P. 1986. "Epidemiological Aspects of Trichuris and Trichuriasis in Caribbean Communities." *Transactions of the Royal Society of Tropical Medicine and Hygiene* 80:706–18.

BUNDY, D. A. P. and E. S. COOPER. 1989. "Trichuris and Trichuriasis in Humans." *Advances in Parasitology* 28:107–73.

______. 1990. "Trichuriasis." Pp. 399–403 in *Tropical and Geographic Medicine,* edited by K. S. Warren and A. A. F. Mahmoud. New York: McGraw Hill.

BUNDY, D. A. P., E. S. COOPER, D. E. THOMPSON, et al. 1987. "Predisposition to *Trichuris trichiura* Infections in Humans." *Epidemiology and Infection* 98:65–71.

BUNDY, D. A. P. and G. F. MEDLEY. 1992. "Immuno-Epidemiology of Human Geohelminthiasis: Ecological and Immunological Determinants of Worm Burden." *Parasitology* 104:S105–S109.

CHAI, J.-Y., B.-S. SEO, and S.-H. LEE. 1983. "Epidemiological Studies on *Ascaris lumbricoides* Reinfection in Rural Communities In Korea. II. Age-Specific Reinfection Rates and Familial Aggregation of the Reinfected Cases." *Korean Journal of Parasitology* 21:142–49.

CONCHEDDA, M. and G. FERRETTI. 1984. "Susceptibility of Different Strains of Mice to Various Levels of Infection with the Eggs of *Taenia taeniaeformis.*" *International Journal of Parasitology* 14:541–46.

COOPER, E. S., D. A. P. BUNDY, T. T. MACDONALD, and M. H. N. GOLDEN. 1990. "Growth Suppression in the Trichuris Dysentary Syndrome." *European Journal of Clinical Nutrition* 44:138–47.

CROLL, N. and E. GHARIDIAN. 1981. "Wormy Persons: Contributions to the Nature and Patterns of Overdispersion with *Ascaris lumbricoides, Ancylostoma duodenale, Necator americanus,* and *Trichuris trichiura.*" *Tropical and Geographic Medicine* 33:241–48.

CROMPTON, D. W. T. 1992. "Ascariasis and Childhood Malnutrition." *Transactions of the Royal Society of Tropical Medicine and Hygiene* 86:577–79.

CROMPTON, D. W. T., M. NESHEIM, and Z. S. PAWLOWSKI. 1985. *Ascariasis and Its Public Health Significance.* London: Taylor and Francis.

CROMPTON, D. W. T. and L. SAVIOLI. 1993. "Intestinal Parasitic Infections and Urbanization." *Bulletin of the World Health Organization* 71:1–7.

DARGIE, J. D. 1982. "The Influence of Genetic Factors on the Resistance of Ruminants to Gastrointestinal Nematode and Trypanosome Infections." Pp. 17–51 in *Animal Models in Parasitology,* edited by D. G. Owen. New York: MacMillan.

DYKE, B. 1989. PEDSYS. *A Pedigree Data Management System.* Users Manual. PGL Technical Report No. 2. San Antonio, TX: Southwest Foundation for Biomedical Research.

ELKINS, D., M. R. HASWELL-ELKINS, and R. M. ANDERSON. 1986. "The Epidemiology and Control of Intestinal Helminths in the Pulicat Lake Region of Southern India. I. Study Design and Pre- and Post-Treatment Observations on *Ascaris lumbricoides* Infection." *Transactions of the Royal Society of Tropical Medicine and Hygiene* 80:774–92.

ELSTON, R. C. and J. STEWART. 1971. "A General Model for the Genetic Analysis of Pedigree Data." *Human Heredity* 21:523–42.

FALCONER, D. S. 1981. *Introduction to Quantitative Genetics,* 2nd ed. London: Longman.

FORRESTER, J. E., M. E. SCOTT, D. A. P. BUNDY, and M. H. N. GOLDEN. 1988. "Clustering of *Ascaris lumbricoides* and *Trichuris trichiura* Infections Within Households." *Transactions of the Royal Society of Tropical Medicine and Hygiene* 82:282–88.

FORRESTER, J. E., M. E. SCOTT, D. A. P. BUNDY, and M. H. N. GOLDEN. 1990. "Predisposition of Individuals and Families in Mexico to Heavy Infection with *Ascariasis lumbricoides* and *Trichuris trichiura.*" *Transactions of the Royal Society of Tropical Medicine and Hygiene* 84:272–76.

GENTA, R. M. 1993. "Diarrhea in Helminthic Infections." *Clinical Infectious Diseases* 16(S2):S122–S129.

GUPTA, M. C. 1990. "Effect of Ascariasis upon Nutritional Status of Children." *Journal of Tropical Pediatrics* 36:189–91.

HALL, A., K. S. ANWAR, and A. M. TOMPKINS. 1992. "Intensity of Reinfection with *Ascaris lumbricoides* and Its Implications for Parasite Control." *Lancet* 339:1253–57.

HAMMOND, M. P. and A. E. BIANCO. 1992. "Genes and Genomes of Parasitic Nematodes." *Parasitology Today* 8:299–305.

HASWELL-ELKINS, M., D. ELKINS, and R. M. ANDERSON. 1987. "Evidence for Predisposition in Humans to Infection with Ascaris, Hookworm, Enterobius and Trichuris in a South Indian Fishing Community." *Parasitology* 95:323–37.

HOPPER, J. L. and J. D. MATHEWS. 1982. "Extensions to Multivariate Normal Models for Pedigree Analysis." *Annals of Human Genetics* 46:373–83.

KEYMER, A. and M. PAGEL. 1990. "Predisposition to Helminth Infections." Pp. 177–209 in *Hookworm Disease: Current Status and New Directions,* edited by G. A. Schad and K. S. Warren. London: Taylor and Francis.

KONIGSBERG, L. W., J. BLANGERO, C. M. KAMMERER, and G. E. MOTT. 1991. "Mixed Model Segregation Analysis of LDL-C Concentration with Genotype-Covariate Interaction." *Genetic Epidemiology* 8:69–80.

LAMAS, D. A., L. A. MITCHELL, and D. WAKELIN. 1989. "Genetic Control of Eosinophilia. Analysis of Production and Response to Eosinophil-Differentiating Factor in Strains of Mice Infected with *Trichinella spiralis.*" *Clinical and Experimental Immunology* 77:137–43.

LANGE, K. and M. BOEHNKE. 1983. "Extensions to Pedigree Analysis. IV. Covariance Components Models for Multivariate Traits." *American Journal of Medical Genetics* 14:513–24.

LEIGHTON, E. A. 1988. "Sources of Variation in and Estimates of Genetic Parameters for Parasite Egg Excretion Rates Observed in Angus Calves." *Journal of Animal Science* 66(S1):222.

MACCLUER, J. W. 1989. "Statistical Approaches to Identifying Major Locus Effects on Disease Susceptibility." Pp. 50–78 in *Genetic Factors in Atherosclerosis: Approaches and Model Systems,* edited by A. J. Lusis and R. S. Sparkes. New York: Karger.

MACKINNON, M. H., K. MEYER, and D. J. S. HETZEL. 1991. "Genetic Variation and Covariation for Growth, Parasite Resistance, and Heat Tolerance in Tropical Cattle." *Livestock Production Science* 27:105–22.

MCCALLUM, H. I. 1990. "Covariance in Parasite Burdens: The Effect of Predisposition to Infection." *Parasitology* 100:153–59.

MEDLEY, G. F., H. L. GUYATT, and D. A. P. BUNDY. 1993. "A Quantitative Framework for Evaluating the Effect of Community Treatment on the Morbidity due to Ascariasis." *Parasitology* 106:211–21.

MITCHELL, G. F., G. R. RAJASEKARIAH, and M. D. RICKARD. 1980. "A Mechanism to Account for Mouse Strain Resistance to the Larval Cestode *Taenia taeniaeformis.*" *Immunology* 39:481–89.

MORO-FURLANI, A. M. and H. KRIEGER. 1992. "Familial Analysis of Eosinophilia Caused by Helminthic Parasites." *Genetic Epidemiology* 9:185–90.

MPAIRWE, J. B. 1991. "Complications of *Ascaris lumbricoides* Infection: Case Reports from Southwestern Uganda." *Journal of Helminthology* 65:286–88.

MULLER, M., R. M. SANCHEZ, and R. R. SUSWILLO. 1989. "Evaluation of a Sanitation Programme Using Eggs of *Ascaris lumbricoides* in Household Yard Soils as Indicators." *Journal of Tropical Medicine and Hygiene* 92:10–16.

NOKES, C., S. M. GRANTHAM-MCGREGOR, A. W. SAWYER, et al. 1992. "Parasitic Helminth Infection and Cognitive Function in School Children." *Proceedings of the Royal Society. London* B 247:77–81.

PAWLOWSKI, Z. S. 1990. "Ascariasis." Pp. 369–78 in *Tropical and Geographical Medicine,* edited by K. S. Warren and A. A. F. Mahmoud. New York: MacGraw Hill.

PERUSSE, L., P. P. MOLL, and C. F. SING. 1991. "Evidence That a Single Gene with Gender- and Age-Dependent Effects Influences Systolic Blood Pressure Determination in a Population-Based Sample." *American Journal of Human Genetics* 49:94–105.

POND, L., D. L. WASSOM, and C. E. HAYES. 1989. "Evidence for Differential Induction of Helper T-Cell Subsets During *Trichinella spiralis* Infection. *Journal of Immunology* 143:4232–37.

PRITCHARD, D. I., R. J. QUINNELL, M. MOUSTAFA, et al. 1991. "Hookworm (*Necator americanus*) Infection and Storage Iron Depletion." *Transactions of the Royal Society of Tropical Medicine and Hygiene* 85:235–38.

REED, N. D., D. WAKELIN, D. A. LAMMAS, and R. K. GRENCIS. 1988. "Genetic Control of Mast Cell Development in Bone Marrow Cultures. Strain-Dependent Variation in Cultures from Inbred Mice." *Clinical and Experimental Immunology* 73:510–15.

ROBERTSON, L. J., D. W. T. CROMPTON, D. SANJUR, and M. C. NESHEIM. 1992. "Haemoglobin concentrations and concomitant infections of hookworm and *Trichurus trichuria* in Panamanian school children." *Transactions of the Royal Society of Tropical Medicine and Hygiene* 86:654–56.

SAVIOLI, L., D. BUNDY, and A. TOMKINS. 1992. "Intestinal Parasitic Infections: A Soluble Public Health Problem." *Transactions of the Royal Society of Tropical Medicine and Hygiene* 86:353–54.

SCHAD, G. A. and R. M. ANDERSON. 1985. "Predisposition to Hookworm Infection in Humans." *Science* 228:1537–40.

SCHAD, G. A. and J. G. BANWELL. 1990. "Hookworms." Pp. 379–92 in *Tropical and Geographical Medicine,* edited by K. S. Warren and A. A. F. Mahmoud. New York: McGraw Hill.

SIEFERT, G. W. 1977. "The Genetics of Helminth Resistance in Cattle." Third International Congress of the Society of Advanced Breeding Researches in Asia and Oceania, Canberra, Australia, 7:4–8.

SMITH, T., K. BHATIA, G. BARNISH, and R. W. ASHFORD. 1991. "Host Genetic Factors Do Not Account for Variation in Parasite Loads in *Strongyloides fuelleborni kellyi.*" *Annals Tropical Medicine and Parasitology* 5:533–37.

THEIN-HLAING. 1985. "*Ascaris lumbricoides* Infection in Burma." Pp. 83–112 in *Ascariasis and Its Public Health Significance,* edited by D. W. T. Crompton, M. C. Nesheim, and Z. S. Pawlowski. London: Taylor and Francis.

THEIN-HLAING, THAN-SAW, and MYINT-LIN. 1987. "Reinfection of People with *Ascaris Lumbricoides* Following Single, 6-Month, and 12-Month Interval Mass Chemotherapy in Okpo Village, Rural Burma." *Transactions of the Royal Society of Tropical Medicine and Hygiene* 81:140–46.

THEIN-HLAING, THAN-SAW, and MYAT-LAY-KYIN. 1991a. "The Impact of Three Monthly Age-Targeted Chemotherapy on *Ascaris lumbricoides* Infection." *Transactions of the Royal Society of Tropical Medicine and Hygiene* 85:519–22.

THEIN-HLAING, THANE-TOE, THAN-SAW et al. 1991b. "A Controlled Chemotherapeutic Intervention Trial on the Relationship Between *Ascaris lumbricoides* Infection and Malnutrition in Children." *Transactions of the Royal Society of Tropical Medicine and Hygiene* 85:523–28.

TINGLEY, G. A., A. E. BUTTERWORTH, R. M. ANDERSON, et al. 1988. "Predisposition of Humans to Infection with *Schistosoma mansoni:* Evidence from the Reinfection of Individuals Following Chemotherapy." *Transactions of the Royal Society of Tropical Medicine and Hygiene* 82:448–52.

VADAS, M. A. 1982. "Genetic Control of Eosinophilia in Mice: Gene(s) Expressed in Bone Marrow–derived Cells Control High Responsiveness." *Journal of Immunology* 128:691–95.

WAKELIN, D. 1985. "Genetic Control of Immunity to Helminth Infections." *Parasitology Today* 1:17–23.

WAKELIN, D. 1986. "Genetic and Other Constraints on Resistance to Infection with Gastrointestinal Nematodes." *Transactions of the Royal Society of Tropical Medicine and Hygiene* 80:742–47.

______. 1991. "Immunology and Genetics: Their Relation to Control of Parasitic Zoonoses." *Parassitologia* 33:61–66.

WALTER, S. D. 1974. "On the Detection of Household Aggregation of Disease." *Biometrics* 32:817–28.

WARREN, K. S. 1988. "Hookworm Control." *Lancet* 2:897.

WARREN, K. S. and A. A. F. MAHMOUD. 1990. *Tropical and Geographical Medicine.* New York: McGraw Hill.

WASSOM, D. L., B. O. BROOKS, J. G. BABISH, and C. S. DAVID. 1983. "A Gene Mapping between the S and D Regions of the H-2 Complex Influences Resistance to *Trichinella spiralis* Infections of Mice." *Journal of Immunogenetics* 10:371–78.

WASSOM, D. L., D. WAKELIN, B. O. BROOKS, et al. 1984. "Genetic Control of Immunity to *Trichinella spiralis* Infections of Mice. Hypothesis to Explain the Role of H-2 Genes in Primary and Challenge Infections." *Immunology* 51:625–31.

WILLIAMS, D., G. BURKE, and J. O. HENDLEY. 1974. "Ascariasis: A Family Disease." *Journal of Pediatrics* 84:853–54.

WORLD HEALTH ORGANIZATION (WHO). 1987. "Prevention and Control of Intestinal Parasitic Infections." Technical Report Series 749. Geneva: World Health Organization.

ZHU, D. and R. G. BELL. 1989. "IL-2 Production, IL-2 Receptor Expression, and IL-2 Responsiveness of Spleen and Mesenteric Lymph Node Cells from Inbred Mice Infected with *Trichinella spiralis.*" *Journal of Immunology* 142:3262–67.

Chapter 18

# Domestic Violence Against Women: A Contemporary Issue in International Health

*Ruth L. Fischbach and Elizabeth Donnelly*

*Soncha (Mexico), pregnant with her third child, resists her husband's sexual advances, but he forces her to have sex, violently and against her will. He reminds her that she is his property so he has the right to enjoy her as he desires. Equally as devastating as his slaps and kicks are José's abusive words, which leave Soncha feeling demoralized and hopeless, with a pain in her heart that throbs long after the bruises fade.*

*Ajita (India, Pakistan) comes from a relatively poor family that has sacrificed greatly to provide a dowry payment for their daughter's husband. Soon after her marriage, Ajita dies an unnatural death in what the police file as "a kitchen accident"; her husband reports that a kerosene stove exploded while she was cooking. Ajita's is the third such "accidental" death of a new bride in 5 months in this village.*

*Fatou (Somalia) is 12 and her family is preparing her for marriage, the only status position available to women in this northeast African society. The central component of her rite of passage involves circumcision; a procedure in which a traditional midwife and elder female kin remove her clitoris and other parts of her external genitalia. The surgery helps ensure her premarital purity, an absolute prerequisite for marriage and social identity.*

*As Jing Wang (China) nears marriage age, she dreads her inevitable, arranged marriage to Rui Xiao. After an unsuccessful attempt to escape with the man she wishes to marry, the reluctant bride is held captive and beaten by her prospective husband and father-in-law, who feel humiliation at her rejection. After several days of torment, Jing*

*Wang returns to her unsympathetic family, who resents her renunciation of traditional values and customs. Later that week, Jing Wang is found dead, an apparent suicide.*

Violence against women is manifest and legitimized in many ways within and across cultures. Gender-based violence has only recently emerged as a crucial global issue that cuts across regional, social, cultural, and economic boundaries. As the data accumulate, the pervasiveness of gender-based violence and its impact on morbidity and mortality are becoming alarmingly clear. Indeed, gender-based violence is a nearly universal phenomenon threatening the health and freedom of women in the streets, in the workplace, and, most troublesome, in the home.

Domestic violence must be viewed as a public health problem that directly damages women's health and well-being. The *World Development Report 1993* indicates that in 1990, domestic violence and rape caused an estimated 5% of the global health burden for women aged 15 to 44 (World Bank 1993). Hence, violence and rape account for 5% of the total years of healthy life lost. Because of underreporting, the magnitude of the global health burden from domestic violence and rape is almost certainly greater than current estimates (World Bank 1993).

Domestic violence must also be viewed as a human rights issue, one that threatens the security of women and their fundamental right to life and liberty as well as freedom from fear and want, as described in the *Universal Declaration of Human Rights* (UN 1948). Although extreme poverty, deprivation, and social and economic oppression increase the potential for the violation of human rights (Jilani 1992), these abuses can occur in any society where disadvantaged groups are oppressed by political and social forces.

This chapter focuses on violence in developing or low-income countries. These countries are dynamic, with rising populations and evolving economies. Much information needs to be exchanged. Only within the last few years have researchers and clinicians begun to compile data on the prevalence, nature, and consequences of domestic violence. Despite the disturbing findings, in countries where infectious disease, malnutrition, or war pose critical challenges to survival, protection from violence in the home has been given a low priority on the health and human rights agenda. Yet, a deeper appreciation of the nature and consequences of domestic violence would reveal its association with myriad serious health and social problems, including depression, chronic pain, substance abuse and dependence, suicide, child abuse, and homelessness. There are compelling reasons why the issue of domestic violence in the developing world is in urgent need of attention and why this issue should be a high-priority item on the health and human rights agenda:

1. Even with the paucity of systematic documentation, the magnitude of reported incidents of domestic violence throughout the developing world constitutes a significant cause of physical morbidity and mortality. And

these health risks affect not only women but future generations; battered women run twice the risk of miscarriage and four times the risk of having a below-average-weight baby (World Bank 1993). One of the most effective means to reduce congenital birth defects and infant mortality is to ensure the safety of pregnant women and mothers.

2. In countries where more extensive data do exist, there are indications of a direct association between domestic violence and psychiatric morbidity. Research from the United States reveals, for example, that "battered women are four to five times more likely to require psychiatric treatment and five times more likely to attempt suicide" (Stark and Flitcraft 1991). Ethnographic data from Oceania, South America, and China provide further evidence that wife-beating is widespread and is associated with depression and suicide (Counts 1987, 1990a, 1990b; Gilmartin 1990).
3. Most violations against women are perpetrated by someone the woman knows and most often in the "privacy" of the home. Historically, in most societies, the criminal justice system has relegated authority in domestic affairs to men as heads of households. Similarly, the human rights community has failed to acknowledge the gender-specific ways in which the rights and dignity of women are violated. Too often, systematic violence and abuse are tolerated internationally as cultural patterns. These are just two examples of the systemic devaluation of women's worth.
4. Domestic violence against women is a global issue requiring global awareness and action. Despite cultural variations in the manifestations, the underlying factors that promote and perpetuate violence are remarkably similar. A cross-cultural perspective allows us to learn not only *about* violence against women in other regions but to learn *from* the experiences of people working to define and combat this problem in their communities. These examples provide the direction and guidance needed to respond to this global problem.

## PURPOSE AND PLAN OF THIS CHAPTER

This chapter consolidates data from low-income countries related to the prevalence and nature of domestic violence. Such data are requisite for the appreciation of the role of domestic violence in the cause of women's physical, mental, and emotional disorders and for the implementation of strategies to alleviate this pandemic.

Three specific experiences faced by many women in the domestic setting—female circumcision, marital rape, and dowry deaths—are discussed in detail to illustrate the complex cultural meanings that these events have. A growing database substantiates our contention that a yet unknown and, to date, unexplained proportion of the physical and mental disorders and emotional distress ascribed to women is likely a response to the systemic physical and sexual violence they have experienced or are experiencing. Much of this violence remains hidden and undisclosed to clinicians and researchers because of the shame, guilt, and social taboos associated with these actions.

The authors suggest research initiatives and provide policy recommendations that emphasize the health care professional's vital position in recognizing, diagnosing, treating, and preventing injury to women living in violent intimate relationships. Health care professionals by themselves, however, cannot resolve the problem of domestic violence. Sustainable strategies for relieving domestic violence depend on an integrated, society-wide approach that involves collaboration between many institutions (e.g., law, government, religious organizations), an approach that entails raising the status of women in society and even altering the existing social and cultural mores. Domestic violence is not just a woman's issue. Therefore, the chapter concludes with a sample of successful strategies from around the world where men and women are acting together to curtail domestic violence against women.

## LEXICON FOR DOMESTIC VIOLENCE

Abuse and violence take many forms, and to date there is little universal agreement on the terminology to describe the experiences of women. Often the terms used become ideological and highly politicized. Recognizing that "violence" may be defined according to particular cultural understandings (Counts 1990a), we consider violence to be "an act carried out with the intention, or perceived intention, of physically hurting another person" (Straus et al. 1980, p. 20). Other definitions focus on power and control, such as that offered by Heise (1993c): Violence against women includes "any act of force or coercion that gravely jeopardizes the life, body, psychological integrity or freedom of women." Abuse includes behaviors that cause harm without the inclusion of physical force, encompassing neglect, psychological and emotional harm, and nonviolent sexual harm. We use the term "domestic violence" in this chapter to encompass harmful behaviors by intimates directed toward females assuming the role of wife in household relationships, with or without the legal sanction of marriage. We broaden the definition to include behaviors that occur while preparing for marriage. We also focus on women, as they are the victims/survivors in more than 85% of cases of domestic violence (Koss 1990).

Taken as an aggregate, the numerous terms used to describe acts of domestic violence form a rich lexicon. These terms demonstrate the degree of variation across cultures while at the same time emphasize the difficulty of conducting research in this field: No standard definition of domestic violence exists. Our lexicon of domestic violence, collected as we reviewed the literature, is comprehensive but by no means exhaustive. We include the following terms: (physical) abuse; wife-beating in all capacities such as slapping, punching, kicking, biting, burning, using a weapon (with intent to injure); wife-battering (defined as repeated attacks, multiple blows); aggravated assault; assault and battery; domestic battery; injurious assaults; intimate assault; wife assault; spouse abuse; sexual assault, rape, attempted rape, forcible rape, marital rape, custodial rape, conjugal violence, intimate violence, sexual violation, unwanted or intrusive experiences, forced prostitution; homicide, honor murder/killing (of rape victims or women suspected of adultery), dowry-related murder or bride burning, sati (widow joins husband in death on his funeral pyre); "acid throwing" (perpetuated by vengeful lovers); and medical violence or social surgical procedures including genital mutilation (circumcision and infibulation). Acts of domestic violence against women are usually categorized under three main headings: physical, sexual and emotional/psychological. Although these categories can be useful as distinct entities, it is problematic to compartmentalize violence. A women raped by her husband is concomitantly physically, sexually, and emotionally harmed. Kicking, slapping, punching, and burning have obvious physical sequelae; less blatant, although nonetheless harmful, are the devastating psychological and emotional effects. By categorizing acts of violence as either physical, sexual, or emotional, the impact that violence has on a women is reduced to a single component, which can lead to trivializing the experience.

Health care professionals and researchers are developing measures to assess the impact of abuse. According to Heise (1993a), once a woman is hit, even one time, the "effectiveness" and fear associated with threats and psychological abuse increase. Thus, women who are assaulted only rarely can suffer long-term effects from the memory of the original incident and ongoing verbal and emotional abuse. The physical and mental health consequences rise dramatically when women are subjected to repeated violence.

## EPIDEMIOLOGY OF DOMESTIC VIOLENCE IN LOW-INCOME COUNTRIES

Historically, cross-cultural information on the extent of domestic violence has been limited by the inadequacy and inaccessibility of international data on women in general and on domestic violence in particular. This constraint is abating. As a consequence of the United Nations Decade for Women (1975 to 1985), a considerable amount of international information on women is available; since 1990, several sophisticated studies have been undertaken to establish prevalences of domestic violence. Accruing data on domestic violence give cause for concern. These data show that domestic violence and rape, even while rarely recognized as public health problems, nonetheless cause substantial damage to women's health through injuries, depression and psychological trauma, sexually transmitted diseases, suicide, and murder. The most endemic form of violence against women is wife abuse, or more accurately, abuse of women by intimate male partners (Heise 1993c). Severe and ongoing violence has been documented in almost every culture in the world; a few small-scale preindustrial societies are notable exceptions to this prevalent pattern (Levinson 1989).

In reviewing cross-cultural data from studies documenting domestic violence, several cautions are advised. First, prevalences of domestic violence may not be directly comparable because investigators are not consistent in the probes used to identify abuse or the nominal and operational definitions of their dependent variables (e.g., violence "over a lifetime" or "in the last year"). Furthermore, a higher rate in a particular culture does not necessarily mean that something intrinsic to that culture is conducive to domestic violence. Rather, it may be that rates in other countries appear low owing to poor ascertainment. In addition, in contrast to the perception that relying on women's self-reports inflates statistics, clinical and research experience suggest that the reverse occurs: Women *underestimate* the level of physical and psychological violence they experience in relationships. Likely explanations for this are (1) women in many cultures are socialized to accept physical and emotional chastisement as part of a husband's marital prerogative, thereby limiting the range of behavior they identity as abusive (Counts 1990a) and (2) women are averse to report abuse out of shame or reluctance to incriminate family members for fear of retaliation (Heise 1993a). Either of these factors, as well as others, may contribute to estimates lacking complete accuracy.

Data on domestic violence have been accruing for several years in the United States, and they can be used as a measure for comparison when examining the prevalence of violence against women on an international scale. These data indicate that for women in the United States, the family is a violent institution (Koss 1990). In the United States, a woman is more likely to be assaulted, raped, or killed by a male partner than by any other assailant (Browne and Williams 1989). Population-based surveys suggest that between 21% and 30% of American women are beaten by a partner at least once in their lives (Kilpatrick et al. 1985; Koss 1990). Based on national probability samples from the United States, 47% of the husbands who beat their wives do so more than three times per year (Straus et al. 1980). Assaults by husbands, ex-husbands, and lovers cause more injuries to women than motor vehicle accidents, rape, and muggings combined (Rosenberg et al. 1986; Stark and Flitcraft 1991). Studies estimate that 22% to 35% of women seeking emergency treatment do so for symptoms related to abuse (Randall 1990) and, because abuse is an ongoing cycle producing increasingly severe injuries over time, battered women are likely to see physicians frequently. One study reported that nearly one in five battered women had seen a physician at least 11 times for trauma, and another 23% had seen a physician 6 to 10 times for abuse-related injuries (Stark and Flitcraft 1979). Health officials estimate that each year more than 4 million women are battered and more than 4,000 are killed by such "intimate assaults" (Royner 1991).

Similar statistics are reported from Canada, which is "at a crisis level," according to the 1993 report by the Canadian Panel on Violence against Women. Based on a random survey of 420 Toronto women between the ages of 16 and 64, 98% reported "some form of unwanted or intrusive experience before they reached 16"; furthermore, 51% of the sample had been the victim of rape or attempted rape and 40% reported at least one rape; 81% of rape or attempted rape victims said they knew their attacker (*Boston Globe* 1993).

Reports by Lori Heise (1993a) for the World Bank and Freda Paltiel (1987) for the United Nations Commission on the Status of Women provide a comprehensive overview of domestic violence, with examples of domestic violence from numerous low-income countries. Table 18–1 draws on their extensive lists of references.

## EXPERIENCES FACED BY MANY WOMEN

Among the many forms of domestic or gender-based violence, we examine three closely in order to illustrate the complex cultural patterns and values that promote and perpetuate the threat to women's lives and welfare. Female circumcision, marital rape, and dowry-related deaths are currently affecting women in epidemic proportions.

### Social Surgery: Female Circumcision and Infibulation

It is only a decade since women in Africa and the Middle East first dared to speak publicly about a procedure known as female circumcision, the cultural practice of surgically altering female genitalia. There has been little reduction in its occurrence during that time. Three procedures exist: The Sunna type (excision) consists of removal of the tip of the prepuce of the clitoris. The simplest, it is considered the type recommended by Islam, yet is the least practiced form of circumcision (El-Dareer 1982). Clitorectomy consists of removal of all of the clitoris. Infibulation, the most extreme form of circumcision (includes the excising of the clitoris, the labia minora, and the inner wall of the labia majora, and the suturing together of the two sides of the vulva except for a small opening for the passage of urine and menstrual blood), is practiced on nine out of ten girls in Sudan and Somalia (Seager and Olson 1986). The surgery may be performed on girls as young as a few days old or in late adolescence. Rarely are surgical instruments or anesthesia used. Gruenbaum (1988) described the operation itself as performed by a woman behind closed doors with only women taking part; men are completely excluded. Moreover, it is the women who strongly defend the propagation of this practice, not surprisingly, because they derive much of their social status and economic security from their roles as wives and mothers.

The derivation of this practice is difficult to trace (WHO 1993). Although it is generally believed that female circumcision was originally an attempt to

**TABLE 18–1. Examples of Domestic Violence in Low-income Countries**

| *NATION* | *SURVEY/SOURCE (YEAR)* | *FINDINGS* |
|---|---|---|
| Bangladesh | World Bank (1993) | Intentional injury during pregnancy—motivated by dowry disputes or shame over a rape or a pregnancy outside of wedlock—caused 6% of all maternal deaths between 1976 and 1986. |
| Bangladesh | Paltiel (1987) | Severe beating usually by husbands, accounts for 49% of deaths. |
| Brazil | Heise (1993a) | State of Pernambuco: Of 415 women murdered, 70% were killed by intimate male partners. |
| Chile | Moltedo et al. (1989)<br>Carrillo (1991) | A survey in Santiago found that 80% of women have suffered physical, emotional, or sexual abuse by male partner or relative; 63% report they are currently being abused. |
| China | United Nations Case Study<br>Kahn (1993) | In the city of Suzhou, Jiangsu Province, the census counted 48,100 women abducted and sold into marriage as slave wives. In one small village called Ninlou, of all married women were slaves to their husbands. |
| Colombia | Demographic and Health Survey<br>Heise (1993a) | From a national sample of 3,272 urban and 2,118 rural women, 20% report being beaten, 10% raped by husbands. |
| Costa Rica | Chacon et al. (1990)<br>Heise (1993a) | 51% of women report being beaten up to several times per year; 35% report being hit regularly. |
| Costa Rica | Canas (1990)<br>Heise (1993c) | Using children as informants, 57% of wives were reported to be beaten by husbands. |
| Fiji | Haynes (1984) | 41% of men cite marital violence as the cause of their loved one's suicide. |
| Guatemala | Coy (1990)<br>Heise (1993a) | Random sample of 1,312 women aged 15–49 yrs., 49% report being abused, 74% of intimate male partner (includes physical, emotional, and sexual abuse in adulthood). |

*(continued)*

**TABLE 18–1.** ***(continued)***

| *NATION* | *SURVEY/SOURCE (YEAR)* | *FINDINGS* |
|---|---|---|
| India | Mahajan (1990)<br>Heise (1993a) | Of 109 households in an Indian village, 22% of higher-caste husbands and 75% of scheduled (lower)–caste husbands admitted to beating their wives. The scheduled-caste wives reported they were "regularly beaten." |
| India | Ahmedabad Women's Action Group<br>Kelkar (1991) | "Bride burning" (under-)estimated to result in 4,835 deaths in all of India, but as many as 1,000 women/year may be burned alive in Gujarat State alone. |
| Jamaica | Paltiel (1987) | Domestic violence was implicated in 22% of the crimes committed against women. |
| Kenya | Centre for Development Research<br>Raikes (1990) | Of 733 women surveyed, 42% said they were beaten regularly by their husbands. |
| Malaysia | Survey Research Malaysia (1990)<br>Heise (1993a) | Random sample of 713 females and 508 males over 15 yrs. report 39% of women have been "physically beaten" by a partner in the last year. This is an annual figure. 15% of adults consider wife-beating acceptable (22% of Malays). |
| Mexico | Valdez and Shrader-Cox (1991) | A survey of a city near Mexico City found 1 in 3 women were victims of family violence; 20% reported blows to the stomach during pregnancy. |
| | Mexican NGO; cited in Carrillo (1991) | It is estimated that domestic violence is present in at least 70% of Mexican families, but most cases go unreported. |

| | | |
|---|---|---|
| Nicaragua | Carrillo (1991) | 44% of men admit to having beaten their wives or girlfriends regularly. |
| Papua New Guinea | PNG Law Reform Commission Bradley (1988) | 67% of rural women and 56% of urban women reported being victims of wife abuse; 18% of *all* wives surveyed in urban areas received hospital treatment for injuries inflicted by their husbands; almost 3 out of 4 women murdered were killed by their husband. |
| Peru | Seager and Olson (1986) | 1 of 3 women seen in Lima's emergency rooms are victims of domestic violence. Lima, population 7 million, had 168,970 rapes reported in 1987 alone. In Peru, 70% of all crimes reported to police involve women who are beaten by their partners. |
| South Africa | Heise in Schuler (1992) | Every 1 minutes a woman is raped in South Africa, totaling approximately 386,000 women raped each year. |
| Thailand | World Bank (1993) | A survey of the largest slum in Bangkok found that 50% of married women were beaten regularly. Also, 25% of children receiving treatment in a nutrition center came from families where the mother is routinely beaten. |

ensure chaste or monogamous behavior or as a means of suppressing female sexuality, some believe that it served to protect adolescent girls against rape. Moslems mistakenly believe that female circumcision is demanded by the Islamic faith, although it has no basis in the Koran (Heise 1993c). Significantly, the WHO closely links this practice with poverty, illiteracy, and low status of women. In such settings, an uncircumcised woman is stigmatized and not sought in marriage, which helps explain the paradox mentioned earlier that circumcised women are among its strongest proponents, along with the traditional midwives who perform the act.

Hicks (1993) offers a series of "indigenous" explanations to justify infibulation: (a) it has religious significance; (b) it preserves virginity until the time of marriage; (c) it is hygienic and purifying; (d) it curbs the (potentially) excessive sexuality of females; (e) it promotes fertility; and (f) it maintains general body health (p. 13). Both clitoral excision and infibulation are seen to relate to Islamic religious tradition and the absolute prerequisite of virginity for a bride-to-be. Indeed, very few men would marry a girl who has not been excised and infibulated, which precludes women's choice in the matter (Forni 1980, cited in Hicks 1993).

***Health consequences of female genital surgery*** Female circumcision—especially infibulation—is a major health problem in Africa and the Middle East. According to the WHO (1993), it is believed that more than 84 million females in more than 30 countries have been subject to female genital mutilation. Health consequences are considerable, including both acute problems of hemorrhage, shock, and tetanus and long-term problems such as pelvic infections leading to infertility, vesiculovaginal fistula, HIV infection from contaminated instruments, chronic urinary tract infections, cysts and abscesses, keloid and severe scar formation, lack of sexual response, and often death (e.g., 10% to 30% estimated mortality of young Sudanese girls) (Heise 1993c). In women who have been infibulated, a cut must be made to enlarge the vaginal opening immediately before marriage and before childbirth. During childbirth, the risk of maternal death is doubled, and the risk of a stillbirth increases severalfold. The long-term morbidity becomes cumulative and chronic. In one country alone, the Sudan, 30% of all Sudanese women have circumcision-related complications, and that figure rises to 83% in Sierra Leone (World Bank 1993). Maternal and infant mortality rates are particularly high where the incidence of circumcision is high (Seager and Olson 1986).

There are two perspectives on the impact of circumcision and infibulation on women. One position argues that while the *medical* consequences are obvious, genital mutilation, in addition, has staggering *mental health* consequences for women. The extent and degree of sexual and mental health problems can only be guessed at, however, because circumcised women are often hesitant to discuss the subject that both means little to them and is embarrassing—that is, their sexuality (Seager and Olson 1986). The other position, articulated by Hicks (1993), contends that after the initial operation, the issue is closed (literally and figuratively speaking). Women do not even correlate their subsequent physical discomfort, pain, and related gynecologic and obstetric problems with having been circumcised. Such physical problems are perceived as being the common lot of women. In short, infibulation is not considered a problem but a badge of merit and identification. It accords girls the right to marriage and the protection and the status this union provides. Individual social identity is based on being infibulated. Women's collective social identity is based on *all* women being infibulated. As long as the tradition holds that men will not marry uncircumscribed women, considered to be promiscuous, unclean, and sexually untrustworthy (Heise et al. 1989), the practice will be perpetuated.

Women are subjected to other gender-related, culturally determined medical or surgical procedures. Forced sterilization and forced abortion (described by Clare 1992) are examples of government policies or cultural beliefs that condone abuses or violence against women.

In addition, certain nonsurgical/medical procedures that are gender-related have been practiced widely. The custom of footbinding ended under the Nationalists in the late 1930s in some areas of China and was outlawed all over China after 1949. Neck elongation in parts of Africa, as well as breast augmentation in the United States, are examples of women subjecting themselves or being subjected to painful and potentially harmful practices to conform to what is considered by local custom to be desirable to their men.

### Rape

Rape is a complex experience for women, as its impact is contingent on the circumstances surrounding the rape, the relationship to the perpetrator, and the cultural meaning attached to rape. It may occur in the form of an assault outside the home by a stranger, as an aftermath of war where the victor gets the spoils, and even within the margins of the marital relationship. The impact of rape on the woman is often additive. The victim of rape is victimized twice (at least)—first by the rapist, physically and emotionally, and then by the consequent stigmatization and rejection by the family, community, and culture. All to frequently, it is the victim who is blamed for the attack.

Rape is probably the most underreported, fastest growing, and least convicted crime in the world. Particularly in low-income countries, few agencies provide services as well as data from which to estimate the prevalence of rape. It has long been considered as a crime only against property—the woman as man's property. "Now rape is beginning to be recognized for what it is: a crime of violence and power, and a violation of women's civil rights" (Seager and Olson 1986).

The Latin root of rape means "theft," and most cultural responses to such violence emphasize reclaiming the woman's lost value, not prosecuting the offender. This helps explain why rape is either seen as a man's prerogative or as a crime against the honor of a woman's family or husband, rather than a violation of the woman (Heise 1993c). As Heise described (1993b), in parts of Asia and the Middle East, the stain of rape is so great that victims are sometimes killed by family members to cleanse the family honor. According to Mollica and Son, in Southeast Asian cultures, a husband often rejects his wife if she has been sexually violated because she is perceived as having been "used" or "left over" by the rapist(s) (Mollica and Son 1989, cited in Heise 1993b). The consequences of rape in societies where a young woman's worth is equated with her virginity are ruinous.

***Marital rape*** There is growing acknowledgment of the extent of marital rape as more women are able to report and discuss its occurrence. Researchers still find, however, that most women are not able to address sexual abuse in their marriage because of the deep shame they experience. Heise's report on rape (1993b) includes the following empirical data: In the United States, whereas 14% of all wives report being raped, the prevalence among battered wives is at least 40%; in severely abusive relationships, forcible rape may occur as often as several times a month. Heise (1993b) also noted that in Bolivia and Puerto Rico, 58% of battered wives report being sexually assaulted by their partner, and in Colombia, the reported rate is 46%. Reports from the Philippines and Guatemala indicate that forced sex with husbands is a common experience.

***Medical consequences of rape*** The medical consequences of rape, including physical trauma and risk of pregnancy, sexually transmitted diseases (STDs), and AIDS, are considerable. Reports from a Rape Crisis Center in Bangkok, Thailand, indicate that 10% of its clients contract STDs as a result of rape and 15% to 18% become pregnant, a figure consistent with data from Mexico and Korea. Where abortion is illegal or restricted, death and infertility are often the sequelae of the resorted to *illegal* abortion (World Bank 1993). Additionally, as discussed below, rape may be a risk factor for the development of risk-taking behaviors (e.g., substance abuse). In cultures where the stigma of rape and subsequent victim blaming are especially powerful, the risk of suicide (and even homicide) rises dramatically.

### Dowry-Related Deaths

A deadly form of domestic violence has been occurring on the Indian subcontinent. "Dowry deaths" or "bride burning" has been reported with alarming frequency amid speculation that the exact magnitude of the mortality statistics remains unknown. This form of violence, visible and sensational, is seen by activists as the extreme symbol of a society where women are considered expendable (Jilani 1992).

By long-established custom, dowry referred to the wealth given to a woman by her family, which she subsequently brought to her husband upon her marriage. This was a Hindu practice that enabled parents to pass on family assets to their daughters, who were not allowed by law or custom to inherit property. The tradition has been transformed into a crucial premarital negotiation and now refers to the money or goods that the bride's parents agree to present to the groom and his family as a condition of the marriage settlement. No longer a gesture of love and devotion, increasingly dowry is seen as a "get rich quick" scheme by prospective husbands (Heise 1993c). Typically the bride is exploited by the husband and his family, who make ongoing demands for her wealth, demands that her parents may not be able to meet. If the demands go unmet, with increasing frequency the bride may be severely abused to a point that culminates in her unnatural death. With her death, the husband (widower) is free to pursue a more profitable marriage.

The most common form of dowry death is by burning, usually by dousing the woman with kerosene and setting her on fire. The murder is disguised, claimed by the husband to be the result of a "kitchen accident" caused by the bursting of a stove used for cooking. Investigations are rarely conducted, as police are loathe to get involved.

Because dowry deaths are notoriously undercounted (Heise 1993c), exactly how many women die as a result of this form of domestic violence can be inferred only from data that are known. In all of India, 999 deaths were registered as dowry-related deaths in 1985; as of 1991, that number had increased to 5,157 registered deaths (Kelkar 1991). Yet the Ahmedabad Women's Action Group estimates that 1,000 women may be burned alive each year in Gujarat State alone (Heise et al. 1989). Given that in two of India's cities, one of every four deaths among women aged 15 to 24 is reported to be due to "accidental burns" (Karkal 1985), one can only hypothesize what the true mortality figures might be.

## DOMESTIC VIOLENCE AND MENTAL HEALTH

"Every woman's mental health is affected by the way her society regards and treats unmarried or married women, childless women, mothers, poor women, assaulted women, divorced women, minority women, disabled women, widows, aged women or women with aspirations" (Paltiel 1987, p. 234). Until recently, mainstream literature has paid little attention to the mental health consequences of domestic violence. Women's lives have remained largely unexamined and their experiences unreported (Paltiel 1987). Currently, physicians rarely, if ever, inquire of their patients whether domestic violence is a significant experience in their lives. They tend to avoid the prospect of "opening Pandora's box" (Sugg and Inui 1992), treating symptoms rather than causes. It is no wonder that the linkage between domestic violence and psychiatric diagnosis is seldom secured.

Many cultures find the concept of mental illness so stigmatizing that they ignore, deny, and ostracize not only the mentally ill person but the entire family. Other cultures simply do not have a concept of mental illness (Wetzel 1991), which means they have no system of treating those in need. Still other societies may acknowledge mental disorders but not give them the proper recognition and required services (Jacobsson 1985). These limitations serve as serious barriers to proper diagnosis, treatment, prevention, and research.

The immediate impact of physical and sexual abuse and violence on women's mental health is increasingly, if belatedly, being recognized. In addition, acceptance is growing that the deleterious effects of abuse can continue to contribute to psychiatric morbidity for many years (Mullen et al. 1988) and is a strong risk factor for the development of lifetime mental health problems (Kilpatrick et al. 1985). These women are significantly more likely than nonvictims to qualify for psychiatric diagnoses, including major depression, alcohol and drug abuse and dependence, generalized anxiety, post-traumatic stress syndrome, and obsessive-compulsive disorder (Koss 1990).

A consistent observation in psychiatric epidemiology is that women are disproportionately represented among patients with depressive and anxiety disorders (Robins et al. 1984). This discrepancy has been ascribed to women's biology, psychology, and social position (Mullen et al. 1988).

In this section, we propose that a significant portion of the mental distress or disorder observed in women is directly related to their experiences as victims of domestic violence. Our position is that the experience of abuse, endemic or even epidemic on a global scale, has been largely ignored or rarely considered by social scientists and psychiatric epidemiologists in studies assessing risk factors for mental disorder.

In addition to psychiatric diagnoses, violence against women has been linked with symptoms of morbidity, including fear, anxiety, fatigue, sleep, and eating disorders. For abused women, the "trauma-related effects are exacerbated by the fact that the aggressor (perpetrator) is someone they love and trust, a reality that compounds the psychological consequences of the abuse. . . and exacerbates their feelings of vulnerability, loss, betrayal, and hopelessness. Abused women frequently become isolated and withdrawn as they try to hide the evidence of their abuse" (Heise 1993a, p. 8).

Specific psychiatric disorders have been linked to experience with domestic violence. We review them only briefly owing to space limitations and because scant data are available to report.

### Depression

Because of the prevalence, persistence, recurrence and interference with well-being and performance, depression is the single most serious mental health problem for women, with a preponderance for females in every age group according to most studies. Sartorius et al. (1980) found that the core symptoms of depression (e.g., sadness, worthlessness, lethargy, decreased interest and concentration) vary little from country to country (p. 204).

Most clinicians regard depression, one of the world's leading mental health problems, as a single entity even though there are at least five classification schemas and over a dozen major theories of depression. Few of these theories recognize the links between women, oppression, and poverty, even though women are three times more likely than men to become depressed, and two thirds of the world's women live in poverty (Wetzel 1991).

Connections are beginning to be made between depressed mood and a history of abuse and/or violence. According to a 1990 American Psychological Association monograph:

> Victimization in interpersonal relationships is a significant risk factor in the development of depressive symptomatology in women. What is presented clinically as depressed mood may be long-standing post-traumatic responses to experiences of intimate violence and victimization, for example, childhood sexual or physical abuse, marital or acquaintance rape, women battering, sexual harassment in the workplace, or sexual abuse by a therapist or health care provider. The contribution of these factors to rates of depressive symptomatology in women has been neglected, partially because victimization histories in most psychiatric patients tend to be ignored or conceptualized as the source of a disordered personality rather than as depressive symptomatology (American Psychological Association 1990).

Even with this recognition, the symptoms of depression customarily may be treated while the causes of the depression remain unexplored.

#### Post-Traumatic Stress Disorder (PTSD)

As defined by DSM III-R (American Psychiatric Association 1987), the essential feature of this disorder is the development of a complex of symptoms in the aftermath of a psychologically traumatic event outside the range of usual human experience which caused feelings of intense fear, terror, and helplessness. The characteristic symptoms involve intrusive memories, depression, sleep disturbance, trouble concentrating or memory impairment, hyperarousal alternating with psychological numbing and withdrawal, guilt about having survived when others did not or about behavior required for survival, and attempts to avoid any reminders of the trauma. The prevalence of PTSD is unknown. Some experts consider female sexual abuse and assault victims to be the largest single group of PTSD sufferers and rape the single most likely event to cause PTSD (Foa et al. 1987). The symptoms may persist or be subject to periodic recrudescences. Kilpatrick (1992) reported that 11% of rape victims still quality for a full PTSD diagnosis 3 years after the rape.

### Nervios

*Nervios*, a frequently used idiom of distress in Latin America, construed as a psychiatric syndrome of post-traumatic stress, can best be seen as an illness experience (Kleinman and Kleinman 1985). It is displayed in the overwhelming and pervasive quality of experiences of violence and social breakdown for women. Social, marital, and family problems, including violence, are the main sources of *nervios*, which is associated with distress experienced in family relations and social functioning and reflects a sense of personal disarray, loss of control, and powerlessness. Farias (1991) offered a series of vignettes of Salvadoran refugees which detailed years of physical and sexual violence leading to experiences of powerlessness and oppression.

### Phobia

The essential feature of agoraphobia is a marked fear of being alone or of being in public places from which escape might be difficult or help not available in case of sudden incapacitation. Normal activities are increasingly constricted as the fears or avoidance behavior dominate the individual's life (American Psychiatric Association 1987). What is considered agoraphobia in some women may have environmental rather than psychogenic explanations. In the United States, agoraphobia, the most severe form of phobia, represents about 85% of all phobia cases, making it also the most pervasive form. "Because of its manifestation of helplessness and dependency, it has been called the prototype of the sex-stereotyped woman or the caricature of the housebound housewife" (Paltiel 1987, p. 240). These situations must be better understood. Helplessness and dependency are symptomatic of the "battered woman syndrome." And because women are *justifiably* fearful of rape and sexual or physical assault in unprotected and unfamiliar surroundings, as well as in some intimate relationships, this could account for their "unreasonable" fear to leave their homes.

### Substance Use and Abuse

It is difficult to disentangle life events caused by drinking and drinking caused by life events. Studies indicate, however, that battered women have higher rates of substance use and abuse than nonbattered women. Furthermore, most of the battered women who drink excessively began to do so only after the onset of abuse, suggesting that women are using substances, including alcohol, to escape an intolerable situation (Heise 1993a).

### Suicide

Suicide is consistently reported in the aftermath of rape and other displays of violence against women. Although men have higher rates of death by suicide, women predominate in attempted suicides, which occur more frequently than completed suicides. A humiliating life event is one factor cited by Blumenthal (1988) as a precipitant for suicidal behavior. Abused women often become isolated and withdrawn as they try to hide the evidence of their victimization, for most a discredited and embarrassing circumstance. One of every four suicide attempts by white American women are preceded by abuse, as are half of all attempts by African-American women (Stark et al. 1981, cited in Rosenberg et al. 1986).

In a community survey of crime victimization in the United States, rape survivors reported more "nervous breakdowns," more suicidal thoughts, and more suicidal attempts than any other category of victim. Although prior to the rape, survivors were no more likely than anyone else to attempt suicide, almost one in five (19.2%) made a suicide attempt following the rape (Kilpatrick et al. 1985). In summary, Stark and Flitcraft (1991) conclude that "in North America, abuse may be the single most important precipitant for female suicide attempts yet identified" (p. 141).

The scant cross-cultural empirical data that have been gathered to address the mental health burden of domestic violence, to a large degree reflect cases resulting in death or suicide. Dorothy Counts's research (1987, 1990a, 1990b) concludes that wife-beating is widespread and is associated with suicide in North American, Oceanic, South American, and African societies. Gilmartin (1990) provides corroborative data from China. In some societies, female suicide is regarded as a socially sanctioned behavior that enables the politically powerless or entrapped to avenge those who have made their lives intolerable. This pattern of behavior signals not only severe personal suffering but society's failure to intervene effectively.

Where virginity determines the woman's worth, the stigma of rape is particularly devastating. Fauveau and Blanchet (1989), for example, conducted a study of rape in rural Bangladesh and concluded that when women are victims of rape, their personhood is spoiled and their reputation can never be restored. Case studies included in their report document numerous women beaten, murdered, or driven to suicide because of the dishonor that rape or illegitimate pregnancy brought upon the family (Heise 1993b).

### Implications of the Proposed Link Between Domestic Violence and Mental Health

The disproportionate prevalences of psychiatric disorders in women—especially depression and suicidal behavior—and the concomitantly high prevalences of women who are victims/survivors of domestic violence suggest a relation that requires urgent empirical study. More clinical data are needed to clearly understand this relationship in order to treat the disorders accurately and comprehensively.

Ultimately, the failure to correctly diagnose and treat disorders resulting from domestic violence could lead to iatrogenic damage (Eisenberg 1987).

The underlying causes remain hidden while the risk of dependence on prescription drugs rises. Moreover, battered women are far more likely than others to be given a pseudopsychiatric label such as "hysteric," "hypochondriac," or "crock" (Stark and Flitcraft 1991). Finally and ominously, the common custom of prescribing tranquilizers for a woman in a battering situation is not only nontherapeutic but can be lethal. Psychotropic drugs can significantly increase her danger when they dull the woman's capacity to recognize life-threatening situations and her ability to take appropriate actions to protect herself or to escape.

## RESEARCH INITIATIVES

In this chapter, using a cross-cultural perspective, we have described various facets of domestic violence, a significant social problem that appears to affect the mental and physical health of a substantial number of women around the world. Because of the complexity of this issue and the paucity of available data, the need for further research is obvious and urgent. The challenges to implement appropriate unbiased studies are great. Direct and indirect causal relationships must be postulated, and attention to multiple causal pathways must be considered (Newberger et al. 1992). Statistical data are needed from every region to document the magnitude and impact of the problem, as well as ethnographic data to enhance our understanding of domestic violence as a social process in different local contexts.

### Who Is the Victim?

Our principal needs are for epidemiologic data at the descriptive level which are prospective as well as retrospective, taken from both communities and treatment facilities. Basic sociodemographic characteristics including age, marital and family status, socioeconomic and education levels, and medical and psychiatric histories should be linked with culture-specific stressful life events (e.g., barrenness, failure to have the right gender or number of children, forced marriages, social surgical procedures) and histories of violence or abuse. Men as well as women should be assessed to elicit gender-associated differences. These data should be acquired through the use of standardized research designs, instruments, and indices. An immediate need is to formulate a standard definition of domestic violence that is acceptable to varied types of researchers so that it can be applied across cultures.

Studies on domestic violence have understandably tended to concentrate on victims who have sought help and on batterers who have sought help, have been incarcerated, or have been remanded to treatment programs. To avoid Berkson's (selection) bias, we need studies of random or probability samples drawn from the community rather than the usual convenience samples recruited from groups seeking help for psychiatric or other problems or those reported to the police. Data from all social strata are essential because domestic violence is socially ubiquitous. Ultimately, both qualitative (including ethnographic) and quantitative data should be gathered.

### Who Is the Perpetrator?

We stress the need for balanced research that includes the perpetrator as well as the victim. The causes and consequences of violence against women are multifactorial in nature, requiring a broad research agenda that examines the issue from varied perspectives. Basic sociodemographic data are also essential here, with links made to early experiences with violence. Studies in the United States suggest that at least 60% of men who batter grew up in homes where they were beaten, sexually abused, or witnessed parental battering, resulting in an ominous cycle of violence. Neglecting to understand the dynamics of interpersonal relations and conflict resolution between intimate partners may perpetuate "band-aid solutions" to the problem and sustain the emphasis on the victim as deviant. Further at the core of the problem lie the cultural values, mores, rights, and practices that condone physical violence as a means of conflict resolution within intimate relationships. Direct assessment of perpetrators (who in a small proportion may be women) is essential. Recruiting an adequate sample undoubtedly poses an enormous challenge.

Research is needed also to better understand domestic violence in homosexual relationships. The accumulating body of research indicates, for example, that approximately 25% to 30% of lesbian relationships have experienced abuse (Jim Shattuck, personal communication).

### Investigating the Association Between Abuse and Mental Disorders

Gender- and culture-sensitive mental health research remain neglected areas of investigation. We urge intensive examination of the association between domestic violence against women and the women's mental health disorders. Protocols need to be developed that can be applied cross-culturally to document prevalences of violence and subsequent mental health disorders so that temporal relationships essential for a causal model can be generated. Researchers must be cognizant of particular concerns of women across cultures and cultural variations in interpretation of violence. For example, is a husband's chastisement of his wife categorized as abuse? In certain settings, focus groups have been an effective means to elicit qualitative information in a culturally sensitive way. In other settings, however, a woman might be reluctant to speak openly in front of a group of women from her neighborhood or community for fear of becoming the focus of local gossip. Survey data alone may fail to capture subtle nuances that reveal both the true impact and the cultural variations of domestic violence in the same way that a medical examination without explicit probing by a sensitized physician fails to detect a history of violence and abuse underlying myriad symptoms.

## ETHICAL CONSIDERATIONS

The fundamental ethical consideration when conducting research in the area of domestic violence is to avoid exacerbating violence against women while attempting to understand it or to reduce its occurrence. *Primum no nocere*—above all, do no harm. Protecting the confidentiality of sources of the data and avoiding the medicalization of social problems experienced by women present significant challenges. By treating social problems as medical or psychiatric disorders, the sufferers lose the context of the experience, the suffering is delegitimated, and society is precluded from responding appropriately (Kleinman and Kleinman 1985).

Sigler (1989) and others have offered caveats about the link between activism and research in which the research is designed to provide support for particular activist positions. Findings may be misleading or slanted, affording only partial understanding that is shaped by activist perspectives. Those who attempt to dramatize the scope and magnitude of violence, for example, can inflate the results by defining domestic violence, broadly stating, for example, that a single act over a lifetime of marriage constitutes domestic violence. Because the results of a research project are likely to have an effect on the way in which people live and the extent to which they are labeled deviant, sensitivity is required to present data objectively, without ethnocentrism, and with respect and appreciation for the culture being studied.

## POLICY IMPLICATIONS

Domestic violence against women destroys women's physical and mental health, diminishes their dignity, and violates their fundamental human rights. This is a problem deeply embedded in the social, cultural, religious, and economic values and mores of a community. In this chapter we have attempted to emphasize the variation and pluralism in the forms and consequences of domestic violence. As local context gives shape and meaning to domestic violence and its ramifications, so too will local context shape appropriate strategies of intervention. No one approach will or should work in every setting.

We must be creative in our interventions and policy initiatives. While recognizing the need for variation in solutions, ultimately the need is for an integrative approach that brings together grassroots organizations and national and international agencies to achieve sustainable social change (World Bank 1993). This integrative approach should include the legal and medical professions, governments, the media, and public education institutions. Accepting that violence against women is a learned behavior that can be changed is a progressive step (Carrillo 1991).

Domestic violence must not be seen as "just a women's issue." Although it affects women primarily, impairment in the woman's physical, mental, and emotional capacity to function adequately resulting from exposure to violence ultimately impairs the care she can give to her family. Consequently the harm spreads to include other family members, particularly her children. Furthermore, the strong correlation between domestic violence and child abuse and mortality suggests that the best protection for a child's well-being is protecting the mother from becoming a victim of domestic violence.

Common to societies in which men exhibit violence against intimate partners is the devalued status of women. All policies that seek to alleviate domestic violence must address the social position of women. Equality of women is, in fact, essential to peace, not only between intimate partners but in the workplace, the political realm, and society in general. In their *Statement on Peace,* the Baha'i Peace Council of Canada eloquently expresses the significance of "equality between the sexes":

> The emancipation of women, the achievement of full equality between the sexes, is one of the most important, though less acknowledged prerequisites of peace. The denial of such equality perpetuates an injustice against one half of the world's population and promotes in men harmful attitudes and habits that are carried from the family to the workplace, to political life, and ultimately to international relations. There are no grounds, moral, practical, or biological, upon which such denial can be justified. Only as women are welcomed into full partnership in all fields of human endeavor will the moral and psychological climate be created in which international peace can emerge (1986, p. 8).

Domestic violence must no longer be a private affair in which public agencies cannot and do not intervene. Governments must be held accountable for the violence to which their citizens are subjected. They must acknowledge the specific experiences of women in order to provide appropriate protection to this half of their citizenry.

In most countries, women have very little legal or actual protection from abusive husbands. Traditionally, law in most societies have denied women equal protection and have often relegated that responsibility to men as heads of households. Men's violence against "their" women is accepted (or ignored) across a wide spectrum of cultures. Activists are now pushing to have domestic violence recognized as a crime distinct from general assault laws, and for police to have powers of arrest and intervention in cases of domestic assault (Seager and Olson 1986). The rape of a man's wife is considered a serious crime only because of the longstanding legal tradition of the wife as property; for this reason wife-rape is rarely prosecutable. How can you violate the rights of someone who has no independent civil rights? (Seager and Olson 1986). In the United States, as recently as the 1970s, husbands had conjugal rights to consummate the marriage which their women did not have the right to refuse (Sigler 1989).

Legal reform is an area where women in a number of societies have succeeded in effecting change, both to extend their rights and to ensure protection of their rights. In Puerto Rico, for example, the Law for the Prevention of Domestic Violence was implemented in 1990, recognizing domestic violence as a felony. After only 7 months, 936 men were arrested on charges of domestic violence (*Women's World* 1991–2). Legal reform alone is inadequate, however, in societies where women have never experienced participation in public affairs. Educating the public about nuances of legal reform (e.g., equal rights to protection) must accompany such change.

Universal education is a key factor in raising women's status and thereby providing them with greater options and with the tools for self-reliance and access to positions of influence in society. Where social resources are limited, however, education of girls is afforded a low priority. Nonetheless, investment in the education of girls may well be the highest-return investment in the developing world (Summers 1993), as women with even an elementary education raise the standard of living in a poor country. Furthermore, studies have repeatedly shown that educating mothers is the single most effective way to reduce child mortality because it mitigates the woman's fatalism, improves her self-confidence, and changes the power balance within the family (Heise et al. 1989). In nearly every society, the medical, legal, and public professions remain male-dominated. Equal access to higher education will facilitate women's entry into such fields, where they will have a stronger voice for the concerns of women in the population they serve.

Education must extend to professionals as well. Raising awareness of police, lawyers, and judges to the magnitude of the problem and the unique needs of abused women is necessary if the law is to be an arm by which women are protected.

Health care professionals are in the best position to identify, counsel, and empower women experiencing domestic violence because the health care system represents the one institution with which almost every woman interacts during her lifetime. But most health care professionals are ill-prepared to provide assistance and need training in effective intervention strategies for caring for abused and battered women. Strategies, taken from Sugg and Inui (1992) and Star and colleagues (1981), include educating professionals to know how to do the following:

Assess the immediate crisis; take an in-depth history, especially inquiring about abuse and violence in the home.

Refer the woman to appropriate resources, including medical assistance, financial and legal aid, emergency shelters, and other alternatives to consider.

Help the woman increase her self-esteem; deal with the battered woman's ambivalence about whether or not to leave the abusive spouse.

Establish a trust relationship with the woman which provides ongoing emotional support, security, practical assistance, and empowerment options.

Viewing domestic violence in the contexts of public health and human rights exposes the pervasive and systematic exclusion of women from public policy. David Christiani links public health and human rights in the following way:

> An issue becomes a public health issue when an individual disease is shown to be more prevalent in a group or among groups of people for social, cultural, or economic reasons—for systemic reasons. A public health issue, in turn, becomes a human rights issue when basic rights to existence are systematically denied to a group or groups of people. Human rights abuses involve issues of coercion, of profound inequality . . . inequalities in the ability to control basic conditions of daily life. When groups of people are denied control of their basic living conditions, and their health and even existence are placed in jeopardy, a public health issue expands to become a human rights issue (Christiani, quoted in Klinger 1993, p. 11).

Women must have a role in determining the policies and programs that affect them (Rodriguez-Trias 1992). Before any strategy to combat certain culturally determined behaviors is initiated, attempts to understand the nature and function of the behaviors in their social context are mandatory in order to determine the appropriateness and feasibility of the intended strategy. Sidel (1993) noted the evolution in thinking from "helping the victim" to "blaming the victim" to the current "organizing the victim." Whereas helping the victim promotes dependence and blaming the victim draws attention away from the societal causes of illness, organizing the victim gives attention to those who have traditionally been socially and economically vulnerable and disenfranchised. Organizing increases the likelihood of the survivors gaining control over their lives and wielding power to make changes that ultimately could lead to improvements in their sense of dignity, their health, and their well-being.

## LESSONS FROM THE FIELD

Although estimates of the prevalence of domestic violence in low-income countries and its burden on the mental and physical health of women paint a grim picture, energy, insight, and hope can be gained from examples of concerned individuals around the world unifying their efforts to combat this problem in their communities. A global perspective on domestic violence allows us to recognize and ultimately to transform the social and cultural underpinnings that condone violence against women in the home.

What follows are examples of innovative strategies from around the world which challenge, on various fronts, the values and structures that have perpetuated domestic violence against women.

***India*** In rural India, where the stigma of rape is great and the status of women is low, women who are raped are no longer considered marriageable. But an unmarried woman in traditional rural communities cannot earn enough money to make a living. Today, rape survivors are turning to the legal system to back their demand for retribution from their rapists. They are lobbying for legal measures requiring rapists to turn over half their annual income or an equivalent in land to their victims (Parikh 1991).

***Mexico*** "Specialized agencies" providing integrated legal, medical, and psychological services to rape survivors were established in Mexico City in 1988 by the Commission on Violence. Centralizing services makes it easier for women to be aware of and take advantage of the services that are available. The commission plans to extend such agencies to assist survivors of family violence and to reach rural areas (Shrader-Cox 1992).

***Malaysia*** In Malaysia, women's organizations representing various disciplines have joined forces to raise awareness of violence against women and to effect legislative and social change. Their focus has been first to dispel the myths surrounding the issue of domestic violence and, second, to draw attention to the inadequacy of present laws to protect women's rights. The Joint Action Group Against Violence Against Women (JAG), established in 1985, includes representatives from a battered women's shelter as well as the Association of Women Lawyers, the University Women's Association, the Malaysian Trade Union Congress Women's Section, and the media. Their campaign has been waged largely through public education programs (Fernandez 1992).

***Jamaica*** A women's theater group, Sistren, has been writing and producing drama-in-education workshops for schools and community groups, primarily in rural areas throughout the Caribbean, in an attempt to raise awareness about the reality of violence in women's lives. Women's Media Watch, a grass roots organization, has been lobbying both politicians and advertisers to create legislation to end sexist advertizing (Parikh 1991).

***Bangladesh/Chile/Thailand*** The Bangladesh Women's Health Coalition and the Chilean Institute of Reproductive Medicine offer integrated family planning services at the same time as child health services, and Thailand is experimenting with mobile health clinics to reach women in their homes (World Bank 1993). Comprehensive health services designed to treat or prevent domestic violence can, similarly, be made more accessible.

***Brazil*** In Brazil, women have responded to police officers' insensitivity to raped and battered women by lobbying for, and eventually establishing, all-women police stations. The first station was established in São Paulo in 1985 and responded to 2,000 cases of abuse. Now, with six stations in the capital city alone, women police, detectives, and social workers respond to more than 7,000 domestic violence and rape cases each year (Parikh 1991).

One feature common to all of the strategies is that they began as grass roots movements that, with concerted effort, succeeded in making their way onto the agenda of national and international agencies. To date, strategies emanating from women's groups have been the most effective in educating the public about the magnitude of the problem and initiating national and international debate.

At the recent Human Rights Conference in Vienna (1993), an unprecedented representation of 950 women's organizations from around the world coalesced into the strongest and most effective lobby grappling with the common concern of violence against women. A significant achievement of the conference was the demonstration that although they came from vastly different social and cultural backgrounds, they could unite around a common issue of violence against women while collaborating on what has become the Global Campaign for Women's Human Rights.

Interaction between different levels of society is crucial to the strength of the movement to bring domestic violence to the forefront of the health and human rights agenda. Community-based grassroots organizations keep the movement alive and in touch with the people most in need. National and international agencies have the clout to effect social and political change and to secure the ever-needed funds that sustain a movement. The effort, however, starts with a steadfast few in the spirit of anthropologist Margaret Mead's well-known words: "Never doubt that a small group of thoughtful, committed citizens can change the world; indeed, it's the only thing that ever does."

## REFERENCES

AMERICAN PSYCHIATRIC ASSOCIATION, COMMITTEE ON NOMENCLATURE AND STATISTICS. 1987. *Diagnostic and Statistical Manual of Mental Disorders, Third Edition—Revised.* Washington, DC: American Psychiatric Association.

AMERICAN PSYCHOLOGICAL ASSOCIATION. 1990. Monograph, p. 28 as cited in Leidig 1992, pp. 151–52.

BAHA'I PEACE COUNCIL OF CANADA. 1986. *To the Peoples of the World—A Statement on Peace.* Ontario, Canada: Universal House of Justice.

BLUMENTHAL, S. J. 1988. "Suicide: A Guide to Risk Factors, Assessment, and Treatment of Suicidal Patients." *Medical Clinics of North America* 72:937–71.

BOSTON GLOBE. 1993. "Reuters Report of Canadian Panel on Violence against Women." August 1, p. 8.

BRADLEY, CHRISTINE. 1988. "The Problem of Domestic Violence in Papua New Guinea." In: *Guidelines for Police Training on Violence Against Women and Child Sexual Abuse.* London Commonwealth Secretariat, Women and Development Programme (cited in Heise 1993c).

BROWNE, A. and K. WILLIAMS. 1989. "Exploring the Effect of Resource Availability and the Likelihood of Female-Perpetrated Homicides." *Law and Society Review* 23:1.

CHACON, K., et al. 1990. "Characteristicas de la mujer agredida entendida en el patronato nacional de la infancia (PANI)." In: *Batres Gioconda and Elaramount, Cecilia. La Violencia contra la mujer en la familia constrarricense: Un problema de salud pública.* San José, Costa Rica: ILANUD.

CARRILLO, ROXANNE. 1991. "Violence Against Women: An Obstacle to Development." Pp. 19–41 in *Gender Violence: A Development and Human Rights Issue,* edited by C. Bunch and Roxanne Carillo. New Brunswick, NJ: Center for Women's Global Leadership, Douglass College, Rutgers University.

CANAS, M. 1990. *Maltrato Fisico a la Mujer Salvadorena.* Unpublished thesis, San Salvador (available from author).

CLARE, ANTHONY. 1992. *Medicine Betrayed: The Participation of Doctors in Human Rights Abuses.* London: Zed Books/British Medical Association.

COUNTS, DOROTHY A. 1987. "Female Suicide and Wife Abuse: A Cross-cultural Perspective." *Suicide and Life-Threatening Behavior* 17:194–204.

______. 1990a. "Domestic Violence in Oceania: Introduction." *Pacific Studies* 13(3):1–5.

______. 1990b. "Beaten Wife, Suicidal Woman: Domestic Violence in Kaliai, West New Britain." *Pacific Studies* 13(3):151–69.

COY, F. 1990. Study cited in Castillo, D., et al. 1992. *Violencia Hacia la Mujer en Guatemala.* Report prepared for the First Central American Seminar on Violence Against Women as a Public Health Problem. Managua, Nicaragua, March 11–13.

EISENBERG, LEON. 1987. "Preventing Mental, Neurological and Psychosocial Disorders." *World Health Forum* 8:245–53.

EL-DAREER, A. 1982. *Women, Why Do You Weep? Circumcision and Its Consequences.* London: Zed Books.

FARIAS, PABLO J. 1991. "Emotional Distress and Its Socio-Political Correlates in Salvadoran Refugees: Analysis of a Clinical Sample." *Culture, Medicine and Psychiatry* 15:167–92.

FAUVEAU, V. and T. BLANCHET. 1989. "Epidemiology and Cause of Deaths Among Women in Rural Bangladesh." *International Journal of Epidemiology* 18:139–45.

FERNANDEZ, IRENE. 1992. "Mobilizing on All Fronts: A Comprehensive Strategy to End Violence Against Women in Malaysia." Pp. 101–20 in *Freedom from Violence: Women's Strategies from Around the World,* edited by Margaret Schuler. Washington, DC: OEF International.

FOA, E. B., B. OLASOV, and G. S. STEKETEE. 1987. *Treatment of Rape Victims.* Paper presented at the State of the Art in Sexual Assault Conference. Charleston, SC.

FORNI, E. 1980. "Women's Role in the Economic, Social, and Political Development of Somalia." *Afrika Spectrum* 15:19–28.

GILMARTIN, CHRISTINA. 1990. "Violence Against Women in Contemporary China." Pp. 203–25 in *Violence in China: Essays in Culture and Counterculture,* edited by J. Lipman and S. Harrell. Albany, NY: State University of New York Press.

GRUENBAUM, E. 1988. "Reproductive Ritual and Social Reproduction: Female Circumcision and the Subordination of Women in Sudan." Pp. 308–25 in *Economy and Class in Sudan,* edited by N. O'Neill and J. O'Brien. Aldershot, UK: Avebury.

HAYNES, R. H. 1984. "Suicide in Figi: A Preliminary Study." *British Journal of Psychiatry* 145:433–38.

HEISE, LORI. 1993a. "Background Data for Establishing the Health Burden from Domestic Violence for the World Health Report of the World Bank." Unpublished.

______. 1993b. "Global Estimates of the Health Burden Resulting from Rape for the World Health Report of the World Bank." Unpublished.

______. 1993c. "Violence Against Women: The Missing Agenda." Pp. 171–95 in *The*

*Health of Women: A Global Perspective,* edited by M. Koblinski, J. Timyan, and J. Gay. Boulder, CO: Westview Press.

HEISE, LORI, R. W. KNOWLTON, and J. STOLTENBERG. 1989. "The Global War Against Women." *Utne Reader* 36:40–49.

HICKS, E. K. 1993. *Infibulation: Female Mutilation in Islamic Northeastern Africa.* New Brunswick, NJ: Transaction Publishers.

JACOBSSON, L. 1985. "Psychiatric Morbidity and Psychosocial Background in an Outpatient Population of a General Hospital in Western Ethiopia." *Acta Psychiatrica Scandinavica* 71:417–26.

JILANI, HINA. 1992. "Whose Laws? Human Rights and Violence Against Women in Pakistan." Pp. 63–74 in *Freedom from Violence: Women's Strategies from Around the World,* edited by Margaret Schuler. Washington, DC: OEF International.

KAHN, JOSEPH. 1993. "Slave brides: Chinese women captured, sold to men to meet demands for wives in village." *Dallas Morning News* Feature Series—Violence Against Women: A Question of Human Rights, April 9, Pp. 1A, 14A–15A.

KARKAL, M. 1985. "How the Other Half Dies in Bombay." *Economic and Political Weekly* p. 1424 (Cited in Heise, 1993c).

KELKAR, GOVIND. 1991. "Stopping the Violence Against Women: Issues and Perspectives from India." Pp. 75–99 in *Freedom from Violence: Women's Strategies from Around the World,* edited by Margaret Schuler. Washington, DC: OEF International.

KILPATRICK, D. 1992. *Rape in America: A Report to the Nation.* Arlington, VA: National Victim Center.

KILPATRICK, D., C. BEST, L. VERONEN, et al. 1985. "Mental Health Correlates of Criminal Victimization: A Random Community Survey." *Journal of Consulting and Clinical Psychology* 53:866–73.

KLEINMAN, ARTHUR and JOAN KLEINMAN. 1985. "Somatization: The Interconnections in Chinese Society Among Culture, Depressive Experiences and the Meanings of Pain." Pp. 1–42 in *Culture and Depression: Studies in Anthropology and Cross-Cultural Psychiatry of Affect and Disorder,* edited by Arthur Kleinman and Byron Good. Berkeley: University of California Press.

KLINGER, KAREN. 1993. "A Voice for Health and Human Rights." *Harvard Public Health Review,* Spring, pp. 6–11. David Christiani quoted in text.

KOSS, MARY P. 1990. "The Women's Mental Health Research Agenda." *American Psychologist* 45:374–80.

LEIDIG, M. W. 1992. "The Continuum of Violence Against Women: Psychological and Physical Consequences." *Journal of American College Health* 40:149–55.

LEVINSON, DAVID. 1989. *Family Violence in Cross Cultural Perspective.* Newbury Park, CA: Sage Publications.

MAHAJAN, A. 1990. "Instigators of Wife Battering." Pp. 1–10 in *Violence Against Women,* edited by Sushma Sood. Jaipur, India: Arihant Publishers.

MOLLICA, RICHARD and L. SON. 1989. "Cultural Dimensions in the Evaluation and Treatment of Sexual Trauma: An Overview." *Psychiatric Clinics of North America* 12:363–79.

MOLTEDO, C., S. CLOTILED, C. ORELLANA, et al. 1989. *Estudio Sobre Violencia Domestica en Mujeres Pobladoras Chilenas.* Santiago, Chile: CUSO.

MULLEN, P. E., S. E. ROMANS-CLARKSON, V. A., WALTON, and G. P. HERBISON. 1988. "Impact of Sexual and Physical Abuse on Women's Mental Health." *Lancet* 1:841–45.

NEWBERGER, E., S. E. BARKEN, E. S. LIEBERMAN, et al. 1992. "Abuse of Pregnant Women and Adverse Birth Outcome." *Journal of the American Medical Association* 267: 2370–72.

PALTIEL, FREDA L. 1987. "Women and Mental Health: A Post-Nairobi Perspective." *World Health Statistics Quarterly* 40:233–66.

PALTIEL, FREDA L. 1993. "Women's Mental Health: A Global Perspective." Pp. 197–216 in *The Health of Women: A Global Perspective,* edited by M. Koblinsky, J. Timyan, and J. Gay. Boulder, CO: Westview Press.

PARIKH, R. 1991. "Violence Meets Its Match." *The Canadian Nurse,* October, pp. 14–15.

RAIKES, A. 1990. *Pregnancy, Birthing and Family Planning in Kenya: Changing Patterns of Behavior.* Copenhagen Centre for Development Research.

RANDALL, T. 1990. "Domestic Violence Intervention Calls for More than Treating Injuries." *Journal of the American Medical Association* 264:939–40.

ROBINS, LEE N., JOHN E. HELZER, MYRNA M. WEISSMAN, et al. 1984. "Lifetime Prevalences of Specific Psychiatric Disorders in Three Sites." *Archives of General Psychiatry* 41:949–58.

RODRIQUEZ-TRIAS, HELEN. 1992. "Women's Health, Women's Lives, Women's Rights." *American Journal of Public Health* 82:663–64.

ROSENBERG, M. L., E. STARK, and M. A. ZAHN. 1986. "Interpersonal Violence: Homicide and Spouse Abuse." Pp. 1399–1426 in *Public Health and Preventive Medicine,* 12th ed., edited by J. M. Last. Norwalk, CN: Appleton-Century-Crofts.

ROYNER, S. 1991. "Battered Wives: Centuries of Silence." *The Washington Post* August 20, p. 7. Cited in Rodriquez-Trias 1992.

SARTORIUS, NORMAN, A. JABLENSKY, W. GULBINAT, and G. ERNBERG. 1980. "WHO Collaborative Study: Assessment of Depressive Disorders." *Psychological Medicine* 10:743–49.

SCHULER, MARGARET. 1992. "Violence against women: An international perspective. Pp. 1–45 in *Freedom from Violence: Women's Strategies from Around the World.* Washington, DC: OEF International. (Available through UNIFEM, New York.)

SEAGER, J. and A. OLSON. 1986. *Women in the World: An International Atlas.* London: Pluto Press Limited.

SHATTUCK, JIM. 1993. (Director of *Men Overcoming Violence*) Personal communication.

SHRADER-COX, ELIZABETH. 1992. "Developing Strategies: Efforts to End Violence Against Women in Mexico." Pp. 175–98 in *Freedom From Violence: Women's Strategies from Around the World,* edited by Margaret Schuler.

SIDEL, VICTOR. 1993. "From 'Helping the Victims' to 'Blaming the Victims' to 'Organizing the Victims': Lessons from China, Chile and the Bronx." Pp. 205–18 in *A New Dawn in Guatemala: Toward a Worldwide Health Vision,* edited by R. Luecke. Prospect Heights, IL: Waveland Press.

SIGLER, R. T. 1989. *Domestic Violence in Context: An Assessment of Community Attitudes.* Lexington, MA: D. C. Heath.

STAR, B., C. G. CLARK, K. M. GOETZ, and L. O'MALIA. 1981. "Psychosocial Aspects of Wifebeating." Pp. 426–61 in *Women and Mental Health,* edited by E. Howell and M. Bayes. New York: Basic Books.

STARK, E. and A. FLITCRAFT. 1979. "Medicine and Patriarchal Violence: The Social Construction of a Private Event." *International Journal of Health Services* 9:461–93, as cited in Council on Scientific Affairs, American Medical Association. 1992. "Violence Against Women." *Journal of the American Medical Association* 267:3184–95.

STARK, E. and A. FLITCRAFT. 1991. "Spouse Abuse." Pp. 123–57 in *Violence in America: A Public Health Approach,* edited by M. Rosenberg and M. Fenley. New York: Oxford University Press.

STRAUS, MURRAY A., RICHARD J. GELLES, and SUZANNE K. STEINMETZ. 1980. *Behind Closed Doors: Violence in the American Family.* Garden City, New York: Anchor Press.

SUGG, NANCY K. and THOMAS INUI. 1992. "Primary Care Physicians' Response to Domestic Violence: Opening Pandora's Box." *Journal of the American Medical Association* 267:3157–60.

SUMMERS, L. 1993. *Women's Education in Developing Countries: Barriers, Benefits and Policies.* Washington, DC: The World Bank.

UNITED NATIONS GENERAL ASSEMBLY (UN). 1948. *Universal Declaration of Human Rights.* Adopted 10 December 1948. G.A. Res. 217A(III), U.N. Doc. A/810.

UNITED NATIONS COMMISSION ON THE STATUS OF WOMEN (UN). 1986. *Expert Group Meeting on Violence in the Family with Special Emphasis on Its Effects on Women.* Vienna, December 8–12 (cited in Paltiel 1987).

VALDEZ SANTIAGO, R. and E. SHRADER-COX. 1991. *Estudio Sobre la Incidencia de Violencia Domestica en una Microregion de Cuidad Nezahualcoyotl,* 1989. Mexico City: Centro de Investigacion y Lucha Contra la Violencia Domestica.

WETZEL, JANICE W. 1991. "Universal Mental Health Classification Systems: Reclaiming Women's Experience." *AFFILIA* 6:8–31.

*WOMEN'S WORLD.* 1991–2. "Wife Abuse: Law and Order." 26:24–25.

WORLD BANK. 1993. *World Development Report 1993: Investing in Health.* The World Bank, Report No. 11778, Washington, DC.

WORLD HEALTH ORGANIZATION (WHO). 1993. "World Health Assembly Calls for the Elimination of Harmful Traditional Practices." Press Release: May 12.